APULEIUS
A Latin Sophist

APULEIUS
A Latin Sophist

S. J. HARRISON

OXFORD
UNIVERSITY PRESS

OXFORD
UNIVERSITY PRESS
Great Clarendon Street, Oxford OX2 6DP

Oxford University Press is a department of the University of Oxford.
It furthers the University's objective of excellence in research, scholarship,
and education by publishing worldwide in

Oxford New York

Athens Auckland Bangkok Bogotá Buenos Aires Calcutta
Cape Town Chennai Dar es Salaam Delhi Florence Hong Kong Istanbul
Karachi Kuala Lumpur Madrid Melbourne Mexico City Mumbai
Nairobi Paris São Paulo Singapore Taipei Tokyo Toronto Warsaw

with associated companies in Berlin Ibadan

Oxford is a registered trade mark of Oxford University Press
in the UK and in certain other countries

Published in the United States
by Oxford University Press Inc., New York

© S. J. Harrison 2000

The moral rights of the author have been asserted

Database right Oxford University Press (maker)

British Library Cataloguing in Publication Data
Data available

Library of Congress Cataloging in Publication Data
Data available

ISBN: 0 19 814053 3
1 3 5 7 9 10 8 6 4 2

Typeset by Invisible Ink
Printed in Great Britain
on acid-free paper by
Biddles Ltd.,
Guildford & King's Lynn

PREFACE

This book is a response to the literary pleasures and scholarly problems of reading the texts of Apuleius—display orator and professional intellectual in second-century North Africa, Platonist philosopher, extraordinary stylist, relentless self-promoter, and versatile author of a remarkably diverse body of work, much of which is lost to us. It is written for those able to read Apuleius in Latin, and Apuleian works are accordingly quoted without translation (though I have indicated suitable translations of each work where they exist); Greek is generally translated. I have aimed primarily to provide a literary handbook to the works of Apuleius other than his well-known novel the *Metamorphoses* or *Golden Ass*, and secondarily to set these works and the *Metamorphoses* against their intellectual background; this means not only Apuleius' career as a performing intellectual, a sophist, in second-century Roman North Africa, but also the larger contemporary framework of the Greek Second Sophistic.

Apuleius' relationship to the Second Sophistic has recently received welcome attention in Sandy (1997), which offers a general assessment of the cultural and literary context; this volume hopes to provide a complementary treatment through a closer concern with the individual Apuleian texts and their interpretation. My interest is primarily literary and literary-historical; some apology is consequently due to specialists in ancient philosophy, who are likely to find my treatments of the philosophical aspects of Apuleius' works and of his important role in Middle Platonism relatively superficial, though I hope I have noted recent work on this topic where appropriate. I had originally planned to include chapters on Apuleian language and the reception of Apuleius in later periods, but space pressed, and there are some good treatments of these topics to be found elsewhere (see the bibliographical references given in the introduction to Harrison (1999)).

I have many obligations to record. First, to Robin Nisbet, who first introduced me to the pleasures of reading Apuleian Latin and has always encouraged me in my work, and to Donald Russell, who first suggested that I should write a book on Apuleius. Second, to Hilary O'Shea and the Oxford University Press, who have patiently encouraged and fostered the project since its inception a decade ago; I am especially grateful to Angela

Blackburn for her meticulous copy-editing. Third, to the colleagues and friends who have given generous practical aid: to those who helped in finding bibliographical items or in supplying copies of their own publications—Fred Brenk, Luca Graverini, Harry Jocelyn, Silvia Mattiacci, and Charles Weiss; and especially to those who read and commented on draft chapters—Mariateresa Horsfall Scotti, Nicholas Horsfall, Michael Trapp, who also kindly let me see material before publication, and Michael Winterbottom, who has also taken a general interest in the project. I should particularly like to thank Keith Bradley for reading sections of the typescript at a late stage and generously sharing his research in various ways, and Vincent Hunink, both for commenting in detail on several chapters and for facilitating my acquisition of his publications; I am also grateful to Kai Brodersen, Marco Fernandelli, and Antoinette Novara for helping me obtain German, Italian, and French publications respectively. Special gratitude is due to Maaike Zimmerman and her colleagues at Groningen, who have always been keen to welcome me to their splendid centre of Apuleian studies and to share information and ideas.

I should also like to acknowledge more personal debts. My classical colleagues and students (undergraduate and graduate) at Corpus have provided a stimulating, supportive, and tolerant environment over the last decade, for which I am very grateful indeed; it is a real privilege to work in such a community. I am especially grateful to Ewen Bowie, who has so often given me kind advice and aid, and not just on matters of the Second Sophistic. But I should like to dedicate this volume to my family: to my wife Louise, for all her love and help amid her own work, and to our sons Alexander and Freddie, whose coming has much heartened (if not much hastened!) the writing of this book.

Finally, though it was not the main project for my tenure of the award, the last stages of assembling this book have been facilitated by a Leverhulme/British Academy Senior Research Fellowship for 1997–8, which has given me precious time for research activity, and for which I am extremely grateful.

Corpus Christi College, Oxford   S.J.H.
April 1999

CONTENTS

ABBREVIATIONS OF APULEIUS' WORKS

Apol.	*Apologia*
DDS	*De Deo Socratis*
Flor.	*Florida*
Met.	*Metamorphoses*
Mu.	*De Mundo*
Pl.	*De Platone*

1

Apuleius in Context: Life, Background, Writings

1. LIFE AND BACKGROUND

Information on the life of Apuleius may be recovered from two main sources—his own works, and the writings of Augustine, another writer from North Africa to whom Apuleius' works were clearly familiar.[1] We can be sure only of his *nomen*; the *praenomen* 'Lucius' attributed to Apuleius in some Renaissance manuscripts of his works is not found in ancient sources, and is very likely to be derived from the apparent identity suggested between Apuleius and his narrator Lucius of Corinth at the end of the *Metamorphoses* (11. 27). A recent suggestion that Apuleius is to be identified with a contemporary L. Apuleius Marcellus known from an inscribed lead pipe in Ostia is an interesting but ultimately unconvincing speculation.[2] We can be sure that he was born in the 120s AD at Madauros, now M'daurouch in Algeria, an inland city then in the Roman province of Africa Proconsularis, situated some 230 kilometres south-west of Carthage (modern Tunis) and some 900 metres above sea level on the southern slopes of the Atlas mountains.[3] The early history of Madauros

---

[1] On Augustine's knowledge of Apuleius see Hagendahl (1967), i. 17–28, ii. 680–9, Horsfall Scotti (1990). On the evidence for the life of Apuleius see now the summary statement by Sallmann (1997), 293–4 and the fuller treatment in Sandy (1997), 1–36.

[2] Coarelli (1989), a fascinating interpretation of an Ostian house, argues that Apuleius resided at Ostia in the late 140s or early 150s and took the *cognomen* 'Marcellus' as a compliment to an Ostian patron of consular family, Q. Asinius Marcellus (*PIR* A 1235/6), and that the latter is also complimented by appearing as the priest of Osiris in the *Metamorphoses* (11. 27). Against this one might argue (a) that Apuleius, generally forthcoming about his career, never mentions residence at Ostia or a connection with this relatively grand family (as one might expect, at least in the *Apologia*) and (b) that the identification with L. Apuleius Marcellus partly depends on the dubious ascription of the *praenomen* 'Lucius' to Apuleius (see above).

[3] Madauros is named as his birthplace by (e.g.) [Apuleius] *De Interpretatione* 4, Augustine *Ep.* 102. 32, *Civ.* 8. 14. 2, Sidonius *Ep.* 9. 13. 3 and Cassiodorus *Inst.* 2. 4. 7; the only certain Apuleian mention of Madauros is the notorious *Met.* 11. 27 *Madaurensem* (for

is obscure: Apuleius relates (*Apol.* 24) that at the time of the Third Punic War it belonged to the dominions of the Numidian king Syphax, who after some indecision joined Carthage in the struggle against Rome. On the Carthaginian defeat in 203 BC, it passed to the great Massinissa, ally of Scipio, whose descendants ruled as kings of Numidia until 46 BC. Then the current monarch, Juba I, a Pompeian in the civil war, was expelled by Caesar, who set up the Roman province of Africa Nova in place of the former independent kingdom, to add to the existing Roman province of Africa based on Carthage. After an unsuccessful return to client-kingdom status under Juba II, protegé of Augustus, in 29–25 BC, Numidia was united with the older province of Africa to form Africa Proconsularis, an arrangement which lasted until repartition by Septimus Severus. Madauros itself was re-settled in the Flavian period as a Roman *colonia*, with the title *Colonia Flavia Augusta veteranorum Madaurensium*; for the next two centuries the city flourished, as its extensive ruins testify.

Punic culture and language remained strong in the area of Madauros as in other parts of Roman North Africa. It is probable that Apuleius spoke Punic as his vernacular first language, like others of similar origin, such as his stepson Pudens (*Apol.* 98) from Oea in Tripolitana (modern Libya), and the emperor Septimus Severus,[4] born a generation after Apuleius in Lepcis Magna, not far from Oea. Understandably, we are not told this in his Latin writings; though Punic might be the usual vernacular of a North African *colonia*, Latin was the language of all formal literary and legal discourse,[5] Fronto, coming from the similar *colonia* of Cirta a generation before Apuleius, similarly does not mention Punic in his writings, though it was probably his vernacular first language too.[6] It is important for a true appreciation of Apuleius to realize that he belongs not to an African sub-culture but to the mainstream of Latin culture and literature, with his much-vaunted fluency in Greek acquired as it would

discussion of this see Ch. 6). For the archaeology and epigraphy of Madauros cf. Gsell (1922*a*), 181–266, Gsell (1922*b*), and Lepelley (1981), 127–39. Note that there is no epigraphical evidence for the spelling *Madaura* (n. pl.?), often found in older Apuleian literature; it is derived from Augustine *Conf.* 2. 5 *a Madauris*, but other sources (e.g. *ILA* 2761) and the evolution into the Arabic *M'daurouch* make it clear that *Madauros* was the standard form— cf. Gsell (1922*a*) 181.

  [4] The evidence is gathered and discussed by Barnes (1967), 94–7, though he wishes to underplay Severus' Punic culture.
  [5] For Latin at Madauros see conveniently the material collected from inscriptions by Harrison (1990*b*), 508 n. 4.
  [6] Cf. Champlin (1980), 8. For the status of Punic in Roman North Africa see Millar (1968) and Röllig (1980).

be by a well-educated Roman.[7] This is the obvious but fundamental difference separating Apuleius and other Roman literary figures with sophistic interests from the contemporary Greek figures of the Second Sophistic, who otherwise appear to match Apuleius in their interests in rhetorical and philosophical performance.[8] Though he, like Fronto, can talk lightly of his African background,[9] Apuleius, through his name, literary culture, and education, is fundamentally Roman in cultural identity and a native speaker and writer of Latin.

The date of Apuleius' birth in the 120s AD is commonly derived from several passages in his works. In *Flor.* 16 he claims to have been a fellow-student of Strabo Aemilianus, who is therefore likely to have been an approximate contemporary and was probably about thirty-two at the time of his consulship in AD 156;[10] in the *Apologia* (89) he states that his wife Pudentilla is about forty at the time of the trial (AD 158–9), and that she is somewhat older than he himself (*Apol.* 27), while he seems older than her son Pontianus, who had earlier studied with him at Athens and thinks him a suitable match for his mother (*Apol.* 72). It is a fair guess that Apuleius was in his early or middle thirties at the time of the *Apologia*, and that he was therefore born in the mid-120s AD. This makes him a contemporary of Aulus Gellius, whom he may have known personally,[11] and of the Greek writers Galen, Lucian, and Aelius Aristides; thus his life falls at the height of the Greek intellectual revival of the Second Sophistic, when Greek writers famously sought to revive the past glories of their culture in the rich cities of the Greek Mediterranean under the protection of Roman rule. As this book's title suggests, that fact is not coincidental; Apuleius' choices of career and literary genres are fundamentally influenced by what was happening to his contemporaries in the Greek world.

---

[7] The notion of 'African Latin' as an identifiable dialect is now largely discredited; but for revised versions of the argument see Lancel (1987) and Petersmann (1998). Fluency in Greek, though normal in the cultured upper classes at Rome in Apuleius' day, may have been more unusual in Roman North Africa outside cosmopolitan cities such as Carthage— cf. Kotula (1969). Apuleius is likely, of course, to present himself as more fluent in Greek than he actually was.

[8] Cf. Bowersock (1969), Anderson (1993). For a recent useful assessment of Apuleius' sophistic links see Sandy (1997).

[9] *Apol.* 24 *seminumidam et semigaetulum*, Fronto *Ad M. Caes.* II. 3. 5 van den Hout ἐγὼ δὲ Λίβυς τῶν Λιβύων with Champlin (1980), 7–8. It should of course be recalled that in the *Apologia* Apuleius is speaking to an African audience in Sabathra.

[10] *Flor.* 16. 36 *a commilitio studiorum eisdem magistris honeste incohata*; it is not clear whether these shared studies were in Carthage or Athens (the latter seems more likely). For Strabo's career cf. *PIR* S 674.

[11] Cf. n. 22 (below).

His family background was prosperous. He tells us that his father achieved the duumvirate, the 'mini-consulate' which was the highest magistracy of a *colonia*,[12] and that he had begun a public career at Madauros by 158–9 (*Apol.* 24. 9). Apuleius and his brother were left the substantial sum of 2,000,000 sesterces (five times the equestrian *census*) jointly by their father when he he died some time before 158–9 (*Apol.* 24. 9), while Augustine, not a friendly witness, states that Apuleius was *honesto patriae suae loco natus* (*Ep.* 138. 19). As a citizen and magistrate of a *colonia* he would have the Roman franchise, and possibly the three names usual in this period, but only his gentile name is certain. The name 'Apuleius' occurs in four different inscriptions found at Madauros; though none of these can be firmly dated except to the Roman imperial period in general, this distribution suggests that the family was well established there at some point.[13]

The family's earlier origins may only be guessed at. Many families in Madauros derived their names from those of Roman senators who had bestowed the franchise on native families after military service,[14] and it is possible that Apuleius' family was indigenous and gained its name and citizenship from the *gens Appuleia*, notable in the early Roman republic and known later for one of its members who married Augustus' eldest sister, but there is no known African connection of that S. Ap(p)uleius or any of his family.[15] Alternatively, Apuleius' family may have come to Madauros as settlers from Italy or elsewhere when the Flavian *colonia* was set up,[16] possibly as former soldiers in the campaigns of Vespasian or Titus. Apuleius' own characterization of himself as *seminumidam et semigaetulum* (*Apol.* 24) seems to refer to the geographical position of Madauros on the border of Numidia and Gaetulia rather than to his own

---

[12] The emperor Septimius Severus' grandfather attained the same office in Lepcis Magna (cf. Birley (1988), 19–22), and Fronto came from much the same class in Cirta (cf. Champlin (1980), 7–11); for the duumvirate in Roman North Africa cf. Lepelley (1979), 151–63.

[13] C. Apuleius Rogatus (*ILA* 2276–7), Apuleius Rufus (2278), Apuleia Quarta (2279), and the spice-merchant Apulaeus Datianus Pomponianus (2236). Ap(p)ulei are also attested in the epigraphic records of two other Roman sites in Algeria—Theveste, modern Tebessa (*ILA* 3178–9, 3601, 3608), and Turbusicu Numidarum, modern Khanissa (*ILA* 1412).

[14] Cf. the material collected in Thompson and Ferguson (1969), 166–7, 178–80. .

[15] Methy (1983) argues that Apuleius was of indigenous African origin. For S. Appuleius cf. *PIR* A 960; his son (A 961) and grandson (A 962) were both consuls, while his great-grandson (A 963) is commemorated as *ultimus gentis suae* (*CIL* 11. 1362). On the earlier history of the family and the (highly variable) spelling of the name cf. *RE* 2. 245. 32 ff.; the only Appuleius with known African connections is the tribune L. Appuleius Saturninus, who assigned land to Marius' veterans in 103 BC (*De Viris Illustribus* 73. 1).

[16] For the patterns of colonization in Roman North Africa cf. Gascou (1972) 136–229, esp. 159–65 on Flavian *coloniae*.

ethnic identity; but even if it does allude to the latter, Roman Africa was a region where 'many prominent aristocrats vociferously claimed indigenous origins when in reality they were, at least in part, descendants of settlers'.[17] Though the question of his family's origin seems insoluble in the present state of the evidence, three essential facts about Apuleius' background are clear: he was a Roman citizen of Latin nomenclature, he belonged to a leading family in his *colonia*, and he was personally wealthy at least at his father's death.

This wealth enabled him to study at a high level: elite literary education was then as throughout antiquity the preserve of the prosperous, and Apuleius' background was similar to those of other literary figures of the period in this respect. Madauros was a centre of teaching by Augustine's time, more than two centuries later (he learnt literature and rhetoric there—*Conf.* 2. 5), but Apuleius himself implies that his studies began at Carthage, the provincial capital and proconsular seat, where he acquired his basic education in letters, grammar, and rhetoric (*Flor.* 18. 15, 20. 3);[18] he also claims that his first instruction in Platonic philosophy occurred there (*Flor.* 18. 15), though here as elsewhere in his statements about Carthage in the *Florida* it needs to be recalled that they are made to a Carthaginian audience to whom such claims would naturally be pleasing. Subsequent study took him to Athens, where he claims with characteristic self-promotion to have imbibed poetry, geometry, music, dialectic, and general philosophy (*Flor.* 20. 4). These subjects, and Apuleius' self-description (*Apol.* 10. 6) and later reputation as a *philosophus Platonicus*, show that he plainly studied in the Platonist tradition: Apuleius speaks of his Platonic studies and *academicis meditationibus* (*Flor.* 15. 26), but does not mention any of his *magistri* (ibid.) by name.[19] Apuleius' philosophical studies clearly reflect the revival of Platonism in

[17] Thompson in Thompson and Ferguson (1969), 145.

[18] Though he might well not mention study at Madauros in the context of the *Florida*, taken from speeches delivered in Carthage and naturally rather stressing his Carthaginian links (cf. Ch. 2).

[19] Apuleius often alludes to himself as a Platonist and is commonly called *philosophus Platonicus* or *Platonicus* by Augustine (*Civ.* 8. 12, 8. 14, 8. 24, 9. 3, 10. 27), and once each by Sidonius (*Ep.* 9. 13. 8), Cassiodorus (*Inst.* 2. 5. 10), and Charisius (*Inst. Gram.* 2. 16 = Keil *GL* 1. 240. 27). Claims that Apuleius studied formally at the Platonic Academy confront the serious problem that the Academy seems to have no formal existence by the second century AD (see Glucker (1978), 139–42), though the title 'Academic' is still used to label Platonic philosophers, and is surely hinted at by Apuleius in *Flor.* 15. 26. Apuleius may well have studied under Sextus, the nephew of Plutarch mentioned as an ancestor of Lucius in the *Metamorphoses* (1. 2. 1); see Dillon (1977) 338, Dowden (1994), 428–9, and Ch. 6 n. 15.

the second century AD,[20] especially if he is the author of the *De Platone* (see Chapter 5), which has an evidently close relationship to other contemporary handbooks of Platonic doctrine.[21]

Apuleius tells in the *Apologia* (23) of his 'distant travels and long studies' undertaken before AD 158–9. This is partly boastful self-presentation as a globe-trotting intellectual in the manner of the great Greek sophists of the time, but apart from his studies in Athens (see above), he certainly spent time in Rome (*Flor.* 17. 4), where he may have met Aulus Gellius,[22] and was on the way to Alexandria at the beginning of the events which led to the *Apologia* (*Apol.* 72); thus he clearly knew some of the major intellectual centres of the Second Sophistic at first hand. He also seems to have gone to Samos (*Flor.* 15. 4 *si recte recordor viam*, implying autopsy) and to Hierapolis in Phrygia (*Mu.* 17 *vidi ipse apud Hierapolim Phrygiae*); he is likely also to have visited the great Greek sophistic centres of Asia Minor such as Pergamum, Smyrna, and Ephesus, if he got as far as Samos and Hierapolis. However, his silence on these great cities (which would be uncharacteristic if he had visited them) provides some counter-evidence; his evident interest in the god Aesculapius in the *Florida* and *Apologia* may owe more to the syncretism of that deity with the Punic *'smun* in Carthage (cf. *Flor.* 18. 36–7)[23] than to a visit to Pergamum, though that city and its cult of Asclepius were much frequented by second-century Greek intellectuals.[24] In general, Apuleius, a Latin speaker competent in Greek but probably unable to compete effectively with the great Greek sophists of his time on their own territory, seems to have had some knowledge of sophistic activity and its centres, but not to have joined the sophistic circus of the Greek East, settling instead for the life of a public lecturer and declaimer in Latin in North Africa. In the *Apologia*, probably the earliest work we have, he appears at the age of thirty or so as a fully-fledged public performer, declaiming *de maiestate Aesculapii* at Oea (*Apol.* 55, 73), and producing in the *Apologia* itself what has been justly termed a masterpiece of the Second Sophistic.[25]

[20] On this revival cf. Whittaker (1987).

[21] On the relation of *De Platone* to other Platonic handbooks see the discussion in Ch. 5.

[22] On well-travelled sophists see Ch. 2 n. 78. For the possible acquaintance between Apuleius and Gellius cf. Holford-Strevens (1988), 16–19, and Sandy (1993). Coarelli's identification with L. Apuleius Marcellus (n. 2) would of course require that Apuleius lived in Ostia for some time in the late 140s or early 150s AD.

[23] Cf. Huss (1985), 516–17, 522, Lipiński (1994).

[24] Cf. Habicht (1969), 1–20, Polemo at Philostratus *VS* 1. 25. 535, and the life-long connection of Aristides with Pergamum—cf. Behr (1968).

[25] So Helm (1955), 86.

During a period of study in Athens, perhaps in the early 150s, he met and shared rooms with a fellow-student named Pontianus, like himself from Roman North Africa, from Oea, the modern Tripoli in Libya (*Apol.* 72). The consequences of this are well known from the *Apologia*; naturally, we have only Apuleius' own forensically-slanted version of events in that famous speech (which will be discussed in detail in Chapter 2). It may be summarized as follows. Several years after his first acquaintance with Pontianus (*Apol.* 72), probably towards the end of 156,[26] Apuleius set out (perhaps from Carthage) on the long journey to Alexandria, and rested with friends at Oea on the way. He was there visited by Pontianus, who persuaded him to stay for a whole year and eventually to marry his mother Pudentilla, a rich widow, in order to protect her fortune for her sons: the marriage seems to have taken place in late 157 or early 158. Subsequently, in the course of appearing for his wife at the proconsular assizes in a case concerning a property dispute, Apuleius was accused by several relations of Pudentilla's of having induced her to marry him through magic means. This case was heard (presumably during the same assizes) at Sabathra, near Oea, by the proconsul Claudius Maximus, apparently in late 158 or early 159.[27] Though we are nowhere told so, it is clear that Apuleius was acquitted; the publication of such a *tour de force* as the *Apologia* is not the act of a defeated party, and it is an impressive advertisement of Apuleius' talents as a public speaker.

Other evidence for Apuleius' rhetorical activities derives from the *Florida,* an extant collection of twenty-three extracts from his speeches (discussed in detail in Chapter 3). Some of the speeches from which these are taken were clearly delivered at Carthage (*Flor.* 9, 15, 16, 17, 18): two extracts are from speeches delivered in the presence of proconsuls of Africa in the 160s AD (*Flor.* 9 for Severianus Honorius, proconsul 162–3, and *Flor.* 17 for Scipio Orfitus, proconsul 163–4),[28] and *Flor.* 16 refers to the hopes of Strabo Aemilianus, consul 156, of becoming proconsul, something to which he might plausibly have aspired in the late 160s or early 170s.[29] Thus no date to be extracted from the *Florida* takes Apuleius' career much beyond the 160s, but it is clear that in that decade at least he was a successful public speaker in Carthage: he mentions in the undated *Flor.* 18 (18. 16) that he has been declaiming at Carthage for some six years.

---

[26] This follows the chronology of Guey (1951).

[27] This follows the dating of Maximus' proconsulate by Guey (1951) and Syme (1959).

[28] Dates according to Syme (1959).

[29] The gap between consulship and proconsulate of Africa seems to have been about fifteen years in this period—see the table in Syme (1959), and Thomasson (1960), i. 31.

Flor. 16 also reflects his established status there, since it renders thanks for the honour of a statue voted by the senate and people of Carthage, and for election to the chief priesthood of the province of Africa Proconsularis, an honour confirmed by the testimony of Augustine (*Ep.* 138. 19).[30] This last fact makes it clear that Apuleius, like contemporary Greek sophists, not only came from a respectable background but also increased his social status by rhetorical activities within his home community;[31] in the 160s he clearly belongs to the elite of Carthage, at least partly because of his talents as a speaker, and no doubt because of his wealth (only the rich could afford the liturgy of a provincial priesthood).

The brilliant lecture *De Deo Socratis* (treated in greater detail in Chapter 4), which discusses the topic, popular in Middle Platonism, of the *daimonion* or guardian spirit of Socrates, is also likely to have been delivered to a Carthaginian audience in the 160s. It seems that after the triumph of the *Apologia,* the publication of which could not have harmed his career, Apuleius spent much time in Carthage, which as a cosmopolitan provincial capital relatively close to Rome served as a good showcase for his talents. He may have retained some kind of connection with his native town; the famous inscription found at Madauros recording the setting-up of a statue to a 'Platonic philosopher' is very likely to honour Apuleius, given that the title was applied to him by himself and others.[32] *Flor.* 16. 37 states that cities other than Carthage had honoured Apuleius with statues, and it would be only natural for the relatively unimportant Madauros to celebrate a son of one of its best families who had achieved fame and success in the province at large.

There is no firm evidence for Apuleius' career after the 160s AD. Two

---

[30] Rives (1994) has recently argued that this may have been the priesthood of Aesculapius rather than the *sacerdotium provinciae,* and that Augustine may have been guessing, but Augustine seems to know more about Apuleius than the latter's extant works reveal (cf. n. 1 above), and there is no reason to doubt his testimony. Other sophists were made provincial priests in the Greek East—e.g. Favorinus (Philostratus *VS* 1. 8. 490), Scopelian (*VS* 1. 21. 515), and Heraclides the Lycian (*VS* 2. 26. 613), while Aristides successfully appealed against election to the high priesthood of Asia—cf. Bowersock (1969), 35 and 38. *Flor.* 16 seems to imply that Apuleius was a member of the Carthaginian senate, who have there voted him the honour of a statue in his absence (cf. Ch. 3 n. 84), and this would be fully consistent with his high social standing in the city; though in the usual manner of Roman elites he, as a magistrate's son, attended the senate of Madauros as an observer (*Apol.* 24. 9 *curiam participare coepi*), there is no evidence that he was himself a magistrate there.

[31] On the social status of the Greek sophists cf. Bowie (1982); for Apuleius' role in the development of Latin education at Carthage cf. Opeku (1993).

[32] *ILA* 2115 (on a statue-base) *ph]ilosopho [Pl]atonico | [Ma]daurenses cives | ornament[o] suo. d(ecreto) d(ecurionum), p(ecunia) [p(ublica)]*; for Apuleius as *philosophus Platonicus* cf. n. 19.

works, *De Mundo* (a version of Aristotle's treatise) and *De Platone* (a summary of Platonic doctrine), are ascribed to Apuleius, with some plausibility (see the treatment in Chapter 5). Both books in their prefaces address *fili Faustine,* most naturally interpreted as the writer's son Faustinus: if Apuleius had a son old enough to be concerned with such matters by Pudentilla or a later wife, then these works would belong to the 170s or (probably) later. Their content would also suggest that the writer was concerned with didactic exposition in Latin of the major authorities of Greek philosophy, a credible development in Apuleius' career given his view of himself (especially in the *Apologia*) as a *philosophus Platonicus* who gives a Latin-speaking audience the benefit of his studies. The evidence of an encyclopaedic trend in his writings (see Section 2 (iii) below) and for the existence of pupils who studied with Apuleius (see Section 2 (ii) 17 below) suggests an interest in education; it is possible to imagine a career of rhetorical performance and teaching for Apuleius continuing at Carthage into the 170s, 180s, or even 190s, but there is no substantial evidence for this, unless we regard the *De Mundo* and *De Platone* as indicative of a particularly didactic phase in Apuleius' later career, as tentatively suggested in Chapter 5. Unlike some writers of the period, such as Fronto, Apuleius does not seem to have pursued a political career after literary or rhetorical successes; Augustine, admittedly a jaundiced witness, records that he never achieved a judicial magistracy in the province of Africa, and that the priesthood mentioned in *Flor.* 16 was the highest public office he attained.[33]

Scholars have disagreed about the dating of the *Metamorphoses* or *Golden Ass,* Apuleius' most celebrated work (treated in Chapter 6). Some regard this exuberant fiction as a youthful work, aimed at a Roman readership with whom Apuleius had greater contact in the earlier part of his career,[34] while others see its consummate style and dense literary texture as belonging to the mature period of his life.[35] Objective dating criteria are hard to find; those which have been suggested from *Realien* are ultimately insubstantial or indecisive.[36] But a number of considerations

[33] Augustine *Ep.* 138. 19; see n. 31.

[34] e.g. Bernhard (1927), 357–60, Dowden (1994). For a detailed argument for a date 158–61 and discussion of other views see Carratello (1963).

[35] e.g. Walsh (1970) 248–51, though he relies on some 'objective' evidence which is inconclusive. I agree with Holford-Strevens (1988), 17 n. 59, who suggests that the *Metamorphoses* was written under Commodus (after 180).

[36] Cf. Bowersock (1965), 282 n. 31, followed by Walsh (1970), 250, essentially inconclusive, and Summers (1973); it is naturally difficult to prove that naturalistic fictional details are in fact specific historical allusions.

suggest with some probability that the *Metamorphoses* belongs at least after the *Apologia* of 158/9. First, the *Metamorphoses*, which contains stories of magic and much obscenity, was apparently not known to Apuleius' accusers in his trial on charges of sorcery: there is no hint at all of it in the *Apologia*. Second, the *Metamorphoses* seems to display allusions to Apuleius' own career in the period of the *Apologia*. Like Apuleius, Lucius in *Met.* 3 faces a trial on trumped-up charges in which he defends himself with brilliant rhetoric, and after which, like Apuleius at Carthage and probably at Madauros, he is rewarded by the honour of a statue.[37] Like the marriage of Apuleius and Pudentilla, that of Cupid and Psyche in the *Metamorphoses* is impugned by opponents for its secretive location in a country villa.[38] Third, Apuleius' own list of the various literary genres he has attempted in *Flor.* 9. 27–8, dated to 162–3, does not include prose fiction, though it mentions a wide range of things (see below). Fourth, as I shall argue in Chapter 6, there seems some reason to date the *Metamorphoses* after the publication of the *Sacred Tales* of Aelius Aristides, which probably dates from the 170s AD. It is thus reasonable to argue that the *Metamorphoses* was written after the *Apologia*, and perhaps at a late stage in Apuleius' career. In the light of the current evidence, there is no reason why the *Metamorphoses* could not belong to the 170s or 180s AD, where I would like to place it as the climax of Apuleius' literary career.

2. WRITINGS

(i) *Extant Works*

The major surviving works firmly or plausibly attributed to Apuleius are all treated later in this book—the *Apologia*, *Florida*, *Metamorphoses*, *De Deo Socratis*, *De Platone*, and *De Mundo*, all already mentioned. Our knowledge of the *Apologia*, *Florida*, and *Metamorphoses* is derived from a single eleventh-century manuscript, F, and the *De Deo Socratis*, *De Platone*, and *De Mundo* likewise descend together through a separate branch of the tradition which would seem to go back to a collected edi-

---

[37] Cf. van der Paardt (1971), 89 and 91, who is cautious about the similarity because of consequent identity between Lucius and Apuleius; but that need not follow, since this is a fictionalized allusion not requiring identity. For further possible links between the character Lucius and the real-life Apuleius see Ch. 6 below.

[38] Cf. Kenney (1990a), 203.

tion of Apuleius' works.[39] Though the authenticity of the *De Platone* and *De Mundo* has been questioned, there is a good chance that these works are Apuleian (see Chapter 5), and they both offer some interest for literary readers.

There are two other ancient works ascribed to Apuleius. The Περὶ Ἑρμηνείας (an original Greek title) is a brief Latin version of Aristotelian logical doctrine in dry and technical language which offers little of stylistic or literary interest; it has a textual tradition separate from that of other Apuleian works, but has been attributed to Apuleius in its manuscript transmission and in the indirect tradition since late antiquity.[40] Added evidence cited for Apuleian authorship is that it uses the name of Apuleius in several of its examples, and seems to cover the logical territory of the otherwise lost third book of the *De Platone* (cf. *Pl.* 1. IV. 189), certainly credible in a Middle Platonist context.[41] However, the case could easily be argued the opposite way:[42] the work's separate textual tradition, its use of Apuleius' name in examples,[43] and its apparent supplying of material missing from the *De Platone* could all equally well indicate a later writer following Apuleius, perhaps a pupil attempting to graft his work on to that of his master or summarizing Apuleian doctrine.[44] Stylistically, though the highly specialized nature of the treatise and its consequent

---

[39] For a good summary of the textual transmission of Apuleius cf. Reynolds (1983), 15–18.

[40] M, the earliest manuscript (seventh/eighth century), attributes the work to *Apuleius philosophus*, and several allusions in Cassiodorus (*Inst.* 2. 3. 12, picked up by Isidore *Et.* 2. 28. 22) take the attribution back to the sixth century. Martianus Capella in the fourth century pillages the work, but without acknowledgement.

[41] See e.g. Londey and Johanson (1987), 12–13.

[42] First by Hildebrand (1842), vol. i, p. xliv, who raised most of the modern arguments against authenticity. The work is not considered genuine by either of the two major modern editors of Apuleius' philosophical works—Beaujeu (1973) (see pp. vii–viii) and Moreschini (1991), who argues for this view in Moreschini (1985), 27–49. For modern supporters of Apuleian authorship see Sullivan (1967), Baldassari (1986), Hijmans (1987), 408–11, Londey and Johanson (1987), and Sandy (1997), 38–41 (who attaches it to Apuleius' early studies in Athens); Sallmann (1997), 301–2 (with useful bibliography) gives a balanced view, cautiously in favour of authenticity.

[43] All in 267: 'Apuleius disserit' . . . *ut si pro 'Apuleio' dicas 'philosophum Platonicum Madaurensem'.*

[44] It also worth observing that the most recent research into the prose-rhythm of the philosophical works attributed to Apuleius finds not only that the *De Mundo, De Platone,* Περὶ Ἑρμηνείας, and *Asclepius* all show accentual rather than quantitative rhythms, differing from other Apuleian works in this (see Ch. 5), but also that the Περὶ Ἑρμηνείας and *Asclepius* show a 'purely' accentual technique (the *cursus*), while the *De Mundo* and *De Platone* show a 'mixed' accentual/quantitative technique (the *cursus mixtus*), another indication that the author of the *De Mundo* and *De Platone* is unlikely to be identical with those of the Περὶ Ἑρμηνείας and *Asclepius*—cf. Oberhelman and Hall (1985), 222, Oberhelman (1988a), 145.

technical language offer relatively little scope for effective comparison, it offers virtually none of the typically Apuleian archaic and poetic vocabulary to be found throughout even the less colourful *De Platone* and *De Mundo*.[45] Though Apuleian authorship of the Περὶ Ἑρμηνείας is not in my view absolutely impossible, and though it played an important role in transmitting Aristotelian logic to the Middle Ages, this work will not be treated in this volume, since its highly technical content is beyond my competence and has been much discussed recently.[46]

The *Asclepius*, a version of a largely lost Greek Hermetic treatise,[47] has the same textual transmission as the philosophical works of Apuleius, but there are three strong reasons for not believing it to be genuinely Apuleian.[48] First, none of the manuscripts which contain it, though within the Apuleian corpus, attribute it to Apuleius; second, none of the several testimonia to the *Asclepius* in Augustine, who knew the Apuleian corpus well, ascribe it to Apuleius; and third, the work shows some fundamental divergences from Apuleian linguistic usage.[49] The ascription to Apuleius might well be motivated as in the case of the Περὶ Ἑρμηνείας by an interest in swelling the already diverse Apuleian canon with appropriate additions; the prominence of Aesculapius in Apuleius' work is a

---

[45] I can find only five Apuleian-type colourful usages, poeticisms, or archaisms in this work of twenty-five Teubner pages: *quispiam* (266), *hinnibilis* (267), *supervacaneus* (272), *hicce* (275) (see n. 74 below), *perquam* (280). The first three pages of the *De Platone* and the *De Mundo* both supply more than this.

[46] See esp. Londey and Johanson (1987), and the very useful annotated bibliography in Bajoni (1992), 374–8. My Oxford colleague Dr Suzanne Bobzien is currently working on an edition of this work.

[47] See Nock in Nock and Festugière (1945), 275–7, Wigtil (1984).

[48] For all these points see the fundamental treatment of Nock in Nock and Festugière (1945), 277–83, and the convincing arguments of Horsfall Scotti (1990), 312–17. For a recent attempt to establish Apuleian authorship, following Hijmans (1987), 411–13, see Hunink (1996); G. Madec in Herzog (1989), 356, and Gersh (1986), i. 218–19 are firmly for inauthenticity. Gersh (1986), i. 329–87, gives a full analysis of the dialogue; for an annotated modern translation cf. Copenhaver (1992), 67–92, 213–60.

[49] To give the most striking examples, supplementing the list of Nock (Nock and Festugière (1945)), the *Asclepius* in forty-eight Teubner pages does not use the words *ceterum, commodum, cur* (in a work framed as questions to a god and his answers), *eiusmodi, ferme, frustra, igitur* (though it uses *itaque*, uncommon in Apuleius outside the *Met.*, very freely), *immo, inquit* (in a work where at least some speech is reported indirectly), *interdum, interim, item*, impersonal *licet, longe, mox, namque, negare, ne . . . quidem, oppido, paene, partim, plerumque, plerusque, praeterea, profecto, prorsus, protinus, rursum/rursus, saltem*, and *sane*, all relatively neutral words occurring frequently in genuine Apuleian works (these figures rely on the accuracy of the *Index Apuleianus*, since *Asclepius* is not included on the PHI CD-ROM). Most striking of all, perhaps, is the fact that the *Asclepius* uses only the name-form 'Asclepius', while the firmly Apuleian works all use 'Aesculapius' (*Apol.* 55. 10, *Flor.* 18. 42, *DDS* xv. 154).

strong motivation for a late antique editor to group the *Asclepius* with Apuleius' works.[50]

Both these works, if they are falsely ascribed to Apuleius as I think certain for the *Asclepius* and likely for the Περὶ Ἑρμηνείας, show the capacity of later writers and editors to compose para-Apuleian works or attach such works to the genuine Apuleian tradition; such pseudepigraphical additions are particularly common for writers in the period of the Second Sophistic with a large and varied output, inviting accretions of this kind.[51] More obviously non-authentic are two further works of late antiquity ascribed to Apuleius—the brief *Herbarius* or treatise on the medical use of herbs, and the longer *Physiognomonia*, a physiognomic treatise. The *Herbarius* claims to be by Apuleius in its preface, but is undoubtedly later and probably from the fourth century AD,[52] and is no doubt ascribed to Apuleius because of his prestige and his lost work on medical botany (see fr. 14 below), just as the anonymous *Medicina Plinii* made similar false claims to be by Pliny the Younger.[53] The *Physiognomonia* interestingly deals with a topic of particular interest in Apuleius' period, with which Apuleius himself shows some connections, and claims the sophist Polemo (whom it calls Palemo) as one of its sources.[54] However, it does not itself claim to be by Apuleius, an attribution which was made as late as the nineteenth century;[55] and, indeed, the most detailed studies of the treatise demonstrates that this ascription is false, and that this work is to be dated to the third or fourth century AD.[56]

Quite apart from these accretions, which suggest that Apuleius' diverse output could easily encourage later additions,[57] the list of genuine

[50] For Aesculapius in Apuleius cf. *Apol.* 55, *Flor.* 18, *DDS* 15, and n. 23 above.

[51] The appreciable number of inauthentic works attached to the canons of Dio Chrysostom, Plutarch, and Lucian are good examples.

[52] This text is also known as *De Medicaminibus Herbarum*: see the full treatment by Maggiulli and Buffa Giolito (1996); a text is to be found in Howald (1927).

[53] See the edition of this work in Önnefors (1964).

[54] For Apuleian interest in physiognomy cf. *Met.* 2. 2. 8–9, *Pl.* 1. 1. 183, and Opeku (1979). For Polemo's interest in physiognomy, the treatise ascribed to him, and the popularity of the topic in the Second Sophistic, see Gleason (1995), 29–81.

[55] See Förster (1893), vol. i, p. cxxxvii.

[56] Kelter (1890), Förster (1893), vol. i, pp. cxxxi–cxlv.

[57] I here mention for the sake of completeness the further works even more improbably ascribed to Apuleius: *De Remediis Salutaribus*, another brief fragment on medical botany found in the medieval tradition of Pliny's *Natural History* and clearly from late antiquity (Schanz, Hosius, and Kruger (1922), 131–2), a medieval *De Monarchia*, and two medieval grammatical treatises *De Nota Aspirationis* and *De Dipthongis* (for these last three see the bibliography in Sallmann (1997), 317). The last two were probably the inspiration for the

extant Apuleian works already shows a remarkable versatility. The four major works, *Metamorphoses, Apologia, Florida,* and *De Deo Socratis,* are written in a characteristically rhythmical style, highly archaic and colourful, but the *De Platone* and *De Mundo* demonstrate a much drier style appropriate to the technical treatise.[58] More generally, Apuleius' extant works are characteristic of his time and place as a Latin writer in the second century AD, influenced not only by contemporary Roman culture but also by the Second Sophistic then flourishing in the Greek part of the empire. Forensic oratory (the *Apologia*) was the field where Fronto and other North Africans had achieved fame at Rome in the previous generation,[59] while epideictic speeches, such as those evidenced by the *Florida,* and popular philosophical lectures, such as the *De Deo Socratis,* were the intellectual life-blood of the Second Sophistic. Works of prose fiction, too, such as the *Metamorphoses,* seem to have been particularly common in Apuleius' time: of the two Latin novels and the seven complete Greek ones, at least four may belong to the later second century AD.[60] Finally, the kind of philosophical doxography found in the *De Platone* reflects the revival of interest in Platonic philosophy in this period, shown in similar contemporary handbooks of Platonic doctrine such as that by Alcinous.[61]

(ii) *Fragments of and Testimonia to Lost Works*

Both Apuleius' literary versatility and his close connections with the intellectual currents of his time are considerably extended if we add the fragments of and testimonia to lost works. He himself, ever keen to proclaim his own talents, speaks of his own versatility in two passages of the *Florida.* First, 9. 27–8:

sed pro his praeoptare me fateor uno chartario calamo me reficere poemata omnigenus apta virgae, lyrae, socco, coturno, item satiras ac griphos, item histo-

---

forged grammatical work circulated in the Renaissance under the name of L. Caecilius Minutianus Apuleius (on which see Jocelyn (1990)).

[58] The best comparative stylistic analysis of individual Apuleian works is still that in Bernhard (1927), though on the different style of the *De Mundo* and *De Platone* there is much helpful material in Redfors (1960).

[59] Cf. Champlin (1980), 18–19.

[60] Longus, Achilles Tatius, and Xenophon of Ephesus may all belong to the second century AD: cf. Hunter (1983), 1–15, Reardon (1991). For a good introduction to the Greek novels and the best modern translations see Reardon (1989).

[61] On second-century Platonism in general see Whittaker (1987); for Apuleius' Platonism see Moreschini (1978), Gianotti (1986), Gersh (1986), Hijmans (1987), Fick-Michel (1991), and Münstermann (1995). For the handbook of Alcinous see further Ch. 5.

rias varias rerum nec non orationes laudatas disertis nec non dialogos laudatos philosophis, atque et alia eiusdem modi tam graece quam latine, gemino voto, pari studio, simili stilo.

Here Apuleius claims to have worked in a wide range of poetic genres (epic, lyric, comedy, tragedy, satire, riddles)[62] and three prose genres—*variae historiae rerum*, probably collections of historical or other narratives in the manner of Aelian's *Varia Historia*, oratory, and philosophical dialogues. Note that prose fiction is not mentioned, some indication perhaps that the *Metamorphoses* had not been written by this date. Of the poetic genres mentioned, lyric, comedy, and satire can arguably be found in Apuleius' known output (below), while each of the three prose genres is there exemplified (the *Epitoma Historiarum*, the *Florida* themselves, and the *Phaedo*—see below). One claim here which appears not to be justified by the evidence is that of equal facility and literary production in both Latin and Greek; in fact, the only firm support for Greek works by Apuleius comes from his own assertions, since all the preserved fragments of lost works are in Latin or are most likely to be taken from a Latin original. Apuleius surely did write Greek poems and declamations as he here claims and Greek scientific works as he states in the *Apologia* (36), just as his fellow-North African Tertullian in the next generation wrote some works in Greek now lost,[63] but the great preponderance of Latin amongst his known works is not merely an accident of survival in Latin sources. His claims of complete bilingualism are likely to be exaggerated for effect and self-promotion; his self-representation as equally at home in Greek clearly reflects the world of the Second Sophistic, where Greek was the language of star rhetorical performers. By claiming the same facility in performance and literary production in Greek as in Latin, Apuleius could present himself to a North African audience as belonging, however tenuously, to the group of greatest international intellectual prestige in the Roman empire of his own day.[64]

The second relevant passage of the *Florida* is 20. 5–6:

canit enim Empedocles carmina, Plato dialogos, Socrates hymnos, Epicharmus modos, Xenophon historias, Crates satiras: Apuleius vester haec omnia novemque Musas pari studio colit, maiore scilicet voluntate quam facultate.

---

[62] *Virgae* refers to the rod (ῥάβδος) wielded by the rhapsode or epic performer—cf. Callimachus fr. 26. 5 Pf.

[63] For the Greek works of Tertullian see Barnes (1971), 68–9.

[64] For the rarity of such bilingualism in Roman North Africa see Kotula (1969); this view seems to fit the evidence better than the over-optimistic approach of Thieling (1911), shared by Sandy (1997), 9–11, who regards Apuleius as 'fully bilingual in Greek and Latin' (ix).

Here the assertion of literary versatility is for once accompanied by a profession of modesty, perhaps because this is clearly a *captatio benevolentiae* at the beginning of a speech. Apuleius is clearly arguing that philosophers have written poetry and other works of literary character in the past, and that he as a philosopher is following this tradition through the variety of his output. The only genre to appear in this list (if *modos* is taken to refer to lyric poems, which is not easy)[65] which was not included in the list in *Flor.* 9 is that of the hymn, but this is justified, since we know that Apuleius wrote hymns to Asclepius in both Greek and Latin (see 13 below).

More detailed evidence for the titles and contents of Apuleius' lost and fragmentary works derives from quotation or allusion in his own works and the works of others. As a public performer in an intellectual age who depends for status on his reputation as a *philosophus Platonicus* and a man of wide learning, Apuleius has every reason to allude to his various literary works, and loses few opportunities for doing so. His extensive output was also clearly a useful repository of knowledge for Latin writers in late antiquity, increasingly unable to read Greek and dependent on convenient summaries of Greek learning such as Apuleius often provided; but there is also apparent evidence that Apuleius' Latin works were read at Byzantium (see 3, 4, 5, 7, 10, and 11 below). In what follows, a complete list will be given of the works which can be identified through such means; Beaujeu's numeration of the fragments will be followed for convenience, and the reader will be assumed to have his Budé edition to hand, though all except the longest fragments will here be cited in full.[66]

1. *Fr. 1. Ludicra*

Nonius (p. 96 Lindsay) cites a trochaic septenarius from Apuleius' *Liber Ludicrorum*:

---

[65] Stramaglia (1996), 192, convincingly questions the reading *modos*, which cannot by itself designate lyric poetry, suggesting Teuffel's *mimos* or *comoedias*, or Rohde's *gnomas*; given that Epicharmus was primarily known as a comic poet to whom philosophical works were also attributed, *comoedias* seems most appropriate here.

[66] Beaujeu (1973) is the best collection of the fragments, though not entirely exhaustive. Useful recent treatments are to be found in Zimmerman (1996) and Sallmann (1997), 293–313; there is a brief survey in Sandy (1997), 36–41. It is notable that many of the citations come from Priscian, who was born in North Africa (in Mauretania), wrote in Byzantium, and may have had a particular interest in the North African Apuleius, whom he seems to cite directly—cf. Stramaglia (1996).

sed fuisti quondam Athenis parcus atque abstemius.[67]

It is no surprise to find Apuleius, who shared the archaizing tastes of his time,[68] using a common metre of early Roman comedy. Further evidence for the *Ludicra* comes from the *Apologia*, where Apuleius quotes some comic iambics of his own sending dentifrice to Calpurnianus *de ludicris meis*, suggesting that a collection of his *Ludicra* is already available at that date (*Apol.* 6):

> Calpurniane, salve properis vorsibus.
> misi, ut petisti, <tibi> munditias dentium,
> nitelas oris ex Arabicis frugibus,
> tenuem, candificum, nobilem pulvisculum,
> complanatorem tumidulae gingivulae,
> converritorem pridianae reliquiae,
> ne qua visatur taetra labes sordium,
> restrictis forte si labellis riseris.

This poem is clearly based on Catullus 39, about Egnatius' dental hygiene, and in a closely related iambic metre, cited by Apuleius shortly afterwards; its occasional nature is clear both from its content and its initial reference to extempore composition (*properis vorsibus*). Though the style owes something to Catullus, the poem is less ambitious metrically,[69] and characteristic Apuleian elements are evident—apparent coinages on archaic models (*nitela, candificus, complanatorem, converritorem*),[70] use of diminutives, a taste of course shared with Catullus (*pulvisculus,*

---

[67] For a detailed discussion of this line and its context in Nonius see Rocca (1978).

[68] On second-century archaizing taste in Latin in general the best work is still Marache (1952); on its effect on the style of Apuleius see (e.g.) Médan (1925), Bernhard (1927), Callebat (1964), Roncaioli (1966), and Sandy (1997), 52–7. On archaizing poetry in particular, see Steinmetz (1982), 295–373, and the brief summary by Courtney (1993), 372–4; on Apuleius' interest in and use of archaic Latin poets in general see Mattiacci (1986), and for further general treatments of his poetry Steinmetz (1982), 336–41, Mattiacci (1985), Blänsdorf (1995), 362–6, and Sallmann (1997), 297–8.

[69] Note that Apuleius' poem is not in the more difficult choliambics of Catullus but in the easier Plautine senarii, which (unlike any of Catullus' iambic poems) permit resolutions of iambi into tribrachs, dactyls, and anapaests (Apuleius' eight-line poem has eight of these); cf. Steinmetz (1982), 340–1.

[70] All appearing for the first time in Apuleius; *candificus, converritor,* and *complanator* are unique, *candificus* and *nitela* occuring only once again in Latin. The first three are compounds with an archaic flavour: for the verbal derivatives *converritor* and *complanator* cf. *coniector* (Plautus *Poen.* 444), *compressor* (Plautus *Aul.* arg. 2), *conquisitor* (Plautus *Am.* 64), and *contortor* (Terence *Ph.* 374), and for the *-ficus* termination cf. Hofmann and Szantyr (1965), ii. 396. For *nitela* cf. *custodela* (Plautus *Merc.* 233, Apuleius *Met.* 9. 1), *fugela* (Cato *Or.* 81, Apuleius *Apol.* 98), and *suadela* (Plautus *Cist.* 566, Apuleius *Met.* 9. 25).

tumidulus, gingivula),[71] and some elements of rhyming at line-end (*vor-sibus/frugibus, dentium/pulvisculum/sordium, gingivulae/reliquiae*).[72]

The other poems of his own reproduced by Apuleius in the *Apologia*, two elegiac erotic epigrams addressed to Critias and Charinus (*Apol.* 9), are likely to have belonged to the *Ludicra* as well, both for their light content (they are clearly in the tradition of Hellenistic erotic epigram) and because Apuleius' accusers (who have raised them against him in the forensic context of the *Apologia*) are likely to have got them from the same source as the nearby poem on dentifrice. Here is the first:[73]

> et Critias mea delicia est, et salva, Charine,
>   pars in amore meo, vita, tibi remanet;
> ne metuas; nam me ignis et ignis torreat ut vult
>   hasce duas flammas, dum potiar, patiar.
> hoc modo sim vobis unus sibi quisque quod ipse est:
>   hoc mihi vos eritis, quod duo sunt oculi.

Once again we see archaism (*hasce*),[74] a pronounced rhyming effect (*dum potiar, patiar*), and some signs of relatively modest poetical ability (note the lack of any medial caesura in the third line, and the slightly convoluted and prosaic ten-word hexameter in the fifth). The second is similar:

> florea serta, meum mel, et haec tibi carmina dono,
>   carmina dono tibi, serta tuo genio,
> carmina uti, Critia, lux haec optata canatur,
>   quae bis septeno vere tibi remeat,
> serta autem, ut laeto tibi tempore tempora vernent,
>   aetatis florem floribus ut decores.
> tu mihi des contra pro verno flore tuum ver,
>   ut nostra exsuperes munera muneribus;
> pro implexis sertis complexum corpore redde,
>   proque rosis oris savia purpurei.
> quod si animam inspires donaci, iam carmina nostra
>   cedent victa tuo dulciloquo calamo.

---

[71] *Pulvisculus* is Plautine (*Rud.* 845, *Truc.* 19), while *tumidulus* and *gingivula* are first found in Apuleius—for Apuleian diminutives see Koziol (1872), 260–6 (still the best collection), Bernhard (1927), 135–8. The latter two features clearly recall the style of Catullus, also fond of diminutives (Ross (1969), 22–6): *gingivula* clearly invents a diminutive for *gingiva* in the Catullan poem imitated here (39. 19 *defricare gingivam*), while *tumidulus* is similar to the Catullan coinage *turgidulus* (3. 18).

[72] For Apuleian rhyming see Bernhard (1927), 224–8

[73] For further commentary on both poems see Steinmetz (1982), 337–40, Courtney (1993), 394–5.   [74] For the archaic colour of *hicce* cf. *TLL* 6. 2694. 58 ff.

The insistent jingling word-plays (*carmina . . . carmina . . . carmina . . . canatur, tempore tempora, florem floribus, verno . . . ver, munera muneribus, implexis . . . complexum*) and the select and archaizing vocabulary (*floreus, remeare, donax, dulciloquus*)[75] are again typically Apuleian. There are also two other preserved poems, too long for full quotation here, but similar in style and erotic content. A risqué adaptation in twenty-four iambic senarii of a speech from Menander's lost Ἀνεχόμενος preserved under Apuleius' name in the *Anthologia Latina* and very likely to be by him may also have come from the *Ludicra*; the same is true of an expansion to seventeen iambic lines of Plato's famous distich on kissing Agathon, quoted by Gellius (*NA* 19. 11. 6), which has also been plausibly attributed to Apuleius.[76]

On this evidence, the *Ludicra* seems to have been a collection of light and amusing poems, perhaps with some erotic flavour. The general sense of the title supports this (the *Metamorphoses* too can be alluded to as *ludicra*, indicating its frivolous and erotic character),[77] since it clearly translates Greek παιγνία, the title of several collections of short poems in the Hellenistic period;[78] similar Latin collections such as the lost *Erotopaegnia* of Laevius, a suitably archaic poet clearly known to Apuleius himself (*Apol.* 30), and the extant but later *Technopaegnia* of Ausonius confirm that the title suits books of light verse, no doubt in a variety of metres as in Apuleius' collection.[79] The *Ludicra*, evidently following in the tradition of Catullus and of earlier Roman poets who adapted Hellenistic epigram,[80] bear little relation to the output of Greek sophists; some of the

---

[75] *Floreus* and *remeare* are both select poetical words with archaic flavour, both first found in Plautus (*Aul.* 385, *Epid.* 662; note that *florea serta* is taken from Martial 8. 77. 4), *dulciloquus* is a hapax, though it is likely to belong to lost archaic poetry (Gellius *NA* 19. 7. 13 cites the similar *dulcioreloquus* from Laevius, and see Skutsch's note on Ennius *Ann.* 304 *suaviloquenti*), and *donax* uses a Greek poetic term for 'reed-pipe' (cf. Theocritus 20. 29) found before Apuleius in Latin only twice without musical connotation (Pliny *HN* 16. 165, 24. 86).

[76] Apuleian authorship of the Menander version is supported by the detailed discussions of Harrison (1992) and Courtney (1993), 397–400, and accepted by Sallmann (1997), 298; for further discussion of the Plato version see Dahlmann (1979), Steinmetz (1982), 334–6, Courtney (1993), 395–7. For Gellius and Apuleius see Holford-Strevens (1988), 16–19.

[77] For *ludicra* describing the *Met.* cf. *SHA Clod. Alb.* 12. 12 *cum ille inter Milesias Punicas Apulei sui et ludicra litteraria consenesceret.* For *ludicra* referring to light verse cf. *TLL* 7. 2. 1763. 70 ff.

[78] For these (including one by Philetas, fr. 10–11 Powell) see Courtney (1993), 119.

[79] For Laevius and his collection cf. Courtney (1993), 118–22. For Ausonius' collection cf. Green (1991), 583–4.

[80] For the links between these poems of Apuleius and the archaic Latin epigrammatists such as Valerius Aedituus see the commentary of Courtney (1993).

latter are known for poetic production, but none seems to have produced a similar collection of short miscellaneous poems.[81] Analogies are rather to be sought in the short poems in trochaics supposedly exchanged by Florus and Hadrian, and the similar works of the Latin poets of the second century in general, sometimes misleadingly referred to as *poetae novelli*.[82]

2. Fr. 2 (+ fr. 19a–d). De Proverbiis

A single firm quotation is known:

Fr. 2. Charisius *GLK* 1. 240:

mutmut non facere audet, ut apud Apuleium Platonicum de proverbiis scriptum est libro II.

This is clearly not an original Apuleian saying but a version of a traditional proverb found in Ennius according to Varro, *LL* 7. 101 *neque, ut aiunt, μῦ facere audent*, and the *De Proverbiis* was clearly a paroemiographical compilation in at least two books. Like many ancient proverbs, the quotation is in verse-form, forming the end of a hexameter as in Ennius.[83]

It is also possible that Apuleius' work contained the five moralizing iambic lines (three single lines and one distich) claimed by Barth as attributed to Apuleius in a manuscript known in the seventeenth century which has since disappeared (the lines are preserved as Beaujeu's fragments 19a–d):

    a. principium vitae . . . obitus meditatio est
    b. non vult emendari peccare nesciens
    c. immoderata ira genetrix est insaniae.
    d. pecuniam amico credens fert damnum duplex
       argentum <enim> et sodalem perdidit simul.

Such short verse maxims were a favourite form of proverbial moralizing in Rome (for example, the extant iambic *sententiae* of Publilius Syrus and

---

[81] On the poetry of Greek sophists cf. Bowie (1989).

[82] For this imaginary 'group' see Cameron (1980), Mattiacci (1982) and (1985), and the useful summary by Courtney (1993), 372–4.

[83] For the use of verse in ancient proverbs cf. Otto (1890), xxxiii–xxxiv, *RE* 18. 1713. 17 ff. Grilli (1982) and Courtney (1993), 21, rightly deny actual Apuleian authorship of this fragment on the grounds that he is simply collecting existing material, but it is still a fragment of an Apuleian work.

[84] For this tradition cf. Roos (1984), 61–74, 178–228.

the hexameter *Disticha Catonis*);[84] these particular examples show Greek philosophical links which would suit genuine lines of Apuleius. Fr. 19a clearly recalls Plato *Phaed.* 81a μελέτη θανάτου, 19b a familiar Platonic idea (e.g. *Gorg.* 479a–c), 19c Epicurus fr. 246 Arighetti = Seneca *Ep.* 18. 14 *immodica ira gignit insaniam.* Fr. 19d is similar to Plautus *Trin.* 340 *et illud quod dat perdit et illi prodit vitam ad miseriam*, and clearly shares much with a proverb circulating under the name of Seneca in the Middle Ages and Renaissance, *amico mutuam roganti me pecuniam si dedero, et amicum et pecuniam perdo.*[85] But suspicion must hang over all four fragments.

More generally, paroemiography was both part of the Greek philosophical tradition of which Apuleius presented himself as an heir (Aristotle and Theophrastus wrote works on proverbs—Diogenes Laertius 5. 26, 5. 45), and operative in the contemporary Second Sophistic. Plutarch wrote a lost work on proverbs (Lamprias catalogue no. 55), as did Favorinus (*Suda* IV. 690. 26 Adler), and the origins of the surviving Greek *Corpus Paroemiographorum* go back to a collection made by Zenobius, a sophist of the reign of Hadrian.[86] Proverbs were clearly useful as convenient rhetorical ornament to Greek writers of the second century AD, especially to those who declaimed extempore.

3. *Fr. 3–8. Hermagoras*

Six short fragments are cited from this work:

Fr. 3. Priscian *GLK* 2. 85:

Apuleius in I Hermagorae: *visus est et adulescens honesta forma quasi ad nuptias exornatus trahere <se> in penitiorem partem domus.*

---

[85] Shakespeare's 'loan oft loses both itself and friend' (*Hamlet* I. iii. 76) has been traced to this 'Senecan' source via its appearance in Renaissance collections of Latin proverbs and vernacular translations (Baldwin (1944), ii. 610–11), but this 'Senecan' proverb is unlikely to be either Senecan or pre-Apuleian: for the large amount of later proverbial material falsely attributed to Seneca in the Middle Ages see Pascal (1908). It is impossible to say firmly whether fr. 19a–d are genuinely Apuleian. On the one hand, the context in which they are quoted by Barth (1624), 815–16, shows clear knowledge of the *Apologia* and *De Deo Socratis*, and gives every impression that the fragments are copied from an old manuscript (*membranae*). On the other hand, Barth is known to have forged at least some supposedly ancient poetic fragments, claiming similar lost sources (cf. Sandys (1908), ii. 363–4, Skutsch (1985), 786). Fr 19a can in fact only be made into a complete iambic senarius if an undesirable hiatus is tolerated in the middle of the line (*vitae *obitus*), but this could be due to corrupt transmission rather than an un-Apuleian verse technique (a word may have been lost between the two words in hiatus).

[86] Cf. Bühler (1987), 33–7.

Fr. 4. id. 2. 111:

Apuleius tamen in I Hermagorae: *verum infirma scamillorum obice fultae fores.*

Fr. 5. id. 2. 135:

'*scius*'—sic Apuleius in primo Hermagorae.

Fr. 6. id. 2. 279:

unde Apuleius in I Hermagorae: *aspera hiems erat, omnia ningue canebant.*

Fr. 7. id. 2. 528:

Apuleius in I Hermagorae: *et cibatum, quem iucundum esse nobis animadvertant, eum adposiverunt.*

Fr. 8. Fulgentius *Exp. Serm. Antiq.* 3:

unde et Apuleius in Ermagora ait: *pollincto eius funere domuitionem paramus.*

Five of the six quotations refer to the first book, indicating a work in more than one book. Earlier scholars inferred from the title that it was a dialogue of Platonic type, a genre in which Apuleius claims to have written (*Flor.* 9. 28, above), but Perry's reconstruction of it as a low-life novel in the manner of Petronius[87] is clearly much more plausible given its details (fr. 3 suggests a romantic scenario, fr. 6 a comic blockading of a door, fr. 7 a meal, fr. 8 a funeral). This would provide another Apuleian work of prose fiction to add to the *Metamorphoses*; attempts to interpret some of the fragments (4 and 6) as metrical, thus matching the prosimetric format of the *Satyrica*, are unpersuasive—they fit no appropriate metrical pattern, and their rhythmical and alliterative nature is the common currency of Apuleian style rather than an indication of verse-form.[88] The title recalls Hermagoras of Temnos, 'the most influential rhetor of the Hellenistic period',[89] and it may be, as Perry suggests, that the work satirized a rhetor just as rhetors and rhetoric are a major target of attack in Petronius' *Satyrica*.[90] It is most unfortunate that its fragments are so few and brief, since this work would have provided a fascinating point of comparison for the *Metamorphoses*.

---

[87] Dialogue: e.g. Hildebrand (1842), vol. i, p. lviii. Novel: Perry (1927).
[88] On rhythm and alliteration as Apuleian stylistic features cf. Bernhard (1927).
[89] Russell (1970).
[90] Cf. Kennedy (1978).

4. *Fr. 9–10. Phaedo*

Clearly a translation of Plato's dialogue, since the two extant fragments loosely render passages of Plato's work:

Fr. 9. Priscian *GLK* 2. 511:

Unde Apuleius ... in Phaedone De anima: *sic auditurum, sic disciturum qui melius sit haec omnia et singula sic agere aut pati, ut patiuntur atque agunt.* [~ *Phaed.* 97e–98a]

Fr. 10. Priscian *GLK* 2. 520:

Apuleius in Phaedone: *et causam gignendi ostensurum et immortalitatem animae reperturum.* [~ *Phaed.* 100b]

Such a translation of a loose kind is very suitable for a *philosophus Platonicus* (above) who may have translated Ps.-Aristotle *De Mundo* and composed a doxographical work *De Platone* (see Chapter 5); both fragments, though very brief, show clear characteristics of Apuleian style—the rhyming isocola *sic auditurum, sic disciturum* and *et ... ostensurum ... et ... reperturum,* and the poetical archaism *gignendi* (cf. *gignitur, Apol.* 8). Here Apuleius follows great Roman writers such as Cicero with his rendering of part of the *Timaeus*,[91] and is once again seen as a purveyor of Greek philosophy for a Latin-speaking readership. It is just possible that the 36–line translation of *Phaedo* 66b–67a quoted anonymously by Claudianus Mamertus *De Statu Animae* 2. 7 belongs to Apuleius' version, but the complete absence in this relatively long extract of the stylistic features so evident even in the short citations of the Apuleian version in Priscian is a strong argument against this.[92]

---

[91] On Cicero as translator of Plato cf. Powell (1995), 272–300. Cicero's *Timaeus* is probably used in the *De Platone* by Apuleius: see Ch. 5.

[92] Here I follow Beaujeu (1973), 173; for further discussion see Bajoni (1994), 1787 n. 4. Without stylistic considerations the evidence might point the other way: the Apuleian version was clearly available to Mamertus' contemporary and correspondent Sidonius (see below; for his correspondence with Mamertus see Sidonius *Ep.* 4. 2, 4. 3, and for Mamertus' knowledge of Apuleius see Alimonti (1975)), and Mamertus cites a passage from Apuleius' *De Platone* as if from Plato's Περὶ Φυσικῆς in the same chapter of *De Statu Animae* (see Beaujeu (1973), 264). The two fragments of the *Phaedo* version cited by Priscian show omissions and loose interpretations (Beaujeu (1973), 172–3), similar to those in the *De Mundo* translation (see Ch. 5); its accuracy as a translation of the *Phaedo* was in fact questioned in the only other ancient reference to it (Sidonius *Ep.* 2. 9. 5).

5. *Fr. 11–12. Epitoma Historiarum*

Fr. 11. Priscian *GLK* 2. 250:

Apuleius in Epitoma: *sed tum sestertius dipondium semissem, quinarius quinquessis, denarius decussis valebat.*

Fr. 12. Priscian *GLK* 3. 482:

secundum Apuleium . . . in Epitomis historiarum *Aeneanica gens.*

Fr. 11 gives information on the value of the Roman currency in some unspecified past period, suggesting that this work was an epitome of Roman history with some Varronian-type antiquarian material. This is fitting for Apuleius, who elsewhere praises Varro,[93] and may here be imitating him in detail.[94] Fr. 12, quoting the unusual phrase *Aeneacica gens*, a typically florid Apuleian adjective,[95] perhaps suggests that this work dealt at some point with the early history of Rome. Epitomes of Livy are known in both Latin and Greek from the imperial epoch; the plural *historiarum* might suggest that Apuleius summarized more than one writer, but all must be conjecture here. The variation between singular and plural titles in Priscian's two citations is typical of the kind of loose references found in ancient grammarians,[96] and it seems economical to assume that the same work is meant in both cases. Epitomizing was especially common in the second century AD, an age where the demands of extensive education, voluminous writing, and rhetorical performance led to the summarizing of learning in various forms. A particular analogue for Apuleius' work from this period may be seen in the extant historical work of Florus, probably written in the Hadrianic period, an account in two books of the wars of Rome from its foundation to the age of Augustus, summarizing Livy and other sources. It is also possible, though by no means sure, that Justin's extant epitome of the *Historiae Philippicae* of Pompeius Trogus, a universal history, belongs to the second century AD.[97]

---

[93] *Apol.* 42 *Varronem philosophum, virum accuratissime doctum atque eruditum.*
[94] See Beaujeu (1973), 174, who draws a close parallel between fr. 11 and Varro *LL* 5. 173.
[95] Cf. e.g. *Met.* 1. 1 *fabulam Graecanicam.*
[96] See the useful evidence in Stramaglia (1996), 193.
[97] For epitomizing in the Imperial period (and second century in particular) cf. *RAC* 5. 944–73, Champlin (1980), 56, Steinmetz (1982), 145–6, Reardon (1991), 160. For the second-century date of Florus cf. Sallmann (1997), 327–9. The common second–third century dating of Justin (see most recently Yardley and Heckel (1997), 8–13) is attacked by Syme (1988) in favour of a late-fourth-century date.

6. *Fr. 13. De Re Publica*

Very little can be guessed from the single remaining fragment, a proverbial saying on the art of government (fr. 13):[98]

Fr. 13. Fulgentius *Exp. Serm. Antiq.* 44:

unde et Apuleius in libro De Re Publica dicit: *qui celocem regere nequit, onerariam petit.*

This treatise may or may not have been a version of the works of the same name by Plato or Cicero, though not a close translation of the former, since this image does not appear in Plato; the archaic *celox* (Ennius *Ann.* 506, Plautus *Asin.* 258), picked up again by second-century archaizing (Gellius *NA* 10. 25. 5), is certainly appropriate for Apuleius, and Fulgentius, who quotes the fragment, clearly had a good knowledge of Apuleius.[99] If not a version of Plato or Cicero, this book may have resembled the shorter handbooks of political advice composed by Plutarch such as the *Praecepta Gerendae Rei Publicae*.[100] A possible context for such a work might be Apuleius' links to the proconsuls of Africa evident in the *Florida*; he might be addressing it to one of them, just as Dio Chrysostom had addressed speeches on kingship to Trajan (*Or.* 1–4), but all is conjecture here.

7. *Fr. 14. Libri Medicinales (?)*

Fr. 14. Priscian *GLK* 2. 203:

Apuleius in medicinalibus: *caepe sucum melle mixtum.*

This single fragment refers to a herbal cure involving onions and honey, plainly derived from the section on the curative powers of onions in Pliny's *Natural History* (20. 39–43), where mixtures of onions and honey are recommended as remedies for the bites of dogs and snakes, and for

---

[98] For its proverbial character cf. Otto (1890), 71.

[99] Fulgentius' *Libri Mithologiarum*, edited by Helm (1898), shows clear Apuleian influence, not just in the famous allegorization of the Cupid and Psyche story (3. 6), but also in the prologue, with several verbal imitations of the prologue of the *Met.* (e.g. Fulgentius 1 *praef.* 3 *lepido quolibet susurro permulceam* ~ Apuleius *Met.* 1. 1 *lepido susurro permulceam*). Fulgentius is also the only writer outside Priscian to show knowledge of Apuleius' *Hermagoras* (see fr. 8 above); like Priscian (n. 67 above) he may favour Apuleius as a North African, since whether or not he is to be identified with Fulgentius the bishop of Ruspe, he is likely to have come from North Africa (on the identification debate see Skutsch in *RE* 7. 215. 58 ff., Whitbread (1971), 3–11).

[100] *Mor.* 798a ff.; see the discussion by Russell (1973), 97–8.

throat infections. The content of the fragment supports Apuleian authorship: Priscian bears witness to other lost Apuleian works (fr. 3–7 and
9–12), while Pliny is an obvious and frequent source for Apuleius in his
works of encyclopaedic information (see 8 and 9 below). Apuleius could
be seen as a medical writer in later antiquity: Marcellus' *De Medicamentis*
(*praef.* 2) seems to list him with Pliny and Celsus as a source for medical
lore.[101] The title of this Apuleian work is not clear: *medicinalibus* perhaps
suggests *libri medicinales*, as in the *Liber Medicinalis* of Serenus, rather
than *medicinalia*.[102] Its content clearly reflects the Roman tradition of
botanical remedies, which goes back as far as Cato (*De Agr.* 70–3), but
may also be connected with contemporary intellectual life. The Greek
culture of the second century AD could show much medical writing:
Galen himself was closely contemporary with Apuleius, while Archigenes, Soranus, and Rufus of Ephesus had all written at the end of the first
or beginning of the second century. Apuleius himself claims in the
Apologia to be *medicinae nec instudiosus neque imperitus* (40), and the
study and practice of medicine were sometimes closely linked to sophistic activity: this can be seen not only in the career of Galen, who wrote a
number of works of conventional Platonizing philosophy and a treatise
on logic, but also for example in the institution of the Asklepieion at
Pergamum, simultaneously hospital and health resort, temple and cultural centre.[103]

8. *Fr. 15. De Re Rustica (?)*

Fr. 15. Palladius 1. 35. 9:

adversus mures agrestes Apuleius adserit semina bubulo felle maceranda, ante-
quam spargas.

[101] For the evidence of Marcellus' preface, which has sometimes been supposed to allude
not to our Apuleius and Celsus but to Apuleius Celsus, the early first-century AD teacher of
Scribonius Largus, cf. Maggiulli and Buffa Giolito (1996), 12–14. It is possible that Priscian
is alluding to this more notably medical Apuleius, but this is unlikely given that this would
be the only instance of 'Apuleius' in Priscian meaning an Apuleius other than ours, and the
reputation of our Apuleius as medical botanist implied by the ascription to him of the
Herbarius (see n. 52).
[102] Cf. also Marcellus *De Medicamentis*, Sextus Placidus *Liber Medicinae*. Beaujeu (1973),
175, following previous scholars, suggests that Apuleius' title was *De Medicinalibus*, while N.
M. Horsfall in Horsfall Scotti (1990), 87, proposes *De Medicina*.
[103] For the date of Soranus cf. Hanson and Green (1994), 981–8; for that of Rufus Sideras
(1994), 1085–9; and for that of Archigenes see his entry in the *Suda*, which puts him under
Trajan. Bowersock (1969), 59–75, and Pearcy (1993) argue for the link of medicine and
sophistic activity (for scepticism cf. Brunt (1994), 38–52, for a firm reply von Staden (1997));
see Habicht (1969), 1–20, on the Asklepieion.

The title is nowhere attested, but seems appropriate; this single preserved quotation advises the dipping of seeds into ox-gall before sowing as a precaution against their being eaten by rodents, very much in the homely manner of Cato and Varro. An evidently agricultural work in Latin by Apuleius is also alluded to on a number of occasions in the Byzantine *Geoponica*.[104] It seems clear from the material in the *Geoponica* that Apuleius here as in his work on medical botany (above) and probably his *De Arboribus* (below) made use of Pliny's *Natural History*;[105] here as in several other works we see a tendency towards encyclopaedic didacticism in the honoured tradition of Pliny, Celsus, and Varro (see below). In his *Res Rusticae* (1. 8), Varro lists amongst his sources Democritus, Xenophon, Aristotle, Theophrastus, and Archytas, so a concern with matters agricultural had an ancestry in Greek philosophers which might appeal to the *philosophus Platonicus* Apuleius, as well as a strong Roman tradition.

9. *Fr. 16. De Arboribus (?)*

Fr. 16. Servius on Vergil *Georg.* 2. 126:

quod negat Apuleius in libris quos de arboribus scripsit.

This sole allusion concerns the identity of the *felix malum* at *Georg.* 2. 126; Apuleius clearly engaged in a controversy which was both scientific and literary, very suitable for a writer who commonly quotes Vergil as a matter of cultural display (cf. e.g. *Apol.* 30, *DDS* 130, *Mu.* 320). The form of citation makes it clear that there was more than one Apuleian book on trees, but allows the possibility that these books were simply a part of the larger agricultural work listed as 8 above, since ancient works on farming usually included substantial sections on the crucial area of arboriculture (the second book of Varro's *Res Rusticae* is devoted to it). On the other hand, the allusion in Servius and the title *De Arboribus* (rather than *De Arborum Cultura*) might suggest that Apuleius' work was a botanical

---

[104] For the use of Apuleius in the *Geoponica*, compiled in the tenth century, cf. the thorough treatment of Gemoll (1883), 98–105, which makes it clear that the *Geoponica* knows Apuleius (whom it quotes more than a dozen times) through the mediation of Anatolius of Berytus in the fourth or fifth century AD, who certainly used Apuleius as a source (Photius *Bibl.* Codex 163). That the original work was in Latin is implied by the designation 'Apuleius the Roman' (*Geoponica* 1. 14. 10); cf. Oder (1890), 80.

[105] Gemoll (1883), 99 n. 104, Oder (1890), 79–81. For Pliny as a source in the *Apologia* too see Ch. 2 nn. 81 and 82.

handbook identifying and classifying particular trees, a parallel to his work on fish, and falling into an identifiable scientific tradition. Theophrastus had devoted the first five of the books of his *History of Plants* to the classification and description of trees, and Pliny had done the same with six books of the *Natural History* (12–17); as in other works, Apuleius may have been using Pliny as a convenient source, though the particular piece of lore attested for his work does not, as it happens, occur in the *Natural History*.

10. Fr. 21. Eroticus

John Lydus *De Magistratibus* 3. 64:

ταύτῃ καὶ Σανδῶν Ἡρακλῆς ἀνηνέχθη, ὡς Ἀπουλήιος ὁ Ῥωμαῖος φιλόσοφος ἐν τῷ ἐπιγραφομένῳ Ἐρωτικῷ. 'For this reason Heracles Sandon was also referred to, as Apuleius the Roman did in his work entitled *Eroticus*.'

Though this one allusion, showing that Apuleius referred to the story of Hercules and Omphale in this work, is found in a Greek text, the Apuleian work was almost certainly in Latin, as Lydus' 'Apuleius the Roman' clearly suggests. Ἐρωτικός (*Amatorius*) is also the title of a dialogue by Plutarch, in which the relative merits of marriage and pederasty are debated; closely related is the pseudo-Lucianic Ἔρωτες (*Amores*), probably from the early fourth century,[106] where a similar dialogue takes place. Given these parallels and Apuleius' own repeated claim to have written dialogues (*Flor.* 9. 28, 20. 5), it seems likely that Apuleius' work was in this dialogue genre: the *exemplum* of Hercules and Omphale could have been used to urge the heterosexual case, since it argued that the power of love for women could overcome even the greatest of heroes.[107] More generally, Apuleius' work clearly stands in the tradition of the ἐρωτικὸς λόγος emanating from the *Symposium* and *Phaedrus* of Plato, two dialogues which similarly discuss homosexual and heterosexual love; several post-Platonic philosophers are credited with works entitled Ἐρωτικός which may have been known to Apuleius—Aristotle and Demetrius of Phalerum (Diogenes Laertius 5. 81), Diogenes (id. 6. 80), Theophrastus (id. 5. 43), and Heraclides Ponticus (id. 5. 87). There is also a moralized ἐρωτικὸς

---

[106] Cf. Macleod (1967), 147–8.

[107] This is its function in the Latin love poets, whence Apuleius no doubt derived it (Propertius 3. 11. 17–20, Ovid *Ars* 2. 221). For a full argument for the probable dialogue character of the *Eroticus* and its links to similar contemporary texts see the detailed treatment of Mantero (1972).

λόγος in Greek in one of Fronto's letters to M. Aurelius, and a homo-sexual/heterosexual debate in the novel of Achilles Tatius (*Leucippe and Clitophon* 2. 35–8); clearly the topic was familiar in the Greek literary culture of the second century AD, of which Apuleius is so often a reflection.[108]

11. *Fr. 22–5. Astronomica (?)*

A title of convenience for the single work likely to underlie four passages, too long to quote in full here, cited by John Lydus (*De Mensibus* 4. 116 = fr. 22, *De Ostentis* 4 = fr. 23, *De Ostentis* 7 = fr. 24, *De Ostentis* 44 = fr. 25) from an unnamed Latin work of Apuleius 'the Roman'. Their content (comets, solar and lunar portents, meteors, lightning) is largely lifted wholesale from Pliny's *Natural History*,[109] already seen as a convenient source for Apuleius' scientific writings.[110] Apuleius' interest in this general area is proved by the *De Mundo*, assuming it is a genuine work of his (see Chapter 5), and such studies were prominent in contemporary writing; the second century AD saw the production of Ptolemy's *Almagest* and Vettius Valens' *Anthologiae* in technical astronomy, and also of paradoxographical works, which included the kind of celestial marvels treated in Apuleius' surviving fragments.[111]

12. *Zoological Work(s) (not numbered in Beaujeu)*

At *Apol.* 36 Apuleius calls for one of his works:

prome tu *librum e Graecis meis*, quos forte hic amici habuere sedulique naturalium quaestionum, atque eum maxime, in quo plura de piscium genere tractata sunt.

The phrase *naturalium quaestionum* here suggests the title *Naturales Quaestiones*, following Seneca's work of the same name, or rather Φυσικὰ

[108] On the Fronto text (= pp. 250–5 van der Hout²) see very fully Fasce (1973), which also gives a good summary of the literary tradition of the ἐρωτικὸς λόγος up to the second century AD. For a stimulating account of the relevant texts of Plutarch, Ps.-Lucian, and Achilles Tatius see Goldhill (1995), 82–92, 102–9, and 144–61.

[109] For the details cf. Beaujeu (1973), 177–80. For some interesting thoughts on other sources for Apuleius' astronomical material cf. Keyser (1994), 644–7, 650.

[110] See n. 105 above.

[111] e.g. Ps-Aristotle *Mir. Ausc.*, parts of which belong to the second century AD (*RE* 2. 1048. 57 ff.), or the work of Phlegon of Tralles, a freedman of Hadrian, for which see Hansen (1996). On paradoxography in the Second Sophistic in general see Reardon (1971), 237–41.

Προβλήματα, since this is a Greek work, a title with an established Greek tradition.[112]

At *Apol.* 38 we seem to be dealing with a Latin book on the same subject:

memento de solis piscibus haec volumina [i.e. the Greek books already mentioned] a me conscripta . . . pauca etiam *de Latinis scriptis meis* ad eandem peritiam pertinentibus legi iubebo.

Apuleius is clearly parading bilingualism for effect. It is not immediately clear whether either of these ichthyological studies is to be included in the Greek and Latin works which Apuleius claims in the same context to have composed as summaries of several Aristotelian zoological treatises at *Apol.* 36: *praesertim cum ordinatius et cohibilius eadem* [i.e. Aristotle *Gen. An.*, *Hist. An.*, and *Anatomy of Animals*, a lost work, all just mentioned] *Graece et Latine adnitar conscribere*; these could be described as *naturales quaestiones*, but they could equally be different works. In any case, it seems more likely that material on fish formed a section of a larger work than that Apuleius wrote separate works on fish in both Greek and Latin, just as fish are the subject of the ninth book of Pliny's *Natural History*: the words *de piscium genere* (*Apol.* 36) suggest a classification of fishes, Pliny's central concern and fundamental to the researches of Aristotle, clearly to be seen as Apuleius' ultimate model in his zoological writings.

13. *Quaestiones Conviviales*

There are two testimonia to this work, which is not mentioned by Beaujeu:

Sidonius *Ep.* 9. 13. 3:

a Platonico Madaurensi saltem formulas mutuare convivalium quaestionum;[113]

and Macrobius *Sat.* 7. 3. 23–4:

suadeo in conviviis . . . magis quaestiones conviviales vel proponas vel ipse dissolvas. quod genus veteres ita ludicrum non putarunt, ut et Aristoteles de ipsis aliqua conscripserit et Plutarchus et vester Apuleius.

---

[112] Cf. Hine (1981), 24–9.

[113] Sidonius clearly knew Apuleius' works well: he also mentions the lost *Phaedo* translation (*Ep.* 2. 9. 5) and the *Apologia* (2. 10. 5), and appreciates his style in general (4. 3. 1 *ponderis Apulei fulmen*).

These passages confirm the title and make clear that this was a Latin work where questions were put and answered in the manner of the Aristotelian Προβλήματα (*Quaestiones*). Given the Macrobius passage, which asserts the serious nature of the work, the term *conviviales* surely refers to a setting at a symposium rather than the content of the questions, just as in Plutarch's wide-ranging work of the same title (Συμποσιακὰ Προβλήματα), adduced by Macrobius as a parallel for Apuleius' book; no doubt this was a fine showcase for the kind of serendipitous learning we see in the *Apologia*. As Plutarch points out in the preface to his work (*Mor.* 612e), such learned symposiastic dialogues go back to Plato's *Symposium* and were favoured by philosophers of many different schools.[114] In Apuleius' own time, we have the parodic *Symposium or Lapiths* of Lucian, and later on the massive *Deipnosophistae* of Athenaeus. In Latin, the contemporary *Noctes Atticae* of Gellius has something of the same character of multifarious and episodic learning; though neither strictly symposiastic or strictly dialogic in overall form, it does supply in *NA* 7. 13 a miniature collection of *quaestiunculae sympoticae* presided over by the philosopher Taurus, which clearly derives from the same tradition. Closer in form (but more distant in date) is the *Saturnalia* of Macrobius, which probably used Apuleius' work as a source.[115]

14. *De Musica (?) (not in Beaujeu)*

Cassiodorus (*Inst.* 2. 10) alludes briefly to an Apuleian work on music:

fertur etiam Latino sermone et Apuleium Madaurensem instituta huius operis [i.e. music] effecisse.

The second century was an age of Greek treatises on music, for example Ptolemy's *Harmonics* and the pseudo-Plutarchan *De Musica*, a trend perhaps influenced (both generally and in the particular case of Apuleius) by the importance of music in Platonic thought. The Neopythagorean Nicomachus of Gerasa, who flourished about AD 100 and whose work on arithmetic Apuleius seems to have translated (see 15 below), also wrote an

---

[114] On the genre of the literary symposium cf. Martin (1931), Relihan (1992). Schmidt in Sallmann (1997), 312 discusses Apuleius' *conviviales quaestiones*, but wants it to be identical with the *naturales quaestiones*. However, there is no evidence in the two allusions to *conviviales quaestiones* that they were scientific in character; indeed, the context in Sidonius 9. 13. 3 (a moralizing exhortation to a young man) rather implies that they included ethical topics.

[115] Cf. Linke (1880), 52.

extant *Handbook of Harmonics*; this was quite possibly the major source for Apuleius' lost work, but all must be conjecture here.[116]

15. De Arithmetica (not in Beaujeu)

There are two testimonia, Cassiodorus *Inst.* 2. 4. 7:

arithmeticam disciplinam . . . quam apud Graecos Nicomachus diligenter expo-suit. Hunc prius Madaurensis Apuleius, deinde magnificus vir Boethius Latino sermone translatum Romanis contulit lectitandum;

and Isidore *Et.* 3. 2. 1:

numeri disciplinam apud Graecos . . . autumant . . . a Nicomacho diffusius esse dispositam; quam apud Latinos primus Apuleius deinde Boethius transtulerunt.

The second would appear to be directly dependent on the first, but it is clear that this work was a translation of the extant *Introductio Arithmetica* of Nicomachus of Gerasa,[117] whose *De Musica* was a possible source for Apuleius' work on music (see 14 above).

16. Lost Speeches and Declamations

A number of these are mentioned by Apuleius in his extant works, as we would expect; such rhetorical performances and their publication were clearly fundamental to Apuleius' literary activity, just as they were crucial for the Greek intellectuals of the contemporary Second Sophistic. Some individual pieces may have been published as separate works like the *Apologia*, but it is also possible that most or even all were included in a collection of speeches, perhaps the original from which the *Florida* were excerpted (see Chapter 3). Here only those specifically said to be pub-lished are mentioned.

(i) *De Maiestate Aesculapii*. Apuleius tells us (*Apol.* 55) that he delivered a declamation on this topic in Oea, probably late in AD 156;[118] the pub-

---

[116] For the history of Greek musicology with translated texts see most usefully Barker (1984) and (1989); for the date of Ps.-Plutarch *De Musica* cf. Lasserre (1954), 104 and *RE* 21. 815. 62 ff., and for a modern translation of and commentary on Nicomachus' work see Barker (1989) 245–69.

[117] A modern translation of Nicomachus' work by M. L. D'Ooge is included in Heath (1990); for a characterization of Nicomachus cf. Heath (1921), i. 97–112.

[118] *Apol.* 55 *abhinc ferme triennium* (speaking in 158–9).

lished version is then produced in court and a passage recited to prove Apuleius' pious character (and his status as a performing intellectual). The god Aesculapius was (as already noted) much worshipped in North Africa owing to his syncretism with the Punic god *'smun*, but he was also widely popular in the Greek East, especially of course at Pergamum, site of the famous Asklepieion (see above) and a major sophistic centre. The title of Apuleius' lost work suggests that it was a rhetorical encomium: such praise of the gods in prose featured in both cult-practice and musical competitions,[119] and Apuleius' lost work may be compared with the extant prose hymn to the same god by his contemporary the sophist Aelius Aristides.[120] It was probably the allusions to this work and especially to a dialogue on Aesculapius (see 17 below) which led to the copying of the Hermetic dialogue *Asclepius* with Apuleius' philosophical works and its false ascription to him (see n. 48).

(ii) *On his Statue.* Apuleius seems to have made a speech about a statue set up to him at Oea, presumably after his spectacular victory in the *Apologia* case. It seems from an informative letter of Augustine (*Ep.* 138. 19) that local opposition to this honour was mounted (perhaps by Pudentilla's defeated relatives), and that Apuleius made and published a speech vindicating the award (*quod posteros ne lateret, eiusdem litis orationem scriptam memorise commendavit*). There may be an allusion to this in *Flor.* 16. 37, where Apuleius, rendering thanks for another statue voted for him in Carthage, remarks that other cities have set up statues to him before now. There are parallels to this statue dispute in the Greek sophistic world: statues were a common honour for successful sophists as for all members of local elites,[121] and disputes concerning their award sometimes arose, such as that charted in the Corinthian oration of Favorinus (transmitted as Dio *Or.* 37).

(iii) *Before Lollianus Avitus.* This speech was delivered before Lollianus (*Apol.* 24 *cum Lolliano Avito C.V. praesente publice dissererem*), very likely

[119] Cf. Bowie (1989), 213–18.
[120] *Or.* 42; on Aristides' prose hymns cf. Russell (1990), 199–219.
[121] A further statue of Favorinus at Athens is known from Philostratus *VS* 1. 8. 490, one of Lollianus at Athens from *VS* 1. 23. 527, one of Polemo at Smyrna from *VS* 1. 25. 543. The tendency to grant statues to sophists is satirized by Lucian *Demonax* 58; see Gleason (1995), 8–20, on this and on Favorinus' Corinthian speech (= Dio *Or.* 37), concerned with the restitution of Favorinus' statue at Corinth. For artistic evidence of statues of sophists cf. Richter (1965), iii. 282–9.

in his proconsular year of 157–8,[122] perhaps on a visit to Carthage from
Oea, where Apuleius was then living (see the *Apologia*). It is cited by
Apuleius *de meis scriptis* at *Apol.* 24, to prove the honourable character of
his region of origin, and must have been published soon after delivery. As
a speech which clearly said something about Apuleius himself and which
was probably delivered in front of a proconsul, it must have been similar
to several of the speeches excerpted in the *Florida* (*Flor.* 9, 16, 17, and 20).

17. *Dialogue on Aesculapius*

This is mentioned as a preface to the hymn on Aesculapius (see 18 (i)
below), and clearly consisted of Greek and Latin parts assigned to different speakers and honouring the god (*Flor.* 18. 39 *dialogum similiter
Graecum et Latinum*). In *Flor.* 18, which forms an introduction to a performance of the dialogue and hymn, the two main parts are to be read by
two friends of Apuleius', one in Latin, one in Greek; the dialogue is said
to begin with an enquiry in Greek from a fellow-student of Apuleius' at
Athens concerning the nature of Apuleius' discourse at the temple of
Aesculapius on the previous day. Such a contrived beginning clearly
recalls the opening of Platonic dialogues,[123] while the bilingual form is
pure intellectual display,[124] and the subject of Aesculapius is highly suitable for a Carthaginian setting (see on 16 (i) above). As with the mention
in the *Apologia* (55) of the speech *De Maiestate Aesculapii* (above), the
mention of this dialogue in the *Florida* may have influenced the ascription to Apuleius of the Hermetic dialogue *Asclepius* (see above).

18. *Lost Poems*

(i) *Hymn to Aesculapius.* At *Flor.* 18. 39 Apuleius mentions a verse hymn
to Aesculapius in both Latin and Greek (*hymnum eius utraque lingua . . .
canam*), clearly matching the bilingual dialogue, already mentioned,
which prefaces it. He promises to perform the hymn for his audience, but
the extract then concludes; the hymn was no doubt delivered in the lost

---

[122] The date is that of Syme (1959). The context in the *Apologia* suggests a fairly recent
performance.

[123] e.g. *Protagoras, Parmenides,* and *Phaedo*.

[124] Cf. also the so-called 'false preface' of the *De Deo Socratis* (discussed as part of the
Florida in Ch. 3) where Apuleius seems to have begun in Greek and switched to Latin. On
literary bilingualism in this period, and the probable limits to Apuleius' own talents in this
direction, cf. n. 64 above.

portion of the speech. Apuleius' sophistic contemporary Aelius Aristides wrote hymns to the same god in verse as well as prose, in lyric and hexameter metres.[125] We can only guess at the metre used by Apuleius, perhaps hexameters; judging by his handling of iambics and elegiacs (see on the *Ludicra*, 1 above) he may not have had complete facility in handling the harder Greek lyric metres.

(ii) *Panegyric of Scipio Orfitus*. *Flor.* 17, itself fulsome in praise of Orfitus, appears to be introducing a performance of this lost poem, *hoc meum de virtutibus Orfiti carmen* (17. 18), apparently towards the end of Orfitus' proconsular year of AD 163–4.[126] Verse panegyric of great men is a fundamental element in Roman literature from the time of Ennius' *Scipio*; an encomium of a later Scipio delivered in Carthage might indeed look back to that work, particularly as Apuleius quotes Ennius elsewhere (*Apol.* 29, *DDS* 121).[127]

19. *Fr. 17, 18, 20, 20 bis (for fr. 19a–d see 2 above). Fragments unattributable to individual works*

Fr. 17. Charisius *GLK* 1. 248 (*deleo deles delui et delevi, tero teris terui et trivi iuxta Apuleium*) refers to a linguistic feature possible in any Apuleian work, while fr. 20 (Scheffer (1654) 261) *Apuleius:* si vado non poterunt, pontonibus transibunt) is a seventeenth-century citation (from no known Apuleian work) on the subject of boats; its source is dubious, but it does contain an archaic word (*ponto*) which was revived by Gellius (*NA* 10. 25. 5).[128]

Frs. 18 and 20 *bis* are more interesting. Fr. 18, cited by Barth from the same lost manuscript source as fr. 19a–d (see 2 above), makes a point in the popular rhetorical style of the *Florida*:

quemadmodum matura os unicum, aures vero duas cuilibet ministravit, ita nos et loqui pauca et audire plurima debemus.

---

[125] Cf. Bowie (1989), 214–21.

[126] For the date see Syme (1959).

[127] On Apuleius' use of Ennius see Mattiacci (1986), 180–90.

[128] Scheffer had clearly read Beroaldus' edition of Apuleius (Scheffer (1654), 146 argues against Beroaldus' interpretation of a passage of the *Metamorphoses*), so his evidence is not that of a writer ignorant of Apuleius' other works. The content of fr. 20 suggests that it is derived from historiography, or perhaps from a military anecdote in a rhetorical context. But Brancaleone (1996–7) argues effectively against the Apuleian attribution, pointing out that Scheffer takes over the relevant citation from N. Perotti's *Cornucopia* (1489), a notoriously unreliable source for classical quotations.

This looks like a genuine oratorical fragment, and (along with Scheffer's citation of fr. 20) intriguingly suggests that genuine Apuleian material otherwise unknown to us could have been circulating as late as the seventeenth century.

Fr. 20 *bis* from Isidore (8. 11. 100) contains a traditional type of etymology (*manes . . . cum sint terribiles et immanes*), and might come from any kind of work, if indeed it is genuine.[129]

Another quotation from an uncertain work is made by Apuleius himself at *Apol.* 33: *interfeminium tegat et femoris obiectu et palmae velamento*. These words, as the context indicates, refer to the pose of a particular statue of Venus, perhaps the Venus of Cnidos, and have been found by Apuleius' accusers *quodam libro meo* (they are quoted by the prosecution as an example of *risqué* language). These words clearly belong to an *ekphrasis* or formal description, and could come from any kind of work; they are clearly related to *Met.* 2. 17,

in speciem Veneris, quae marinos fluctus subit, pulchre reformata, paulisper etiam glabellum feminal rosea palmula potius obumbrans de industria quam tegens verecundia,

but that passage cannot be alluded to in the *Apologia* because the word picked up by Apuleius' opponents is *interfeminium*, which does not occur in the *Metamorphoses* description; Apuleius is probably reusing a previous work in the novel. Such descriptions are common in the *Metamorphoses* and in many contemporary works of other authors, since they were highly fashionable in the literature of the era of the Second Sophistic.[130] It is tempting to think that Apuleius might have written a work describing real or imaginary statues or paintings in the sophistic manner of the *Imagines* of Lucian or Philostratus, perhaps plundering the sections on art in Pliny's *Natural History*, but this must remain pure speculation.

(iii) *Conclusions*

Consideration of this long list of extant and lost works leads to several points. First and most obviously, Apuleius' literary output shows an

---

[129] For the etymology see Maltby (1991), 364. Beaujeu (1973), 177, suggests that the citation may be a misreading of *DDS* 153, but different points seem to be made in the two passages; Brancaleone (1996–7) argues that Isidore's citation is a misremembering of Servius' commentary on the *Aeneid* and not a genuine Apuleian fragment.

[130] Cf. Bartsch (1989), 3–39.

extraordinary variety and versatility: there seems to have been almost no branch of ancient learning in which Apuleius had no interest, almost no genre in which he did not write a work. Indeed, it has been suggested that a number of the didactic works represent the remnant of an encyclopaedic whole assembled by Apuleius in the manner of Varro's *Disciplinae* or Celsus' *Artes*.[131] In favour of this is the fact that several of the works discussed above fall into the categories covered by the nine books of Varro's *Disciplinae: grammatica, dialectica, rhetorica , geometria, arithmetica* (15 above), *astronomia* (11 above), *musica* (14 above), *medicina* (7 above), and *architectura*.[132] Against an Apuleian encyclopaedia is the fact that all the books are always cited individually, and that we are never given a title of an overall work. This seems decisive. If Apuleius aimed at a form of encyclopaedic coverage, it was through a number of separate works rather than a single *magnum opus*.

It is also clear from the evidence considered above that Apuleius was more of a compiler of existing materials than an original investigator: his didactic books usually relate to a recognizable literary tradition, often being Latin translations or versions of Greek works, and provided an easy path to the reputation for polymathy which Apuleius promotes in the *Apologia* and elsewhere. The clear didactic slant suggests perhaps that Apuleius wrote many of his works for educational purposes as well as self-promotion and self-display; *Flor.* 18 suggests that he had pupils in Carthage (see Chapter 3), and like almost all the contemporary Greek sophists he is likely to have engaged in instruction as well as performance.

Finally and perhaps most importantly, the range and nature of Apuleius' works establishes him firmly as an intellectual child of his time. Almost every known work of his finds an analogue in contemporary Greek or Latin literature, and especially in the productions of the Greek Second Sophistic. His very polymathic display reflects the character of an age where learning and its demonstration were required for literary and worldly success. But such success as Apuleius achieved in his lifetime seems to have been limited to his chosen home base of Carthage. Roman North Africa, though Carthage itself was in many ways a cosmopolitan city, was clearly something of a cultural backwater when compared to

---

[131] By Otto Jahn—cf. Schanz, Hosius, and Kruger (1922), 129.

[132] The common suggestion that the nine *disciplinae* of Varro are the source of the late antique 'seven liberal arts', all of which they can be argued to include, is vigorously resisted by Hadot (1984) and (1997); she argues that the seven liberal arts derive from a Middle Platonist/Neoplatonist context, independent of Varro, which would make an interesting connection with the Middle Platonist Apuleius.

Rome or the great cities of the Greek Mediterranean. However, this gave Apuleius many advantages. He is able to present himself as the purveyor of Greek intellectual culture to an audience for whom he himself is the major source for such material; and though there were clearly rival performing intellectuals at Carthage, he could there avoid many of the problems of the sharp competition amongst contemporary sophists in the Greek world.[133] One of these problems was whether to proclaim oneself a sophist or a philosopher; generally speaking, most Greek sophistic intellectuals felt obliged to choose one name or the other.[134] Apuleius, on the other hand, though he never uses the word *sophista* of himself, can freely compare himself both implicitly and explicitly with the great sophists of the fifth century, a characteristic sophistic move, while also maintaining his status as a *philosophus Platonicus*.[135] Such things were clearly permissible in the Latin West, where the cultural polemics of the Greek Mediterranean found only a distant echo. But though Apuleius proclaimed himself a philosopher, his status as a star performer in Carthage, his obvious self-promotion and cult of his own personality, and his prodigiously displayed literary and scientific polymathy plainly allow us to designate him a Latin sophist.

[133] For Apuleius' Carthaginian rivals see Ch. 3 n. 26; for the rivalries of Greek sophists, a continual feature of Philostratus' *Lives of the Sophists*, see Ch. 3 n. 49.

[134] Modern interpreters sometimes disagree with the labels chosen by particular writers: for a discussion of the choice and the critical problem cf. Stanton (1973).

[135] Apuleius himself uses *sophista* only twice, of the fifth-century sophists Hippias (*Flor.* 9. 15) and Protagoras (*Flor.* 18. 19), to both of whom he implicitly compares himself; for the connections made between the 'First' and Second Sophistic see Philostratus' *Lives of the Sophists* with e.g. Anderson (1993), 13–16. For Apuleius himself as *philosophus Platonicus* see n. 19 above.

2

A Sophist in Court:
The *Apologia*

1. BACKGROUND AND DATE

A partial view (in all senses) of the circumstances surrounding Apuleius'
Apologia[1] is given us in some detail in the work itself, at *Apol.* 72–98, the
main narrative section of the speech. This view need not be taken as
wholly truthful, but provides a convenient guide to the sequence of
events from Apuleius' own perspective, certain to be strongly biased in
his own favour, and is summarized here in the absence of other evidence.
In the winter of AD 156–7,[2] Apuleius arrived at the town of Oea, modern
Tripoli in Libya, travelling eastwards to the sophistic centre of
Alexandria. There he stayed with some friends, the Appii, for a number
of days, recovering from exhaustion brought on by the journey (perhaps
from Carthage, a major journey whether by land or sea, or perhaps even
from Athens or Rome). At the house of the Appii he was visited by his former room-mate and protegé at Athens a few years previously, Sicinius
Pontianus. Pontianus was in search of a suitably honourable husband for

---

[1] The *Apologia* is still most easily found in the Budé edition of Vallette (1924), whose text
with its paragraphs and convenient sections is cited here; there is also the important
Teubner edition by Helm (1905). The commentary of Butler and Owen (1914) is still useful;
most useful of all is the recent text and commentary by Hunink (1997), with its excellent
bibliography, to which I owe much. Vincent Hunink is currently working on a new English
translation of the *Apologia*; otherwise the most recent is Butler (1909). I have been unable
to consult the Italian editions of Marchesi (1914) and Augello (1984); Moreschini (1990) is
an Italian bilingual edition with an introduction but no notes. Vallette's book (1908) still
provides much useful and detailed material, while Norden (1912) and Abt (1908) remain
essential on their topics; lively appreciations of the work as a whole are to be found in Helm
(1955) and Tatum (1979), 105–19. Most recently, there is a good survey of some of the main
issues by Hijmans (1994), a helpful piece on the narrative texture of the speech by Sallmann
(1995), informative considerations of its social and cultural background by Bradley (1997)
and (forthcoming), and a useful general account in Sandy (1997), 131–48.

[2] This and other datings of events surrounding the *Apologia* given here largely follow the
chronology of Guey (1951).

his widowed mother Pudentilla, in order to preserve her considerable
fortune for himself and his brother Sicinius Pudens, rather than delivering it into the hands of the strangers or unscrupulous relations who had
for some time been pursuing Pudentilla as suitors.[3] With Apuleius in
mind for this role, but without directly proposing it to him as he saw that
he was keen to continue his journey and disinclined to settle down, he
urged him to stay in Oea until the following winter, to avoid the dangers
of travelling in high summer; he also prevailed upon the Appii to let the
sick Apuleius be transferred from their house to that of Pudentilla,
located in a more salubrious position beside the sea. There, over a period
of months, Apuleius recovered well, and began to give rhetorical performances in Oea.

After the success of one of these, Pontianus raised the notion of marrying Pudentilla directly with Apuleius. After a long discussion, in which
Pontianus applied considerable pressure and Apuleius urged again his
desire to travel as a barrier to marriage, Apuleius was persuaded to agree
to the union; having lived in Pudentilla's house for a year by then, he was
willing to marry her to help his friend. Pontianus was keen for the marriage to take place as quickly as possible, but it was eventually decided that
it should take place after Pontianus' own marriage and his brother
Pudens' taking of the *toga virilis*, thus putting the social and financial
future of the family on a clear and firm footing. But Pontianus' marriage
changed his mind; he married the daughter of Herennius Rufinus, who,
having thus acquired an interest in the property of Pudentilla which
would pass to his son-in-law in due course, persuaded Pontianus that
Pudentilla's marriage to Apuleius would be undesirable. But Pudentilla
remained firm in her resolve to marry Apuleius, despite the entreaties of
Pontianus and the railings of Rufinus (represented by Apuleius as a
vicious and disreputable money-grubber). The couple were married in
one of Pudentilla's suburban villas rather in the town itself, perhaps late
in 157 or early in 158.

After the marriage, Apuleius (he claims) persuaded Pudentilla to settle considerable portions of her assets on her sons; they had already been
reconciled with Apuleius, who was now asked by Pontianus for his previously promised good offices with Lollianus Avitus, the proconsul of

---

[3] On the status and wealth of Pudentilla and her family see Gutsfeld (1992), Fantham
(1995), Bradley (forthcoming). For sensible caution on how far we should believe the highly
rhetorical presentation of Pudentilla in the *Apologia* see Hunink (1998*b*).

157–8 (we are now probably in the first half of 158).[4] Armed with Apuleius' recommendation for his oratory, Pontianus set off for Carthage, the proconsular seat, but died either there or on his return journey. At that point, his younger brother, Sicinius Pudens, left his mother's house and moved to that of his uncle, Sicinius Aemilianus, portrayed by Apuleius as a bad influence. After some time, Aemilianus, allied with Rufinus, used Pudens to attack Apuleius in the courts, the two hoping no doubt to gain control of Pudentilla's fortune through her only remaining son; Apuleius alleges that Rufinus was planning to marry Pudens to his daughter, Pontianus' widow, and Pudens was clearly under the effective control of his uncle Aemilianus. Some time afterwards, perhaps in the winter of 158 or spring of 159, Apuleius arrived at the assize session being held by the proconsul Claudius Maximus (158–9) at the town of Sabratha, modern Sabratah in Libya, not far from Oea, to defend his wife's interests in a suit against the family of the Granii. There he found himself suddenly accused of having induced Pudentilla to marry him by magical means, and even of murdering Pontianus, a charge which was soon dropped.

So far the background, or at least Apuleius' own version of it in the speech. The charge may seem bizarre, but that would be misleading. Prosecutions for malevolent magic in general were clearly common enough in Roman law and notionally at least carried the death penalty, and the allegations about love-philtres clearly made against Apuleius brought the case within the scope of Sulla's *lex Cornelia de sicariis et veneficis* (cf. Justinian *Inst.* 4. 18. 5).[5] Greek sophistic figures of the same period could also be presented as 'magicians', no doubt because their rhetorical skills could be represented as supernatural influence;[6] this kind of slur against clever speakers was no doubt part of the prosecution's view of Apuleius, though (as in the case of Ciceronian speeches) we should naturally be cautious in reconstructing the prosecution's case from the highly biased evidence of Apuleius' defence. The official accuser was the young Pudens, but since he was a minor the case was conducted in court by Aemilianus, and also by hired advocates. By this means Aemilianus avoided any possibility of the severe penalty for false accusation under the *lex Remmia*, which could apply neither to him, since he was not the accuser, nor to Pudens, since he was still a minor.[7]

---

[4] On Lollianus and the date of proconsulship see Syme (1959), Hunink (1997), ii. 82.

[5] On the legislation and other charges under it cf. conveniently Moreschini (1990), 16–19, and Hunink (1997), i. 13; on questions of Roman law in the *Apologia* in more detail see Norden (1912).

[6] See Section 5.   [7] For the issue see conveniently Hunink (1997), i. 15.

2. THE SPEECH: CHARACTER AND STRATEGY

It seems fundamentally unlikely that the text we possess is an essentially unrevised version of the speech Apuleius gave at the trial.[8] This is not because of its length, which at a reading time of three hours, with further time added for hearing evidence and witnesses,[9] is not unreasonable for a Roman forensic speech, at least in a published version; it is not much longer than Cicero's *Pro Cluentio* and shorter than the (undelivered) *Third Verrine*.[10] The strongest argument for extensive revision between delivery and publication, a regular practice of ancient orators such as Cicero, is the complex texture of the speech, stuffed with allusions to philosophical and literary texts. While the memory of Apuleius, a professional performer, for quotations was no doubt good, the copious number of allusions and the careful way in which they are applied to the argument strongly suggest that the text we have is a final post-trial version finely honed by Apuleius for circulation rather than the *ipsa oratio* of the court-room. This is also argued by a more general consideration: like certain speeches of Cicero, the *Apologia* gives the impression of being coloured by later events, in particular the likelihood that Apuleius won his case; had he lost, the stakes were high, and there is no sense at all of this in the speech that we have, a supremely confident performance. Indications in the text that the speech is an exact transcript of what was said at the trial, such as space for the reading of evidence and references to time running out (28. 1, 37. 4, 69. 6–8, 94. 8), could simply be the trappings of the original forensic context inserted for verisimilitude in a later reworking, just as in the highly elaborated undelivered speeches of the *actio secunda* of Cicero's *Verrines*.[11]

I join most modern scholars in referring to Apuleius' speech as the *Apologia*, but there is in fact no ancient evidence for that title, which seems to occur first in the Aldine edition of 1521;[12] the work's title in the

---

[8] *Contra* Hijmans (1994), 1715–19, who usefully reviews the issue and argues (partly following Winter (1969)) that the extant *Apologia* results from a direct copy made at the trial. For a balanced discussion see Vallette (1908), 115–21. I would side with those who argue for a complete reworking, e.g. Gaide (1993).

[9] Abt (1908), 6, reckons three hours without time for the testimony of witnesses and the reading of documents; Steinmetz (1982), 203, six hours with witnesses and documents.

[10] *Apologia* = 123 Budé pages; *Pro Cluentio*, 118; *Verrine* 3, 136.

[11] For such realistic allusions to the reading of evidence, etc., in the undelivered second *actio* of the *Verrines* (in which the absent Verres, who had fled Rome already, is addressed throughout), cf. e.g. *Verr.* 1. 37, 57; 2. 24, 183; 3. 37, 45; 4. 12, 53; 5. 54, 61.

[12] Cf. Hijmans (1994), 1713. Augustine refers twice to the speech (*Civ.* 8. 19, *Ep.* 138. 19), but never gives a title or anything which could be a paraphrase of one.

oldest manuscripts F and ϕ is *Apuleii Platonici Madaurensis Pro Se Apud Claudium Maximum Proc. De Magia Liber.* This latter label looks like a scribal convenience rather than a preserved feature of the original (note *Liber* rather than *Oratio*), but it is the only transmitted title before the Renaissance. Many have felt that Apuleius, a writer of high literary ambition, is unlikely to have given his work such a pedestrian name, and that even the shorter version *Pro Se De Magia* seems too colourless, though similar titles are known in antiquity, such as the speeches of Antonius and Cotta *Pro Se Lege Varia* (Cicero *Tusc.* 2. 57, *Brut.* 205). The title *Apologia* certainly has relevant literary affinities, which have no doubt contributed to its appearance in texts of Apuleius' speech: in particular, its use for the two *Apologias of Socrates* of Plato and Xenophon suggests a Socratic model which Apuleius the literary Platonist might be keen to follow, and there are certainly moments at which the Apuleius of the *Apologia* echoes the Socrates of the *Apology*.[13] But significant resemblances between the *Apologia* and Plato's *Apology* are necessarily limited: both are speeches which present a philosopher on trial for his life and in some sense defending philosophers and philosophy in general (cf. *Apol.* 3. 5, 103. 4), but Plato's Socrates and Apuleius are in very different situations. Apuleius, facing a sympathetic judge known to be interested in philosophy, cannot (unlike other intellectuals of the Imperial period) make too much use of the case of Socrates, the archetypal unjust conviction in a hostile court of a misunderstood and oppressed philosopher. Moreover, if the speech was revised retrospectively (as argued above), Apuleius' presumed acquittal[14] means that the condemned Socrates is of little use as a literary role model. The title *Apologia* would also provide interesting links with contemporary Greek Christian apologetic, for example with the contemporary *First Apology* of Justin, written about AD 155–7, where we find not dissimilar elaborate defences of belief and practice backed up with Platonic learning. On the other hand, there is little firm evidence that Apuleius knew much of contemporary Christianity and its literature; though this has been argued, it can remain only an interesting speculation.[15] Though the

[13] Cf. *Apol.* 1. 3, 5. 2–5.

[14] The publication of the speech is surely evidence that Apuleius was not convicted: The arguments are conveniently summarized by Hijmans (1994), 1714–15 and Hunink (1997), i. 19–20.

[15] On Justin's and other Christian *Apologies* of the second century cf. Grant (1988), esp. 50–73. Justin resembles Apuleius not just in his Platonic interests, but in his claim to be a philosopher and his concern with *daimones* (Eusebius *HE* 4. 8, 4. 11, 4. 18). On the possibility of Apuleius' connection with contemporary Christianity see the discussions at Walsh (1970), 186–9, and Schmidt (1997).

evidence for the title *Apologia* is poor, I retain it here for convenience and because it is not entirely improbable.

In its basic texture, the *Apologia* combines tight court-room argument with expansive elements more naturally at home in sophistic declamation.[16] In terms of Aristotle's tripartite typology of rhetoric (*Rhet.* 1. 3. 2, 1358b), it mixes the forensic with the epideictic. The model on the forensic side is Cicero;[17] in the *Apologia* Apuleius takes the opportunity to emulate the greatest orator of the Roman courts, and his language, though close to the jingling and colourful style of the *Metamorphoses*, is profoundly influenced by that of the speeches of Cicero. More particularly, the colourful characters and charges of the *Apologia* recall some of the more vivid criminal cases in which Cicero appeared, in particular the *Pro Cluentio*, where the scheming Oppianicus, impoverished and acquiring funds through marriage, inheritance, and a series of poisonings, is a more vicious and successful ancestor of the villains Aemilianus and Rufinus in Apuleius. The pillorying and ridicule of Apuleius' opponents in the *Apologia*, one of its fundamental techniques, recalls Cicero not only in rehearsing the standard topics of invective used (for example) in the *Verrines* and *Second Philippic* (e.g. drunkenness, venality, sexual insatiability),[18] but also in its use of humour as a forensic weapon. The charges made are often laughed out of court, just as they were in the *Pro Caelio*, where Cicero's comic presentation of Clodia as the villain of the piece and as a 'Medea of the Palatine' is similar to Apuleius' ridicule of the rustic Aemilianus and use of mythological figures from literature in attacking him (see Section 4 below).[19]

But, as already indicated, the *Apologia* is not only an imitation of the Ciceronian forensic manner. Its many didactic digressions mark the speech out as (at least in part) an epideictic performance in the manner of the *Florida* and the *De Deo Socratis*. This is clearly the work of a sophis-

---

[16] On this mixture see Vallette (1908) and Sallmann (1995).

[17] Cf. esp. the long list of reminiscences in Helm (1910), XXII–XXVIII, and in the commentary of Butler and Owen (1914), the article by Carbonero (1977), which compares the *Apologia* to the *Pro Archia,* and the resemblances to the *Pro Caelio* stressed by Sallmann (1995), 148. Hijmans (1994), 1711 n. 7, and Hunink (1997) are in my view unduly sceptical on Ciceronian links, as the further examples brought forward in this chapter show; for a more balanced view, still too sceptical for my taste, cf. Callebat (1984). Cicero was admired by Fronto and Gellius, despite his relatively unarchaic style (Holford-Strevens (1988), 143–5), another motive for Apuleian imitation.

[18] On these invective topics the standard treatment is still Süss (1912).

[19] Cf. Cicero *Cael.* 18 *Palatinam Medeam* with R. G. Austin's commentary, Quintilian 8. 6. 53 (on the *Pro Caelio* and the *Apologia* see Sallmann (1995), 148 n. 17).

tic speaker (see Section 5 below), anxious to demonstrate his learning and intellectual interests and to produce a stylistic *tour de force*, just as much as the self-defence of a man accused of serious charges in a court of law. Some have criticized the *Apologia* for its learned digressions and found them inimical to Apuleius' defence, but it is clear, on the contrary, that these are at the centre of Apuleius' forensic strategy, based according to the traditions of Greco-Roman rhetoric on the character and situation of the audience which the orator needs to persuade. Just as (for example) the *Pro Caelio* depends for much of its effect on the fact that it was delivered to reluctant jurors on what was normally a holiday, with Cicero providing his own brand of comic entertainment visibly related to the comedies which the jury might otherwise have the pleasure of witnessing, and which flatters the presiding praetor Cn. Domitius Calvinus, or as the *Pro S. Roscio* similarly flatters the presiding praetor M. Fannius,[20] so the *Apologia* aims at convincing and entertaining the one man on whose judgement the issue of the case depended—the proconsul of Africa Proconsularis, C. Claudius Maximus.

Here Apuleius had a natural ally. This Maximus, consul in 142 and proconsul in 158–9, is surely to be identified with the Claudius Maximus who was one of the teachers of Marcus Aurelius in Stoic philosophy (Marcus Aurelius *Med.* 1. 17. 5).[21] Apuleius' constant appeals to Maximus' philosophical learning and knowledge of the texts of Plato and Aristotle might have baffled a proconsul who had no philosophical interests, and the allusion to Maximus as *virum tam austerae sectae tamque diutinae militiae* (19. 1) fits well with his long and distinguished military career, possibly stretching back to the Parthian campaigns of Trajan, as well as his Stoic interests (cf. Cicero *Mur.* 74 *at enim agit mecum austere et Stoice Cato*). It is also notable that Apuleius applies *severus*, appropriate to philosophers (cf. e.g. Lucilius fr. 754 M *tristis ac severus philosophus*),[22] to Maximus on

---

[20] On this aspect of the *Pro Caelio* cf. Geffcken (1973), on the context of the *Pro S. Roscio* May (1988), 21–33; for Cicero's flattery of Domitius cf. *Cael.* 32, of Fannius cf. *S. Rosc.* 11–12, 85.

[21] The identification is doubted by Butler and Owen (1914), 1, while admitting that the references to Maximus' learning would suit the Stoic, but seen as possible in the entry in *PIR* C 933 (which conveniently summarizes Maximus' military career) and by Hunink (1997), i. 18. There is no reason why in this period a successful soldier and politician cannot also have strong Stoic interests (cf. Marcus Aurelius himself). For a recent good account of Maximus' career and connections, and an examination of Apuleius' relationship to him in the *Apologia*, suggesting plausibly that Apuleius is casting himself as philosophical adviser to Maximus, see Bradley (1997).

[22] For *severus* of philosophers elsewhere cf. Cicero *Fin.* 2. 29 *severus et gravis philosophus.*

two occasions in the speech (25. 3, 59. 5). One of Apuleius' fundamental strategies is to praise and flatter Maximus in every way, lauding his moral virtues as well as his intellectual qualities; here we get a glimpse of the Apuleius who was later to compose the lavish tributes to proconsuls at Carthage to be found in the *Florida* (cf. *Flor.* 8, 9, 17). The prosecution is accused of wasting Maximus' precious time and trying his patience with their frivolous and ill-educated calumnies (1. 1, 1. 6, 23. 3–4, 35. 7, 46. 5), and Apuleius seeks to develop a complicity between himself and Maximus, men of literary education, philosophical learning, and elegant taste (cf. 41. 4 *ego et Maximus*), against what he presents as the ignorance and rusticity of his accusers. Passages of Greek are cited *in extenso* to assert their mutual close acquaintance with the classic philosophical texts (10. 9–10, 22. 5, 25. 10, 26. 4, 31. 5–6, 38. 8, 65. 5–7, 82. 2, 83. 1), whereas in the *De Deo Socratis*, addressed to a larger and less select audience, only Latin literature is quoted, apart from a brief passage from Homer which is given in Latin translation rather than the Greek original.[23] Thus the so-called 'digressions' are strategically important to Apuleius as a continued *captatio benevolentiae* directed towards the presiding magistrate, and (as I shall argue) many are also tactically important in their particular contexts.

Just as Apuleius and Maximus share an understanding and appreciation of high intellectual culture, so Apuleius' opponents are represented as ill-educated and uncivilized; just as Maximus is continually praised for his wisdom and other qualities (2. 5, 11. 5, 19. 1, 25. 10, 36. 5, 38. 1, 41. 4, 48. 5, 53. 4, 63. 6, 64. 4, 81. 2, 84. 6, 85. 2, 91. 3, 98. 8), so Apuleius' opponents are repeatedly pilloried for their ignorance and lack of comprehension of higher things (5. 6, 9. 1, 9. 6, 16. 7, 23. 5, 30. 3, 33. 2–3, 34. 5, 42. 1, 66. 6, 74. 7, 86. 3, 87. 4, 91. 1). This is not purely gratuitous invective, but like the common ground between defendant and proconsul is essential for the details of Apuleius' argument in making his case. His defence asserts above all that the charges of magic have been brought through ignorant misunderstanding and wilful misinterpretation of harmless and indeed highly respectable scientific, philosophical and medical activities. These are the kind of activities appropriate to Apuleius' concept of a *philosophus*, a wider term than the modern 'philosopher'; *philosophus* seems to

---

[23] *DDS* 11; for the audience of the *De Deo Socratis* cf. Ch. 4. At *Apol.* 4. 4 a passage of Homer is given a Latin translation in the transmitted text, a feature which does not otherwise occur in the speech's Greek quotations. The translation is retained by Butler and Owen, but excised by Vallette, following Scriverius; I would favour the latter course, for the reasons already given.

include a wide range of intellectual activities together with their public presentation, and which as often is used to describe things which might also be associated with sophists. Apuleius takes his stand on the high ground of the omnicompetent intellectual, discoursing with the proconsul of their mutual literary and philosophical interests, while despising and ridiculing the peasants who have misunderstood and maligned his harmless and indeed useful activities.

3. THE SPEECH: STRUCTURE AND COMPOSITION

The structure of the speech can be set out as follows, with Roman numerals marking the main sections (my divisions), arabic numerals the traditional chapters:

   I. 1–3. *Exordium.*

  II. 4–24. Refutation of non-magical allegations.
     (i) 4–5. Apuleius' beauty and eloquence.
    (ii) 6–13. 4. His amusing and erotic poems.
    (iii) 13. 4–16. His possession of a mirror.
    (iv) 17. 1–6. His freeing of three slaves.
    (v) 17. 7–23. His poverty.
    (vi) 24. His origins.

 III. 25. 1–4. Summing-up of refutation of non-magical allegations.

 IV. 25. 5–28. Introduction to refutation of 'minor' magical charges.

  V. 29–65. Refutation of 'minor' magic charges.
     (i) 29–42. Apuleius' interest in fish.
    (ii) 42–52. The epileptic slave Thallus and the epileptic woman.
    (iii) 53–6. Apuleius' 'magic' talisman.
    (iv) 57–60. His alleged nocturnal sacrifices.
    (v) 61–5. His statuette of Mercury.

 VI. 66–7. Introduction to refutation of 'major' charges concerning Pudentilla's marriage.

VII. 68–101. Refutation of 'major' charges concerning Pudentilla's marriage.
     (i) 68–78. Narration of main events before the marriage.
    (ii) 79–87. 9. The letter written by Pudentilla to Pontianus, and the forged letter ascribed to Apuleius.
    (iii) 87. 10–88. The marriage in the country.

The break marked by F at chapter 66, dividing the speech into two books, was no doubt in part a mechanical necessity owing to the length of a papyrus roll, recorded at the point of former division when the text was copied in codex form. But given that the first publication of the *Apologia* in antiquity is likely to have been in two papyrus rolls, this particular division might well have been authorial, since it occurs at a very suitable point in the structure of the speech (see the scheme above); 65–6 is an important internal transition, and 66 a marked new beginning.[24] The speech is so constructed that 1–65 deal with the apparently 'minor' charges and allegations associated with the indictment for magic, allowing many learned disquisitions in a part of the speech where the charges, though answered, are more ridiculed than refuted, while 66–103 conclude the work with a substantial and detailed rebuttal of the 'major' charges concerning the alleged enchantment of Pudentilla forcing her into marriage with Apuleius. In this organization of the speech, Apuleius creates a deceptive dichotomy between such 'minor' charges as the use of fish for magic purposes and the 'major' issue of the marriage; it is likely that aphrodisiac potions derived from fish were one of the magic means alleged by the prosecution for the enchantment of Pudentilla, and so the major charge is undermined beforehand in both general and specific terms in dealing with the minor charge. The strategy is clearly to separate out two things which the prosecution has intimately interrelated, of which the first allows an entertaining refutation; if Apuleius can give an innocent and amusing explanation for minor incidents alleged to be magical, his innocence of the major charge will seem more probable in a later and more serious treatment.

Within chapters 1–65, there is a clear break at chapter 25. There Apuleius moves from miscellaneous allegations of a non-magical kind to the formal charges of magic before the court, a transition carefully marked in the text (25. 5 *aggredior enim ad ipsum crimen magiae*). The

---

[24] Hijmans (1994), 1726 n. 42, favours the idea that the division might have been an authorial one (followed by Hunink (1997), i. 174), but rightly says that the evidence on the question is insufficient.

preceding allegations are dismissed as insubstantial and incoherent calumnies (25. 1 *frivola et inter se repugnantia*, 25. 3 *vana haec convicia*). This division between magical and non-magical charges is an obvious one, but as in the division at 66 Apuleius draws a distinction here for his own strategic purposes; much of the material in section II is in fact directly relevant to the later charges concerning the marriage of Pudentilla, dealt with in section VII. The accusations of beauty and eloquence (4–5), composition of erotic verses (9–13), and use of a mirror (13–16) are not merely assertions of a levity and vanity inappropriate for a philosopher, as Apuleius presents them; beauty (with the mirror that aids it) and eloquence were no doubt raised by the opposition as unfair advantages which Apuleius used along with magic to enchant Pudentilla, while composition of erotic verses could have been presented as evidence for Apuleius' interest in the art of seduction. Similarly, the aspersions evidently cast on Apuleius' apparent extravagance in freeing three slaves of Pudentilla's, his poverty, and his origins (17–24) are directly relevant to the marriage with Pudentilla, and are clearly aimed at establishing a mercenary motive on Apuleius' part. By separating them from the main consideration of the marriage in section VII, Apuleius undermines the force of these allegations, and turns them to his own advantage by representing them as casual slurs rather than part of a coherent case brought by the prosecution.

The structure of the speech, though not corresponding to the traditional four- or six-part forensic pattern, shows careful organization and symmetry.[25] The audience, and Maximus in particular, are 'warmed up' by the entertaining and relatively superficial refutation of miscellaneous non-magical charges and allegations in section II, conducted through to the consideration of minor magical charges in V, and then presented with the crucial arguments about the marriage in the penultimate main section, VII. The sections on magic which contain the most important argumentation (V and VII) are each prefaced with an introduction (IV and VI), which orientates the reader and carefully individuates the allegations made; section II on non-magical allegations, presented already in I as mere insults to be cleared away before the main business of the speech

---

[25] For the four-part *principium, narratio, confirmatio,* and *peroratio* cf. Cicero *De Part. Or.* 27; for the six-part version (adding *divisio* after *narratio* and *confutatio* after *confirmatio*) cf. (the anonymous) *Ad Herennium* 1. 4, Cicero *De Inv.* 1. 19. For brief views of the structure of the *Apologia* cf. Helm (1955), 107, Moreschini (1990), 21–4, and Sallmann (1995); for a useful outline of points made in sequence and basic analysis of the work's strategy cf. Hijmans (1994), 1726–30 and 1760–8 (his further identification of 'macrorhythms', 1739–43, may not convince all).

(3. 4 *priusquam ad rem aggrediar*), is summed up and dismissed as frivolous in the following section, III, so as to be removed from consideration before the major section on magic (IV–VIII), and sections V and VII are briefly summed up in the final section, VIII. The listener (and reader) is always aware of what is going on through the use of such signposts, as commonly in Cicero.

Notable too is the way in which each of the major sections which deals with a string of charges is designed to finish with a climactic flourish, which itself gives a natural punctuation and relief after a period of close attention to detailed argument, and which on each occasion serves to present Apuleius himself in a highly positive light and denigrate his opponents. Section II ends with the presentation of Apuleius' origins (24), raised against him by the prosecution, but used by Apuleius to stress both his own high status and that of his birthplace of Madauros, and to contrast with the barbarously named and obscure Zarath, birthplace of the rustic Aemilianus, whose attack on Apuleius' birthplace thus backfires. Section V ends with the discussion of the statuette of Mercury (61–5), which allows Apuleius to present himself as a devoutly religious person who will not reveal the name of the god he worships even to Maximus (64. 5), and to stress further his knowledge of and following of Plato, who is enlisted as an advocate in his defence. Indeed, a quotation from Plato is presented as bringing the house down (65. 8). Finally, section VII ends with the testimony of two respected locals as to Apuleius' innocence in a minor financial dealing, concerned with a small estate bought for Pudentilla, possibly the original case against the Granii (*Apol.* 1) for which Apuleius had been attending the proconsul's assizes. This is a crowning instance of the section's main point, his lack of covetousness towards Pudentilla's wealth; Pudentilla's will, just read, left Apuleius a small legacy, but here he has no financial interest whatsoever, even in such a tiny and insubstantial matter.

4. ANALYSIS OF SECTIONS

I. *Exordium* (1–3)

Here Apuleius presents his general view of the case, that it is a collection of rash and ill-thought-out allegations characteristic of Aemilianus, the main accuser. This identifies two main strategies of the speech, to stress the prosecution's ignorant and hasty misinterpretation of the innocent actions of an intellectual, and to expose their vindictive and rapacious motives. He presents himself as the defender of philosophy as well as of himself against the prejudices of the ignorant (1. 3), playing for a moment the part of Socrates in Plato's *Apology*, who similarly claims that he is being accused of charges levelled at all philosophers (*Apol.* 23e). But, as stressed in Section 2 above, the main model here is Cicero. Not only does the speech begin with an address to the presiding proconsul and his *consilium* which picks up a Ciceronian formula (1. 1 *Maxime Claudi quique in consilio estis*—cf. *Quinct.* 10 *te, C. Aquili, vosque, qui in consilio adestis*),[26] but the detailed situation, where Apuleius claims to have had only a few days to prepare a response to the charges (1. 5), also corresponds to that in the *Pro Quinctio*, where the young Cicero is similarly faced with a complex case at short notice (*Quinct.* 3–4). In the case of Cicero, this is a *captatio benevolentiae*, asking for consideration in a difficult situation; for Apuleius, member of a sophistic culture where 'improvization' and unprepared performance were highly admired,[27] it is also a challenge which he is keen to answer, and his claim to have encouraged his opponents to lay formal charges is not incredible.

Even at this initial stage, the case against Apuleius is already presented as poor and doomed to failure. Aemilianus is even now preparing a fall-back position, dropping the charge of killing Pontianus which originally formed part of the indictment (1. 5, 2. 1), and assigning the accusation of magic to Pudens (2. 3), in order to avoid the risk of a severe penalty for false prosecution, despite the righteous indignation of Maximus, already evoked in Apuleius' favour (2. 1–5). Aemilianus is described in a vivid and developing military metaphor as a cowardly skirmisher rather than direct heroic challenger, as a deserter from the battle, and as a plotter behind the scenes (2. 6–8 *comminus . . . eminus . . . velitatur*);[28] the phrase *professor et machinator* (2. 8) recalls Cicero's identification of Chrysogonus as the contriver of the case against S. Roscius, *omnium architectum et machinatorem* (*S. Rosc.* 132), another allusion which stresses the Ciceronian character of Apuleius' speech. At 2. 11–12 a distinguished local who had risen to prominence in Rome, Lollius Urbicus, consul *c.* 135 and *praefectus urbi*

---

[26] The parallel is noted by Helm (1910), XXII; Helm also points out (XXVIII) that the *Pro Quinctio* and *Pro S. Roscio* are particularly well used by Apuleius in the *Apologia* (the more abundant style of these earlier orations (cf. Cicero *Orat.* 108) may have appealed to Apuleius).

[27] See the references cited in Ch. 3 n. 118.

[28] For the metaphors of these early chapters cf. McCreight (1990).

in the mid-150s,[29] is flatteringly mentioned twice (2. 11–12); like that of the preceding proconsul Lollianus Avitus later on (94. 5 ff.), this important name is dropped in Apuleius' favour, as a proof of Aemilianus' villainy, and indeed as a parallel for Maximus' already-expressed disapproval of Aemilianus' underhand tactics; Aemilianus has already been reproved by Urbicus for similar bad behaviour in a legal context, having falsely challenged his uncle's will, so good and distinguished men are at one in their hostility to him. The case of the uncle's will clearly presents Aemilianus as a man who will do anything for money, a factor crucial to the present case, which is really about the wealth of Pudentilla. It also emphasizes that he has already mounted another dishonourable legal challenge which has ended in failure; Apuleius hopes for a similar verdict in his own case (3. 1), the implication being that Maximus will find against Aemilianus as Urbicus did.

Apuleius concludes his *exordium* by presenting himself as an honourable man, in contrast to the known disrepute of Aemilianus (3. 2–3), and by justifying the inclusion of section II, the refutation of the minor allegations against him. As he stressed at the opening (1. 3; note the element of ring-composition), he is defending philosophy in general as well as himself; even the slightest slur on the name of philosophy is the greatest crime, and needs to be countered (3. 4–12). Indeed, the good man, unused to being attacked, is all the more offended when it happens (3. 11); but the refutation of slurs will cause them to rebound on their authors and will reinforce the honour of the good man (3. 12). Thus we are left with a final dichotomy between Apuleius, occupying the high moral ground as the innocent philosopher, and Aemilianus, pilloried as a vicious and groundless accuser—the essential polarity of the case as seen by Apuleius.

II. *Refutation of Non-Magical Allegations* (4–24)

(i) *Beauty and Eloquence* (4–5)

Here Apuleius begins at the beginning of his opponents' allegations, claiming to quote the first words of the speech of Tannonius Pudens, one of the *patroni* speaking for the young Pudens alongside Aemilianus:[30]

---

[29] On Lollius' career see *PIR*² L 327, Vidman (1977), Champlin (1980), 13–14.

[30] Nothing is otherwise known of this character; his cognomen Pudens is not uncommon in Roman North Africa (cf. *ILA* I, p. 423) and need not suggest that he is related to the young Pudens.

*accusamus apud te philosophum formosum et tam Graece quam Latine...
disertissimum.* Thus the topics of good looks and eloquence are immediately introduced, allegations by the prosecution which can be turned to
Apuleius' favour—he can both admit them to be true and show that they
are characteristic of the prosecution's frivolity. As so often in the
Apologia, Apuleius initially adopts a hypothetical method redolent of the
rhetorical schools—if he had both these advantages he would quote
Homer (4. 4) to the effect that one should not cavil at the gifts of the gods.
Beauty and eloquence are then separated out in his detailed response. On
beauty (4. 5–9), he argues that if he had beauty he would not be the first
philosopher to do so, but in fact he is not handsome, and his devotion to
literature has led to neglect of his person (4. 1–11). The quotation from
Homer and the details of handsome philosophers deploy for the first
time the literary learning of the speech; the beauty of Pythagoras is a
standard feature of his biography, that of Zeno of Elea (note the place of
origin, carefully distinguishing him from Zeno the Stoic) is taken from
Plato's *Parmenides*.[31] Interesting too is the longish description of Apuleius' hair (4. 11–13), which is presented as dull and unkempt rather than
the slick coiffure imagined by the prosecution, showing the insouciance
of the intellectual for personal appearance;[32] this builds up to the characteristic clever alliteration of *crinium crimen* (a 'hearing on hair') and
the pun of *capitale* (Apuleius' *caput* has led to a 'capital' charge). The allegation of eloquence is then treated more seriously, with a passage (5. 1–6)
that presents Apuleius as the ideal Ciceronian orator, recalling Cicero's
intellectual autobiography in the *Brutus* in its evocation of his dedication
to literature and oratory from an early age, his days and nights of study,
and the damage to his health.[33] He then moves back to the higher moral
ground, claiming that innocence is his true eloquence (5. 2–5), and quoting in his support the poet Caecilius, here stressing once again his literary learning and revealing for the first time in the speech the archaizing
taste of his age.[34] Innocence means that one can defend all one's actions
in public.

---

[31] Cf. Iamblichus *Vit. Pyth.* 10, Plato *Parm.* 127b.
[32] This links up with contemporary busts of philosophers with similarly unkempt hair—
cf. Zanker (1995), 233–42.
[33] Dedication to literature and oratory: *Brut.* 309. Days and nights of study: *Brut.* 308.
Damage to health: *Brut.* 314.
[34] For archaizing taste in Apuleius cf. Ch. 1 n. 68.

(ii) *Amusing and Erotic Poems* (6–13. 4)

This last section makes a neat transition (5. 6) to the allegations about his amusing and erotic poems, horribly mangled in pronunciation by his ignorant opponents. The poem on dentrifice to Calpurnianus from Apuleius' *Ludicra* (6. 3),[35] a casual but effective first advertisement of the fact that he is an established writer, is first implicitly justified by its cleaning-up of a well-known poem from Catullus (39 to Egnatius), as Apuleius implies by quoting that same poem and recalling its interest in urine a few lines later (6. 5). This is meant to display both laudable imitation of a classic and higher moral standards than the original, important to Apuleius' self-characterization as a blameless intellectual, but the disquisition on the cleanliness of the mouth which follows (7. 1) clearly goes beyond any forensic necessity. Here we have a sophistic set piece of the kind we find in the *Florida* (e.g. the praise of the human voice in *Flor.* 17. 6–14), moralistic in tone and elaborate in style, carefully extending the Homeric metaphor of *dentium muro* with similar terms (*animi vestibulum et orationis ianua et cogitationum comitium*), and making full use of characteristically Apuleian alliteration and word-play (7. 1 *oris . . . orator*, 7. 6 *libero et liberali*, 7. 7 *mortuis . . . morsum*). This epideictic window-display then turns into invective at 8. 1, the clean mouth of the philosopher being contrasted with the filthy orifice of Aemilianus, perhaps with an amusing hint at Catullan dentifrice amongst others, and back to epideictic at 8. 6, with the evocation of the oral hygiene of the crocodile, a snippet (as so often in Apuleius) from Pliny's *Natural History* appropriate to the miscellaneous learning of the Second Sophistic,[36] and preparing for the zoological knowledge which Apuleius will display later on (29–41).

The amatory poems to the sons of a friend, again barbarously mispronounced by the opposition (9. 1), receive similar justification as being in the classic tradition (9. 1–13. 4);[37] here Apuleius can point not only to a series of honoured love poets in Latin and Greek (9. 6–8), unknown to the uncouth prosecutors (including the early Aedituus, Porcius, and Catulus, for whom his archaizing age had a marked taste),[38] but also to

---

[35] On this poem and the collection of *Ludicra* see Ch. 1.

[36] Pliny *HN* 8. 90, suggested as source by verbal similarities and convenience, rather than Herodotus 2. 68 or Aristotle *Hist. An.* 1. 2. For Pliny as a frequent source for Apuleius cf. Ch. 1 n. 105.

[37] For pederastic epigrams in the Hellenistic period see Book 12 of the *Palatine Anthology*, and for pederastic poetry intended as a compliment to the boy's family cf. Pindar fr. 123 Snell/Maehler.

[38] The same poets appear in Gellius *NA* 19. 9; for the difficult question of who is using

philosophers who did the same (9. 9–11); his use of pseudonyms in love-poetry is also justified by classic examples (10. 1–10), evidently drawn from the Latin scholarly tradition for which they are early evidence.[39] The penultimate of these, the supposed use of Alexis in Vergil's second *Eclogue*, is cleverly turned into an attack on the prosecution: Aemilianus is more rustic than the humble peasants portrayed by Vergil in the *Eclogues* (10. 6 *vir ultra Vergilianos opiliones et busequas rusticanus*)— hence his accusation that erotic verses do not suit a philosopher. This accusation is then answered by the knock-down example of Plato himself, philosopher and writer of homoerotic poems with pseudonyms,[40] a precise parallel for Apuleius, even down to the epigram form used by both; what was good enough for Plato is clearly justifiable for a *philosophus Platonicus* (cf. 11. 5).

At 11. 1 the possibility of irrelevance is raised for the first time (*sed summe ego ineptus, qui haec etiam in iudicio?*). The *Apologia* is aware of the possibility that its more digressive parts may be taken as irrelevant to the matter in hand, and concerned to prevent such an impression. Here the relevance of evidence from erotic poetry is strongly asserted: the accusers must be made to agree with Catullus and even the emperor Hadrian that erotic poetry is no sure indicator of an immoral life— Aemilianus is dared to disagree with the divine Hadrian, a masterly stroke in front of the proconsul and protector of imperial status (11. 3–4). As if it were not enough to argue that literature is one thing, reality another, Apuleius goes on to justify the love expressed in his poetry through an account of Plato's own theory of love, again appealing to Maximus' philosophical knowledge (11. 5). He summarizes the famous bipartite division of love in Plato's *Symposium* (12. 1–5), and implies that his own love expressed through homosexual love poetry is of the higher divine kind, attained by mortals through the reminiscence of celestial Forms. To this brief course in Platonic theory are added a couple of casual quotations from Afranius and Ennius, showing both his own learning and the archaizing taste of the age.[41] At 13. 3 Apuleius again professes anxiety

---

[39] whom and the issue of a common source (poetic anthology or critical work) cf. Holford-Strevens (1988), 16–17.

[39] This is famously the earliest identification of the various *puellae* of Latin love poetry with historical individuals; given that the ultimately Suetonian *Vita Donati* of Vergil assigns the same 'real' identity to the Alexis of *Ecl.* 2 (*Vit. Don.* 9), Suetonius' lost *De Poetis* is an obvious possibility for the source for this information.

[40] For the epigrams attributed to Plato cf. Hunink (1997), ii. 49–50, Page (1981), 161–81, Ludwig (1963).   [41] Cf. above, n. 34, and Ch. 1 n. 68.

about the relevance of all this material, but justifies it as a detailed reply to detailed allegations (*appendices defensionis meae iccirco necessarias, quia accusationi rependuntur*), and takes the opportunity to flatter Maximus for listening so attentively, no doubt entranced by the learning in which he so notably shares.

(iii) *Possession of a Mirror* (13. 4–16)

To this repeated accusation of the foolish Pudens, Apuleius answers with impeccable logic that possession of a mirror does not necessitate its use for admiring oneself, but allowing that he had looked at himself in it: self-contemplation is a natural human activity. This then develops into a set piece on the superiority of reflection to other means of figural representation of men, embroidered with traditional anecdotes actually derived from handbooks or convenient sources rather than classic Greek originals, the kind of short-cut to learning familiar in Apuleius; the story of Agesilaus comes from Cicero, that of Socrates from the biographical tradition, that of Demosthenes from Quintilian.[42] These great orators and philosophers justify the use of the mirror for self-contemplation. But, he goes on, there are other reasons for using a mirror; scientific theories such as Epicurean physics (here clearly with details garnered from Lucretius, unmentioned, rather than the cited Epicurus) and Archimedean optics require them. Here fun is poked at the rustic Aemilianus (16. 7) for not having read the Κατοπτρικά of the great Archimedes (had Apuleius himself, one wonders?),[43] a gibe which would hardly have been effective in a Ciceronian speech but which marks the importance of recondite learning for Apuleius, Maximus, and the culture of the period in general. The treatment of the mirror concludes with a neat contrast between the unknown obscurity of Aemilianus, engaged in rustic activity, and the open and public life of Apuleius; the former's attempt to attack Apuleius' life, known to all the world, is likened to a man lurking in the dark and gazing at another bathed in sunlight. Apart from the suggestion of envy of Apuleius' fame on Aemilianus' part, this clearly classes Apuleius with the great Greek sophists of his era, whose lives, personalities, and quarrels were decidedly public;[44] Apuleius is, or wishes to class himself as, a

[42] Cicero *Fam.* 5. 12. 7, Diogenes Laertius 2. 33, Quintilian 11. 3. 68 (cf. Plutarch *Dem.* 11. 1); all these are noted by Butler and Owen (1914).

[43] Hunink (1997), ii. 65, plausibly suggests more easily found Latin sources, including Lucretius.

[44] On the publicity of sophists' lives cf. Anderson (1993), 13–36.

denizen of the limelight, while Aemilianus is a lowly creature[45] of no significance who can only gaze at the great man from the shadows. The imagery of light and dark is of course appropriate in a treatment of mirrors.

(iv) *Freeing of Three Slaves* (17. 1–6)

This allegation was presumably raised as a token of Apuleius' extravagance with his new-found wealth after marrying Pudentilla, and a pointed contrast was clearly made by the prosecution with the single slave with which he had first arrived at Oea. Here Apuleius seems deliberately to elide the crucial time-gap and change of circumstances between the two occasions, accusing the opposition of simple incoherence in alleging both only a single slave for Apuleius and his manumission of three, as if the two were said to be true at the same time and in the same situation. This is clearly in order to discount the charge of extravagance, potentially a serious one, and both to separate it from the other material about the marriage in section VII and to connect it with the traditional material on poverty which immediately follows, and into which the charge provides a convenient launching-pad.

(v) *Apuleius' Poverty* (17. 7–23)

Apuleius needs to argue that the philosopher is poor and that this is honourable, but the long disquisition which we find here clearly transcends the immediate requirements of the forensic context, and is indeed the most extensive epideictic digression in the whole speech. It has been plausibly argued that Apuleius is here in effect taking a break from forensic argument, and giving his audience some relief, by recycling standard material.[46] The section begins (17. 7–11) with a list of famous Romans with minimal numbers of slaves, a traditional topic of Roman moralizing, and with an allusion to the speeches of Cato, highly praised by Fronto and favoured reading at Rome in the archaizing literary culture of Apuleius' time;[47] Pudens is admonished for not knowing these last,

---

[45] *Lucifugus* suggests an insect (Vergil *Georg.* 4. 243, Arnobius *Nat.* 6. 16), and is used insultingly of humans by Lucilius (468 Marx) and Cicero (*Fin.* 1. 61). Hunink (1997), ii. 67, notes that the term is used in early anti-Christian polemic, but is rightly hesitant to argue that Aemilianus is depicted as a Christian in the *Apologia* (there is no real evidence for this).

[46] See Hunink (1997), ii. 68.

[47] On the popularity of the works of Cato in the second century AD see Holford-Strevens (1988), 145.

anticipating future attacks on his lack of culture. The following formal *locus de paupertate* (18–21), commending poverty as suitable for a philosopher, is highly expansive in style and strongly redolent of declamatory education.[48] Apuleius is here placing himself in the grand tradition of virtue despising wealth, and of poverty producing virtue; his catalogue of the virtuous poor begins with various Greek worthies (18. 7: Aristides, Phocion, Epaminondas, Socrates, and Homer), no doubt citing the first three for their general moral qualities,[49] the last two for their relevance to himself as philosopher and man of letters, but the more lengthy of his examples are taken from the great men of Roman history (18. 9–11: Fabricius, Scipio, Curius, Publicola, Menenius Agrippa, Regulus) and drawn from much the same sources as before.[50] This greater stress on the Roman gallery of public men seems to be chosen as particularly suitable for the audience in Sabratha.

The turn back to philosophy, crucial for the argument, and the link between these Roman worthies and Apuleius, is accomplished through a further appeal to the sympathies of Maximus, who combines the role of a public man (like those just mentioned) with that of a follower of philosophy (like Apuleius): *virum tam austerae sectae tamque diutinae militiae* (19. 2). Though as a member of the governing class Maximus is naturally well off himself, as a philosopher he will oppose attacking a philosopher for poverty, as Aemilianus is doing (19. 1); the mention of Aemilianus here keeps some grip on the forensic context in this passage, which otherwise follows the traditional groove of popular moralizing. Excess wealth is compared in traditional images with an ill-fitting tunic which impedes the wearer and an outsize tiller which overbalances a ship (19. 2–5).[51] Similarly traditional is the praise of unostentatious wealth and

---

[48] For the *locus de paupertate* in this section, and its connection with Roman declamation, see the full treatment of Vallette (1908), 129–57, Stok (1985), and the additional references in Hunink (1997), ii. 68. That the virtuous early Romans had only a few slaves is a topic of moralistic writing found at Seneca *Cons. Helv.* 12. 5–7 (naming Menenius Agrippa, Regulus, and Scipio Africanus), and Athenaeus 6. 105 (naming Scipio Africanus and Julius Caesar); cf. also Valerius Maximus 4. 4. 6 and 10, indicating that this is a part of the traditional Roman praise of poverty in great men. None of Apuleius' examples in fact occur in the passages just quoted, but the poverty of Curius and Cato is mentioned in Valerius Maximus' chapter *De Abstinentia et Continentia* (4. 3), including the same detail that the Elder Cato went to govern Spain with only three slaves (4. 3. 11).

[49] Aristides and Phocion appear together in Valerius Maximus 5. 3. 3, Epaminondas in id. 3. 2. 5 and 3. 7. 5, all praised for other virtues than poverty; all three were also included in the book on foreign generals which survives from Nepos' *De Viris Illustribus*.

[50] See n. 48; for the two additions Fabricius and Publicola cf. Seneca *De Prov.* 3. 6 (together), Valerius Maximus 4. 3. 2 (Fabricius), Valerius Maximus 4. 4. 1 (Publicola).

[51] See Butler and Owen (1914), 56.

the assertion that poverty cannot be shameful since some of the rich choose to maintain its appearance (19. 6–7).[52]

The argument then turns to the definition of poverty, argued to be in the mind (20. 1–21. 6): he who is content with a few necessaries is not poor, while the rich think of themselves as poor since their wants are excessive. The examples of the rich are again Roman: Philus, Laelius, Scipio, and (inevitably) Crassus (20. 5).[53] This idea is turned against Aemilianus (20. 9), again as at 19. 2 recalling the reader to the forensic context, in a clever and amusing paradox: if Aemilianus wants to prove that Apuleius is a poor man, he must first prove that he is greedy (for his few wants are already supplied). Another turn follows, recalling the argument of 19. 7, and giving a novel turn to the *argumentum ex bestiis*: even if Apuleius admits poverty, why should poverty be a reproach to a man, when it is not a reproach to a beast (21. 1)? Animals and men are self-sufficient in their own virtues, physical and moral respectively, and neither class is to be blamed for lack of material comfort and prosperity. More traditional is the following assertion that reduction in worldly goods is desirable for independence and happiness (21. 3–6): Senecan pointed style as well as thought is conveyed in the pithily expressed moral of *prorsus ad vivendum velut ad natandum is melior, qui onere liberior* (21. 5), and the argument is led to its climax (21. 6) in the Socratic idea that man is more like god the less he requires.[54]

Finally, the argument turns more specifically to the poverty of the philosopher (22. 1), introduced by Aemilianus' taunt that Apuleius' family fortune consisted only of his bag and staff, the traditional philosopher's equipment. Here with the wandering poor philosopher we are firmly in Cynic territory,[55] and it is no surprise to find here a well-known anecdote or rather χρεία (anecdote with pithy remark) of popular sophistic type about the cynic Crates, the central figure in two of the extracts in the *Florida* (14 and 22),[56] in which Crates modifies a Homeric line to praise his philosopher's bag. The explicit parallel between Crates and Apuleius is that of the high value they put on their philosopher's dress and status, but given what is coming in sections 23 and 24 there are surely

---

[52] Cf. Seneca *Cons. Helv.* 12. 3.
[53] Philus and Laelius seem to come from Cicero *Arch.* 16 (so Butler and Owen). The Crassus here is evidently the triumvir: so, rightly, Hunink (1997), ii. 75.
[54] Cf. Xenophon *Mem.* 1. 6. 10.
[55] See Vallette (1908), 152–7, and the further references of Hunink (1997), ii. 76.
[56] On Crates cf. Ch. 3 n. 73, and on the χρεία, Ch. 3 n. 20.

further links to be drawn: both are philosophers of good family whose wealth has been honourably used, Crates' in donations to the poor (22. 2), Apuleius' in travel and study as well as charitable giving (23. 2). The Cynic connection is further extended by mention of Diogenes and Antisthenes, alluding to Diogenes' traditional disparagement of Alexander,[57] but the passage ends in the climax of Hercules, whom the Cynics claimed as their hero for his peripatetic benefactions to mankind (cf. *Flor.* 22), and whose club and lion-skin are here seen as analogous to the Cynic philosopher's staff and bag.[58] This passage in praise of Hercules may have been aimed at the local audience: there was a prominent cult of Hercules (syncretized with the Punic Melqart) at Sabratha, and the god was featured on its coins in the first century and honoured with a major new temple there in the 180s AD.[59]

This passage on poverty is not just an opportunistic lecture. It replies directly to the most dangerous assertion of the prosecution, that Apuleius married Pudentilla for her money; Apuleius must stress the lack of material interest of philosophers in general and of himself as a member of the species. This same point of lack of monetary concerns is neatly made in the final part of this section (23), dealing with Apuleius' personal background. The information given here is valuable for Apuleius' biography (see Chapter 1), but it is also carefully presented; his moneyed background, with the careful calibration of his joint patrimony at the very respectable 2 million sesterces, five times the equestrian *census* (23. 2), is reconciled with his philosophical poverty through his generosity in spending money both on his friends and teachers. Apuleius is rich by birth, and poor by choice—both reasons for lack of monetary ambitions. This both matches the liberality and philosophical poverty of Crates just described, and contrasts with the 'uncultured' Aemilianus (23. 5), who can produce no intellectual fruit, like a barren tree good only for firewood: the use of agricultural imagery for his lack of 'culture' is neat, especially when it is followed by the comic picture of Aemilianus working his own plot with a single ass (23. 6).

In this last vignette, pointing out that Aemilianus is hypocritical in accusing others of poverty, we are reminded not of the common idealization of working one's own land but of the contempt Roman culture could show towards the practice of manual labour in the fields.[60]

---

[57] Cf. e.g. Diog. Laert. 6. 38.   [58] On the moralized Hercules cf. Ch. 3 n. 133.
[59] Cf. Mattingly (1995), 126.
[60] Cf. Cicero *Fin.* 1. 3 *inliberali labore*; for the more usual praise of personal involvement

Aemilianus is an insignificant and disreputable son of the soil, and his humble farm at his obscure home of Zarath (23. 6 *agellum Zarathensem*) is here mentioned for the first time before Apuleius' more explicit attack on it at 24. 10. This stress on Aemilianus' poverty is not mere reciprocal abuse, but important to Apuleius' later argument in VII, where he presents the case against him as motivated wholly by the financial hopes of Aemilianus and Herennius. The Vergilian joke in making the foul-faced Aemilianus a Charon (23. 7) is a good one, but compressed. Aemilianus resembles the ferryman of the dead not only in his unpleasant features (cf. 56. 7), but also in his greed and in making money from corpses: Charon gets his fare across the Styx and is rapacious to boot,[61] while Aemilianus gets undeserved legacies. This form of mythological abuse will reappear and intensify later in the speech (see below), and is a Ciceronian technique (cf. Section 2 above).

(vi) *Apuleius' Origins* (24).

The final part of this section describes Apuleius' *patria* of Madauros, evidently attacked by the prosecution as insignificant; Apuleius is a freebooting nobody from nowhere. Having proved his social status in 23, Apuleius here presents a dilemma for the opposition, first presenting the charge as true but harmless (with another self-promoting reference to his own written works and public performances elsewhere) and then denying it. First, he argues that even if his *patria* is obscure, he shares this with other great men such as Cyrus,[62] and place of birth takes second place to character; this point is neatly put across by clever verbal jingles (24. 3 *non ubi prognatus, sed ut moratus quisque sit spectandum, nec qua regione, sed qua ratione vitam vivere inierit, considerandum est*). Second, he presents Madauros as a fine place in its own right, adopting the first person plural of the proud citizen (24. 8 *sumus*): not only is it long established under Roman rule, but it has been refounded as a *splendissima colonia*, in which Apuleius has followed his father as a leading participant in political life.

---

in agriculture cf. e.g. Cicero *Off*. 1. 151, *Sen*. 51–60, and on the rhetorical manipulation of rusticity in various ways in Cicero cf. Vasaly (1993), 156–66.

[61] At least in Apuleius' own version in *Met*. 6. 18. 6 (Vergil's Charon does not show greed); the rapacity of Charon belongs to the comic/satiric tradition followed by Lucian's second *Dialogue of the Dead*, where Charon demands his fee from Menippus.

[62] The terms *Semimedus* and *Semipersa* (for Cyrus' famous mixed parentage cf. Herodotus 1. 107, Xenophon *Inst. Cyr.* 2. 1) are found before Apuleius in Greek in the second-century Cynic Oenomaus of Gadara (*fl. c.* AD 120), quoted by Eusebius *PE* 5. 21: ὁ μὲν ἡμίμηδος ἢ ἡμιπέρσης Κῦρος.

Cur ergo illa protuli? (24. 10) is a purely rhetorical question, and the possibility of irrelevant self-promotion is here dismissed; Apuleius' praise of his *patria* and associated self-praise is not self-generated but a reply to the allegations of the prosecution. As in the accusation of poverty in 23, the accusation of obscurity is finally turned on Aemilianus himself: who has heard of his barbaric birthplace of Zarath, with its evidently Punic name?[63] Thus the two chapters 23 and 24 are neatly held together by similar structures, providing a firm ending to the consideration of the non-magical allegations.

III. *Summing-up of Refutation of Non-Magical Allegations* (25. 1–4)

The summing-up is cleverly done in a series of seven successive rhetorical questions, powerfully implying that there is no possible counter to Apuleius' refutation. The allegations are presented as frivolous and incoherent, but the incoherences presented here are of course of Apuleius' own construction, deliberately misinterpreting and rearranging the prosecution's case (25. 3). The staff and bag of the philosopher were not accusations of austerity but of poverty as a motive for the marriage, and could indeed be coherent in the prosecution's mind with erotic interests and personal vanity, evidenced by the poems and the mirror; likewise, the contrast between Apuleius' possession of a single slave and his manumission of three is criticized for inconsistency by again blatantly ignoring the different circumstances on the two occasions. The supposed inconsistency between eloquence in Greek and 'barbarous' origins, though propounding a neat paradox for those conversant with the Greek definition of βάρβαρος as non-Greek-speaker,[64] has little effect in the context of the *Apologia*; it merely combines the first and last of the allegations to be treated in a superficial makeweight, no doubt added to ensure three pairs of contrasts here.

The summary closes with a complimentary allusion to Maximus, *virum severum et totius provinciae negotiis occupatum* (25. 3), and a transition to the charges of magic, still within the overall framework of the series of rhetorical questions. The call to the prosecution to wake up to

---

[63] Who indeed? The place is also unknown to modern scholarship or archaeology, though Hunink (1997), ii. 80, is no doubt right in guessing that it was 'a small village near Oea'.

[64] Cf. conveniently Weidner (1913).

reality (25. 3 *quin igitur tandem expergiscimini . . .?*), though echoing more closely a famous passage of Sallust,[65] also recalls Cicero's similar address to Verres (*Verr.* 5. 38 *si forte te expergefacere posses . . .*), and suggests that in these initial allegations Aemilianus is wasting the time not only of the distinguished and busy Maximus but also of anyone of sense; Apuleius challenges his opponent to proceed to the real business, to the charges of magic themselves, as he had claimed to do when the prosecution was first raised. The whole of the speech so far has been in effect a deviation from the central matter, caused by the waywardness of the prosecution. Here Apuleius carefully conceals the fact that many of the points already made in the opening section contribute significantly to his overall defence and prepare the ground for later argumentation—cf. Section 2 above.

IV. *Introduction to Refutation of 'Minor' Magical Charges* (25. 5–28)

The transition to the magical charges is accomplished with a Ciceronian formula: *aggredior enim ad ipsum crimen magiae* (25. 5) echoes the beginning of the treatment of charges in the *Pro Cluentio* (8 *aggrediar ad crimen*), a speech with which the *Apologia* has parallels both general and specific (see Section 2 above). This opening of a crucial stage of the defence is prominently marked with a literary fire-image to characterize the spreading of a baseless accusation; this is an important idea in the speech, since the charge of magic is presented by Apuleius from the very beginning as more a matter of rumour than of proof (2. 2 *facilius infamatur quam probatur*). The image is transfused from the metaphor of *accensum* and *defraglavit* (25. 5) to the simile of an insubstantial blaze in straw (25. 6), with vast noise but little destruction, an appropriate meiosis of the epic simile of a devastating fire in a cornfield, where there is at least something to burn (cf. Vergil *Aen.* 2. 304–5).

Apuleius then begins in the manner of the Socratic elenchus by asking his opponents what they mean by the term *magus*, with which they have characterized him (25. 9). Once again he impales them on the horns of a carefully constructed dilemma, fleshed out with a display of learning and condescension. If the accusation is of being a *magus* in the strict scholarly sense (it is the Persian for 'priest'), that is no crime, indeed a

---

[65] Sallust *Cat.* 20. 14 (Catiline's speech to the conspirators) *quin igitur expergescimini?* Hunink (1997), ii. 86, cites the parallel, adding *Cat.* 52. 6 (Cato to the Senate) *expergiscimini aliquando.*

distinction, and this is proved by the testimony of a minor dialogue of Plato (*Alcibiades* I), cited in the original for the delectation of the learned Maximus, backed up by name-dropping allusions to Zoroaster and Oromazes, again drawn from Plato, and a short quotation of the appearance of the Thracian Salmoxis in Plato's *Charmides* (25. 11–26. 5);[66] but if the accusation is of being a *magus* in the vulgar sense, that is of communing with gods and having personal divine powers, then he is surprised that they dare bring the charge, since such a *magus* could destroy them at any moment; therefore, paradoxically, only he who disbelieves the charge will dare to bring it. The term *magus* is a difficult one to negotiate, since philosophers and *magi* could be easily associated; thus Apuleius needs to provide a respectable type of *magus* with which he could be harmlessly identified, and to distinguish it from the kind of *magus* disapproved of by Roman law.[67]

Apuleius then (27. 1–4) presents himself as the latest in a long line of philosophers maligned as irreligious by the ignorant; if such great men are irreligious, he is happy to be in their company. The charge of irreligiosity seems not to have been part of the accusation in the *Apologia*, or at least only present by implication in that of magic, but Apuleius may use it in order to align himself with the Socrates of Plato's *Apology*, where it is undoubtedly one of the charges and Socrates similarly asserts that it is traditionally made against philosophers (23d); here Apuleius is again keeping his promise to defend philosophers in general. The list of philosophers is in two parts and chosen with the forthcoming argumentation in mind; Anaxagoras and the natural scientists (27. 1) are anticipatory parallels and justifications for Apuleius' investigations of fish, about to be discussed, while Epimenides and the theologians look forward to Apuleius' interest in the nature of the gods and devotion to them, an important theme in section V, where Apuleius (as in the *Florida*) will present himself as religiously devout, which will not only explain many of the elements dubbed magical by the prosecution, but also give a favourable impression to Maximus and the audience; appeals to one's own religious belief, a belief at least notionally shared by one's hearers, are an evident *captatio benevolentiae*.

Chapters 27. 5–28. 8 provide an appropriate transition to the detailed answering of the charges. First, in a technique repeated at 103. 2–3,

---

[66] For Apuleius' manipulation of the Plato passage here see Hunink (1997), ii. 90.

[67] For the links between philosophers and *magi* see Vallette (1908), 298–301. For *magi* and Roman law cf. Vallette (1908), 34–9, G. Kleinfeller in *RE* 14. 396. 30 ff., Norden (1912).

Apuleius gives short and pithy responses to a series of imaginary questions and allegations from Aemilianus, which summarize the argumentation which follows (27. 5–12), and whose brevity both provides
amusement and suggests that the prosecution's allegations may be swiftly
dismissed by persons of common sense. The technique is again
Ciceronian (cf. e.g. Cicero *S. Rosc.* 54, 92). 'Why investigate fish?'—
'Philosophical interest.' 'Why did Pudentilla remarry after such a long
widowhood?'—'Ask rather why it took so long.' 'Why did she write her
thoughts in a letter before the wedding?'—'How should I know the reasons for another's thoughts?' 'An older woman did not turn down a
younger husband.'—'No need for magic there.' 'Apuleius has something
at home which he worships.'—'Surely worse not to.' 'A boy fell over when
Apuleius was present.'—'So what?' The more serious points about
Pudentilla's marriage, which will in fact be treated not in the next section
but in the final section of 68–101, are carefully sandwiched within the
more frivolous minor magic allegations which Apuleius is about to attack
in 29–65: the implication is evidently that all the allegations are equally ill
founded and ridiculous.

This is followed by a pseudo-realistic allusion to the time remaining
for the speech (28. 1),[68] and then a reassertion of his innocence as a philosopher: even if all the things alleged by the prosecution happened, the
innocent philosopher can explain and defend them. This largely covers
the tactics adopted by Apuleius in refuting the lesser magical charges in
29–65. At 28. 4–5, Apuleius provides a formal *divisio* (as again later at 67.
2–4): he will first refute the prosecution's lesser charges of magic (i.e. in
29–65), then turn to the matter of Pudentilla's marriage (i.e. in 68–101).
This is followed by an attack on the motives of the prosecution (28. 5–9),
which forms a useful preface to a detailed defence: Aemilianus is furious
at the marriage, while Pudens, the official accuser, has broken with his
family and decent upbringing by his stepfather Apuleius under the corrupting influence of Aemilianus. The charges are the fabrications of a
rapacious and disappointed man and a rebellious teenager.

V. *Refutation of 'Minor' Magic Charges* (29–65)

(i) *Apuleius' Interest in Fish* (29–41)

Apuleius begins (29) by stressing the normal nature of his interest in
fish—it is surely not suspicious to ask fishermen to catch them (who else

---

[68] On the function of such indications see n. 11 above.

would do so?), or to pay money for them (how else would one obtain them?). If the assertion is that fish themselves have magic uses and properties (30. 2), then Aemilianus is once again faced with an invidious dilemma: either he knows this himself and is a *magus*, or he is making a blind and unrealistic guess. The latter is clearly the case. But the true reason for the fishy allegations is a significant one, stated at 30. 4 *ad amoris ardorem accendendum*; though Apuleius never mentions the charge directly, it is clear that he was accused of using on Pudentilla an aphrodisiac derived from fish, and that fish could readily be associated with magic generally.[69] Apuleius naturally wishes to disprove this, and does so with a barrage of literary evidence, beginning with Vergil and Laevius, the latter again showing the contemporary taste for archaic Roman literature;[70] had the prosecution read these texts, and indeed other Greek texts which they are too ignorant to appreciate (30. 11), they would have known that it is other substances which are used in aphrodisiacs, and framed their calumnies accordingly (31. 1). Evidence for the magical uselessness of fish, rather against the general view of antiquity, is cited in an anecdote (also found in Plutarch)[71] about Pythagoras, who bought a catch from fishermen and ordered it to be thrown back; this actually illustrates his belief in transmigration, but Apuleius suggests that had fish been useful for magic Pythagoras would have kept them. This anecdote about a philosopher, a favourite topic of the *Florida*, matches the earlier tale of Crates (*Apol.* 22. 2).[72] Homer too is cited (in untranslated quotations from *Il.* 11 and *Od.* 4) in support of the terrestrial origins of drugs, and their lack of connection with the sea is presented in a wittily false verbal association: the gods of the sea are to be invoked in the manufacture of love-philtres, and *ab* aestibus *fretorum ad* aestus *amorum transferentur* (31. 9).

At 32. 1 Apuleius, having rebutted the magical use of fish, once more applies a hypothetical strategy: though he has proved the opposite, let it be conceded that fish can have magic properties—does that mean that anyone interested in fish is a magician? This is clearly absurd—those who catch fish need not do so for magic purposes, a point learnedly illustrated

---

[69] On fish-aphrodisiacs and the whole magical background to 39–41 see exhaustively Abt (1908), 135–231, and the references added by Hunink (1997), ii. 98.

[70] Laevius is quoted several times by Gellius (*NA* 2. 24. 8, 12. 10. 5, 19. 7. 2–16) and once by Fronto (*Ad M. Caes.* 1. 5. 5 van den Hout); on his importance for Apuleius see Mattiacci (1986), and for discussions of this fragment Bartalucci (1985), Courtney (1993), 140–1.

[71] Plutarch *Quaest. Conv.* 8. 729d; this dervies from the biographical tradition about Pythagoras—cf. Iamblichus *Vit. Pyth.* 36, Porphyry *Vit. Pyth.* 25.

[72] Pythagoras himself is the subject of *Flor.* 15, Crates of *Flor.* 14 and 22.

from Homer (32. 5), carrying on the Homeric theme from 31, just as those
who buy weapons or tools need not use them in a criminal way. Apuleius
then (33. 1) attacks the ignorance of the opposition, who have mistaken
the identity of some fish and deliberately misinterpreted the nature of
others; he has some fun with Tannonius Pudens, who, wishing to allege
that certain fish resembled human genitals and were therefore likely to be
used in aphrodisiacs, could not bring himself to pronounce the anatomical names, but was forced to quote a euphemism from the works of
Apuleius himself (33. 7). As well as being yet another casual allusion to
Apuleius' prestigious status as an established writer, this last point clearly
inverts the opposition's use of the defendant's works; they must have
hoped to imply that he was interested in the anatomy of sex and, by association, in sexual persuasion and aphrodisiacs. Such associations of the
names of marine life with sexual functions are absurd, claims Apuleius,
and, though he shows off his knowledge of their names in producing a
long catalogue (35. 1–6) to instruct the ignorance of the prosecution (cf.
34. 5), he is simply not interested in most of the creatures mentioned,
which can be picked up for free on the seashore and do not need to be
purchased. The list of marine names concludes with a quartet of comic
word-plays, a *reductio ad absurdum* of the prosecution's method of associating sea-creatures with effects on the human body: *calculus ad vesicam,
testa ad testamentum, cancer ad ulcera, alga ad quercerum.*[73]

Having completed the proof necessary for forensic purposes, at least
for the moment, Apuleius commends the patience of Maximus for having listened to such vacuous accusations (35. 7), but then embarks on a
didactic disquisition on fish for the benefit of the ignorant Aemilianus
(cf. 36. 2 *accipiat doctrinam*); clearly, the implication is that Maximus will
enjoy Apuleius' learned epideictic in contrast with his mere endurance of
the opposition's stupidity, and Maximus' own reading of the relevant
philosophical works is duly pointed out in what follows (36. 5, 38. 1).
A recital of learned sources follows, the last being Apuleius' own works
in Greek and Latin; these are presented as the justification for his

---

[73] The puns are unpacked by Butler and Owen (1914), 86–7: *calculus* means both 'pebble'
and 'gall-stone' (hence the gall-bladder, *vesica*), *testa* ('potsherd') clearly resembles *testamentum*, an Apuleian variation on *testis*, 'testicle' (Butler and Owen rightly compare the
similarly unparalleled use of *detestatio* at *Met.* 7. 23. 3 to mean 'castration'), *cancer*, 'crab', in
Greek is κάρκινος, cognate with καρκίνωμα, the Greek equivalent of *ulcus*, 'sore', while *alga*
puns on *algere*, a supposed cooling effect on fever (*quercerum*). For the last word *quercerum*
is the manuscript reading, retained by Vallette, but the word is an adjective, and the feminine (sc. *febris*; cf. *quartana*) would be expected; Helm rightly reads Colvius' *querceram*, followed by Butler and Owen.

anatomical researches on fish.[74] While a Greek work of Apuleius is being fetched for the benefit of the court, one of several elements in this context alluding with artful realism to the details of forensic procedure,[75] he offers another anecdote of the type so common in the *Florida* (37),[76] this time of the poet Sophocles, the well-known tale of the aged poet's soundness of mind, impugned by his son, being proved in a court of law by the reading of the *Oedipus at Colonus*.[77] The parallels with Apuleius' own case are clear; he too is a literary man under unjustified attack, his innocence too will also be proved by a consideration of his written work, in Latin as well as Greek, and he too is being accused by a member of his family (his stepson Pudens).

Apuleius' Greek book is brought into court and shown to be a scientific work in the manner of Aristotle, being concerned with the techniques of fish reproduction and their classification (38. 1–4). Apuleius then follows this up by allusion to a similar Latin work in which he has personally invented Latin equivalents for Greek fish names. A long list of Greek fish names is put in to ridicule the prosecution, wittily imagined as thinking that these exotic labels belong to the realm of magic; a matching list of Apuleius' Latin equivalents is asked for, but does not appear in the text.[78] All this is of course to present Apuleius as an impressive bilingual intellectual, doing original ichthyological research, and showing an interest in the natural world appropriate to a learned Platonic philosopher. This work is further justified as literature (as well as philosophy) by an appeal to Ennius' *Hedyphagetika* (39. 2), lengthily cited on the best places to obtain fish;[79] this is not only a reminder of the archaizing taste of the age, but also a careful assertion that interest in fish is Roman as well as Greek.

At 40. 1 Apuleius' tack changes, to deal with the further detailed charge that he dissected fish (cf. 40. 5, 41. 1). Here, in defending an action which

[74] For these works see Ch. 1 above, 2 (ii) 12.

[75] For such pseudo-realism cf. nn. 11 and 68 above.

[76] Compare esp. *Flor.* 16, where the dramatist Philemon is similarly used to parallel the situation of Apuleius himself.

[77] Cf. Sophocles *Test.* O 81–9 Radt; Apuleius may well get it from Cicero *De Sen.* 22.

[78] This seems not to be textual damage as some have thought, but another piece of pseudo-realism (cf. n. 11): the Latin translation (even though it is to be by Apuleius himself) is omitted as ancillary like the recitations of other documents and witness-statements (cf. 69. 6–8), showing that the Greek text, with its impressive impact and the ability of the elite few to understand it, is the crucial thing.

[79] Apuleius' quotation is in fact the only firm evidence for this work of Ennius, evidently a version of the hexameter poem of the same name by Archestratus of Gela. For a discussion of these lines see Courtney (1993), 22–5.

looks dangerously like the preliminaries to making an aphrodisiac, he feels it necessary to generate a further positive response: his dissection was indeed for pharmacological purposes, but beneficial rather than harmful, since it involved the search for medical remedies, and the works of Aristotle, also read by Maximus, are called to witness this aspect of dissection (40. 5, 41. 4). Here we find for the first time Apuleius the practitioner of medicine (40. 1 *medicinae neque instudiosus neque imperitus*). This is not a long step from Apuleius the biologist and anatomist; we know that Apuleius composed a work of medical botany, and the stress on medicine here reflects its prestige in the second century BC and the close proximity of the skills of medical expert, philosopher, and sophist.[80] In context, it also prepares the reader for Apuleius' medicinal contacts with epilepsy in the case of Thallus (42–52). At 41. 5 a new objection is wittily made—Apuleius was not even present at the time of the alleged application of the aphrodisiac to Pudentilla, but was away in his home country, mountainous and far from the sea or any fish. He congratulates himself that the opposition are unaware of his wide reading on poisonous creatures, including Theophrastus and Nicander, or they would accuse him further; this, with further allusion to the reading and imitation of Plato and Aristotle (41. 7), not only makes yet again the point of his learning and the prosecution's ignorance, but importantly stresses that it is precisely that learning and intellectual investigation that have brought him undeserved trouble, something of a Socratic pose.

(ii) *The Epileptic Slave Thallus and the Epileptic Woman* (42–52)

The matter of fish dismissed, this new charge is presented as more ignorant misinterpretation. The supposed collapse of Thallus under Apuleius' enchantment is first compared (somewhat gratuitously) with learned accounts of prophecy by possessed children (42. 5); two anecdotes are self-consciously cited from Varro, the first concerning a hydromantic boy at Tralles predicting the outcome of the Mithradatic war, the second about boys who revealed the whereabouts of a lost sum of money under the influence of Nigidius Figulus.[81] Apuleius, though confirming his Platonic belief in divine intervention in the world through the agency

---

[80] On Apuleius' work of medical botany see Ch. 1, 2 (ii) 7 above; on the affinity between medicine, philosophy and rhetoric in the second century AD see Ch. 1 n. 103.

[81] It is not clear which (lost) work of Varro is cited (perhaps a part of the *Res Divinae* on prophecy). For Varro as an Apuleian source elsewhere cf. Ch. 1, 2 (ii) 6.

of possessing δαίμονες, the topic of his *De Deo Socratis* (see Chapter 4 below), professes some doubt of this phenomenon, but points out that even so Thallus could not be such a child owing to his physical imperfections and epilepsy, the real reason for his frequent collapses (43. 10): here once again Apuleius presents himself as capable of authoritative medical diagnosis. Thallus' absence in court (44), a possible disadvantage to Apuleius' case, is explained by reasons of health: he has been sent to the country to avoid contact with his fellow slaves, and a chariot has been dispatched to bring him back. Instead, Apuleius offers fourteen other slaves to support his claims, slaves also alleged to have been enchanted by him (45–6), and makes much of the prosecution's refusal to examine them on the point, contrasting with their stress on Thallus: in a typically pithy Apuleian word-play, the case is summed up as *quattuordecim servi petitu tuo adsunt, eos* dissimulas; *unus puerulus abest, eum* insimulas (45. 2). Apuleius then claims (45. 4) that had he wished to make Thallus collapse, he could have done so from his learned scientific reading on the properties of jet (the allusion here, as so often, is to the elder Pliny);[82] this might seem a risky admission, but Apuleius is once more pursuing the dual strategy outlined at 28. 4, arguing both that the boy's collapse was nothing to do with him, and that even if it had been the reasons could have had nothing to do with magic. Finally, it is pointed out in a humorous climax that the only witness now testifying to the 'enchantment' of Thallus is the boy Pudens. The point in the final *puer cecidit, puer vidit: num etiam puer aliqui incantavit?* (45. 8) seems to be that the boy Pudens is a better suspect for the alleged enchantment than Apuleius given that he shares Thallus' age: is the whole thing a childish pretence dreamt up by the two boys?

Both Tannonius Pudens (who evidently dealt with the matter of Thallus) and Aemilianus are then subjected to a lively passage of browbeating in the best Ciceronian style (46. 3–6): the repeated staccato rhetorical questions *quid taces, quid cunctaris, quid respectas?* (46. 4) and *quid expalluisti, quid taces?* (46. 5) recall Cicero *Planc.* 48 *quid taces, quid dissimules, quid tergiversaris?*, *Quinct.* 79 *quid taces?* and *Cat.* 1. 8 *num negare audes? quid taces?* Some time and stylistic expansion are devoted to the common-sense point that magic is not the kind of crime to have had fifteen witnesses (47), with a casual citation of the definition of *magia* in the Twelve Tables (47. 3), drawn from Pliny rather than real antiquar-

---

[82] Pliny *HN* 36. 142 records the use of jet to test for epilepsy. For Pliny as an Apuleian source cf. Ch. 1 n. 105.

ian research,[83] and a learned joke on the coincidence that fifteen is both the number of alleged witnesses to the magic and the number of the *quindecimviri sacris faciundis*. This lively section then ends with a *reductio ad absurdum* (47. 7): the only sacrificial victims mentioned by the prosecution for the magic ceremonies involved in the enchantment of Thallus are chickens—were they there to count the grains of incense, or to knock Thallus over ?

A further allegation that Apuleius bewitched a woman brought to him for a cure is also dismissed (48); it was a referral by a reputable doctor, and she was also an epileptic with the added symptom of tinnitus. Apuleius jokes that they must think he is a wrestler, not a magician, since everyone who sends for him falls over. As earlier, Maximus is praised for his scepticism towards the prosecution's evidence, and also for his severe cross-examination of them with regard to Apuleius' motives; Apuleius then uses this address to Maximus for a springboard to explain in a didactic digression (promising brevity and perhaps conscious of possible irrelevance) why he is interested in epilepsy and tinnitus (48. 11–51. 8), a learned topic which refers to the teachings of Plato and other philosophers and which will therefore please Maximus (48. 12).

The beginning of the digression is marked by a promise of brevity (48. 13) and a complimentary witticism: Maximus needs only to be reminded of these things, not informed (*admonendus es mihi, non docendus*), not only because he is already expert but also because according to a famous Platonic doctrine all knowledge is merely recollection (ἀνάμνησις).[84] It proceeds by citing the *Timaeus* on the origin of disease and the particular pathology of epilepsy, and then moves to the work of Aristotle and Theophrastus, using philosophers in order to show to the court that interest in such phenomena is a philosophical trait (51. 8), and ends once again with a humorous and punning flourish: the prosecution's allegations about Thallus and the woman will fall to the ground just like the persons themselves (51. 10 *fateantur se in puero et muliere caducis vanas et prorsus caducas calumnias intendisse*). This punning association is further pursued in the following section, which rounds off the whole passage on Thallus (52) by a clever comparison between the disability of Thallus and the inability of Aemilianus to make his case, which, like the epileptic boy, falls to the ground, shows symptoms of madness, suffers

---

[83] Cf. Pliny *HN* 28. 17, which similarly selects crop-enchantment and the making of spells from the Twelve Tables.

[84] Cf. Plato *Men.* 81d ff., *Phaed.* 72e ff., *Phaedr.* 249c ff.

distortion, and is prone to collision; but Thallus cannot help his condition, while that of Aemilianus and his prosecution is malevolently self-
manufactured.

(iii) *Apuleius' 'Magic' Talisman* (53–6)

The prosecution is again attacked for raising an issue of which it is
entirely ignorant; no one has actually seen the object wrapped in the
linen cloth which they mention, not the dead Pontianus, who lived so
closely with Apuleius, not even the slave who looks after Apuleius' chest
where it is kept, who seems to have testified for the prosecution at the
trial, so how can they know its identity? Platonists mistrust the evidence
of the senses, but Aemilianus makes assertions about something he has
never seen or heard. It is unlikely in any case to be a magical object if
Apuleius entrusts it to the care of others such as a slave. Here Apuleius'
strategy is to stress both the hearsay nature of the allegation and his own
personal devotion to religion in order to dismiss suspicions about an
object which is undoubtedly mysterious and potentially damaging in a
case *de magia*; the object in the cloth, he implies (55. 8), belongs to the
mysteries of Dionysus, one of the many Greek cults into which Apuleius
has been initiated, and for that reason Apuleius will not divulge its identity.[85] Here Apuleius adds to religious devotion the glamour of travel and
exotic experience, designed to impress a provincial audience, and once
more not only takes the chance for self-promoting autobiography but
also calls his writings to evidence, this time a declamation given on his
arrival in Oea *De Aesculapii Maiestate*, presented as now published and
well known (55. 10–11). His stress on his own personal piety enables him
to attack Aemilianus as irreligious—he is not only a Charon, foul-look-
ing and greedy, but also a Mezentius, an opponent of the gods (56. 7);[86]
the allusion to Vergil both stresses Apuleius' literary leanings and follows
a Ciceronian technique of using mythological characters in invective.[87]
Finally, the topic of the talisman is effectively closed by an appeal to fel-
low-initiates (56. 9); they alone can hear the identity of the object in the

---

[85] 55. 8 *quid domi conditum celetis* clearly implies to the audience that Apuleius' image
belongs to the cult of Dionysus; on that cult in the Roman empire cf. Turcan (1996), 291–327.
Münstermann (1995), 196–203, argues that the image referred to here, as well as the Mercury
of 61 and 63, is actually Hermetic, and this is not impossible given Apuleius' lack of explicit
statement about its identity; for Hermetic links here see n. 90 below.

[86] On the Mezentius parallel see further Harrison (1988). Hunink (1997), ii. 152, notes that
this fittingly makes Apuleius parallel to Aeneas, pious victor over Mezentius.

[87] Cf. n. 19 for this technique.

cloth. This neatly combines exclusivism with a profession of open defence and personal piety.

(iv) *Alleged Nocturnal Sacrifices* (57–60)

The initial humour of *quod ad sudarium pertineat, omnem criminis maculam detersisse*, referring to the linen cloth so hotly and recently discussed, both provides a neat transition from the previous section and sets the tone here; the treatment of this charge will be broadly comic, and will invoke the low-life world of satire and Roman comedy. The principal prosecution witness, Junius Crassus, is described as a *gumia, lurco,* and *helluo*, all colourful archaic terms for a glutton (57. 2, 6),[88] and he is characterized with many of the topics of Ciceronian invective (cf. esp. 59. 6–7, where his drunken habits and sordid appearance strongly recall those of Piso in the *In Pisonem*);[89] and it is made clear at the beginning that he did not even see the alleged nocturnal sacrifices in his house, being in Alexandria at the time, and claims only to have witnessed the later damage made by their smoke. The answering of the charge is therefore relaxed, since it is not a serious threat, and Crassus is clearly a disreputable witness whose testimony Maximus has (Apuleius claims) already rejected; much is made of a parodic comparison between Crassus' supposed perception at Alexandria of the sacrificial smoke from his house at Oea hundreds of miles away and Odysseus' spying of Ithaca from a distance (57. 4). Here for once Apuleius has a co-defendant, a certain Quintianus who is in court with him and a talented speaker (58. 4), who is accused of sharing in these nocturnal rites. Crassus is presented as much less interested in the truth than in eating, drinking, and the bribe administered to him through the seedy agency of Herennius Rufinus, an important character later in the speech and here introduced with a foretaste of the invective Apuleius will later range against him. Rufinus is represented as all the more keen to help in bribing Crassus since he is conniving at his own wife's provision of sexual services to Crassus, and she will probably receive most of the bribe (60. 2). Furthermore, Crassus

[88] *Gumia* and *lurco* are found in Lucilius (1066 Marx and 75 Marx respectively), *helluo* in Terence (*Hau.* 1033). All three are found in Festus (88. 15, 99. 21, 107. 26 Lindsay), perhaps suggesting that Apuleius got them from a similar compilation, though *helluo* is found in Cicero (*Pis.* 41, a speech clearly known to Apuleius—see n. 89). For comic elements in the *Apologia* and their function see now Hunink (1998*a*).

[89] Cf. 59. 6 *belua* ~ *Pis.* 1 *belua*, 59. 6 *ructus popinam* ~ *Pis.* 13 *cum isto ore foetido taeterrimam nobis popinam inhallasses . . . ructando eiecisse*, and the whole splendid description of the hungover Piso in *Pis.* 13.

has given only written evidence (57. 2 *ex libello*) and like Thallus before him is not produced as a witness in court, even though he was seen the day before in Sabratha; thus Aemilianus has wasted his money in bribing him, or rather Crassus *fumum vendidit*, 'has sold him a pup', a splendid application of a familiar proverb[90] to the particulars of the situation (Crassus has of course sold Aemilianus a story all about *fumus*) which brings a knockabout passage to a rousing close.

(v) *His Statuette of Mercury* (61–5)

This alleged magical image is presented by Apuleius as a legitimate and well-known token of religion. Its maker, Cornelius Saturninus, a worthy local artisan, is produced in court (61. 5) and can testify to its harmlessness; its material of dark ebony, particularly objected to, was due to the kind intervention of Apuleius' stepson Pontianus (61. 6). This stress on the good relations between Apuleius and the late Pontianus is an important point, since the prosecution had initially alleged that Pontianus had been killed by Apuleius; the repetition of Pontianus' name in 62. 1–2 also stresses that it was he (a respectable knight—62. 4 *splendidissimus eques*) and not Apuleius who was largely responsible for the statuette's manufacture on his stepfather's behalf. The statuette has been misrepresented by the prosecution: it is not an infernal or ghostly image (63. 1), but a statue of Mercury for Apuleius' personal devotions, which he takes with him wherever he goes (63. 3). As in the case of the secret talisman above, a potentially suspicious element is neatly turned into evidence for Apuleius' personal piety; Hermes was the patron god of magic, and Apuleius' statuette clearly reflects his Hermetic interests.[91]

Apuleius then backs up his assertions by producing the statue in court, flattering Maximus that he at least is pious enough to handle it (63. 6), and providing a detailed verbal description (63. 7–8), showing the taste for ἔκφρασις familiar in Apuleius and elsewhere in the age of the Second Sophistic.[92] The statue's religious authority is employed in a splendidly melodramatic curse on Aemilianus for his fabrications (64. 1–2), not unlike the great curse called down on Verres at the close of the *Fifth Verrine* (184–9) from the gods of Sicily, whose statues he has violated. The

---

[90] Cf. Otto (1890), 149, no. 730, Baldwin (1985).

[91] On Hermes and magic see the references cited by Hunink (1997), ii. 165. The title βασιλεύς (61. 2, 64. 3) firmly indicates a Hermetic link; on Apuleius' Hermetic interests and links with the *Corpus Hermeticum* see Münstermann (1995), 130–74.

[92] Cf. Bartsch (1989), 3–39.

curse is naturally in the name of Mercury, the traditional divine connection between upper and lower worlds, and appropriately involves the evocation against Aemilianus of the sinister elements with which the prosecution has associated Apuleius' statue (63. 1 *formam diri cadaveris* ~ 64. 1 *obvias species mortuorum*, 63. 1 *larvalem* ~ 64. 1 *larvarum*). This is a neat reversal of the opposition's strategy; indeed, the quasi-magic colouring of the curse suggests that Apuleius is playing up to the magic powers attributed to him in order to terrify the ignorant prosecution.[93]

The charge that Apuleius addressed the statue as βασιλεύς, mentioned at the outset (61. 2), is dealt with last (64. 3 ff.) by an appeal to Plato's *Second Epistle*, a suitable authority for Maximus, invoking its mystical concept of the 'king' divinity who controls all things; the splendidly rhythmical and hymnic language of 64. 7 is very similar to the self-description of Isis in *Met*. 11.[94] The effect of this magnificent passage is to introduce a genuine numinous atmosphere, appropriate to Apuleius' rhetorical purposes here; as in the parallel case of the identity of the mystic object wrapped in the linen cloth, Apuleius presents himself as truly pious in his ability to divulge the identity of this ineffable being, not to be included in mere time, space, or nomenclature, even on the request of Maximus, a request which Maximus is of course too cultured to make (64. 8). Finally, even the the wooden material of the statue, clearly a cause of suspicion, is justified by an appeal to Plato's *Laws* (65. 5–7), again quoted *in extenso*; Plato is both the directing force in Apuleius' life as a *philosophus* and a support in this case (65. 8 *ut vitae magistro, ita causae patrono*), a suitable flourish to round off the section.

VI. *Introduction to Refutation of Charges concerning Pudentilla's Marriage* (66–7)

Here both the essential matter of the letters written by Pudentilla and the crucial question of whether Apuleius married her for mercenary reasons are at last approached. The placing of the most serious charges at the end

---

[93] This is the attractive suggestion of Hunink (1997), ii. 169—better than the alternative interpretation that Apuleius is joking here (see Hunink). This is of course a somewhat risky strategy (some of the court as well as the prosecution might be convinced by such a pose), and is one of the many elements in the speech which suggests rewriting after acquittal.

[94] Cf. (e.g.) *Apol*. 64. 7 *quisnam sit ille basileus*, totius rerum naturae causa et ratio et origo initialis, summus animi genitor with *Met*. 11. 5. 1 *en adsum tuis commota, Luci, precibus, rerum naturae parens, elementorum omnium domina, saeculorum* progenies initialis, *summa numinum, regina manium, prima caelitum* . . . . The two contexts would repay a more detailed comparison.

of Apuleius' defence no doubt reflects both their gravity and their similar climactic position in the prosecution's case; it also shows that the
audience is first to be conciliated, amused, and impressed by the sympathetic self-presentation, verbal pyrotechnics, and intellectual display of
the response to the minor charges, and then brought to share the views
of the defence on the major accusations, less entertaining but more
important. Apuleius begins by stressing that he has made no personal
profit from the affair, and that Aemilianus' prosecution is motivated by
sheer ill feeling, not by any offence on Apuleius' part: the prefatory
emphasis on the low motivation of the prosecution balances the same
feature at 28. 6–9, in the introduction to the defence against the lesser
charges. Nor is Aemilianus prosecuting to make a career, as many great
men have done (the list which follows at 66. 4 seems to be drawn from
Cicero, with several slips);[95] he is too ignorant and unskilled for that, and
too old to want to begin a forensic career. There then follows a further
divisio in classic Ciceronian style (67. 2—cf. the earlier *divisio* at 28. 4–9):[96]
there are five charges to be replied to in connection with Pudentilla—(i)
that Pudentilla had previously not wished to remarry but had been
bewitched by Apuleius into doing so, (ii) that her letters were evidence
for her bewitching, (iii) that she had remarried for sheer sexual gratfica-
tion (not child-bearing) at the age of sixty, (iv) that the marriage was
deliberately concealed by having taken place in the country, and (v) that
the dowry given by Pudentilla to Apuleius was very large. These charges
are indeed all dealt with, if not exactly in the order stated, in the last section of the speech which follows; Apuleius lays most stress on the prosecution's concern with Pudentilla's dowry, a stress which is essential to his
claim that the whole case is about money and is motivated by the misplaced financial jealousy felt by Aemilianus and his fellow-accusers
against him.

VII. *Refutation of Charges concerning Pudentilla's
Marriage* (68–101)

(i) *Narration of Main Events before the Marriage* (68–78)

Most of this section of the speech is in essence a postponed *narratio*,
telling the story of Pudentilla and her family and Apuleius' involvement

---

[95] See Butler and Owen (1914), 131, for Apuleius' garbling of several details such as the correct *praenomina*, typical of his hasty and vicarious learning.
[96] For similar enumeration in a *divisio* cf. e.g. Cicero *S. Rosc.* 35 *tres sunt res, quantum ego*

with them, but this narrative element is heavily interspersed with refutations of particular charges, dealing in some degree with all of the five identified in Apuleius' *divisio*. Like Ciceronian *narrationes*, that of Apuleius is highly tendentious, and supports his own version of events. Pudentilla's long delay in remarriage, potentially a strong point against Apuleius, is explained by family pressure to marry a relative and her father-in-law's threat to disinherit her sons if she married outside the family (68. 4), while her actual decision to remarry is motivated by pressing physiological factors (Apuleius, once again putting on his medical hat, here applies Platonic theory),[97] and she does so on doctors' orders (69. 3). Even Aemilianus, by his correspondence with Pontianus in Rome (read in court and much dwelt on by Apuleius—69. 6–70. 4), is proved to have encouraged a marriage and to have persuaded Pontianus to that end; this is a palpable hit against one who had clearly accused Apuleius of coercing Pudentilla out of fourteen years of widowhood by magic. Also read out (70. 8) is Pudentilla's own letter to Pontianus, stating her desire to remarry and promising that this would not affect the disposition of her property; this reinforces the same point about her marriage plans and adds implicit support to the central argument that his marriage with Pudentilla brought no great financial benefit to Apuleius. Thus Pudentilla's desire to remarry is firmly established before Apuleius arrived in Oea, a crucial point in his attempt to prove that he had not forced her into marriage.

Apuleius' appearance on the scene (72. 1) appeared to be an answer to the prayers of Pontianus, who after Pudentilla's letter had not unnaturally returned from Rome to try to ensure that his mother chose a husband who would preserve the family fortune for her sons. After narrating the illness which led to his extended stay at Oea and lengthy acquaintance with Pudentilla (important in order to show that he was not simply a freebooter and that he had a genuine chance to get to know the virtues of his future wife), Apuleius (73. 3) represents Pontianus as inviting him to be his stepfather, and himself as at first reluctant but then yielding on consideration of Pudentilla's virtues. This places the responsibility for the marriage firmly and conveniently with the dead Pontianus, and absolves Apuleius himself from the charge of actively seeking Pudentilla for her money.

---

existimare possum, quae obstent hoc tempore Sex. Roscio . . . de hisce omnibus rebus me dicere oportere intellego.

[97] Cf. *Tim.* 91b ff., quoted by Butler and Owen (1914), 135.

Pontianus' later change of heart is attributed firmly to the influence of his new father-in-law Herennius Rufinus, whose role begins at 74. 3, a dramatic entrance flagged by two previous anticipatory mentions (60, 67). In a purple passage of invective which casts him firmly as a villain (74. 5–7), he is said to pimp for his wife like the immoral husbands of satire (75. 2 ff.),[98] and his alleged past as a pantomime actor allows a special class of abuse (74. 7, 78. 4).[99] Like the unfortunate Crassus before him (57. 2 ff.), he is characterized as a satiric/comic glutton; his immoral earnings are consumed by his belly (75. 9). This attack on Rufinus is important, for Apuleius needs not only to discredit a major figure of the prosecution, but also to give a convincing explanation of why his former pupil and room-mate Pontianus turned against him. Rufinus, having married Pontianus to his daughter, much abused by Apuleius in satirical mode as debauched like her mother (76. 2–6), persuades and threatens him into a different view of the Apuleius/Pudentilla marriage (77. 1–7). Apuleius allows himself a brief tirade of righteous manly anger,[100] against the behaviour of the worthless and effeminate ex-pantomime Rufinus in abusing Pudentilla in front of her son (78. 3–4), but he returns to his narrative with a Ciceronian-type formula (78. 5 *sed ne longius ab ordine digrediar*).[101] This confrontation elicits the all-important letter from Pudentilla to Pontianus, in which (so the prosecution allege) Pudentilla reveals that Apuleius is a *magus*, which forms the subject of the next set of arguments.

(ii) The Letter Written by Pudentilla to Pontianus, and the Forged Letter Ascribed to Apuleius (79–87. 9)

In dealing with the crucial letter of Pudentilla, Apuleius delays the most convincing proof (the citing of the letter in full) until last, and builds up to it with arguments of increasing probability and with a certain amount of suspense. First, using his now familiar hypothetical method, he argues

---

[98] An accusation already made at 60. 2 and a traditional mark of male immorality: cf. Mayor and Courtney on Juvenal 1. 55.

[99] For the low status of actors in the Roman empire cf. Edwards (1993), 123–36, Csapo and Slater (1995), 275–85.

[100] *Vix hercule possum irae moderari, ingens indignatio animo oboritur.* This is heroic impatience couched in specifically epic terms: *ingens* is the classic epic epithet in Latin (cf. conveniently Harrison on Vergil *Aen.* 10. 127), while the phrase as a whole recalls Homeric expressions such as *Il.* 9. 136 χόλος ἔμπεσε θυμῷ.

[101] Cf. Cicero *Caec.* 55 *verum ne nimium multa complectamur atque ab eo, quod propositum est, longius aberret oratio.*

that even if Pudentilla had accused him of magic, the statement of a woman in love need not be strictly believed, and her love for him need not be the product of magic (79); this is followed by a section of self-conscious logic-chopping, the inheritance of a dialectical training (80. 3 *mitto dialectica*)—if she was of sound mind when she wrote, she could not have been bewitched, if of unsound mind, her word is not to be relied on. The reading of the letter itself is dramatically interrupted at some length (80. 4–82. 1) by Apuleius, to indicate to Maximus that the next passage is the most significant, and to comment on the cunning of Rufinus, comparing him expansively to mythological tricksters and traitors from Greek history (81. 3).[102] All this is plainly a means of creating suspense, and the suspense is not ended when the next passage is read, for it seems to convict Apuleius clearly (82. 2); the letter, written in Greek,[103] apparently says, 'Apuleius is a magician, and I have been enchanted by him and am in love. Come now to me, while I still have my reason.' Before continuing, Apuleius again attacks Rufinus, this time for the way he showed the letter around Oea as proof of Apuleius' guilt (82. 3–9), and the truth only comes out at the last moment, when Apuleius supplies the full context to the quotation excised by Rufinus and shows that it actually means the opposite of what he claimed (83. 1): the apparent statement of Pudentilla's enchantment is in fact merely a report of the calumnies spread by Rufinus, while the clause 'while I still have my reason' is later interpreted as Pudentilla's ironic ridicule of these falsehoods (87. 6). The grand prosopopoeia of the letter itself (83. 2) is very much in the Ciceronian manner;[104] had it a voice, it would have revealed Rufinus' crimes, but they are now laid open in any case. The subtle Vergilian colouring of this attack on Rufinus, likening him to the Cacus of the *Aeneid*,[105] is clearly for the learned reader rather than the immediate audience.

The continuation of the letter (84. 2) with Pudentilla's explicit statement that she is neither enchanted nor in love makes Apuleius' point beyond doubt, and Maximus is congratulated for ensuring that copies of all documents were swiftly made. After another attack on Rufinus for publishing a private letter from mother to son (84. 7–8), Apuleius turns his attention to his stepson Pudens in a dramatic passage which accuses

---

[102] For their literary origins cf. Hunink (1997), ii. 202.

[103] On Pudentilla's use of Greek as a sign of her high social standing cf. Fantham (1995), 226, and Ch. 1 n. 7 above.

[104] Cf. e.g. Cicero *Cael.* 60 *nonne ipsam domum metuet, ne quam vocem eiciat, nec parietes conscios . . . perhorrescet?* with R. G. Austin's note.   [105] Cf. Harrison (1988).

him of impiety and ingratitude towards his mother (85. 2–9); he is compared to a snake eating its way out of the womb, not only a view of ancient
science but also a version of Clytemnestra's dream of Orestes—he is as
bad as a matricide.[106] The villainy of reading private correspondence is
illustrated by an anecdote from Athenian history (86. 1), taken from
Plutarch;[107] a pun on *litterae*, referring to both correspondence and the
letters of the alphabet, adds the slur of ignorance to the accusation of
misbehaviour (Pudens' ignorance clearly matches that of the rest of the
prosecution—cf. 98. 8). Pudens is also berated for his own letter to
Pontianus, full of unfilial sentiments towards his mother (86. 4–6).

The topic of letters provides a transition to the last part of this section,
in which all the important documentary evidence is treated. Here (87.
2–6) Apuleius deals with a forged letter purporting to have been sent by
himself—palpably fabricated, with its poor and faulty style and bar-
room endearments; its bad Greek is even inconsistent with the prosecution's earlier charge that Apuleius is eloquent in that language, and its
smooth delivery by the prosecution confirmed their authorship. Finally
(87. 7–9), Apuleius returns again to the crucial letter of Pudentilla: she
could not have been in the state of madness claimed by the prosecution's
interpretation of the letter, since after the letter she spent two months in
the country with her sons and daughter-in-law, capably managing her
property as usual,[108] and made very clear her views on Rufinus and his
bruiting abroad of her private correspondence (thus underlining the
view of this offence much stressed by Apuleius in this section).

(iii) *The Marriage in the Country* (87. 10–88)

It is at this point, presumably because it was the next event chronologi-
cally, that Apuleius inserts a brief account of the marriage itself. The justification he gives for its being in the country, to avoid the expense and
bother of large-scale entertainments and popular distributions, is sensible enough, but given that this is one of the five main charges highlighted
in his earlier *divisio*, the point is made in a rather unemphatic way.
Perhaps, having given such a long and dramatic treatment of Pudentilla's
letter, Apuleius is varying the pace and duration of his different refuta-

---

[106] For this ancient view of the viviparous viper cf. Pliny *HN* 10. 170; in this context of
filial ingratitude the 'snake in the bosom' of Aeschylus' *Choephoroe* (327–34) may be
alluded to.
[107] Plutarch *Demetrius* 2.
[108] On Pudentilla's management of her property cf. Fantham (1995).

tions. The point is lengthened a little by a joke at the rustic Aemilianus' expense (88. 2: as a yokel he should not object to the country), by a witty parody of a nonexistent law against rural weddings (showing Apuleius' legal pretensions),[109] and by praise of the country as the place of fertility and ancient Roman life. Apuleius self-consciously stops himself from pursuing further the praise of rural life (88. 7), that well-established Roman topic which was no doubt beloved of declamation; this is professedly to avoid giving pleasure to Aemilianus by praising his natural rural element, but is also motivated by the desire to drive his case forward.

(iv) *The Age of Pudentilla* (89)

This again is one of the five points identified by Apuleius in his *divisio*, and again treated briefly and efficiently by reference to public records, which show she is around forty rather than sixty; the literary joke on Aemilianus' adding of ten years (89. 4 *Mezentius cum Ulixe erravit*) is effective and coherent with other mythological witticisms in the speech,[110] while much fun is had with the idea that Aemilianus could not have confused different number-gestures (89. 6–7). Pudentilla's age is important in Apuleius' defence for two reasons: first, Roman marriage laws prohibited marriage for women over fifty, and second, the marriage of a younger man to a much older woman of property could in the Roman world attract accusations of legacy-hunting on the man's part and of sexual indulgence without the excuse of child-bearing on the woman's.[111]

(v) *The Charge of Mercenary Motives on Apuleius' Part* (90–2)

This question is again stressed as the central point of the accusation, continuing Apuleius' assertion throughout that the whole case is to do with money and financial jealousy. Apuleius faces his accusers with a crucial question: what profit did he stand to make by marrying Pudentilla? As with the treatment of Pudentilla's letter, the final documentary refutation, the reading of Pudentilla's will, is held back for some time, though its contents are foreshadowed more than once. If Apuleius married her

---

[109] For Apuleius' knowledge of Roman law and its deployment in his works cf. Norden (1912), Summers (1967), (1970), (1972), and (1973), Elster (1991), and Keulen (1997).

[110] The joke puns on *erravit* ('erred'/'wandered'): Aemilianus is *wrong* by ten years, Odysseus *wandered* for ten years.

[111] Cf. Hunink (1997), ii. 218.

for financial profit, he is happy to be classed with a whole series of *magi* (90. 7: the list, drawn from Pliny and other sources, interestingly includes Moses).[112] The imagined exclamations of the prosecution at these unholy names lead to an important restatement of the general thrust of Apuleius' case: knowledge of such persons does not mean a sharing of their activities, and is a product of his high education, which he shares with Maximus (91. 3 *tua doctrina, Claude Maxime, tuaque perfecta eruditione fretus*), while the prosecution's misunderstandings come from their ignorance and lack of literary culture (*stultis et impolitis*).

As for the money of Pudentilla, the figure of the dowry conveyed to Apuleius, imagined as huge by the opposition, is now revealed; it was the relatively modest sum of 300,000 sesterces (92. 1; less than 10 per cent of her large wealth—cf. 71. 6, 77. 1), and was in any case effectively a loan, reverting wholly to her children (whether by first or second marriage) after her death. This arrangement is proved by the *tabulae nuptiales*, produced in court (92. 2). Pudentilla, Apuleius jokes, is indeed lucky to get a husband at such a cheap rate, especially given her age and relative lack of beauty; his description of himself as *iuvenem neque corpore neque animo neque fortuna paenitendum* is both generally self-complimentary and an assertion that Apuleius did not need Pudentilla's money. An elaborate rhetorical comparison is then set out between the virgin bride and the previously married woman, in which the first comes off rather better (this passage is hardly complimentary to Pudentilla, even in its generalized form). The crucial point is made last: Pudentilla has been fortunate enough to pick on a philosopher, who is not interested in money (92. 11 *philosophum spernentem dotis*).

(vi) *Narration of Events after the Marriage* (93–8)

Having introduced himself again into the argument, Apuleius then turns back to his chronological narrative, and to his own behaviour (93). In such a situation, where all the money was to revert to the children, his financial interest would have been served by alienating his wife from her family. And yet his behaviour was the opposite of this; he tried to keep the quarrelling family together (93. 2 *ego vero quietis et concordiae et*

---

[112] All the *magi* here mentioned except for Carmendas and Damigeron (for whom see Butler and Owen (1914) 162) are found as such in the catalogue of Pliny *HN* 30. 3–11; on the possible restoration of the name of Jesus here (very unlikely in my view) see Hunink (1997), ii. 223. For Moses' reputation as a *magus* see (apart from Pliny) Strabo 16. 2. 39, Juvenal 14. 102, Gager (1972).

pietatis auctor), and encouraged his wife to make generous financial set-
tlements for her sons, against her own inclinations (93. 6). Thus Apuleius
is firmly presented not as a hostile and grasping stepfather, as he might
easily have been, but as a beneficial addition to the family who improved
the financial lot of his stepsons. The stepsons are accordingly reconciled
with Apuleius and with their mother; Apuleius' recommendation of
Pontianus' oratory to Lollianus Avitus, Maximus' predecessor as proconsul, shows not only the generous stepfather but also the literary man with
friends in high places. Avitus' support for Apuleius is demonstrated by
the reading of a letter from him, seen as a climactic point in the case (94.
7–8, cf. 95. 1). It is of course a parallel for Avitus' successor Maximus' support for Apuleius in the case in progress; the panegyric pronounced on
Avitus matches the praise of Maximus already frequently expressed in
Apuleius' speech, and the oratorical virtues here ascribed to him through
comparisons to the great speakers of the Roman republic (95. 5), climax-
ing in the praise of Cicero's *opulentia*, echo Cicero's commendations of
fine orators of the past in the *Brutus*.[113]

At 95. 8 (*in causa prorsus ad finem inclinata*) comes the second hint
that Apuleius is drawing to a conclusion (the first was at 95. 1). He then
attacks the prosecution for maintaining that Pontianus continued hostile
to Apuleius, despite the evidence of an ex-proconsul to the contrary; this
is a neat touch in the presence of the latter's successor. Pontianus' grateful letters from Carthage before his untimely death are quoted in support
of this (96. 7), and Rufinus is blamed for suppressing the last version of
Pontianus' will, which not only made laudatory mention of Apuleius, but
left an insultingly small legacy to his wife, Rufinus' daughter, showing
that he had recognized her true worthlessness. The main heirs were his
mother and brother; this allows Apuleius to present Rufinus as now
launching his daughter, Pontianus' widow, at Pudens, and joining with
Aemilianus in corrupting and trying to control a young man with great
material expectations. This is an important point, since it not only
stresses once again the mercenary motives and disreputable actions of the
opposition, but also explains why Pudens has turned against Apuleius,
who by his own account has done him only good. Pudens' pastimes under

---

[113] The links with the *Brutus* are listed by Hunink (1997), ii. 234–5, who nevertheless here
as elsewhere wants to play down the importance of Cicero for Apuleius; against this one
might argue here that Cicero is in climactic final position in the list, and that the literary
virtue of *opulentia* ascribed to him is one that Apuleius might particularly admire. For other
echoes of the *Brutus* in the *Apologia* see n. 33.

his uncle Aemilianus' tutelage, drinking, whoring, and going to gladiatorial fights, traditional marks of the wayward young man, differ dramatically from the good education he was receiving under the influence of Apuleius; now he has become as ignorant as Aemilianus, using the despised vernacular of Punic, speaking a little Greek learnt from his mother, and hardly able to utter a syllable in Latin (98. 8).[114] The waste and loss of education is the ultimate degradation for Apuleius and for the intellectual values of his time.

(vii) *Pudentilla's Will: Final Refutation of Mercenary Motives on Apuleius' Part* (99–101)

The corruption of Pudens by his uncle and prospective father-in-law leads on to his place in his mother's will, again ensured by the generosity of Apuleius, who struggled (partly in his own interest) to persuade Pudentilla not to disinherit her only remaining but ungrateful son. This information is presented (99. 5) as a sudden and unanticipated blow to the opposition, removing any ground for accusing Apuleius of mercenary motives; no other stepfather would have been so self-denying towards an undutiful stepson. The will is then produced in court (100. 1). This is in many ways the climactic point of Apuleius' case, and effectively reserved until last; having proved that he did not profit greatly by the marriage settlement, he can now dispel all suspicion that he stood to profit after Pudentilla's death, likely to occur before his own given the age gap between them. If the seals of the will are broken, its provisions will be found to be as Apuleius states; Pudens, not Apuleius himself, is the main heir, despite his appalling behaviour towards his mother, described in another dramatic attack (100. 6–10) which reveals for the first time the reason for Pudens' separation from his mother after his brother's death (100. 6)—the fact that he was not Pontianus' sole heir but was joint heir with his mother. Thus Pudens, as well as failing in filial duty, matches Aemilianus and Rufinus in greed as well as ignorance; but by the revelation of the details of Pudentilla's will, the financial motive presented by Apuleius as the main reason for the prosecution has now vanished (101. 3 *radicem iudicii huius, id est hereditatis quaesitae invidiam, funditus sustuli*).

---

[114] This remark, made in a highly tendentious context, has been overestimated as evidence for language use in Roman North Africa. For laudable caution on this front see Millar (1968), 130–1, and for other relevant evidence Ch. 1 nn. 4–7.

Apuleius then takes advantage of this climactic point to dispel quickly a minor financial charge, that he bought an estate for himself at great cost with Pudentilla's money. As in other charges, local worthies are brought forward to testify on Apuleius' behalf, namely Pudentilla's legal guardian (probably appointed under her husband's will) and a minor magistrate. It is made clear that the purchase was in Pudentilla's name, and small in scale (60,000 sesterces, less than 2 per cent of her total wealth). Thus he has now refuted all possible modes of mercenary behaviour with which he was charged—a large marriage settlement, a large legacy in his wife's will, and the misuse of his wife's funds.

VIII. *Summing-up of Charges and* Peroratio (102–3)

Apuleius now claims to have answered all the charges, and sums up his responses to those about the marriage and to the earlier magical allegations. He begins the first with the most important point: what could be his personal profit in applying magic to Pudentilla? The marriage has brought him little financial benefit, and indeed he has persuaded Pudentilla not to give money to himself but to distribute it to her sons, which she had refused to do before her marriage to him. This is encapsulated in a characteristically alliterative word-play (102. 3 *o grave* venefi-cium *dicam, an ingratum* beneficium?); Apuleius' intervention in the family's affairs has been no black magic but a real help, and his persuasive powers have been used in the interests not of himself but of Pudentilla's sons, even though the ungrateful Pudens has repaid his kindness with an accusation at law. Even with a judge much worse than Maximus and, unlike him, sympathetic to their case, it barely stands up—the charges of mercernary motives have been completely refuted by documentary evidence.

The charges of magic are given similar short shrift in a devastatingly brief set of questions and answers (repeating the technique of 27. 5–12) which expose their inadequacy but also vividly remind the reader of a set of arguments made much earlier in the speech (103. 2–3); his good teeth are the product of dental hygiene, mirrors are the tools of philosophers, writing poetry is perfectly acceptable, the investigation of fish and the use of wood for a statue are justified by Aristotle and Plato respectively, his marriage obeys the encouragement of the laws, that his wife is older than him is no crime, and the documents prove that he did not marry for money. This is followed by a brief but recognizable *peroratio* (103. 4–5), a single rolling period of multiple conditional clauses: if he has rebutted all the groundless charges made against him and maintained the honour of philosophy as well as his own reputation, he has nothing to fear from Maximus, whose good opinion he seeks even more than acquittal. The structure of this final paragraph, its language, and its direct appeal to the judge, rounding off the flattery which has been a constant feature of the speech, fittingly recalls the close of a Ciceronian oration;[115] Apuleius has produced a self-defence which is a worthy imitation of the greatest defence counsel in Roman literature.

5. APULEIUS' *APOLOGIA* AND THE SECOND SOPHISTIC

An elaborate self-defence on a charge of magic is not a particularly surprising literary work to find in the age of the Second Sophistic; self-presentation and occasional self-justification against attack, whether forensic or other, were central to the activities of the Greek sophists for whom Apuleius is a Latin parallel. Philostratus in his *Lives of the Sophists* narrates a number of cases where sophists were accused in law-suits, and they were well known for their highly publicized disputes with each other, which sometimes ended in court.[116] The particular charge of magic is also not astonishing. Magical abilities were also suspected or alleged in the case of one or two of the more extraordinary sophistic performers, whether from malice or sheer astonishment at their capacity to persuade; persuasive rhetoric had been viewed as a form of magic since the days of Gorgias.[117] In his obituary for Hadrian of Tyre, pupil of Herodes Atticus and an older contemporary of Apuleius (he is said to have died at the age of eighty in the reign of Commodus), Philostratus says that he 'had attained to such high honour that many actually believed him to be a magician' (*VS* 2. 10. 590), and another sophist, Dionysius of Miletus, was thought to have used 'Chaldean arts' to train his pupils in the art of memory (*VS* 1. 22. 523).

In terms of content, the *Apologia* bears the unmistakable stamp of sophistic discourse. As noted in Section 2 above, its most notable feature

---

[115] Cf. e.g. the peroration of the *De Domo* (147), with its similar multiple conditional clauses.

[116] Cf. Bowersock (1969), 89–100, Anderson (1993), 35–9.

[117] Gorgias himself had famously compared rhetoric and magic in their capacity to enchant (*Enc. Hel.* 10), and Plato regularly equates sophistic powers of persuasion and magic (*Symp.* 203d, *Soph.* 235a, *Pol.* 291c).

is its constant mixture of forensic argumentation and strategy with epideictic and didactic digression, a mixture which is not merely inevitable
from its speaker but also carefully calculated in terms of its audience,
above all Claudius Maximus; for a proconsul unsympathetic to literary
and philosophical concerns, Apuleius might well have produced a
defence rather different from the extant *Apologia*. The constant deployment of material from literature both Greek and Latin shows that
Apuleius, like all sophistic speakers, is anxious to impress with the
breadth of his reading, which can sometimes be traced to handbooks and
summaries rather than original texts, but nevertheless shows a considerable width of knowledge. The interest throughout in philosophical topics, and in particular Plato, is not only forensically important in
supporting Apuleius' view of himself as a misunderstood *philosophus* and
appealing to the personal tastes of Maximus (see Section 2 above), but
also stresses Apuleius' considerable reading in the works of one of the
central intellectual and stylistic inspirations of the Second Sophistic.[118]
The *Apologia* shows a complete command of all rhetorical techniques,
both forensic and epideictic, the everyday tools of the performing
sophist. Apuleius can be seen demonstrating his ability in narrative,
comparison, invective, encomium, description, and anecdote, all προγυμνάσματα, the basic elements of speaking and composition taught to students in ancient rhetorical schools.[119] He is also skilled in diatribe,
popular moralizing on the Cynic model, a type of writing much favoured
by sophistic writers such as Dio Chrysostom and Aelius Aristides, and
which is found again in the final section of the *De Deo Socratis* (see
Chapter 4).

Thus Helm's claim that the *Apologia* is a 'masterpiece of the Second
Sophistic' seems thoroughly justified.[120] But though Apuleius may share
much with the Greek sophists, he is also a writer in Latin who had studied in Rome and was strongly influenced by Roman literary fashion. Thus
the *Apologia* is a rich quarry for fragments of archaic Latin poets, popular after Hadrian who had famously claimed to prefer Ennius to Vergil,
and for archaic and poetic vocabulary in general, the central feature of
the Latin style of the age.[121] These characteristics are also markedly shared

---

[118] On the particular importance of Plato for sophistic literature cf. e.g. Anderson (1993),
173; for the general prominence of Plato in the intellectual culture of the second century AD
cf. Whittaker (1987).

[119] On the προγυμνάσματα cf. Ch. 3 n. 20.

[120] Helm (1955), title (86): 'Apuleius' *Apologia*: Ein Meisterwerk der zweiten Sophistik'.

[121] On Apuleius' use of archaic poetry see Mattiacci (1986); on the contemporary taste
for archaizing see Ch. 1 n. 68.

by the contemporary work of Aulus Gellius, who may well have known Apuleius in Rome.[122] The *Apologia*, like all Apuleius' works, bears the mark of its time and of the particular culture of its author (see Chapter 1), one who had some experience of Athens and other Greek sophistic centres, but who had also studied in Rome and returned to live in his home province of Roman Africa.

---

[122] For the possibility that Gellius and Apuleius met in Rome see Ch. 1 n. 22, and for the character of Gellius' work cf. Holford-Strevens (1988), 20–60.

3

Sophistic Display:
The *Florida*

1. INTRODUCTION

The version of Apuleius' *Florida* transmitted by the manuscript tradition,
containing some forty pages of modern text, is evidently a collection of
excerpts; the more than twenty sections distinguished in modern texts
within these forty pages are clearly disparate extracts rather than a continuous whole, extracts which vary in length from six or seven lines (*Flor.*
5) to six or seven pages (*Flor.* 9, 16, and 18). This chapter will consider the
transmission and title of the collection, analyse its contents with a view
to establishing links with the literary culture of the Roman empire in the
second century AD, especially Greek sophistic texts, and finally suggest
the principles upon which it was excerpted. There is as yet no published
commentary on the *Florida*, remarkable given its literary quality and cultural interest, though there has been much useful work;[1] for reasons of
space, this account cannot offer an extensive commentary, especially on
the longer pieces, but will aim to give the reader some idea of the character of the work and of each extract. The reader is assumed to have
Vallette's Budé text (1924) to hand (references are to its sections).

---

[1] The most useful editions of the *Florida* are Helm (1910) and Vallette (1924). Apart from
the notes in Vallette and in older commentaries on the whole of Apuleius (esp. Hildebrand
(1842)), there is a more recent unpublished commentary by Opeku (1974), and a few notes
are to be found in Augello (1984); we hope for a commentary soon from Vincent Hunink.
Tatum (1979), 163–77, provides a translation of selected fragments from the *Florida*; otherwise the most recent English translation is Butler (1909), but John Hilton is currently
preparing an English translation. Hijmans (1994) and Sandy (1997), 148–73, provide useful
general treatments; Mras (1949*a*) provides a helpful discussion of the literary genre of the
Florida, De'Conno (1958–9) of its place in Apuleius' works, and Ferrari (1968, 1969) of elements of its verbal style. The paragraphs of the 'false preface' are usually edited along with
the other philosophical works, and may be found conveniently in Beaujeu (1973) and
Moreschini (1991).

2. TRANSMISSION AND TITLE

In modern editions of the *Florida* twenty-three separate extracts are usually identified, ranging in length from a few lines to half-a-dozen pages. This separation into individual extracts, largely accomplished by scholars in the sixteenth century,[2] is not found in F and the manuscripts descended from it, which divide the *Florida* into four books, each described as the appropriately numbered *liber Floridorum* (extracts 1–9. 14, 9. 15–15, 16–17, 18–23 in the modern numeration). It is likely that these book-divisions preserve in some sense those of an original collection of the same name, not those of the extant *Florida*, since the four books thereby produced in our extant collection are not of realistic length for ancient prose books and contain rather different numbers of items (each contains between ten and twelve pages of modern text, and Book 1 contains nine items, Book 3 two).[3] Given this, there is one curious feature: the division between the first and second books occurs in the middle of what is plainly a continuous piece, that known to modern editors as *Flor.* 9. The most likely explanation is some form of error in the transmission. It has been argued that the *subscriptio* marking the book-division was copied in the wrong place, perhaps a page late: a book-division between *Flor.* 8 and 9 makes good sense, and the existing division occurs something like a codex-page into *Flor.* 9.[4]

One might also argue that the division of the work into four books of very much the same length but different numbers of items (nine in Book 1, two in Book 3), one of which plainly cuts across a unified piece, looks suspiciously even (Book 1 in Helm's edition contains 253 Teubner lines, Book 2, 262, Book 3, 246, and Book 4, 261); our modern *Florida* may simply have been a collection of material divided into four sections of approximately equal mass by an ancient editor with the knowledge that it somehow represented four books and with a desire that those books should be roughly the same length. If this is so, some credit should be given to an ability to produce coherent units within the limits of such a mechanical division. Though the division between Books 1 and 2 falls in the middle of a piece and therefore cannot be authorial, it is at a point where modern editors usually mark a paragraph, and the division

---

[2] Scioppius (1594) already divides the pieces in a way very similar to modern editors, though he does not separate *Flor.* 20 from 21 or *Flor.* 22 from 23; see further Opeku (1974), 15–16.

[3] Cf. Hijmans (1994), 1719–20.   [4] Cf. Mras (1949a), 217–18.

between Books 2 and 3 clearly falls at the end of a piece. Such exact location of divisions suggests some conscious editorial activity at some stage
in the work's copying. The incompleteness of *Flor.* 11 and 22 could be
taken to indicate an excerptor with little interest in extracting complete
sentences or paragraphs, but could equally well reflect physical damage
in textual transmission.

An error in the transmission of the *Florida* also appears to be responsible for the so-called 'false preface' transmitted at the beginning of the
De Deo Socratis, which, as has long been recognized, belongs, partly if not
wholly, not to that work but to the *Florida*.[5] This 'preface' is composed of
five separate sections which in my view are discontinuous rhetorical
excerpts of similar character to the *Florida*, and most scholars would
attach all of them to it, though there has been some disagreement about
the fifth section, which some have wanted to retain as the prologue to the
De Deo Socratis.[6] These five excerpts seem to have become detached from
the *Florida* and wrongly attached to the *De Deo Socratis* at some point in
the textual transmission of Apuleius, very likely at the time when the
philosophical works were separated from the other works.[7] Two pieces of
evidence point this way. First, the collection of the *Florida* as we have it
contains no final *subscriptio* signalling the end of the fourth and last
book, though these are present for the other three books. This suggests
that at some point the work lost its final section, and that the five excerpts
may have constituted that final section. Second, the division between
works in the manuscript transmission of Apuleius is essentially bipartite,
placing the *Apologia*, *Metamorphoses*, and *Florida* in that order in one
group, and the *De Deo Socratis*, *De Platone*, *De Mundo*, and *Asclepius* in
that order in another.[8] This suggests that the *Florida* and the *De Deo*

---

[5] The first four sections of the 'false preface' were attached to the *Florida* as early as
Pithoeus (1565), bk. 12, ch. 10; for a history of the discussion see Beaujeu (1973), 161–2, and
for the most important contributions cf. Helm (1900), Thomas (1900), Barra (1960–1),
Mantero (1973), Tomasco (1992), and Bingenheimer (1993), 67–9. The most recent work
defends the whole of the 'false preface' as a genuine part of the *De Deo Socratis* (Hunink
(1995) and Sandy (1997), 192–6), though neither in my view allows enough weight to the
internal discontinuity of the 'false preface', a contrast with the well-organized structure of
the *De Deo Socratis* (see Ch. 4 below), or to the arguments of Thomas (1900) on textual
transmission. For a more detailed discussion of Extract V as a possible preface to the *DDS*
(which rejects this idea) see Ch. 4, Sect. 2.

[6] For a modern supporter of this view cf. Hijmans (1994), 1781–2, following the detailed
arguments of Mantero (1973), who provides an excellent summary of scholarship on the
issue. For the counter-arguments against this position, see Ch. 4.

[7] See the important discussion by Thomas (1900).

[8] See conveniently Beaujeu (1973), xxxvi–vii.

Socratis were juxtaposed in an original collection of these seven works together, and that the division of that original collection into two parts which our two manuscript groups represent simply made the separation between the *Florida* and the *De Deo Socratis* at the wrong point, a few pages before rather than at the end of the *Florida*. By this means the final part of the *Florida* was isolated from the rest of its work and became attached to the beginning of the *De Deo Socratis*. For convenience, and in the belief that they were originally the final part of the *Florida*, the five sections of the 'false preface' will be analysed at the end of this chapter.

The meaning of the title *Florida* is closely bound up with the issue of the nature of the collection. The evidence of its transmission and original book-divisions already discussed makes it certain that our *Florida* derives by a later act of excerption from an original work of the same title in four books attributed to Apuleius. The absence of any preface or conclusion (though these could theoretically have been lost in transmission) suggests this, as does the unevenness of selection: a self-respecting sophistic writer seems to me unlikely to have composed an anthology from his own works in the form we have, in which extracts of six or seven pages (*Flor.* 16 and 18) were set next to extracts of six or seven lines (*Flor.* 5). The nature of the original four-book work may be guessed at from its title as well as from the content of the extant collection. *Florida* means literally either 'flowery parts', which might indicate choice selections culled from a longer original without stylistic reference, or pieces with 'flowery' style; these are the alternative explanations of the title offered since the Renaissance.[9] The adjective *floridus* can certainly be applied to style (cf. *TLL* 6. 1. 925. 72 ff.). Quintilian uses it of a middle style of writing which is full of pleasing ornament and digression, the verbal equivalent of a *locus amoenus* (12. 10. 60):

medius hic modus et translationibus crebrior et figuris erit iucundior, egressionibus amoenus, compositione aptus, sententiis dulcis, lenior tamen ut amnis lucidus quidem sed virentibus utrimque silvis inumbratus.

This is not inappropriate for the ornamental language of the most epideictic parts of the *Florida*, as some have argued.[10] However, it is not clear

---

[9] Already found together in Scioppius (1594), 84: *sunt enim hi Floridorum libri nihil nisi mera fragmenta, ab aliquo Apulei studioso ex diversis eius libris in unum comportata, tamquam ἔκλογαι et floridiore dicendi genere expressa.*

[10] On the Quintilian passage see the useful discussion of Austin (1948), 199, especially his reference to Cicero *Orat.* 96, where an *insigne et florens orationis pictum et expolitum genus* is associated with the epideictic style of the fifth-century sophists. For a summary of views on the meaning of *floridus* for the *Florida* see Hijmans (1994), 1719–23.

that flowery style is the criterion for selection for the *Florida*: our collection includes extracts which have little stylistic colour of this kind and
which seem to be chosen for their function or subject matter (e.g. *Flor.* 5
and 11). Moreover, the weight of the linguistic evidence for *floridus* and
its cognates *flos, flosculus,* and *florens* suggests that the title *Florida* should
indicate primarily an anthology on any principle; though style will naturally play an important role in selection, the selection will not be limited to the stylistically 'flowery'.[11]

Three passages in particular point this way. The first occurs in the
preface to Justin's epitome of the *Historia Philippica* of Pompeius Trogus,
an epitome possibly contemporary with Apuleius[12] (Justin *praef.* 4):

horum igitur quattuor et quadraginta voluminum . . . cognitione quaeque dig-
nissima. excerpsi et . . . breve velut florum corpusculum feci.

Here *flores* is applied to the excerpts made by Justin, excerpts analogous
to those of the *Florida*, particularly in the matter of retaining the books
of the original, reduced in Justin to a few paragraphs each. The second
passage is in the preface to Aulus Gellius' *Noctes Atticae,* itself a collection
of varied selections and excerpts from Apuleius' period (Gellius *NA
praef.* 6):

namque alii Musarum inscripserunt, alii Silvarum, ille Πέπλον, hic Ἀμαλθείας
κέρας, alius Κηρία, partim Λειμῶνα, quidam Lectionis Suae, alius Antiquarum
Lectionum atque alius Ἀνθηρῶν et item alius Ἐρωτημάτων.

Here Gellius, in listing titles of other (lost) works of miscellaneous compilation like his own, mentions ἀνθηρά, of which *Florida* is a translation
(cf. Quintilian 12. 10. 58 *floridum (nam id ἀνθηρὸν appellant)* . . .): the
term clearly refers to an anthology, and there is no necessary link with
style given the other titles mentioned.[13]

The final passage is from a letter of Claudianus Mamertus, presbyter
of Vienne in the fifth century AD (Claud. Mam. *Ep.* p. 205. 14 ff. Engel-
brecht):

e summis auctoribus . . . doctiora quaeque velut thyma fraglantia et fecundiora
veluti quaedam florida praecerpens.

This is the only other occasion in classical Latin apart from Apuleius' title

---

[11] *TLL* 6. 1. 925. 72 ff. (*floridus*), 936. 45 ff. (*flos*), 938. 15 ff. (*flosculus*), 923. 24 ff. (*florens*).
[12] On the date of Justin see above, Ch. 1 n. 97.
[13] For discussions of the Gellius passage cf. Holford-Strevens (1988), 20–2, and Vardi
(1993).

Florida that the neuter plural adjective *florida* is used substantivally. Again it describes excerpting activity, this time applied to the teaching activities of the writer's correspondent, the rhetor Sapaudus, who selects the best passages of the classics in instructing his pupils, on the grounds of learning (*doctiora*) and intellectual richness (*fecundiora*) rather than flowery style. Claudianus Mamertus may well be influenced by Apuleius' title *Florida* here; he knew Apuleius' works well, and another of his correspondents was Sidonius Apollinaris who similarly had access to the works of Apuleius.[14] In any case, the use of *florida* and similar terms to describe choice passages culled from larger works seems beyond dispute, and these passages indicate that the title *Florida* suggests 'choice blooms' collected in an anthology. Our *Florida* is thus a collection of excerpts itself excerpted from a choice collection; further definition of the principle of excerption must await a full analysis of the extant *Florida*, together with the excerpts falsely attributed to the preface of the *De Deo Socratis* (see Section 4 below).

3. ANALYSIS OF THE *FLORIDA*

Florida 1

In these fifteen lines Apuleius, in an elaborate simile, compares stopping at a city to give a speech with stopping at a shrine while travelling: this is clearly meant as a compliment to the city concerned, which is not named. Carthage has been suggested as a possibility,[15] and this could be so if *Flor.* 1 predated Apuleius' residence at Carthage in the 160s; it is unlikely that Apuleius would talk in this way about his home city, since the passage clearly concerns a visit to a city en route to somewhere else (2 *ita mihi ingresso sanctissimam istam civitatem, quamquam oppido festinem . . .*). Here Apuleius is shown as the professional travelling speaker in true sophistic manner, just as in *Flor.* 21 (below) and in the *Apologia*, where he mentions a speech given at Oea where he stopped on the way to Alexan-

---

[14] Claudianus Mamertus *Anim.* 2. 9, p. 137. 1 Englebrecht *cernas hic alium situ fetutinarum turpium ex olenticetis suis ac tenebris . . . oris inhalare sentinam*: the noun *olenticetum* is otherwise found only at Apuleius *Apol.* 8, which also joins it with the otherwise very rare noun *fetutina*: *nocens lingua mendaciorum et amaritudinum praeministra semper in fetutinis et olencetis iaceat.* For Mamertus' substantial knowledge of Apuleius see Alimonti (1975).

[15] So Scotti (1988), 126 n. 2 (her brief article is the nearest thing to a commentary on *Flor.* 1 and is very useful); other North African cities with major cults (e.g. Lepcis Magna or Alexandria) are possible.

dria (55). Allusions to travelling and compliments to the city where the speaker has arrived are naturally common topics in the opening of sophists' speeches,[16] and there is every indication that this passage constitutes the beginning of a speech. Aelius Aristides, in a recognizably cognate conceit, begins a speech to a Roman audience by claiming that he had vowed that very speech as an offering to the gods for safe passage on his journey (*Or.* 26. 1 K), and a similar extended simile is used by Lucian to open the first book of the *Verae Historiae:* Lucian compares readers/audiences and athletes, Apuleius speakers and travellers, and the two similes are articulated in a closely similar way.[17] These similarities suggest that this type of structure is a typical kind of sophistic opening, though the style is very much Apuleius' own: in the opening sentence, the characteristic jingle of *aliqui lucus aut aliqui locus* and the rhyming asyndetic isocola of *votum postulare, pomum adponere, paulisper adsidere* are typically Apuleian.[18] Strongly Apuleian too are the two similarly rhythmical and carefully balanced sets of four isocola in the second sentence which list with careful learning and colourful language the various types of sacred site a traveller might encounter (*aut ara floribus redimita* | *aut spelunca frondibus inumbrata* | *aut quercus cornibus onerata* | *aut fagus pellibus coronata,* | *vel enim colliculus saepimine consecratus* | *vel truncus dolamine effigiatus* | *vel caespes libamine umigatus* | *vel lapis unguine delibutus*). This yields not only verbal pyrotechnics but also an impression that the speaker is both learned and pious, matching Apuleius' similar self-projection in the *Apologia.*[19]

---

[16] Allusions to travel: Dio *Or.* 7. 2, 9. 1. Encomium of place arrived at expected: Dio *Or.* 33. 2.

[17] Lucian *VH* 1. 1 'Just as athletes (Ὥσπερ τοῖς ἀθλητικοῖς) and those who are seriously concerned with the care of the body do not care only for good physical condition or the gymnasia, but also for relaxation at the appropriate time (indeed they suppose it the most important element in their training), so (οὕτω) in my view it is fitting for those concerned with literature (τοῖς περὶ τοὺς λόγους ἐσπουδάκοσιν) to relax the mind after extensive reading of more serious works and to prepare it to be readier for subsequent exertions'. The word of comparison begins the work in both cases (ut/ Ὥσπερ), followed by a similar long and elaborate *comparans*, and picked up by a correlative *comparandum* (ita/οὕτω), both *comparans* and *comparandum* being in the dative case (*religiosis ... mihi/*τοῖς ἀθλητικοῖς *...* τοῖς περὶ τοὺς λόγους ἐσπουδάκοσιν).

[18] For these features of Apuleian style see Bernhard (1927).

[19] Learning in *Apologia passim*, piety e.g. *Apol.* 54–6. The detail about sacred objects has a feel of Varronian antiquarianism: the seventh book of Varro's *Res Divinae* was devoted to *loci religiosi*, the twelfth to *sacra privata* (cf. Augustine *Civ.* 6. 3). For Apuleius' knowledge of Varro cf. Ch. 1 n. 93.

Florida 2

This forty-line fragment begins with an implied reference to something which has gone before (*at non itidem*), indicating that it is not the opening of a speech and suggesting that the collection is not composed simply of rhetorical openings (see Section 4 below). The reference by the speaker to Socrates as *maior meus* says not just that Socrates lived before him, but also that Socrates is a spiritual ancestor of Apuleius the *philosophus Platonicus*: here, as in some parts of the *Apologia*, Apuleius may have presented himself as a Socrates reborn—as with many of the other anecdotes about philosophers in the *Florida* (cf. Hippias in 9, Crates in 14 and 22, Pythagoras in 15, Protagoras and Thales in 18) the purpose of the comparison is likely to have been self-description. The story concerning Socrates is a χρεία, a short anecdote concluding with a pithy punch-line attached to a historical or literary character, and is clearly an aphoristic development of the scene in Plato's *Charmides* where Socrates is shown the physical beauty of Charmides but wishes to talk to him to establish whether he is truly beautiful (154d ff.): *ut te videam, aliquid et loquere*, says Apuleius' Socrates to a similarly good-looking young man.

Socrates, following the interest of the Second Sophistic in Plato and in the great philosophers of the classical age of Greece, is elsewhere the subject of similar stories, and this anecdote form in general is much favoured by sophistic writers. Instruction in the writing of the χρεία was one of the προγυμνάσματα or *exercitationes primae*, the preliminary exercises which formed part of the standard Greek (or Roman) rhetorical education in the Imperial period.[20] The citation from Plautus (*Truculentus* 489), cleverly reworked by interchanging *auritus* and *oculatus*, paradoxically inverts the ancient truism that sight is much more reliable than hearing, and allies Apuleius with the Latin archaizing movement of his time; both Fronto and Gellius were admirers of Plautus.[21] Notable too is the paraphrase of Homer, the *poeta egregius* of 2. 7 (cf. *Il*. 3. 12): Homer's literal darkness is here turned into the idea of obscured earthly human vision (*obtutum istum terrenum*), clearly Platonic in its notion of the imperfection of earthly existence and the idea of the obscuring *nebula*, a kind of

[20] On the χρεία in general see Gow (1965), 12–15, Lausberg (1960), 536–40, and Hock and O'Neil (1986). On the προγυμνάσματα cf. Kennedy (1983), 54–70, and on their use in sophistic rhetoric Anderson (1993), 47–53.

[21] On Fronto and Plautus cf. Marache (1952), 157; on Gellius and Plautus cf. Holford-Strevens (1988) 157–8; on Apuleius and Plautus cf. Desertine (1898), Mattiacci (1986), 191–200.

allegorical reading of Homer common in Middle Platonism.[22] Finally, the lengthy comparison between the sight of man and that of the eagle, expressed with baroque fullness (it continues for twenty-three lines to the end of the extract) recalls another προγύμνασμα or basic rhetorical exercise, the σύγκρισις or formal comparison,[23] undertaken in classic handbook style in order to praise one of the parties compared, here the eagle. It is carefully constructed: the resumptive *aquila . . . cum igitur eo sese aquila extulit* retains the attention of the audience, while careful repetition helps the drawing of the comparison (6 *cernere* and 7 *obtutum* are picked up by 11 *uno obtutu cernens*). Thus this relatively short fragment shows intellectual affinity with both the Greek sophistic and the Latin archaizing movements, and embodies in practice two basic rhetorical exercises, an element which will be of some interest when considering the principles of selection in the *Florida* as we have it (see Section 4 below).

Beaujeu in his text clearly believes that *Flor.* 2 ends in mid-sentence, but Helm is surely right in supposing that *obtulit* ends a sentence as well as the extract. Grammatically incomplete extracts are certainly possible in the *Florida*, especially given its problematic transmission (*Flor.* 22 is a case in point), but in *Flor.* 2 the syntactical and rhetorical structure clearly argues for completeness. The syntax of the final part of the long last sentence beginning *at cum igitur eo sese aquila extulit* is certainly complex, but there seems to be a balance: the first main verb *labitur* has the participles *advertens, despiciens,* and *eminens* hanging from it, and the second pair of main verbs *circumtuetur et quaerit* similarly has a pendant participle *cernens.* The phrases *rostro transfodiat* and *unguibus inuncet* both govern the following objects *vel agnum incuriosum vel leporem meticulosum vel quodcumque esui animatum vel laniatui fors obtulit;* and the three object clauses beginning with *vel* form a neat tricolon, with the last element both being by far the longest and moving from the particular to the general, all closural signs.

Florida 3

This fifty-line passage tells the story of the legendary aulete Hyagnis, and of the unfortunate musical contest of Marsyas, Hyagnis' son and pupil, with the god Apollo. Plato had named Marsyas as the inventor of the

---

[22] On this type of Homeric interpretation elsewhere in Apuleius cf. *DDS* XXIV. 177–8, and for the general background Lamberton (1986), esp. 233 and 261–2.

[23] On the σύγκρισις as a προγύμνασμα cf. Kennedy (1983), 64.

double-aperture *aulos* (*Rep.* 399c, *Symp.* 215c). Apuleius' ascription of this invention to Marsyas' father Hyagnis follows the later version of Aristoxenus in his lost περὶ μουσικῆς (fr. 77 Wehrli), a version which had become standard by the third century BC (cf. Dioscorides *AP* 9. 340), and which appears again in the pseudo-Plutarchan *De Musica*, which uses many standard sources.[24] That it should appear in a speech in Apuleius is unsurprising; Apuleius was himself probably the author of a work *De Musica* (cf. Chapter 1 n. 116), and Menander Rhetor encourages speakers in the more informal and prefatory λαλία to mention famous auletes as analogies for the speaker himself (II. 392. 18 ff.); Apuleius may have been doing just that in the original context of this fragment, which as in *Flor.* 1 looks like the beginning of a speech. Stories of auletes providing points of comparison for the speaker are similarly found as opening gambits in other sophistic orations, in Dio of Prusa's first oration and Lucian's *Harmonides*, and the sophist Alexander Peloplaton's use of Marsyas in a preface seems likely from a parody of his openings, 'Ionias, Lydias, Marsyases, foolishness, give me subjects', cited by Philostratus (*VS* 2. 5. 574).

The story of the contest of Marsyas and Apollo, which follows the treatment of Hyagnis, is most familiar from Ovid's *Metamorphoses* (6. 382 ff.), and is told by Apuleius in a lively narrative which has some points of connection with Ovid's. Once again influence from a προγύμνασμα may be seen, that of the διήγημα, where a familiar narrative, usually a myth from a poet, is written in the pupil's own words.[25] But particularly interesting is the slant put on the story by Apuleius, which seems to be original and adapted to a particular context. Much is made of the barbarous and uncivilized appearance of Marsyas (3. 6 *phryx cetera et barbarus, vultu ferino, trux, hispidus, inlutibarbarus, spinis et pilis obsitus*) and its contrast with the divine elegance of Apollo (3. 9 *coma intonsus et genis gratus et corpore glabellus et arte multiscius et fortuna opulentus*). Marsyas also attacks Apollo for his ability to prophesy equally easily in prose or verse (3. 10), and claims that the god's many surface attractions are *blandimenta nequaquam virtuti decora, sed luxuriae accommodata* (3. 12). The point of this emerges from the Muses' view that

---

[24] [Plut.] *De Mus.* 5. This treatise probably dates from the first or second century AD; for a modern translation with commentary see Barker (1984), 205–57, and on the date Ch. 1 n. 116.

[25] On the διήγημα as a προγύμνασμα cf. Kennedy (1983), 61, and for its application in Apuleius, Sandy (1997), 156–60.

Marsyas' criticisms are *crimina sapienti exoptanda* (3. 13), the kind of charges which a wise man would be delighted to be guilty of: the characteristics criticized by Marsyas are those which should be regarded as advantages by persons of good judgement. The passage is evidently an attack on Cynic-type mistrust of elegance of appearance and multiple accomplishments in someone who claims to be a *sapiens*.

The obvious candidate for the *sapiens* is Apuleius himself, and the criticisms of Apollo's personal appearance and range of talents clearly recall the attacks on those same characteristics of Apuleius in the *Apologia*,[26] though the reference may be to later local rivals in Carthage rather than to the specific circumstances of the *Apologia* (for other attacks on rivals at Carthage cf. *Flor.* 4, 7, and 9). Furthermore, the ability to write in both prose and verse picks up Apuleius' own claims in *Flor.* 9 (27–8). *Flor.* 3 seems to be a symbolic reprise of the *Apologia*: the opposition of the boorish Marsyas (though he is given an eloquent speech) and the ease of Apollo's victory (3. 14) reflect Apuleius' forensic strategy in the *Apologia*, where he presents the case as an unequal match between his own talents and the rustic barbarism of his opponents, who are similarly attacked for their unkempt appearance, the chief prosecutor Aemilianus being pilloried as the Vergilian Charon to make this very point.[27] Though the passage ends abruptly before any explicit comparison is made, it seems very likely that Apuleius went on to link himself through shared characteristics with Apollo, just as he links himself explicitly with the sophist Hippias in *Flor.* 9, or the philosopher Pythagoras in *Flor.* 15, or the poet Philemon in *Flor.* 16; indeed Hippias is said to be *tam numerosa arte multiscium* (9. 24) in order to compare him to the multi-talented Apuleius, just as Apollo is said to be *arte multiscius* here (3. 9). Envy of Apuleius' prosperity after his marriage to Pudentilla might also lie behind Marsyas' objection that Apollo is *fortuna opulentus* (3. 9), otherwise an oddly anthropomorphic comment to make about a god . We may here have some form of reply to Apuleius' critics, which fits with attacks on him in the *Apologia* and with the apparent controversy about his statue in Oea (Ch. 1, p. 33): like the great Greek sophists, Apuleius could clearly defend himself against detractors through the medium of public declamation.[28]

---

[26] Attacks on personal appearance of Apuleius: *Apol.* 4. Attacks on his eloquence and multiform literary talents: *Apol.* 5–10.

[27] *Apol.* 23, 56; on Vergilian invective in the *Apologia* cf. Harrison (1988).

[28] For Apuleius' attacks on his rivals cf. n. 49.

Florida 4

In these fifteen lines Apuleius moves swiftly through several themes by skilled transitions: the story of the virtuoso aulete Antigenidas, who complained that lowly funeral musicians were thought of as equivalent to great auletes like himself, leads eventually through examples of very different characters wearing the same dress to a discussion of the *pallium*, the cloak worn by philosophers, the subject of Tertullian's *De Pallio* in the next century. The anecdote about Antigenidas, reporting the content of his complaint, is in effect a χρεία as in *Flor.* 2 (see above). Once again, as in *Flor.* 3, initial discussion of a musician seems to be leading up to a comparison with Apuleius himself, with the added hint of the *pallium*, which Apuleius ostentatiously claimed to wear as befitting a *philosophus Platonicus* (cf. *Flor.* 7. 9–15); again, as in *Flor.* 3, this passage is likely to come from the beginning of a speech. The allusions to theatrical and amphitheatrical entertainments suggest that Apuleius is speaking in the context of a festival where such things took place, very likely in Carthage (*munera nostra* suggests the speaker's home territory); similar allusions to rival attractions are found elsewhere in the *Florida* (5. 1, 18. 1) and in other sophistic speeches, since sophists often performed at festivals, and they are also to be found in Roman comedy.[29]

The fact that this fragment about the (historical) aulete Antigenidas follows closely on *Flor.* 3 about the (legendary) aulete Marsyas has led to suggestions that the two passages were drawn from the same original speech.[30] This is not impossible. As already noted, both extracts could be openings from different speeches, brought together in the extant *Florida* because of their common concern with auletes, but the two could equally well be openings of sections in the same speech; the polemical point of the Marsyas/Apollo dispute seen above in *Flor.* 3 (Apuleius overcoming his rivals or detractors) could be directly connected with the snobbish complaint of Antigenidas (Apuleius might similarly complain that his rival speakers unjustly claimed parity with him). The issue must remain unresolved in the present state of the evidence. Antigenidas, like Hyagnis and Marsyas, is mentioned in Ps.-Plutarch *De Musica* (21) and in Aristoxenus περὶ μουσικῆς (fr. 77 Wehrli), showing that Apuleius is once again using readily available material on musicians.

---

[29] Cf. Dio *Or.* 12 and Lucian *Peregrinus*, both delivered at the Olympics, Philostratus *VS* 2. 27. 617, and Terence *Hecyra* 3–5, 33–42.

[30] Cf. Opeku (1974), 24–5.

Florida 5

These six lines, the shortest fragment of the *Florida*, compliment an audience assembled in a theatre and compare the discourse of a philosopher with the shows of other performers which might be seen in the same place. The apparent theatrical context is shared with *Flor.* 4; though it is possible that the two passages come from the same original speech (*enim* as second word makes it clear that *Flor.* 5 is not itself an opening), similar references to a theatrical context and alternative attractions are found in *Flor.* 4 and 18.[31] Like *Flor.* 4, this passage builds up to a mention of the word *philosophus*, and in both cases it seems extremely likely that Apuleius went on to talk about himself under that head. We can see a similar technique in Dio Chrysostom *Orationes* 12. 5, where Dio congratulates his hearers for assembling in the context of the Olympics to listen to him, a philosopher, rather than other more glamorous literary performers, and then goes on to compare himself famously with the owl of Athene, admired for its wisdom. Perhaps the two passages *Flor.* 4 and 5 are set together editorially in our collection as examples of how to introduce oneself at or near the beginning of a speech.

Florida 6

These fifty lines constitute a description of the Indians, and particularly of their philosophers, here referred to vaguely as the 'gymnosophists'; in *Flor.* 15. 16 Apuleius gives them the more specific name of *Brachmanni*, i.e. Brahmins. This material on India is a sophistic favourite, connected with the travellers' tales which were so common in the period and burlesqued in Lucian's *True History*,[32] but also linked with the figure of Alexander, another favourite in the Second Sophistic, since Alexander's campaigns had revealed the wonders of India to the Mediterranean world, and the king himself was reputed to have met with its philosophers.[33] A similar passage on India and its philosophers is found in Dio *Or.* 35. 18 ff., while India is the subject of Arrian's *Indica* (based on the accounts of Alexander's expedition) and is a popular topic in the writings

---

[31] Cf. also n. 29.

[32] On the sources of the *True Histories* cf. Morgan (1985); on India as a sophistic topic cf. Stadter (1980), 115–32, Jones (1986), 56–7, Anderson (1986), 199–215. For Roman interest in India cf. André (1986).

[33] On Alexander and India cf. Max. Tyr. *Dial.* 2. 6, Bowie (1970), 7, Stadter (1980), 123, and esp. Romm (1992), 82–120, Karttunen (1997).

of Lucian, not to mention the meetings of Apollonius of Tyana and the Indian philosophers recounted by Philostratus.[34] We should remember, too, that Pliny's *Natural History*, Book 8 of which is clearly drawn on here for the combat of elephants and snakes, has a substantial Indian section in Book 7.[35]

Apuleius is thus reworking common literary material here, but several devices are used to vary this familiar fare. First, the material on the combats of elephants and snakes (6. 4–5) may be taken not from a Greek work but from a favourite Latin source of Apuleius, Pliny's *Natural History*:

bellantesque cum iis [*i.e. elephants*] perpetua discordia dracones tantae magnitudinis et ipsos ut circumplexu facili ambiant nexuque modi praestringant. commoritur ea dimicatione, victusque conruens complexum elidit pondere. (*HN* 8. 11)

Apuleius typically elaborates Pliny's report with more colourful language, but elements of the original may be detected: Apuleius' final phrase *toto corpore oblidere* looks like a reworking of Pliny's final phrase *elidit pondere.*

Second, Apuleius cites three Latin hexameters on the Ganges delta, in a pastiche of Vergilian style:[36]

> Eois regnator aquis in flumina centum
> discurrit, centum valles illi oraque centum,
> oceanique fretis centeno iungitur amni. (*Flor.* 6. 3)

Ornamentation of declamation by poetical quotation from major authors has been seen already in *Flor.* 2 (citing Plautus) and *Flor.* 3 (citing Vergil), and is a common technique in Greek sophistic writers. But these three lines are not ascribed to a particular author or attested elsewhere, which leads to the assumption that they are either the work of Apuleius himself or of a poet familiar to his audience. It has been suggested that they belonged to the poem on the deeds of Alexander by Clemens cited in the following *Flor.* 7;[37] the fact that Alexander did not reach the Ganges need not exclude this, since it was commonly said to be Alexander's eventual objective and could therefore come into a poem on

---

[34] Philostratus *VA* 1. 2, 3. 15–50.

[35] Pliny *HN* 7. 21–30, mentioning *gymnosophistae* (7. 22). For Greek and Roman interest in the naked philosophers of India cf. Karttunen (1997), 55–64.

[36] See Courtney (1993), 401.

[37] By F. Marx; cf. Blänsdorf (1995). 367.

his deeds.[38] If this is so, there is some likelihood that *Flor.* 6 and 7 are related, and that they come from the same speech.

Apuleius' third device of variation is to attach to the gymnosophists of India a moral story derived from Pythagorean tradition, reflecting the *interpretatio Graeca* which could be applied to these wise men who, like the Pythagoreans, practised asceticism, silence, and vegetarianism.[39] Apuleius claims that at meal-times each is obliged to give an account of the good he has done that day, and is turned away empty if he can think of none. Much the same precept, differing only in the occasion of this account and the method of punishment (the account is placed before sleep rather than before food, and the punishment is self-chastisement), appears in the Pythagorean *Carmina Aurea*, a text which was known at least as early as the first century AD and quoted by Plutarch and Arrian.[40] Thus here too Apuleius is manipulating a topic of the Second Sophistic.

It is possible that this description of the Indians and their way of life constituted the opening of a speech: the second-century sophist Alexander Peloplaton seems to have begun a speech with a similar description of Arabia (Philostratus *VS* 2. 5. 574) while Lucian's extant *Dipsades* opens with an account of Libya. But of course such descriptions need not always have occurred at the beginning of a speech, since they were part of the standard speaker's armoury: ἔκφρασις was one of the techniques included in the προγυμνάσματα already mentioned,[41] the fundamental exercises of Greco-Roman rhetorical training.

Florida 7

In some fifty lines Apuleius praises Alexander, and reports his well-known wish, turned by Apuleius into a command, to be depicted only by artists of the first quality; such a command should also exist for

[38] Cf. Curtius 9. 2. 1, Diodorus 17. 93, Plutarch *Alexander* 62, Arrian *Anab.* 5. 26. 1. The average sophistic auditor may not in any case have been aware that Alexander did not reach the Ganges; he could indeed be represented as doing so in poetry—cf. Lucan 3. 229–39 with Hunink (1992), 123–4.

[39] Cf. Strabo 15. 1. 59, where a clear link is made between the beliefs of the Brachmanes about transmigration and those of the Platonic/Pythagorean school; see also Karttunen (1997), 55–64.

[40] The latest edition of the *Carmina Aurea*, Thom (1995), does not include Apuleius in its list of testimonia (14) or in its list of the frequent citations of the relevant passage (lines 40–4) in the writers of the Second Sophistic (163), though the resemblance is a clear one, presumably because of the transfer from a Pythagorean to a gymnosophist context.

[41] Cf. n. 20 and Kennedy (1983), 65.

philosophy, in which false and insincere practitioners often arise. Alexander's popularity in the literature of the Second Sophistic has already been noted.[42] The story about his wishes for his own artistic depiction is of course familiar in both Greek and Latin before Apuleius: it has been convincingly argued that Apuleius (as often) uses the convenient material of Pliny the Elder (*HN* 7. 175), but he also seems to take something from Horace *Epistulae* 2. 1. 239 ff.[43] There Horace contrasts Alexander's laudable discrimination in choosing artists with his lack of discrimination in choosing poets, and congratulates Augustus that with Vergil and Varius he has done better than Alexander with Choerilus; Apuleius' use of the Alexander story similarly contrasts Alexander's discrimination between true and false artists with the world's lack of discrimination between true and false philosophers.

As with *Flor.* 6, this may or may not be the opening of a speech; it may also be part of the same speech from which *Flor.* 6 is taken (see above). The resumptive *Alexandro illi . . . eius igitur Alexandri* (7. 1, 7. 4) is simply a standard Apuleian way of introducing a character, and need not belong to an opening;[44] on the other hand, anecdotes and praise of famous historical or mythological characters (and of Alexander in particular) are a standard type of sophistic proem. The praise of Alexander again recalls the basic rhetorical exercises of the προγυμνάσματα, one of which was that of the encomium (ἐγκώμιον);[45] but it is also used to introduce an honorific mention of the poem on Alexander by Apuleius' friend Clemens, which may be that cited in *Flor.* 6 (see above). The last section on true and false philosophers plainly shows the relevance of the Alexander material to the speaker's purpose: as in *Flor.* 3, an ornamental passage seems to be leading up to a comparison between the speaker and his rivals, to the disadvantage of the latter—he is the true philosopher, they are inferior and counterfeit. Once again, we can see Apuleius about to attack the opposition in full sophistic style. As in *Flor.* 4, the wearing of the *pallium* is stressed as the mark of the philosopher, though it is also made clear that mere dress does not make a philosopher.

---

[42] Cf. n. 33.

[43] Cf. Brink (1982), 247–8. Apuleius here makes a minor error about Polycletus (cf. Vallette's note *ad loc.*) as he does in the biography of Pythagoras in *Flor.* 15 (Leodamas/Hermodamas), a similar sign of rapid reprocessing of tralatician information.

[44] Cf. *Flor.* 4. 1–2 *Antigenidas . . . is igitur*, 18. 19–20 *Protagoras . . . eum Protagoran*, 19. 1–2 *Asclepiades ille . . . is igitur*, with a fuller list at Hunink (1997), ii. 25, and n. 124 below. The pattern itself is as old as Herodotus (1. 23–4): Ἀρίονα τὸν Μηθυμναῖον . . . τοῦτον τὸν Ἀρίονα.

[45] Cf. Kennedy (1983), 63.

Florida 8

These seven lines, with *Flor.* 5 the shortest of the fragments, constitute an encomium of an unnamed grandee of consular but not proconsular rank (*consularibus*), a man similar to Strabo Aemilianus in *Flor.* 16. The opening words *hic enim* (cf. *Flor.* 5) indicate that this passage is not the opening of a speech (presumably the honorand had previously been identified). The compliment to the learning and virtue of the *laudandus* is an element found in all Apuleius' praises of senators and proconsuls, especially in his continual flattery of Claudius Maximus in the *Apologia*,[46] and does not serve to identify a particularly intellectual consular, despite the argument that *ex consularibus pauci boni et adhuc ex bonis pauci eruditi*. The stress on erudition reflects the value placed on a reputation for learning even by non-intellectuals in the high culture of the Roman West in the second century AD, matching the Greek cultural revival of the Second Sophistic. Though a location is not specified, this passage, like *Flor.* 9, 15, 16, and 17, is likely to reflect Apuleius' relations with the great in the provincial capital of Carthage, where men of consular rank were to be found. As in the praise of Alexander in *Flor.* 7, this is a brief but useful model for the rhetorical technique of encomium.

Florida 9

In this six-page piece, with the seven-page *Flor.* 16 the longest in the collection, Apuleius begins by referring to possible detractors in the audience, compliments his listeners on their learning, compares himself to the proconsul in the matter of his words being irrevocable, and then launches into an elaborate comparison between himself and the sophist Hippias: just as Hippias showed himself versatile in many arts, so Apuleius shows himself versatile in many literary forms. This literary versatility he then wishes to dedicate to praising the proconsul Severianus. It becomes clear that the speech celebrates the end of Severianus' year as proconsul, which it praises as an ideal period of government; it looks forward at the end to the hopes of Carthage that Severianus' son Honorinus will reach the proconsulship of Africa like his father.

Here for once a date and place can be assigned with some confidence for the delivery of a piece from the *Florida*. The proconsul Severianus is clearly Sex. Cocceius Severianus Honorinus (suff. 147), probably

---

[46] Cf. Ch. 2, p. 46.

proconsul of Africa in AD 162–3, the year before Scipio Orfitus, the addressee of *Flor.* 17,[47] and *favor Caesarum* at 9. 40 suggests the joint rule of M. Aurelius and Verus (AD 161–9). Apuleius' speech, clearly an honorific farewell at the end of the year of office, would have been given at the proconsular seat of Carthage, as its allusions to Carthage (9. 37, 9. 40) confirm. It also seems very likely that this piece is the first complete speech to appear in the collection, as the seven-page and probably complete *Flor.* 16 confirms, provided that *illis* in the opening sentence refers simply to persons known to the audience rather than to something preceding in a lost portion of the text; in terms of length it is closely comparable with a number of brief Greek sophistic orations.[48] The reference to the future prospect of Severianus' son Honorinus himself becoming proconsul like his father (9. 40) certainly provides a fitting form of closure, with a firm clausular rhythm.

The references at the beginning to *invisoribus meis* and *lividis* recall *Flor.* 3, 4, and 7, where similar allusions to inferior and envious detractors appear to be made: as already observed, Apuleius' need to represent himself as superior to local rivals in speaking reflects in the culture of Carthage the intense competitiveness of contemporary sophists in the Greek East.[49] Prominent initially too (as in the similar opening of *Flor.* 16) is flattery of the audience, presumably comprised of most of the Carthaginian elite, an evident *captatio benevolentiae* (*in hoc pulcherrimo coetu, splendidissimo huic auditorio*), and remarks on its great size (*incredibilem sessum, frequentiam tantam*): the quality and quantity of the audience reflects, of course, the status of the speaker. This is then followed by another prefatory topic, the potential inadequacy of the speaker to maintain his reputation before such a formidable gathering;[50] Apuleius' reputation for faultless speaking is here at risk, as he states in a series of rhetorical questions which pay a compliment to the high linguistic and cultural standards of his audience:

quis enim vestrum mihi unum soloecismum ignoverit ? quis vel unam syllabam barbare pronuntiatam donaverit? quis incondita et vitiosa verba temere quasi delirantibus oborientia permiserit blaterare? (9. 7)

[47] The dating is that of Syme (1959).

[48] With the six Teubner pages of *Flor.* 9 we may compare the similar length of *Flor.* 16 (~5. 5 pages) and those of Dio *Or.* 29 (~7. 5), 43 (~4. 5), 46 (~6), Max. Tyr. *Dial.* 19 (~6) and 24 (~6. 5) (all Teubner pages).

[49] On the rivalries of sophists cf. Bowersock (1969), 89–100, Anderson (1986), 43–50, 64–6, Anderson (1993), 35–9, and for this theme in Apuleius cf. Sandy (1997), 164–9.

[50] Inadequacy of speaker as prefatory topic: Janson (1964), 124–41.

The stress on correct Latinity reflects the contemporary concern with correct style in writers like Fronto and Gellius and matches the promotion of correct Attic in the contemporary Greek Second Sophistic,[51] but the critical terms used by Apuleius here (*soloecismus, barbarus,* and *vitiosus*) go back to traditional stylistic criticism of the first century BC and before.[52] This prefatory section (9. 1–9) concludes with yet another derogatory mention of those who wear the *pallium* of the philosopher but who are unworthy of it (*palliata mendicabula*), presumably Apuleius' rivals again.

At 9. 10 (*praeco proconsulis*) a new section begins (9. 10–13), giving a dramatic *mise-en-scène* which develops into a comparison for the speaker. The loud clamour of the *praeco*, the public crier who obtains silence for the magistrate,[53] is contrasted with the moderate volume of the proconsul's pronouncements; the proconsul's use of written texts (i.e. edicts and the like) is contrasted with the crier's oral communications— the sayings of the latter are by implication ephemeral, whereas those of the former are official, unalterable, and deposited in the provincial archives.[54] Apuleius compares himself not to the crier but to the proconsul: his words too will be taken down at once and read, and hence he must be careful about what he says, since, like those of the proconsul, his words cannot be subsequently corrected. This is interesting both for the speaker's characteristically high view of his own importance and for the evidence it provides on contemporary note-taking.[55] Apuleius then introduces one of the two major sections of the speech, a comparison of himself with the sophist Hippias (9. 14 29): both were extremely versatile in their productions, Hippias in different types of manufacture, Apuleius in different types of writing (9. 14 *plura enim mea exstant in Camenis quam Hippiae in opificiis opera*).

The choice of Hippias has a contemporary flavour. He is commonly mentioned in the Greek literature of the period: as Philostratus confirms

---

[51] On correct Latinity in this period cf. Marache (1952), 138–82, 218–50, Marache (1957), Holford-Strevens (1988), 35–46. On the Greek equivalent cf. e.g. Anderson (1993), 86–100, and for links between the two Sandy (1997), 50–60.

[52] Cf. esp. *Rhetorica ad Herennium* 4. 17 soloecismus *est cum in verbis pluribus consequens verbum superius non accommodatur,* barbarismus *est cum verbis aliquid* vitiose *effertur;* for the ancient uses of *soloecismus* and *barbarismus* cf. Lausberg (1960), 259–74.

[53] For *praecones* attendant on magistrates cf. *TLL* 10. 2. 497. 9 ff.

[54] *Instrumentum*, 'document', is here used metonymically for the *tabularium*, the archive where documents are kept—cf. *TLL*. 7. 1. 2013. 84 ff.

[55] For such simultaneous noting down (*excipere*) of speech cf. Cicero *Div*. 2. 50, Manilius 4. 199, Seneca *Ep*. 90. 25, Quintilian 1 pr. 7.; Winter (1969), in my view improbably, argues for Apuleius' *Apologia* as a simultaneous transcript.

by honouring him with a biography (*VS* 1. 11. 495–6), he belonged to the group of fifth-century sophists regarded as models by the Second Sophistic.[56] The story of his personal manufacture of all his own clothing and accoutrements derives originally from the *Hippias Minor* of Plato (368 b–d), but it is found in similar extended form in Dio (*Or.* 71. 2), suggesting that in this detail too Apuleius is employing a sophistic commonplace. Shorter versions of Hippias' multiform talents are also to be found in Latin in Cicero (*De Or.* 3. 127) and Quintilian (12. 11. 1), accounts which Apuleius does not detectably echo. Characteristically, perhaps, Apuleius harnesses this traditional material to his own positive self-presentation: he is unlike Hippias in being uninterested in making things (appealing no doubt to the Roman contempt for artisan activity), but like him in his versatility in a different area, literature—many types of poetry and prose in both Latin and Greek (9. 27–9).[57]

This stress on Apuleius' literary versatility introduces the encomium of the proconsul Severianus in the second major part of the speech (9. 30–40): all these talents will be used to praise the proconsul and thereby secure his lasting good opinion (no doubt useful, since he was presumably about to return to Rome, where he could add to Apuleius' fame), just as Apuleius had been approved of by all Severianus' predecessors in the post (a point made again at 15. 27, showing the natural importance of the good opinion of the proconsul in literary patronage in Carthage). The encomium then begins. Apuleius claims that he is praising Severianus for his public benefits, since he himself has received no private benefit from him. Severianus' virtues are those of the kindly and austere ruler, a humane form of Stoicism no doubt chosen as much for its resemblance to the views of Marcus Aurelius, then emperor, as for its individual relevance to Severianus: *tua ista gravitas iucunda, mitis austeritas, placida constantia blandusque vigor* (there seems to be a pun in *austeritas*, pointing to the element of the equivalent *severitas* in the name Severianus—we may compare the similar pun on Honorinus in 9. 40).[58] Severianus' administration has been effective through moral virtue rather than repression, he has spent more time at Carthage than any pre-

---

[56] Apart from Philostratus and Dio, see the mentions of Hippias in Plutarch *Numa* 1, *Lyc.* 23, Lucian *Herod.* 3, Aristides *Or.* 3. 602, 614, 4. 44, Pausanias 5. 24. 5, Athenaeus 5. 218C, 11. 506F.

[57] For an analysis of the types of writing described here and their relevance to Apuleius' output see Ch. 1, Sect. 2 (ii).

[58] *Austeritas* may also suggest Stoicism as in the case of Claudius Maximus, *virum tam austerae sectae* (*Apol.* 19. 2: see Hunink (1997), ii. 73).

decessor (a good point for a Carthaginian audience), and even in the time when he was doing his proconsular tours of the province, his equally virtuous son Honorinus (his *legatus*) stood in for his father. The pair are cleverly linked in praise, while avoiding elevating the son too much at the father's expense: Honorinus' virtues are so like those of his father that his presence afflicted the Carthaginians with desire for their absent proconsul, but those virtues derive from being his father's son. The speech closes with a complaint that the terms of good proconsuls are too soon finished (the element which confirms that this is a farewell speech), and a hope that Honorinus, soon to advance in his public career (9. 40 *et honos suus ad praeturam vocat*: *honos* surely puns on his name, as *suus* suggests),[59] will emulate his father in achieving the proconsulate of Africa.

In the manuscript tradition, this speech is wrongly divided between two books; a mechanical explanation for this has been suggested at Section 1 above. The *subscriptio* to be found after 9. 14 in the manuscript F, in effect the sole source for the text, reads *Apulei Platonici Floridorum Lib. I explic. incip. II.* As argued in Section 1, the mechanical book-divisions recorded in the *Florida* cannot themselves represent complete ancient books within the extant version, though it is likely that they record from which books of an earlier collection our modern extracts are taken. But *Flor.* 9 is clearly a coherent unit, and would not have been divided across two original ancient books. The evidence of its contents is clear and unambiguous. First, section 14 promises a comparison between Apuleius and Hippias, which is delivered at section 27; second, section 30 hopes that the mention of the proconsul will lend glory to *omnem nostram Camenam*, thus picking up *plura enim mea extant in Camenis . . . opera* at section 14. Both these elements pull together the two parts of the extract wrongly sundered after section 14, and serve to confirm that the book-division was misplaced by a scribe at some stage in the transmission.

Florida 10

This fourteen-line fragment begins with an ornamental (mis-)quotation of an address to the Sun from the *Phoenissae* of Accius.[60] Like the

---

[59] The word *honos* not only picks up *Honorinus* but also perhaps plays on its double sense of 'status, honour' and 'public office' (Honorinus' name guarantees both his status and his future electoral success).

[60] Apuleius' manuscripts give *fervido cursu* in the first line of the quotation, but Priscian (*GLK* 3. 424. 19) gives *candido curru*, and this is the most plausible reading: Apuleius seems

quotations from Plautus and an unnamed tragedian in *Flor.* 18, this is taken from a dramatic prologue, which might suggest that *Flor.* 10 itself is the beginning of a longer piece (very likely, given that invocation of divine powers is a common ancient prefatory mode). To Accius' Sun Apuleius adds the Moon and gives a list of the planets with their characteristics; this is followed by an assertion of the existence of intermediate divine powers and their fundamental contribution to the shaping of the earth and its creatures, described in a typically Apuleian elaborate list with much rhythmical alliteration. Here again the content shows Apuleius very much as a child of his time. The quotation of Accius, an author cited again at *DDS* 176, aligns him with the contemporary Roman archaizing movement (compare the use of Plautus in *Flor.* 2 and 18): Accius is cited several times by Gellius, who also tells an anecdote about him, and is recommended as suitable reading by Fronto to his pupil Marcus Aurelius.[61] The fact that Accius is not named here (compare *DDS* 175, where a second unsignalled Accian allusion may be operating) is probably due merely to the fact that the extract begins immediately with the quotation, and not to the speaker's assumption that the audience will identify it without aid (as they might the Vergilian quotation in *Flor.* 11).

The list of astral powers presents the speaker as versed in astronomy; this coheres well with Apuleius' own probable treatise on astronomy.[62] The concern here with intermediate divine powers or δαίμονες is very characteristic of Apuleius, author of the *De Deo Socratis* on the δαιμόνιον of Socrates (see Chapter 4), and also typical of the literary Platonism of the Second Sophistic, since the idea of the δαίμων, though long present in Greek culture, derived most of its force from consideration of passages in Plato.[63] Indeed, Apuleius here, in taking Amor as the prime example of an intermediate divine power, clearly echoes a famous passage of the *Symposium* where Diotima identifies Eros as a δαίμων (*Symp.* 202d). The control of nature by the life-force of intermediate powers, described in a colourful and rhythmical paragraph (10. 4),[64] recalls the opening of

---

to have conflated Accius' line with one from Ennius' *Medea* (*Trag.* 243 Jocelyn)—see Maragoni (1988) and Dangel (1995), 218 and 359, and for the use of Accius in Apuleius in general cf. Mattiacci (1994), 53–68.

[61] Gellius *NA* 13. 2 (cf. Holford-Strevens (1988), 159); Fronto *De Fer. Als.* 3. 1. (= p. 227. 11 van den Hout).

[62] Cf. Ch. 1, Sect. 2 (ii) 11.

[63] Cf. Ch. 4, Sect. 1.

[64] Note especially the rhyming clause-ends *fluores/virores* and *volatus/volutus*, all four words being first found in Apuleius.

Lucretius' *De Rerum Natura*. The influence of Lucretius' Venus over
mountains, rivers, and plains (1. 17–18), birds (1. 12), and beasts (1. 14) is
matched by Apuleius' list of mountains, plains, rivers, meadows, birds,
serpents, beasts, and men, though there are no close verbal echoes.
Perhaps the two are simply separate and unrelated forms of the topos
'divine control over nature', usually ascribed to Eros or Aphrodite;[65] the
fact that Apuleius has just named Amor as the most notable of the intermediate powers may suggest that this literary tradition is in play here.

Florida 11

A short, eight-line piece, an extended simile: he who is barren in respect
of his own virtue is like those who cultivate poor land, illustrated by an
unattributed quotation from Vergil's *Georgics* (1. 154), who cannot grow
crops themselves and steal the flowers of their neighbours. The image is
striking, and such an extended simile might suit a preface as in *Flor.* 1; but
this cannot be the very first section of a speech since *enim* appears as its
second word (cf. *Flor.* 5, 8, and 13). As in *Flor.* 2, 3, and 4, this passage seems
to form part of an attack on Apuleius' rivals. The extract concludes just
as the comparison is being drawn, but it is evident that the thieving farm-
ers are an image for those who plagiarize Apuleius' own works: the fact
that they pluck *flores*, flowers, in a simile otherwise concerned with grain
production, suggests that those *flores* stand for choice flowers of speech,
as in the title *Florida*.[66] Such charges of plagiarism played a part in sophistic quarrels,[67] and Apuleius once again presents himself as a gifted public performer with untalented and envious competitors. The unmarked
quotation appeals to the audience's knowledge of a standard literary text,
while the choice vocabulary of *scruposus* (Plautine), *rupinas* (a diminutive first in Apuleius), and *senticeta* (Plautine) indicates Apuleius' fashionably select and archaic lexicon.[68] The extract as we have it ends
syntactically incomplete (cf. *Flor.* 22), whether through damage in transmission or editorial choice.

---

[65] For the world-domination of Eros cf. e.g. Sophocles *Ant.* 781–90, fr. 941. 9 Radt; for that
of Aphrodite cf. *Hom. Hymn. Aphr.* 1–5 and *Orphic Hymn* 55.

[66] Cf. n. 11 above.

[67] Cf. Stemplinger (1912), 17.

[68] *Scruposus*: Plautus *Capt.* 185; *rupinae*: again *Met.* 6. 26 and 7. 13; *senticeta*: Plautus *Capt.*
860. On Apuleian use of Plautus see n. 21 above, and on Apuleian archaizing in general cf.
Ch. 1 n. 68.

Florida 12

A thirty-five-line description of the parrot and its ability to mimic the human voice. The parrot had been familiar in Roman literature since Ovid, whose epitaph for Corinna's pet parrot (*Am.* 2. 6) was later echoed by that of Statius for the parrot of Atedius Melior (*Silvae* 2. 4), and Apuleius' description here owes something (as often) to Pliny's *Natural History* (*HN* 10. 117).[69] The parrot also attracted interest in the Second Sophistic: Philostratus records a lost *Encomium of the Parrot* by Dio Chrysostom (*VS* 1. 7. 487), and a description of the parrot occurs in Aelian's *De Natura Animalium* (13. 18–19). It is closely connected with the common sophistic topic of India (cf. *Flor.* 6), where Greeks first encountered the bird.[70] In form the passage is a description or ἔκφρασις, like *Flor.* 6; it is possible that it too was an opening—Philostratus records (*VS* 2. 27. 617) that the Severan sophist Hippodromus of Thessaly began a speech with a description of the peacock, which was then applied to his theme. The stress throughout the passage on the parrot's learning to speak naturally picks out its most striking characteristic, but might also suggest that this passage is part of an argument on education, for which the training of the parrot might provide an analogy. The point might be that pupils (like parrots) absorb what they are taught, and if they are taught improper things (as parrots can be taught insults), they will reproduce them, so that much care should be taken in education. But any such reconstruction must remain speculative given the lack of evidence for how the passage continued. Alternatively, the parrot might have been applied to the frequent Apuleian topic of the inadequacies of his rivals: they are only inferior plagiarists, while he is the speaker of true talent.[71]

Florida 13

In this twelve-line fragment Apuleius contrasts his philosophical eloquence with the various brief songs of birds (and the cicada) which occur at different hours of the day: philosophical reasoning and speech is suitable at all times, and as versatile as all these bird-songs. This comparison raises at least implicitly the analogy between philosophical performer and bird, which occurs famously in sophistic literature at the beginning

---

[69] On these classical parrots, dead and alive, cf. Van Dam (1984), 336–42.

[70] Cf. Bigwood (1993), and especially Karttunen (1997), 202–5.

[71] Cf. *Flor.* 3, 4, 7, and 9 (above). Such polemic goes back to Pindar, *Olympian* 2. 86–8, where Pindar compares himelf to the eagle and his rivals to crows.

of Dio Chrysostom's Olympic oration (12. 1–6). Like *Flor.* 1 and 11, this passage is an elaborate comparison reflecting on the speaker; given the parallel with Dio, it is fitting for the opening of a speech, but as in *Flor.* 5, 8, and 11 the initial presence of *enim* guarantees that these are not the very first words of a piece. The versatility of philosophical eloquence, clearly the point of the bird comparison, is similarly stressed in the opening of the *Dialexeis* of Maximus of Tyre (1. 1–4), suggesting that it is a sophistic commonplace.[72] This extract may have been editorially juxtaposed with *Flor.* 12 because of a common concern with birds.

Florida 14

In these twenty-three lines Apuleius relates the story of the Cynic Crates' conversion to philosophy, of his marriage to Hipparche, and of its consummation in public. Crates, from the fourth century BC, turns up again in *Flor.* 22 and in the *Apologia* (22. 2), and was a figure of interest in the Second Sophistic generally.[73] In his life of Crates, written in the early third century AD, Diogenes Laertius (6. 85–98) records, like Apuleius, that Crates was converted to philosophy by Diogenes, but does not include the saying attributed to Crates on that occasion by Apuleius: *Crates Cratetem manu mittit.* The saying occurs in other Greek sources, and was no doubt derived from existing tradition about Crates.[74] Like the words attributed to Socrates in *Flor.* 2 and the complaint of Antigenidas in *Flor.* 4, this is a classic χρεία or pithy saying assigned to a famous figure; such laconic pronouncements were particularly associated with Diogenes and the Cynics.[75] The curious nuptial arrangements of Crates are also commented on by Diogenes Laertius (6. 96), but not the element of public consummation; that this too belongs to the established tradition about Crates is confirmed by its occurrence in other Greek sources later than but independent of Apuleius.[76]

Apuleius' account represents Zeno of Citium, the pupil of Crates later to become the founder of Stoicism, as covering his master's public

---

[72] Cf. n. 28. For the links between Dio *Or.* 12 and Apuleius see Sandy (1997), 154–5.
[73] Apart from Diogenes Laertius, cf. Plutarch *De Vit. Aer. Al.* 8, *Quaest. Conv.* 2. 1. 6, Athenaeus 10. 422C.
[74] Cf. Diels (1901), 222–3. The text is mildly corrupt here, but these Greek parallels for the third-person statement (Κράτη Κράτητα Θηβαῖον ἐλευθεροῖ) argue strongly for *manumittit* rather than (e.g.) *Crates, Cratetem manumitte*, the conjecture of Hunink (personal communication, January 1998).
[75] Cf. Hock and O'Neil (1986), 3–4.
[76] Cf. Clement *Strom.* 4. 19, Sextus *PH* 1. 153, 3. 200.

copulation with his cloak. This is perhaps a hint that Zeno's own works are ultimately behind the story, since Zeno wrote not only a book of χρεῖαι in which sayings by Crates were included (Diog. Laert. 6. 91), but also Ἀπομνημονεύματα Κράτητος, *Recollections of Crates* (id. 7. 3), no doubt in imitation of Xenophon's Ἀπομνημονεύματα, *Recollections of Socrates*. These two books may be the eventual source for Apuleius, perhaps mediated through the homonymous Ἀπομνημονεύματα of Favorinus, a miscellaneous compilation which certainly included stories about Crates (Diog. Laert. 6. 89) and which was certainly known to Gellius and very likely to the latter's contemporary Apuleius.[77]

Florida 15

A four-page fragment which begins with a description of the island of Samos, of its famous sanctuary of Hera, and of a statue in that sanctuary of Bathyllus, the favourite of the great Samian tyrant Polycrates (1–11). By a neat transition, the assertion that some have identified the statue as that of another great Samian, Pythagoras, leads on to an account of that philosopher's life and doctrines, concluding with the practice of silence (12–25). Finally, Apuleius claims that he too has learnt the lesson of silence in his own Platonic studies, Plato being strongly Pythagorean, and has applied it in knowing when to praise the addressee's predecessors and when to be unforthcoming (26–7). A phrase in the last sentence, *ab omnibus antecessoribus tuis* (15. 27), makes it practically certain that, as in *Flor.* 9 and 17, Apuleius is addressing a proconsul of Africa, very likely in Carthage (cf. *Flor.* 9. 31 *per omnes antecessores tuos*). The description of Samos, like the account of India in *Flor.* 6, fits the opening of a speech, as does Apuleius' clear claim to have seen the sights of Samos himself (15. 4 *si recte recordor viam*, 6 *qua nihil videor effectius cognovisse*): sophistic orations could often begin with material drawn from the speaker's journeys, thereby presenting the speaker as an impressively well-travelled and cosmopolitan figure.[78]

The material on Samos evidently combines two forms of ἔκφρασις, that of a place and that of a work of art. Both these types are common in the literature of the Second Sophistic, and are famously conjoined in

---

[77] Cf. Holford-Strevens (1988), 81–2, Sandy (1997), 77–84; though the *De Mundo* appears to quote the views of Favorinus as mediated by Gellius rather than from Favorinus himself—cf. Ch. 5, p. 186.

[78] Cf. *Flor.* 1 and e.g. Lucian *El.* 2, Dio *Or.* 36. 1. For well-travelled sophists see Philostratus *VS* 2. 9. 582 (Aristides), 2. 15. 596 (Ptolemy), 2. 33. 627 (Aspasius).

Pausanias' *Description of Greece*, describing both famous tourist sites and their treasures, a text probably roughly contemporary with the *Florida*.[79] Pausanias, like Apuleius, includes an account of the Heraion on Samos and its monuments, but his text unfortunately has a lacuna at the very point where the statue of Bathyllus might have been described (7. 4. 1–7). The description of a work of art is perhaps the classic mode of sophistic writing, culminating in the *Imagines* of Philostratus, a whole book of such descriptions, and is prominent not only in sophistic speeches but also in the fictional writing of the period: in Apuleius' own *Metamorphoses* we have the famous description of the sculptural group of Actaeon and Diana (2. 4. 1–10), and there are many examples in Greek novels. This is another reminder of the close links between sophistic discourse and the ancient novel seen so prominently in the career of Apuleius himself, both sophistic performer (*Florida*, *De Deo Socratis*) and novelist (*Metamorphoses*).[80]

The biographical account of Pythagoras presented here is very similar to that found in Diogenes Laertius (8. 1–50); there were a number of Greek lives of Pythagoras available for use in the second century,[81] and all the elements found in Apuleius' account may be paralleled from them, except one, which looks like an error. Apuleius names as one of Pythagoras' teachers a certain Leodamas, pupil of Creophylus (15. 21); in most other accounts this figure is Hermodamas, son or descendant of Creophylus. Apuleius seems to have an anomalous version both of this man and of his relation to Creophylus, which suggests either a mistake on Apuleius' part or one in an unknown source; the former is perhaps more likely.

Here, as in *Flor.* 14, Apuleius follows a sophistic interest in the careers of philosophers, with the implication of analogy between the famous figure considered and the speaker himself. Though the point is not explicitly made in the extract we possess, two elements point this way. First, the description of Pythagoras as *tot ille doctoribus eruditus, tot tamque multiiugis calicibus disciplinarum toto orbe haustis* (15. 22) is very like the account of Apuleius' own well-travelled and broad education given by him elsewhere (cf. *Flor.* 18. 15–16, 20. 4, *Apol.* 23. 1, 55. 8–9), even down to the traditional metaphor used of drinking: *ego et alias creterras Athenis*

[79] Cf. Habicht (1985), 1–27.
[80] On sophistic *ekphrasis* and the Greek novel cf. Hunter (1983), 38–52 and especially Bartsch (1989), 3–79. On the sophistic connections of the novel more generally see Reardon (1974).
[81] See the material collected in Cuccioli Melloni (1969) and Guthrie (1987), 57–156.

bibi, states Apuleius at *Flor.* 20. 4, talking of his philosophical education. Second, the argument that Pythagoreans and Platonists are essentially the same school (15. 26) might point to an impending analogy between Apuleius the *philosophus Platonicus* and Pythagoras.[82]

Florida 16

This piece of some 5. 5 Teubner pages, a similar length to that of *Flor.* 7, has every appearance of being a complete composition, and there are many sophistic speeches of comparable brevity.[83] Apuleius begins by thanking the leading men of Carthage for voting him the honour of a statue in his absence; though this speech is plainly not delivered in the *curia* (cf. 16. 41), it may imply that Apuleius was a member of it.[84] He excuses himself for having failed to speak for several days for health reasons by telling an anecdote about the comic poet Philemon (1–18). This is followed by further details about his health (19–24), and the piece concludes with further praise of Carthage for the grant of the statue and of the consular Strabo Aemilianus for his support of the proposal (25–47); Strabo has apparently promised a statue for Apuleius from his own resources (39) and asked the senate for a prominent location for it (41), thereby pressing them to grant a public statue. Apuleius' speech seems to aim to ensure that his statue will be erected at public cost, and only the prominent site requested by Strabo seems to have been granted so far (cf. 16. 46). Apuleius also promises full written encomia both for the chief men of Carthage (16. 29) and for Strabo individually (16. 32), but this may be purely rhetorical, providing an inducement to Carthage to grant the full cost of the statue: at the end of the speech it is clear that the full thanks will be forthcoming when the decreed statue actually materializes (16. 47 *sed de hoc ego perfectius, cum vos effectius*). In his caution here Apuleius may be influenced by previous controversy over the award of a statue to himself at Oea, chronicled by Augustine (*Ep.* 138. 19).

The hope expressed at 16. 40 that Strabo will soon be proconsul gives an approximate date: Strabo, consul *ordinarius* in 156, might therefore aspire to the proconsulship of Africa in the late 160s or early 170s,[85] and the speech may thus belong to a slightly later date than the other datable

---

[82] For Apuleius' comparison of himself with Pythagoras elsewhere cf. *Apol.* 4. 7, 27. 2, 31. 2, De'Conno (1958–9), 67–9, Sandy (1997), 149–50.

[83] Cf. n. 48.

[84] Which he must have been if he was a provincial priest; for this issue see Ch. 1 n. 30.

[85] Cf. Ch. 1 n. 29, and Ch. 1 n. 10 on Strabo's career.

pieces in the *Florida* (9, above, and 17, below). The award of a statue was a standard civic honour in the Roman empire, and was bestowed on sophists and other intellectuals just as much as on others who had brought more tangible benefits to their city.[86] In this speech Apuleius cleverly alludes to statues given him by other cities (probably Oea and his home city of Madauros)[87] by summarizing Strabo's letter to the senate which mentions them (16. 37), thus pointing out the existence of these honours without apparently introducing the topic himself.

Most of the first part of the speech is taken up with the Philemon story, which after a brief didactic account of the comic poet gives a version of his death. Philemon fails to turn up to recite to an expectant audience a new part of a play he is writing; eventually he is found dead in his bed, slumped over the work (6–18). Apuleius has not chosen the usual version of Philemon's end, found for example in Lucian (*Macr.* 25), in which Philemon dies of excessive laughter, as befits a comic poet; his story seems to match that of Aelian in his lost Περὶ Προνοίας, in which Philemon died in his sleep after finishing a play and seeing a vision of the Muses (note the book in Philemon's hand in Apuleius' version—16. 15).[88] The analogy between the end of life and the end of a play, on which Apuleius lays such stress (16. 17–18), is a frequent commonplace which is no doubt brought in here as (again) particularly appropriate for the death of a dramatist.[89] The poets of the New Comedy are prominent in the Second Sophistic, looking back to the great eras of Attic literature; Philemon himself is quoted by Plutarch, Lucian, Aelian, Athenaeus, and Diogenes Laertius, is the subject of an anecdote in Gellius (*NA* 17. 4), and received an honorific statue in Athens in the second century AD.[90] Apuleius' own knowledge of Philemon seems to be tralatician and garbled: he identifies him as a poet of the Middle Comedy rather than the New (16. 6 *mediae comoediae scriptor*), while his literary comments on the writer (16. 7–8) are conventional commonplaces very likely borrowed from another source.[91]

---

[86] Cf. Ch. 1 n. 121.   [87] Cf. Augustine *Ep.* 138. 19, and Ch. 1. n. 32.

[88] For the various versions of Philemon's death see the testimonia in Kassel and Austin (1989), 221–3, and the discussion in Lefkowitz (1981), 115–16.

[89] Cf. Cicero *De Sen.* 5 with J. G. F. Powell's note, Seneca *Ep.* 77. 20, Suetonius *Div. Aug.* 99, Max. Tyr. *Dial.* 1. 1, Helm (1906), 45–53, Dodds (1965), 8–11.

[90] Cf. Kassel and Austin (1989), 221–317, and *Inscr. Att.* 4266.

[91] For the conventional view of Philemon as equal or second to Menander, cf. Quintilian 10. 1. 72; for comments on Menander similar to those of Apuleius on Philemon cf. Quintilian ibid., Plutarch *Comp. Ar. et Men.* 853a ff. The list of stock characters in Apuleius (16. 9) recalls the lists of such characters in Terence's prologues (*Eun.* 36–8, *Heaut.* 37–9).

The real point of the Philemon anecdote (as with the Hippias material of *Flor.* 9) is a comparison of Apuleius himself with an analogous
celebrity. There is no evidence that the plays of New Comedy were ever
recited solo by the poet in an auditorium; Philemon's declamatory performance is likely to be invented in order to aid the analogy between
Philemon and Apuleius as great performers of literary quality, both of
whom are prevented by ill-health from making a public appearance, at
least according to Apuleius. Apuleius' version is in fact the only one in
which Philemon's ill-health plays a role, a detail surely invented to suit
Apuleius' own context and comparison with himself. The topic of ill-
health provides an explicit link to the speaker's account of his own injury
which has kept him from the auditorium (16. 19); indeed, Apuleius claims
that he nearly suffered Philemon's fate, but was able through treatment
to recover (16. 21–2). The description of Apuleius' symptoms (16. 20–5) is
very much in the sophistic mode: the self-absorption of virtuoso performers led to the writer's health, the care of the self, becoming a literary
topic.[92] This can be most famously seen in the Ἱεροὶ Λόγοι of Aelius
Aristides, one of the great hypochondriac journals of the age,[93] but is also
notable in such authors as Gellius and Fronto;[94] Apuleius may also be
looking back to the literary valetudinarianism of Horace in his talk of
recreation at watering-places.[95] The contemporary prestige of medicine
as an intellectual discipline is also brought out here:[96] Apuleius uses
quasi-technical terminology in describing his illness,[97] and not only was
the author of a work on medical botany but elsewhere shows an active
interest in the practice of medicine.[98]

Flor. 16 is a good example of Apuleius' high epideictic style; as an
apparently complete piece it also allows a rare strategic perspective in the
Florida on Apuleius' deployment of stylistic variation. It begins with a

---

[92] Cf. Bowersock (1969), 71–3, and esp. Gleason (1995), 84–7, against the background of
Foucault (1986).
[93] Cf. Behr (1968) and (1994); for a translation see Behr (1986), and on Apuleius' possible knowledge of this work cf. Ch. 6, Sect. 2 (ii).
[94] Fronto's valetudinarianism is a constant feature of his letters; Gellius' use of the theme
also shows its contemporary literary currency—cf. Holford-Strevens (1988), 224.
[95] e.g. Horace *Ep.* 1. 7, 1. 15.
[96] Cf. Ch. 1 n. 103.
[97] Cf. 16. 20 *tamen articulus loco concessit exque eo luxu adhuc fluxus est. Luxus* (only here)
is an Apuleian coinage for the technical *luxum* (Cato *De Agr.* 160, *TLL* 7. 2. 1934. 32).
[98] Gaide (1993), 42, suggests that Apuleius studied medicine in Rome, a possibility supported by the medical details of the *Apologia*—cf. *Apol.* 69. 2, 40. 1, Hunink (1997), ii. 123
and 183 n. 1.

rolling period of twelve lines with multiple subordination in the best Ciceronian tradition, but the trademarks of Apuleian diction are also very evident. Rhyming isocolon, both syndetic and asyndetic, is frequent (16. 1 *quam mihi praesenti honeste postulastis et absenti benigne decrevistis*), especially in ornamenting the tralatician information on Philemon's works (16. 7 and 16. 9). The brief asyndetic clauses of the description of the crowd waiting for Philemon (16. 12–13) both contrast with longer clauses elsewhere and vividly convey the atmosphere of expectation (we await both the star's appearance and the end of the sentence), while the prolonged reported obituary of the poet (16. 17–18), playing on the analogy of the end of a play and the end of life, gives an opportunity for further witty balances and word-plays, ending with the splendid *legenda eius esse nunc ossa, mox carmina* (16. 18).[99] The intended analogy between Philemon's death and Apuleius' near-death is reflected in the continuation of these witty word-plays and balances in the description of the latter at 16. 22 *ante letum abire quam lectum, potius implere fata quam fanda, consummare potius animam quam historiam.*

Following this is a somewhat 'philosophical' passage on the ethics of asking for, receiving, and giving thanks for gifts (16. 25–8). The flavour here is very much that of Roman theoretical debates on benefits and gratitude, a link encouraged by the evident logic-chopping in this passage.[100] The formal thanks to Carthage and Strabo appropriately reintroduces a more formal periodicity (16. 31–2), with several encomiastic topoi—e.g. 'you are the best of men who have ever lived'[101] or 'how can I find the words to thank you ?'[102] This is followed by the more businesslike argumentation about the statue (33–44), but at the end of the speech the peroration is again suitably lofty and periodic (16. 47–8), with the traditional literary personification of the book, travelling the Roman empire to praise not (as elsewhere) its author but its addressee.[103]

The speech gives a good view of Apuleius' status at his home city of Carthage. His excuse of absence is given to justify himself in the eyes of

---

[99] For similar puns on *legere* cf. Seneca *Ep.* 24. 21, *Priapea* 68. 2, *TLL* 7. 2. 1133. 13 ff.

[100] Cf. e.g. Cicero *Off.* 2. 52–71, Seneca *De Ben.* 2. 18–35.

[101] Cf. similarly Catullus 21. 2–3, 24. 2–3, Plautus *Persa* 777, *Bacch.* 1087, Cicero *Post Red. ad Quir.* 16, *Fam.* 11. 21. 1.

[102] Cf. e.g. Cicero *Phil.* 5. 35 *quibusnam verbis eius laudes huius ipsius temporis consequi possumus?*, Vergil *Aen.* 11. 125 *quibus caelo te laudibus aequem?*

[103] 16. 47 *gratias canam eique libro mandabo . . . uti per omnis provincias . . . laudes benefacti tui . . . repraesentet.* Cf. e.g. Horace *Ep.* 1. 20 (personified book travels the empire to commend its author), Ovid *Tr.* 3. 1. (personified book comes from farthest empire to Rome to commend its author).

his audience, whom he presents as continual witnesses of his civic dedication (16. 3). This notion has evident affinities with the Socratic idea of
the philosopher's life as wholly open to scrutiny, both by himself and by
his city,[104] but also shows Apuleius largely based at Carthage rather than
pursuing the semi-permanent travels typical of some contemporary
Greek sophists. He clearly regards himself as an instructor of his local
community: after first flattering them by assuming they know about
Philemon, he then proceeds to give them a potted account of his life and
works (16. 5–9). The status he seeks in an age when intellectuals are honoured is evident from the issue of the statue: like other sophists, Apuleius
is keen to extract marks of distinction from his city,[105] and the speech
makes it clear that this was not a formality. The speech also mentions
Apuleius' schooling (in Rome, presumably) along with Strabo (16. 36–7
commilitio studiorum . . . condiscipulum), and his election to a priesthood
(16. 38), which was probably the supreme priesthood of the imperial cult
in Africa Proconsularis; these details clearly represent the speaker as
belonging to the highest level of his society (the speech indeed implies
that he was himself a member of the Carthaginian senate). Clearly, like
most of the Greek sophists, Apuleius was an important member of his
local elite.[106]

Florida 17

A three-page prefatory discourse in praise of the proconsul Scipio
Orfitus, introducing a missing poem on the same topic. Apuleius opens
by disapproving of those speakers who (unlike himself) thrust themselves upon the attention of a proconsul, stresses his personal connection
with Orfitus, and discounts any previous criticisms he may have made of
Orfitus for his infrequent presence. By a neat implied transition of
thought (Orfitus' absence means that Apuleius cannot use his voice in
praise), the speech introduces a passage on the human voice, best exer-
cised in such activities as praising Orfitus in public, and after a brief contrast of Orpheus and Arion, singers in the wild, with himself, singer in the
city, Apuleius prepares to deliver a panegyrical poem of his own composition on Orfitus' virtues.

---

[104] Cf. Plato *Apol.* 33a–38b.
[105] Cf. Bowersock (1969), 26–9.
[106] On the question of Apuleius' priesthood cf. Ch. 1 n. 30; on the high social status of
sophists cf. Bowersock (1969), 17–25, Bowie (1982).

Here as in *Flor.* 9 the named proconsul yields a date: Ser. Cornelius Scipio Salvidienus Orfitus seems to have been proconsul of Africa in the year 163–4,[107] and the speech from which this extract is taken was evidently delivered in Carthage (17. 19 *Carthaginensium*) during that period, perhaps at its end (cf. 17. 19 *serum*) as a farewell panegyric to its governor (compare *Flor.* 9). The extract may be an opening, beginning from a reference to rival speakers (*quibus mos est . . .*) as from detractors in *Flor.* 9, and initially giving the full name *Scipio Orfite* (17. 1), perhaps a first address (*Scipio*, by contrast, at 17. 21). It matches *Flor.* 16 in being concerned with the praise of a great individual, and *Flor.* 18 in being an introduction to the performance of another Apuleian work.

The opening of the extract is clearly an implied criticism of Apuleius' rival speakers at Carthage, which has already been seen to be a frequent theme in the *Florida*.[108] This may be linked with the following double assertion of his high status, both as a well-known speaker at Carthage and as a long-standing connection of his proconsular addressee. Apuleius' apparent previous complaints about Orfitus' absence (17. 5) might perhaps reflect the discontent of the Carthaginian elite with a proconsul who had paid them insufficient attention (contrast the praise of the proconsul Severianus for his constant presence at Carthage at 9. 36), but are also calculated to demonstrate the familiarity between Apuleius and Orfitus through mutual connections at Rome (17. 4); thus they are cleverly turned to a compliment and assertion of friendship—Orfitus' absence has been lamented since friends ought to be together (a topic of Greek philosophy as well as of common social life).[109] All this implies Apuleius' high status, both as an honoured intellectual and representative of his community, and as one who is in some sense on a social level with the grand proconsul (we may compare the common schooling of Apuleius and Strabo in *Flor.* 16. 36).

The central section on the need of the human voice for exercise (17. 6–13) develops a number of commonplaces with typical Apuleian elaboration of both theme and style: note the ever-present rhyming isocolon (6–7) and the splendid image of the voice as a sword which will rust in disuse (8 *profecto ut gladius usu splendescit, situ robiginat, ita vox in vagina silentii condita diutino torpore hebetatur*).[110] Thematically, the comparison

---

[107] Cf. Syme (1959).   [108] Cf. n. 71.

[109] Cf. Aristotle *EN* 9. 12. 1–2, Cicero *De Am.* 15, 103.

[110] The image of sword and sheath for oratory seems to be drawn from Quintilian 8 pr. 15 *sine quo supervacua sunt priora* [i.e. precepts on *inventio*] *et similis gladio condito atque intra vaginam suam haerenti.*

of the public speaker with the tragic actor, implicit at 17. 8, goes back at least as far as Cicero, but it is also found in Dio Chrysostom, suggesting a sophistic currency;[111] Cicero, again, several times contrasts animal noises with the human voice,[112] a point which Apuleius ornaments with characteristically rhythmical isocolon in a list of animal noises (17. 11). For vocal performers like Apuleius and the contemporary Greek sophists, the human voice and its proper exercise and modulation was an important issue.[113] Also conventional is the use (introduced by an unmarked Vergilian quotation (here of *Ecl.* 8. 56), as in *Flor.* 3, 11, and 16) of the legendary lyre-players Orpheus and Arion (17. 15) as comparisons for the speaker, as recommended by Menander Rhetor (II. 392. 18 ff. R/W); there is clear contemporary interest in both these figures,[114] but their comparison with the speaker also recalls the similar use of the auletes Marsyas and Antigenidas in *Flor.* 3 and 4 (above). The implicit comparison of speaker and bird, a commonplace already noted in *Flor.* 13, is introduced by a characteristically balanced and colourful isocolon (17. 17) .

The reference in the last sentence to *cives ab eo servati* (17. 22) might at first sight suggest that Scipio had engaged in a military campaign in Africa; but there is no record of military activity in the peaceful Africa Proconsularis of the 160s, and the phrase may simply be a high-flown rhetorical compliment simply referring to a good and just governorship. The phrase recalls the traditional granting of the *corona civica* at Rome *ob cives servatos*, perhaps with an eye on the great and homonymous Scipiones of the Republic who really had saved their fellow-citizens, and who had been lauded by great literary men such as Ennius, as Apuleius is here praising Scipio Orfitus.[115] The extract clearly stops just at the point where the promised poem is to be recited.

Florida 18

In these six pages Apuleius compliments a Carthaginian audience for coming to hear a philosopher rather than less dignified rival attractions

---

[111] Cicero *De Or.* 1. 128, Dio *Or.* 19. 4.

[112] *De Or.* 1. 33, *De Inv.* 1. 5, *ND* 2. 148 with Pease's note; cf. Quintilian 2. 16. 12–18.

[113] Cf. Gleason (1995), 103–30.

[114] Orpheus and Arion: Dio *Or.* 19. 2, 32. 61. Orpheus alone: Aristides *Or.* 22. 1, Fronto *Ad M. Caes.* 2. 3. 3 (a Greek letter). Arion alone: Fronto *Arion*, a brief retelling of the Herodotean story (1. 23–4) which is very like the anecdotes of the *Florida*.

[115] On the Scipiones as saviours of Rome cf. e.g. Cicero *Rep.* 6. 12–13; on Ennius' *Scipio* see Vahlen (1903), 22–4. Apuleius might here be encouraging an assimilation of himself and Ennius—for his interest in Ennius see Ch. 1 n. 127.

(1–5). Apuleius will not provide a tragic or comic prologue evoking far-away scenes, but will rather call up the civic buildings of Carthage; his discourse is worthy of its senate-house and library (6–9). He claims that his improvisatory eloquence is inhibited by the large audience, although he is on home ground, in the place where he studied as a boy (10–14). He gives an account of his education, thanking Carthage for its part in it and promising the city a reward (15–18); he then tells anecdotes of Protagoras and Thales, repaid for their instruction of others in rather different ways (19–35). Finally, Apuleius states that he will sing a hymn in both Greek and Latin in honour of the god Aesculapius, prefaced by another work of his, a dialogue in the same two languages performed by two learned friends, which will depict the original context of Apuleius' performance of the hymn in the temple of Aesculapius (36–43). Like *Flor.* 17, this piece is clearly an introduction to another performance of a different kind, and looks to be complete as an introduction. The only indication of date comes at 18. 16, where Apuleius claims to have been performing in Carthage for some six years. Given that he was certainly performing there around 163–4 (*Flor.* 9 and 17), and probably could not have taken this up regularly before 158 since he was largely living in Oea in 156–8, this puts *Flor.* 18 some time in the mid- to late 160s, at much the same time as the securely dated pieces of the collection. The piece is a valuable source for the details of Apuleius' education, and he is clearly pleased to parade his cosmopolitan studies before his fellow-citizens.

The initial reference to other rival forms of entertainment matches those in *Flor.* 4 and 5, and as in those places suggests the context of a festival, perhaps (given the content of the lost hymn and dialogue, and the reference to Aesculapius' temple at 18. 42) a festival of Aesculapius, much worshipped at Carthage.[116] The quotations in sections 6–7, from an unidentified Republican tragedy (possibly the *Antiopa* of Pacuvius), and from Plautus' *Truculentus* (also cited in *Flor.* 2. 4), are both from prologues, stressing the introductory nature of the extract as well as Apuleius' fashionably archaic tastes (compare the quotation of Accius in *Flor.* 10, also from a prologue).[117] The section on Apuleius' professed

[116] Ch. 1 n. 23.

[117] On a less elevated level, quotation of openings sometimes shows that no more than the beginning of a work has been read. The attribution of the anonymous tragic fragment to the *Antiope* is the suggestion of Ribbeck (1897), 310, partly supported by Mattiacci (1994), 53 n. 5, who stresses that there is no firm evidence that the fragment is Pacuvian (it is not included as such in D'Anna (1967)). It is certainly similar to Euripidean prologues which combine a prayer to a god with an allusion to geographical setting—e.g. *Suppl.* 1, *Phoen.* 1.

nervousness before a massed audience is clearly a form of *captatio benev-olentiae* (10–14), not unlike the opening of *Flor.* 9, but also suggests that the speaker is presenting his discourse as previously unprepared. Such 'improvization' was one of the most admired techniques of the contem-porary Greek sophists,[118] and Apuleius is pointing out that he can do it too; three of the five sections of the 'false preface' to the *De Deo Socratis* (see pp. 130–2 below) seem to introduce 'impromptu' performances. The reference at 13 to performances elsewhere (*qui penes extrarios saepenu-mero promptissime disceptavi*), where *promptissime* again suggests 'improvization', is clearly put in to impress the Carthaginian audience, this time with the idea that the speaker is a celebrated international per-former, though the vagueness of *extrarios* is convenient. Apuleius had clearly spoken at Oea in the period 156–8 (*Apol.* 55), but we may reason-ably doubt whether he spoke much outside North Africa once he was set-tled in Carthage.

The anecdotes about Protagoras (19–29) and Thales (30–5) match those about Socrates (*Flor.* 2), Hippias (*Flor.* 9), Crates (*Flor.* 14 and 22), and Pythagoras (*Flor.* 15) in being concerned with famous Greek sophists or philosophers with whom Apuleius the *philosophus Platonicus* is keen to compare himself, and who were naturally popular figures in the liter-ature of the Second Sophistic. Both Protagoras and Thales receive biogra-phies in Diogenes Laertius' *Lives of the Philosophers* (1. 21–44, 9. 50–6), and Protagoras is also included in Philostratus' *Lives of the Sophists*. Further, the stories told of them here by Apuleius, evidently χρεῖαι, anec-dotes with attached witty sayings (as in *Flor.* 2, 4, and 14), are found else-where in sources that are likely to derive from some sophistic collection such as the Ἀπομνημονεύματα of Favorinus: that about Protagoras is found in part in Diogenes Laertius (9. 56) and wholly in Gellius (*NA* 5. 10), while that about Thales occurs in Julian (*Or.* 3. 162. 2).

The last section which formally introduces the forthcoming hymn and dialogue is informative. As in *Flor.* 1 and the *Apologia* (54–5), Apuleius presents himself as a man of religion (38 *sum enim non ignotus illi sac-ricola nec recens cultor nec ingratus antistes*), and as ever he claims that he is highly versatile, equally fluent in both Latin and Greek and in prose and poetry (cf. *Flor.* 9. 27–8, 20. 5–6, *Apol.* 4. 1). The hymns to Aesculapius are

---

[118] Gleason (1995), xix, 53, Philostratus *VS* 1. 8. 491 (Favorinus), 1. 21. 521 (Scopelian), 1. 25. 536 (Polemo), 2. 1. 565 (Herodes), 2. 4. 571 (Antiochus), 2. 17. 598 (Rufus); for improvization as an initial topic cf. Dio *Or.* 73. 1, for its appearance in Apuleius as a link with Greek sophists Sandy (1997), 150–1, and for it as a feature of the fifth-century sophists cf. Alcidamas *Soph.* 14–21 (though Philostratus *VS* 1. 18. 509 claims that it became popular only with Aeschines).

not described in detail except that they are to be in verse; for the bilingual dialogue we are given a self-promoting scenario which evidently owes much to the settings of some famous dialogues of Plato (18. 42).[119] An old schoolfriend of Apuleius from Athens is to ask someone who had been there what Apuleius said the day before at the temple of Aesculapius (was this the lecture on Aesculapius also said to have been delivered at Oea at *Apol.* 55. 10?), a conversation in Greek which is then joined by a Latin-speaking character. The two named participants in the dialogue (perhaps the otherwise unidentified schoolfriend was played by Apuleius himself?) are named as Sabidius Severus and Julius Persius (18. 39). It is possible (but unprovable) that these characters are pupils of Apuleius, something not perhaps inconsistent with their description, which suggests that they have already achieved a respectable position in Carthaginian public life (18. 40).[120] Apuleius might well have pupils in the true sophistic mode (the poetical Clemens of *Flor.* 7 may be another), but these two may again simply be worthy local friends enlisted for this special performance. The unusual bilingual dialogue indicates the relative strength of Greek at the cosmopolitan city of Carthage, not matched in the more distant parts of Africa Proconsularis, but it also of course demonstrates the proclaimed (if not complete) bilingualism of Apuleius himself.[121]

Florida 19

This thirty-four-line extract contains an anecdote about the doctor Asclepiades of Prusa, who practised in Rome in the first century BC. Asclepiades is praised for his use of wine as a restorative, and the story told, apparently set in Rome (note the bare *civitatem* at 19. 2—*the* city), concerns an occasion on which he revived an apparently dead man. Once more Apuleius presents an anecdote concerning a famous name from the past with whom he might himself seek comparison: Apuleius is clearly interested in the technicalities of medicine here and elsewhere, at least on

---

[119] Plato's *Symposium, Parmenides*, and *Protagoras* all open by presenting a meeting at which an earlier conversation is reported. This kind of framework plainly presents Apuleius as analogous to major philosophical figures such as Socrates, Parmenides, and Pythagoras whose discourses are worth preserving.

[120] Persius (or some member of his family) could be identical with the T. Julius Perseus recorded as one of the four public contractors for the province of Africa in an inscription on a bath complex near Carthage (*CIL* VIII 997); for this character's further links see Ch. 6 n. 190.

[121] For the extent of the bilingualism of Apuleius, and for Greek in North Africa, cf. Ch. 1 nn. 7 and 64.

one occasion seeming to have been consulted on medical matters (*Apol.* 48), and we are told in other sources that Asclepiades began as an orator and then turned to medicine.[122] The details of Asclepiades' medical methods and his curing of the apparently dead are both elements drawn from Pliny's *Natural History* (7. 124 and especially 26. 12–15), here as elsewhere a convenient source for Apuleius,[123] who seems simply to be ornamenting the plain tale found in Pliny: Pliny's two clauses *cum occurrisset ignoto funeri, relato homine ab rogo et servato* (26. 15) are fleshed out into more than a page with Apuleian circumstantial details. The resumptive *Asclepiades ille . . . is igitur* is a traditional narrative pattern that Apuleius often uses:[124] once again the passage looks like an opening (the *ille* in such contexts does not look back but rather suggests Asclepiades' general fame), for which such an anecdote would be suitable.

Florida 20

This thirty-line fragment opens with Apuleius' citation of a saying of an unknown sage concerning the various stages of drinking, a χρεία which is then cleverly applied to the stages of Apuleius' own education. The subject of varied education leads naturally to that of varied literary output: Apuleius celebrates his own versatility here, citing other examples of philosophers who have also written non-philosophical works. He concludes by praising the learning of his Carthaginian audience and of that city in general, with the splendid climax *Carthago provinciae nostrae magistra venerabilis, Carthago Africae Musa caelestis, Carthago Camena togatorum* (20. 10).

The striking image, the self-presentation, and the compliments to the audience suggest that once again this is the opening of or the prefatory discourse to a speech given at Carthage in praise of the city. The claims of literary versatility and references to education are repeated elsewhere, and provide important evidence for Apuleius' life and works (see Ch. 1, Sect. 2 (ii)). The unnamed sage at the beginning is the Scythian Anacharsis of the sixth century BC, a popular figure in the Second Sophistic who is the main character in Lucian's *Anacharsis* and receives a biography in Diogenes Laertius (1. 101–5); the fact that he is not named suggests that he was less familiar in the Roman West than the Greek East.[125] Several

---

[122] For Asclepiades in general cf. Vallance (1990); on Apuleius' medical interests cf. n. 98 above; on the career change of Asclepiades cf. Cicero *De Or.* 1. 62, Pliny *HN* 26. 12.

[123] On Pliny as a source for Apuleius cf. Ch. 1 nn. 105 and 109. [124] Cf. n. 44.

[125] On Anacharsis in the Second Sophistic cf. Kindstrand (1981), 3–4.

Greek versions of the χρεία given by Apuleius exist; no doubt he got it from a Greek source.[126] The list of subjects studied by Apuleius at Athens is suitably impressive and climaxes appropriately in philosophy (*[creterram] poeticae comptam,*[127] *geometriae limpidam, musicae dulcem, dialecticae austerulam, iam vero universae philosophiae inexplebilem scilicet <et> nectaream*), presenting the speaker in familiar Apuleian mode as an encyclopaedic intellectual and man of letters who is primarily a *philosophus*; the implied comparison with the list given here of Empedocles, Plato, Socrates, Epicharmus, Xenophon, and Crates suggest that versatility in learning and publication has a long and honourable tradition. This list names figures who are either used by Apuleius elsewhere as implied parallels for himself as a versatile philosophical intellectual, or who are seen as important philosophers in the age of the Second Sophistic.[128] The subjects named in the whole list include five of the complete set of nine found in Varro's *Disciplinae*[129]—grammar, dialectic, rhetoric, music, and geometry (the four omitted are the more technical arithmetic, astronomy, medicine, and architecture, on three of which Apuleius is reported to have written).[130]

Florida 21

This twenty-five-line piece argues that even pressing haste admits of honourable causes for delay, a point illustrated by a line of Lucilius (fr. 1278 Marx); this quotation, like those from Accius and Plautus in *Flor.* 2, 10, and 18, once again shows Apuleius demonstrating fashionably archaic tastes.[131] Even those riding rapidly to a destination will stop to salute an important and respectable man. Since the extract concludes before the subject of this analogy is revealed, the context of these remarks is unclear;

---

[126] Cf. the same version at Stobaeus 3. 18. 25; for an earlier and different version cf. Eubulus *PCG* 94. 6–12 with R. L. Hunter's note.

[127] Here I depart from Vallette's text: *comptam*, 'polished', is Leo's conjecture for the transmitted *comta*, while Vallette reads *commentam*, 'fictional' (apparently his own conjecture, but inappropriately derogatory here?). See Helm's apparatus for further suggestions; Helm himself prints Leo's conjecture.

[128] Empedocles, Plato, and Socrates are similarly named together as implicit comparisons for Apuleius at *Apol.* 27; for Xenophon in the Second Sophistic cf. Müncher (1920), 106–81. Most of Epicharmus' fragments (edited by Kaibel, 1899) are cited by Athenaeus, and a number from the lexicographer and sophist Julius Pollux, favourite of Commodus (on whom cf. Philostratus *VS* 2. 12. 592–4). On Athenaeus as a sophistic author cf. Reardon (1971), 226–7, Anderson (1993), 176–9.   [129] Cf. Simon (1968) and Ch. 1 n. 132.

[130] For this encyclopedic aspect of Apuleius' output cf. Ch. 1 n. 131.

[131] For Lucilius' popularity in Fronto and Gellius cf. Holford-Strevens (1988), 159–60, Marache (1952), 245 n. 2.

it suggests that the intention of Apuleius' discourse is diverted to praise an important personage who requires suitable honour from him—the emphatic *ex principalibus viris nobilem hominem, bene consultum, bene cognitum* (5) surely makes a pointed compliment to a real person. One ready identity for the important personage in the context of the *Florida* is a proconsul: perhaps a provincial governor has arrived unexpectedly where Apuleius is, whether in Carthage or another city, thereby impelling him to speak in his honour rather than on another planned topic, and so showing Apuleius' improvisatory powers. The gnomic opening certainly suggests that (as in *Flor.* 20) this is the beginning of a longer piece, and the slightly mysterious context would no doubt have been explained in what followed. The piece matches *Flor.* 1 in its elaborate comparison of speaker and traveller through an extended simile; it may have been an opening like *Flor.* 1 or the beginning of a major section within a speech. The elaborate description of the obstacles on the road for a rider shows typical rhyme and isocolon (21. 2–3): *propter molestias sarcinarum et pondera vehiculorum et moras orbium et salebras orbitarum —adde et lapidum globos et caudicum toros et collium clivos*; closely comparable in theme and style is the description of Lucius' bumpy ride to Hypata in the first book of the *Metamorphoses* (1. 2. 2 *ardua montium et lubrica vallium et roscida caespitum et glebosa camporum <emensus> emersi*). The passage is a massive single sentence, a syntactical *tour de force* articulated by parenthesis (*adde et*) and resumptive use of pronouns, a common Apuleian technique (*hisce, cum eo equo*),[132] as well as the standard expansive and rhythmical lists.

Florida 22

Like *Flor.* 14, this twenty-line passage concerns the Cynic Crates. As in *Flor.* 14, Apuleius is using common material: the detail that Crates was universally welcomed is found in Plutarch and Diogenes Laertius, and Plutarch also makes the comparison of Crates with Hercules, the hero adopted by the Cynics as model, while the analogy between Hercules' purging the world of monsters and Crates' ridding it of undesirable emotions follows the moralistic allegorization of the Labours of Hercules in Hellenistic philosophy.[133] Once again, Apuleius is selecting a famous philosopher from the past as his topic, perhaps as a comparison for him-

---

[132] Cf. n. 44.
[133] Plutarch *Quaest. Conv.* 2. 1. 6, Diogenes Laertius 6. 86, Plutarch *De Vit. Aer. Al.* 8. On the Cynic and moralized Hercules cf. Hoistad (1948), 33–73, and Galinsky (1972), 101–8.

self. This extract may be the opening of a speech: *Crates ille* recalls other openings of extracts in the *Florida* which may be prefatory (*Alexandro illi* in *Flor.* 7, *Asclepiades ille* in *Flor.* 19), with the pronoun looking forwards rather than backwards. It breaks off at a point where the topic is plainly Crates' conversion to philosophy, and may have been followed by more biographical material on Crates such as we find in *Flor.* 14. It is not impossible that *Flor.* 14 and 22 were part of the same speech, but the surviving book-divisions of the original *Florida* apparently put them in different books, assuming (perhaps unwarrantedly) that the extant *Florida* retains the order of the original four-book collection (see Section 1 above); it seems therefore more probable that Apuleius simply used similar material on Crates in two different places. Finally, *Flor.* 22 matches 11 in being evidently syntactically incomplete (the subordinate clause introduced by *ubi* (22. 6) has no following main verb); this may be due to damage in transmission, or to an excerptor who felt no need to extract complete sentences (compare the ending of *Flor.* 11).

Florida 23

This twenty-line passage contains two concrete illustrations elaborately developed: even a well-built and highly decorated ship will get into trouble without a helmsman to guide it, and a rich man surrounded by luxury still needs a doctor to forbid him food in order to get well, his wealth thus being no advantage. The principle being illustrated is clearly the vanity of external appearance and worldly prosperity: it seems very likely that the helmsman and doctor are presented as analogies for the philosopher, directing the lives of others to good effect and curing their ills, since both the philosopher as helmsman and the philosopher as doctor are well-known comparisons from the time of Plato and Platonizing writers contemporary with Apuleius.[134] This kind of moralistic self-presentation is common in the more philosophically inclined sophistic performers, for example Dio, Aristides, and Maximus.[135] The striking illustrations, developed fully like the elaborate simile of *Flor.* 1 or the elaborate scenario of *Flor.* 21, strongly suggest that this extract is another

---

[134] Cf. on these images of medicine and navigation in Plato, Wehrli (1951), Plato *Phil.* 56b, *Polit.* 299b–c; on the same in Aristides cf. Schmid (1887), ii. 260. They are especially common in Maximus of Tyre—cf. *Dial.* 8. 7, 13. 3–4, 30. 1–3 (with Trapp (1997a), 75 n. 33 and 352).

[135] On the moralizing stance of Aristides cf. Moreschini (1994a), on that of Dio see Desideri (1978); for Maximus see Trapp (1997a), xxxii–xlvii, Trapp (1997b). For popular moralizing in Apuleius and its contemporary context cf. Sandy (1997), 84–6.

opening. Finally, it is notable that F and the other manuscripts contain no *explicit* or formal mark of ending for the fourth book at the end of this last extract, suggesting that the *Florida* collection of our manuscripts is incomplete (see Section 1 above).

The 'False Preface' to the De Deo Socratis

As argued in Section 2, I believe that this material, transmitted continuously at the beginning of the *De Deo Socratis*, consists of five separate extracts accidentally sundered from the *Florida* in the course of its textual transmission. Their analogous length and content makes it clear that they belong with the *Florida* as excerpts from speeches: three allude to extempore speaking (cf. *Flor.* 18), one is a χρεία (cf. *Flor.* 2, 4, and 14), and the fifth is a passage marking a transition from Greek to Latin (cf. *Flor.* 18); some at least of them are prefatory, like many of the *Florida*, and one quotes Lucilius as in *Flor.* 21, possibly from the same context. These texts are here quoted in Beaujeu's numeration.

Extract I

A twenty-five-line passage, clearly a preface to an extempore discourse given its opening (103 *qui me voluistis dicere ex tempore, accipite rudimentum post eventum*); such 'improvization' was of course a key skill for a sophistic performer.[136] It is spoken to an audience which has heard Apuleius give non-improvized rhetorical performances (104 *postquam re probata meditata sunt*), very likely his habitual Carthaginian hearers; it also suggests that his improvizations are not uncommon before the same audience (104 *si qui tamen vestrum nondum subitaria cognostis*). The quotation of Lucilius (104) conveys the same archaizing flavour as that in *Flor.* 21, while the final comparison of the work in hand to a ship under sail is a common image in poetry, as Pliny notes (*Ep.* 8. 4. 5), but is also found in Cicero (*Tusc.* 4. 9) and Quintilian (10. 7. 23, 12. 10. 37), more likely models for Apuleius here.[137]

Extract II

A mere seven lines, citing a pithy χρεία of Aristippus, founder of the hedonist Cyrenaic school, and a frequent figure in sophistic literature

---

[136] Cf. n. 118.   [137] Cf. Fedeli (1985), 134 (on Propertius 3. 3. 22).

(though mentioned only here by Apuleius);[138] the same χρεία is otherwise first found in Diogenes Laertius (2. 68), and has a long subsequent history.[139] Its concern with the philosopher's relations with the great perhaps suggests that the story is intended to illustrate the dealings of the philosopher Apuleius with the great men of his own time, such as proconsuls (cf. *Flor.* 16 and 17), but all must remain speculation. The passage might be an opening, beginning a piece with a striking quotation from a famous philosopher as in *Flor.* 20; the initial *at ego*, apparently abrupt, would be paralleled by the similar opening of the *Metamorphoses* (1. 1 *at ego conseram . . .*).

Extract III

Sixteen lines, clearly from a prefatory *captatio benevolentiae* of a common self-depreciatory type. Whether these words actually constitute the opening of a speech seems excluded by *sententia sumpta est*, meaning 'I have taken up this idea', which implies that the nature of the idea has already been expressed by the speaker. The speaker apologizes for the crude nature of what he is about to deliver, comparing his speech to a roughly constructed building, a common type of metaphor:[140] nothing can be both hasty and well weighed. This image, together with the stress of the passage on haste (*verbo subito, de repentino, festinata, celeritatis*), strongly suggests that the speech is improvized, as in Extract I.

Extract IV

Forty-five lines; the first sentence indicates that this extract comes from the opening of an extempore discourse (cf. Extracts I and III), probably preserving its initial words (cf. Extract I). Apuleius wishes that what happened to Aesop's crow may not happen to him, and this introduces the well-known Aesopic fable of the fox and the crow, of which Apuleius' version is considerably the longest:[141] no doubt as in several of the *Florida* Apuleius is providing his own expanded version of a traditional story.

---

[138] Dio *Or.* 8. 1, Lucian *Dem.* 5, Max. Tyr. *Dial.* 1. 9.

[139] Cf. Beaujeu (1973), 167. No doubt it came from the kind of source tapped in *Flor.* 18—Favorinus or a similar collection of philosophical anecdotes.

[140] The metaphor of speech as architecture, though found in Cicero, is most extensively developed by Quintilian, a likely influence for Apuleius here (cf. n. 110 above); see Assfahl (1932), 46–7, a useful collection of material.

[141] For other versions cf. Babrius 77, Phaedrus 1. 13, *Aesopica* 124 Perry.

The narration of Aesopic fables (μῦθοι) is a standard rhetorical exercise in the handbooks of προγυμνάσματα and in the schools of the Roman empire, and a number appear in sophistic discourses;[142] this passage may be excerpted as a model for the technique.

Extract V

Twelve lines, clearly introducing the Latin part of a bilingual discourse which has up to this point been delivered in Greek; the link with *Flor.* 18, prefatory to a bilingual performance, is clear, though this performance is clearly a standard speech (113 *oratio*) rather than the dialogue of *Flor.* 18. The implication is that Apuleius is equally fluent in Latin and Greek, as he claims elsewhere,[143] and that his audience as in *Flor.* 18 will understand both languages (as they would do in Carthage, perhaps the most likely location for the speech). There is no indication of which Latin discourse this passage introduced; it is unlikely in my view to have been the *De Deo Socratis.*[144] The assertion that the Latin part of the discourse will be no worse than the Greek is appropriately cast in classic Apuleian rhyming isocolon, giving a foretaste of stylistic treats to come (113): *nec argumentis sit effetior nec sententiis rarior nec exemplis pauperior nec oratione defectior.*

4. PRINCIPLES OF SELECTION

I conclude from the evidence of transmission (Section 2 above) and the evidence of content (Section 3) that our extant *Florida* is a collection of extracts from a previous collection of the same title in four books. This, if accepted, entails that it is not itself an Apuleian selection, something also suggested by its crude state (for example, the incompleteness of *Flor.* 11 and 22). The original *Florida*, very likely issued by Apuleius himself, surely had the preface and other evidence of authorial care which are missing from the extant collection, and its original books surely contained more than ten or twelve pages each. Apart from the evidence of the title (see Section 2) and the fact that it contained rhetorical writing in

---

[142] Cf. Max. Tyr. *Dial.* 15. 5, 19. 2, 32. 1, 36. 1, Dio *Or.* 12. 7, 72. 13, and material in Lucian and Plutarch—cf. Holzberg (1993), 29–35.

[143] *Flor.* 9. 28, 18. 16; cf. also *Apol.* 36. 7–8.

[144] See Ch. 4, Sect. 2.

four books, the nature of the original *Florida* can only be conjectured. It seems unlikely to have been a complete collection of Apuleius' speeches; the *Apologia* by itself takes up two books according to the divisions in the manuscript F, and the collected speeches of Apuleius, who clearly enjoyed an extensive rhetorical career at Carthage, are likely to have occupied more than four books. The original four-book *Florida* was probably either a select group of speeches or an anthology of shorter passages similar to but larger than the extant *Florida*; such an anthology of καιρία, 'choice passages' from declamations, is mentioned for Herodes Atticus (Philostratus *VS* 2. 1. 565).

It has been argued that the extant *Florida* derive from an original collection of Apuleius' more informal prefatory discourses, *prologi* or *praefationes*, counterparts of the προλαλίαι or λαλίαι of Lucian or Dio.[145] Many of the *Florida* are clearly opening passages, and many share elements of content with extant προλαλίαι, for example the use of anecdotes and references to the speaker himself; but though most of the *Florida* would in some sense conform to this type, it is difficult to fit all its elements into this category, since several seem to belong to self-sufficient pieces tailored to a particular formal occasion rather than acting as introductions for other speeches or as personal short pieces. In particular, it would be difficult to see the elaborately contextualized and formally encomiastic 9 and 16 as in any sense προλαλίαι. The original collection may well have contained many such pieces, but plainly did not exclude other types of rhetorical performance.

What then are the elements which link the twenty-three extracts of the *Florida* and the five extracts of the 'false preface' of the *De Deo Socratis*, treated here as part of the *Florida*? Apart from being largely taken from proems and prefaces, all the extracts provide useful models of particular rhetorical techniques (for example, the extended simile or metaphor— *Flor.* 1, 11, 13, 20, 23). In particular, as already noted individually, many of the extracts can be related to known rhetorical training through the basic preliminary exercises (προγυμνάσματα, *primae exercitationes*) universally taught in the schools of the empire.[146] One notable exercise is that of the

---

[145] By Mras (1949*a*) and Steinmetz (1982), 192–202. There is an extant collection of Demosthenic prefaces (Clavaud (1974)), and Cicero had a collection of (his own) prefaces which he used for his *philosophica* (*Att.* 16. 6. 4). For sophistic προλαλίαι cf. Stock (1911), Mras (1949*b*), Russell (1983), 77–9, 83, 85, and Nesselrath (1990): some were evident introductions to other pieces, others could have stood alone without the longer pieces which they in fact introduced; but pieces like *Flor.* 9 and 16 simply do not fit this model.

[146] Cf. n. 20.

anecdote about a famous character, either in the form which contains a pithy remark by the famous person, the χρεία (*Flor.* 2, 14, 18, 20, 'false preface II'), or in the straight story, διήγημα or narration (*Flor.* 7, 9, 15, 19, 22). The four extracts praising distinguished men (*Flor.* 8, 9, 16, 17) give examples for the ἐγκώμιον or panegyric, while the retelling of the Aesopic fable of the crow and the fox in 'false preface IV' is a classic example of the μῦθος or narration of a fable, and there are several prominent instances of ἔκφρασις or formal description (*Flor.* 6, 12, 15).

There are also broader links of subject matter between the extracts. Many mention Carthage, reasonably enough since it was clearly Apuleius' main base in the relevant period, but its prominence, especially in *Flor.* 20, suggests that our selection may have been made by someone based at or with an interest in Carthage. There are some apparent sequential groups.[147] *Flor.* 3 and 4 both begin from famous auletes, 6 and 7 concern India and Alexander who first reached it, 12 and 13 talk of birds, 16 and 17 are both praise of great men at Carthage; these reflect Apuleian interests, but also possibly the tastes of a later editor. The large number of extracts about famous philosophers (2, 14, 15, 18, 22) suggest, as we have seen, a concern of the Second Sophistic and of a *philosophus Platonicus* to talk about other philosophers, but again may also show an editorial interest. It has also been been argued that the order of the extracts preserves a chronological sequence;[148] but if *Flor.* 16 is to be dated to the late 160s, as seems likely, this structure cannot hold (*Flor.* 9 is plausibly dated to 162–3, 17 to 163–4—see above).

It seems likely to me that these extracts are selected by a post-Apuleian editor as in some sense technical models for the rhetorical instruction of later generations. One piece of evidence in this direction is the common ground which has emerged in the above analysis between the extracts of the *Florida* and the προγυμνάσματα, the basic techniques of composition as taught in the Roman empire.[149] The evidence of transmission (see Section 1) suggests that the selecting hand which produced the extant *Florida* (as opposed to the original four-book collection) was not that of the author. The interests shown in the selection of the extant *Florida* are

---

[147] Cf. Opeku (1974), 24–5. The argument of Elsom (1984) that the *Florida* is a continuous, coherent, and unified literary work is difficult to accept given its character as an anthology (cf. Sect. 1 above).

[148] By Opeku (1974), 22–4.

[149] Of the fourteen προγυμνάσματα listed by Kennedy (1983), 60–6, from the late Greek empire but unlikely to have changed much since Hellenistic times, at least seven have been identified in my analysis of the *Florida*.

not those of a sophistic speaker wishing to preserve his best work in an impressive anthology, but those of someone whose fundamental interest is education in rhetorical technique. This has led to a suggestion of an identity for the editor—Crispus Sallustius, the known editor of Apuleius' *Metamorphoses* and *Apologia*, who was working in Rome at the end of the fourth century AD, and was a known rhetorical teacher.[150] The suggestion is not implausible, especially if he were a North African, interested in Carthage and drawing from an existing four-book collection by the greatest African stylist an uneven gathering of convenient passages for use in the instruction of pupils.

---

[150] So Pecere (1984); for Crispus Sallustius' activities as a teacher of rhetoric in Rome cf. Canfora (1980). Pecere's view (see also Pecere (1987)) that the *Florida* is acephalous because copied into F from an exemplar different from that of the *Metamorphoses* is fascinating but unprovable.

4

Popular Philosophy: *De Deo Socratis*

1. GENRE, SOURCES, DATING

The *De Deo Socratis* is the only one of the three extant philosophical books transmitted together under the name of Apuleius of which the authenticity is not disputed. It is neither a tralatician doxographical treatise like the *De Platone*, nor a translation of a known Greek philosophical text like the *De Mundo* (for these two works see Chapter 5), but a popular philosophical lecture of the kind widespread in the Greek Second Sophistic, adapted for a Latin-speaking audience.[1] This chapter will not engage with the extensive technical discussions of the philosophical colour and influences shown in the *De Deo Socratis*, though it assumes a generally Platonist stance consistent with Apuleius' self-presentation as a *philosophus Platonicus*; nor will it deal with the finer points of ancient demonology raised by the Apuleian text, which have been more than adequately treated by others. What follows will be mainly directed towards the literary aspects of the work, which have been less often discussed and which have considerable interest.[2]

---

[1] For a summary of work on the *De Deo Socratis* for the period 1940–90 see Bajoni (1992), 362–5, and for an account of earlier work Beaujeu (1973), 16–18. Of more general treatments, Rathke (1911) and Barra (1960–1) are still useful; the best introduction is Beaujeu (1973), 3–18. Modern scholarly texts of the work are to be found in Beaujeu (1973) and Moreschini (1991); the most useful commentary is that in Beaujeu (1973), 201–47, and there are useful notes and an extensive introduction in the German translation of Bingenheimer (1993). The brief Italian editions of Barra and Pannuti (1962–3), Del Re (1966), and Portogalli Cagli (1992) contain a few notes, sometimes useful. There is no English translation currently in print, or any that I can discover more recently than Anonymous (1893); I am preparing one myself at present.

[2] Apart from a limited amount in Beaujeu (1973), only the brief treatments of Barra (1960–1) and Di Giovine (1981) have much of interest here (and both concentrate on Lucretian influence). On the philosophy and demonology of the *De Deo Socratis* the collection of material by Vallette (1908) remains very helpful; see also more recently Beaujeu (1973), 183–201, Dillon (1977), 317–20, Moreschini (1978), Gersh (1986), 228–36, 309–15, Bingenheimer (1993), 35–84, Bernard (1994), and Habermehl (1996).

Some works of this type in Greek are to be found in the so-called *Moralia* of Plutarch, for example the short declamation on superstition, *De Superstitione* (*Mor.* 164e–171e),or that on the Epicurean motto 'live unnoticed', *De Latenter Vivendo* (*Mor.* 1128a–30c),[3] both lively rhetorical treatments of philosophical commonplaces, presented in the first person rather than dialogue form and embellished with poetical quotations, elements (as we shall see) central to Apuleius' own technique in the *De Deo Socratis*; Plutarch's contemporary Dio Chrysostom also produced a number of short works of a similar kind, for example his discourses on greed (*Or.* 17) or on retirement (*Or.* 20), and many of the sophistic discourses of which we have only sketchy reports must have been of this nature.[4] Later, in the second half of the second century, a notable exponent of this type of writing is Maximus of Tyre. His forty-one *Dialexeis*, covering a wide range of issues in ethics, are brief philosophical sermons of a distinctly personal kind, shorter, less polished, and more informal than the *De Deo Socratis*, but similarly lively, ornamented with tags from the poets, and concerned with promoting the doctrines associated by the writer with Plato, which in second-century Middle Platonism included many views adapted from other philosophical schools.[5]

Two of Maximus' *Dialexeis* (8 and 9) in fact concern the same subject as Apuleius' work, the *daimonion* of Socrates. This is the personal divine voice or guardian recorded in the works of Plato and Xenophon as giving Socrates advice on crucial occasions,[6] and was a favourite topic of writers of the Greek Second Sophistic; this is unsurprising given their interest in Plato's works and in the character of Socrates,[7] and the general concern of intellectuals in the first few centuries AD with ideas about intermediate divine powers.[8] Discussion of the *daimonion* of Socrates usually led on to the discussion of the associated class of *daimones* in general, beings commonly characterized as having a status somewhere

[3] Both to be found in useful annotated English translations in Russell (1993).

[4] e.g. the lost discourses of Favorinus, from the generation before Apuleius, on popular wisdom, prayer, old age, Socrates the lover, the philosophy of Homer, and the character of philosophers (fr. 6–23 Barigazzi).

[5] On Maximus see the excellent annotated translation with introduction in Trapp (1997a), and the illuminating general account in Trapp (1997b); I am very grateful to their author for the opportunity to see both these works before publication.

[6] Plato *Euth.* 3b, *Apol.* 31d, 40b, *Phaedr.* 242b–c; [Plato] *Theages* 128e, 151a; Xenophon *Mem.* 4. 8. 1–5, *Apol.* 4, *Symp.* 8. 5.

[7] For the *daimonion* of Socrates in the Second Sophistic cf. Trapp (1997a), 67–8; for literary interests in Plato in the period cf. e.g. Anderson (1993), 173.

[8] See conveniently Beaujeu (1973), 195–201.

between gods and men, and prominent in Plato and the early Academy. Plutarch, already mentioned as a precursor in the field of the philosophical lecture, also composed a treatise on this same subject, commonly known as *De Genio Socratis* (*Mor.* 575a–598f). Here, in the form of a Platonic dialogue, Plutarch expounds ideas about the *daimonion*, without much interest in the larger question of *daimones*; this material is surrounded and indeed eventually overtaken by a melodramatic historical plot concerned with the liberation of Thebes from Spartan domination in 379 BC.[9] Plutarch's work shows that Socrates' *daimonion* was well established as a literary topic before Apuleius, but his treatment does not contribute much to the *De Deo Socratis,* though it shares some basic elements of exposition of Platonic doctrine. Much closer to Apuleius' approach is that to be found in the linked *Dialexeis* 8 and 9 of Maximus, which move on from Socrates' *daimonion* to *daimones* in general (8. 1–6 concern Socrates, 8. 7–8 and 9 the general issue, without indeed returning to the question of Socrates), and make a number of points and arguments also to be found in Apuleius, including one striking verbal parallel at *De Deo Socratis* 8. 1.

The clear similarities between Maximus and Apuleius raise the question of the date and sources of the *De Deo Socratis.* The *Dialexeis* are usually dated to the reign of Commodus (AD 180–92), which suggests that they are later than the *De Deo Socratis* unless that is a very late work of Apuleius; but Maximus seems to have been an exact contemporary of Apuleius who was born in the 120s AD and achieved literary reputation as early as the 150s, and some of the *Dialexeis* may well have been available earlier than 180.[10] Though an Apuleian *De Deo Socratis* from the 180s or 190s is by no means impossible,[11] it seems more likely to belong some twenty years earlier with Apuleius' other datable epideictic performances in the *Florida*. The original audience of the *De Deo Socratis* is clearly Latin-speaking, since at one point the speaker says he will discourse in Latin for the clearer understanding of his addressees;[12] all the quotations with which it is liberally sprinkled are from Latin writers, and even a line from such a well-known Greek text as Homer is cited somewhat ostenta-

---

[9] See the useful annotated translation in Russell (1993).

[10] See Trapp (1997a), xi–xii.

[11] For our uncertainty about the later career of Apuleius see Ch. 1, Sect. 1.

[12] *DDS* 150 *id potius praestiterit, latine dissertare.* Bingenheimer (1993), 68–9, argues that the work must have had a bilingual audience for Apuleius to achieve just credit for his Latin version of a Greek doctrine, but this seems unconvincing.

tiously in Apuleius' own translation rather than in the original.[13] This, combined with a group of honorific references to Africa, Egypt, and the god Aesculapius, particularly prominent as we have seen in Carthage, strongly suggests that the *De Deo Socratis* matches the *Florida* in being delivered to a Carthaginian audience[14] in the 160s or 170s; its close affinities with the language and style of the *Florida* also indicate this—it too shows a highly ornamented epideictic style leavened with anecdotes and literary quotations.[15] Thus, unless the Greek Maximus is using the Latin text of Apuleius, inherently unlikely given the traditional Greek subject matter (there would no doubt be a ready array of Greek sources for easier use) and the general tendency of Greek sophists not to use Latin sources, the similarities between the two will be due to a common (Greek) source.

This is perhaps supported by the differences between the two works, which are most economically explained by the two authors' different use of the same material. As we have seen, Maximus moves from the specific case of Socrates to general *daimon*-theory, while Apuleius, as we shall see, does the opposite; the case of Socrates is mentioned for the first time at *DDS* 150 and first substantially discussed at 157, well over half-way through the work, which opens with Plato's general classification of beings. The striking verbal echo already mentioned also suggests mutual dependence on a third source. Maximus begins *Dialexis* 8 with the words:

You seem surprised (θαυμάζεις εἰ) that Socrates should have enjoyed the company of a benevolent prophetic *daimonion*, which was his constant companion and an all but inseparable element of his mind—even though he was a man pure in body (ἄνδρι καθάρῳ) and blessed with a virtuous soul, meticulous in the conduct of his life, a shrewd thinker, an eloquent speaker, pious towards the gods and holy in his dealings with men.

It is difficult to believe that this is not related to *DDS* 157 *igitur mirum si Socrates, vir adprime perfectus et Apollinis quoque testimonio sapiens, hunc deum suum cognovit et coluit . . .?*[16] The matching opening expressions of wonder (θαυμάζεις εἰ ~ *igitur mirum si*), the incredulous rhetorical questions, and the stress on the great virtue of Socrates similarly expressed

---

[13] *DDS* 145 *versum Graecum* [i.e. *Il.* 1. 198], *si paulisper opperiamini, latine enuntiabo: 'soli perspicua est, aliorum nemo tuetur'.*

[14] So also Bingenheimer (1993), 67 and 171; on Aesculapius at Carthage cf. Ch. 1 n. 23.

[15] On the stylistic affinities of *De Deo Socratis* and *Florida* cf. Bernhard (1927), 344–5.

[16] The translation is from Trapp (1997a). The striking echo has not, I think, been noted elsewhere.

(ἄνδρι καθάρῳ ... ~ *vir adprime perfectus*) all suggest a common origin; both authors are also raising an obvious problem, why the wise Socrates needed a *daimonion* in the first place, which is likely to have featured in previous writing on the subject. Both are also doing so at the start of their treatment of the *daimonion* in particular, Maximus at the beginning of his work, Apuleius half-way through. The most persuasive explanation is that the two are both adopting a standard introduction to the discussion of Socrates' *daimonion*.

Thus, as so often, Apuleius takes up a traditional theme prominent in the contemporary writing of the Greek Second Sophistic and turns it into a Latin and Roman form for a Western audience. Though it is not impossible that it is a translation of a particular lost Greek work, it seems more likely to be an adaptation for a specific occasion of general Greek material.[17] The didactic character of the *De Deo Socratis* is clear; interesting here is the large number of allusions it makes to the work of Lucretius, whom Apuleius might well have seen as an illustrious predecessor in the didactic presentation of Greek philosophy to a Roman audience, though the philosophical works of Cicero and Seneca are also laid under contribution, no doubt for the same reason.[18] Apuleius is also pursuing a topic which he as a writer finds intriguing; apart from *De Deo Socratis*, the issue of *daimones* exercises him in the *Apologia*, and is prominent in the *De Platone*.[19] *Daimones* do not find a place in the worlds of Fronto and Gellius. They fit much more the colourful and exotic image of Apuleius and his notionally pious interest in esoteric religions, well documented in the *Apologia*, where *daimones* also make a brief appearance,[20] and of course they fit his self-proclaimed character as a *philosophus Platonicus*, since *daimon*-theory had since Xenocrates been the accepted province of Platonism.

---

[17] For discussion of whether the *De Deo Socratis* could be a translation of a Greek work see Bingenheimer (1993), 74–6. The dichotomy *Graecus aut barbarus* at 119 may look like good evidence of a text deriving from a Greek original, but in context *Graecus* refers to Plato, while *barbarus* picks up *Chaldaei* (117).

[18] On Lucretian echoes see Barra (1960–1), 110–13, Di Giovine (1981), and the useful notes in Beaujeu (1973). Lucretius is also quarried in the *De Mundo*: for details see Bajoni (1994) and Ch. 5 below. For echoes of Cicero and Seneca see the notes in Beaujeu (1973) and the *index fontium* in Moreschini (1991); further parallels are suggested in this chapter. On the more generally didactic character of the *De Deo Socratis* see Bingenheimer (1993), 73.

[19] For Apuleius' consistent interest in *daimones* see Vallette (1908), 221–90, and for his demonology and its contemporary context see the works listed in n. 2 above.

[20] For *daimones* in the *Apologia* see *Apol*. 43. 1; for piety and religious interests cf. *Apol*. 55. 8–56. 2, 61–5.

2. PROBLEMS OF TEXTUAL TRANSMISSION

The manuscripts of the philosophical works of Apuleius present us with five paragraphs as a preface to the *De Deo Socratis*, sometimes known as the 'false preface'. As suggested in Chapter 3, these paragraphs clearly belong to the *Florida*, and should be treated as further extracts from the end of that collection, wrongly placed at the head of the *De Deo Socratis* through an incorrect division of manuscripts when the philosophical works of Apuleius were separated from the *Metamorphoses*, *Apologia*, and *Florida*. Some scholars have argued that the fifth and final paragraph deserves more consideration as a possible preface to the *De Deo Socratis*, and their assertions merit scrutiny.[21] The fifth paragraph, as we saw in Chapter 3, introduces the Latin part of a discourse which has until then been given in Greek. That this discourse is the *De Deo Socratis* seems fundamentally unlikely, given its clear direction towards a Latin-speaking audience which requires Apuleius to translate even Homer (see above).[22] Advocates of the fifth paragraph have, however, pointed to *DDS* 150, where Apuleius refers to having discussed already (*ut iam prius dictum est*) the reason why the prosperous and happy are called εὐδαίμονες in Greek (because of having a good *daimon*). This discussion does not occur in the extant *De Deo Socratis*, and this leaves five possibilities: (i) the cross-reference is careless and erroneous, (ii) it is a deliberate ploy by Apuleius to give the impression in his written text of an improvized discourse, improvization being so highly prized by sophistic performers, (iii) it is an allusion to the earlier Greek part of the speech imagined by advocates of the fifth paragraph as preface, (iv) it is an allusion to a work of Apuleius other than the one in progress, or (v) it is an allusion to another part of the *De Deo Socratis* now lost. Of these, (i) seems unlikely in the context of a lecture-performance, where the speaker is otherwise clear about what he has said, and (ii) is over-subtle and would be a double-bluff of a kind unparalleled in Apuleius' extant works, while (iii) is again unpersuasive given the intrinsic improbability of an original Greek part of the *De Deo Socratis* (see above). Option (iv) could be true if it refers to a previous speech before Apuleius' habitual Carthaginian audience, but this requires an unacceptable stretching of the sense of *iam prius dictum*, which surely means 'spoken by me in this speech' (*scriptum* would be different). This leaves (v), the least unattractive possibility, and

---

[21] For a bibliography of the issue see Ch. 3 n. 5. The view that the fifth paragraph alone belongs to the *De Deo Socratis* is that of Hijmans (1994), 1781–2.

[22] This crucial point has not been stressed enough in the discussion.

plausible because it is likely on other grounds that there is an earlier section of the *De Deo Socratis* which has been lost and in which such a passage about *daimones* might have occurred.

For the *De Deo Socratis* shows every sign of being an acephalous work. It begins abruptly with Plato's division of the world into various types of beings, with no introduction of the theme to the audience, no explanation of terms, and no indication at all of how all this fits into the general argument about the *daimonion* of Socrates. Such a brusque beginning and lack of connection with the title of the work (assuming that it *is* the original title)[23] is inappropriate for a sophistic writer such as Apuleius, whose concern for elaborately worked prefaces is clear in his other works, especially in the fragments of the *Florida*, many of the items in which are clearly prefatory (see Chapter 3). It seems therefore as if the original preface has been lost, easy enough at the beginning of a work; the same may well have happened at the beginning of the disputed *De Platone* (see Chapter 5). Such a preface might well have contained a passage to which the cross-reference at *De Deo Socratis* 150 alludes, a discussion of the term *eudaimon*; this would easily have fitted into an initial definition of what a *daimon* or *daimonion* was, a necessary preliminary for the non-Greek-speaking audience of the *De Deo Socratis* and indeed to any discussion of the *daimonion* of Socrates. This information is given in the extant text at *DDS* 132–3, but might well have been briefly mentioned at the outset; there is every reason why definition of terms should occur in a preface. Thus the empty cross-reference at *DDS* 150, far from supporting the idea that the fifth paragraph of the 'false preface' might be the real preface of the *De Deo Socratis*, leads us to the conclusion that the real preface has been lost in transmission. The same conclusion is indicated by the very abrupt way in which the *daimonion* of Socrates is mentioned for the first time more than half-way through (150), introduced as if already defined as the subject of the work.

It is also possible that the work has lost not just its original preface but also its original conclusion; the ending of a work, like its beginning, is particularly apt to vanish in transmission. As it stands, the *De Deo Socratis* draws to a close (176–8) with an examination of the figure of

---

[23] Beaujeu (1973), 201–3, discusses the title, plausibly suggesting that Apuleius used the word *deus* instead of *daimonion* as more familiar for his Latin-speaking audience. *Deus* is also perhaps less invidious: as Augustine in fact suggested (*Civ.* 8. 14), *daimon/daimonion* may also have been excluded in the title since it refers to evil spirits by Apuleius' time, as in New Testament usage—cf. E. Schweizer in *RAC* 9. 692–700.

Ulysses as philosophical sage, a traditional topic,[24] and actually ends strikingly but rather suddenly (178) with an impressively epigrammatic paragraph of balanced sentences on the subject of Ulysses' virtues (see Sect. 3 (ii) III below). There is no attempt at a formal conclusion or a return to addressing the audience, the kind of overt closural markers which we find in the longer speeches in the *Florida* and would expect here.[25] The most obvious interpretation is that the work has broken off before its appointed close, though it is always possible that the extant ending is that originally intended, given that the final paragraph with its well-marked formal structure has some closural effect.

One final piece of evidence which has been used to argue for textual damage in the *De Deo Socratis* is 119, where Apuleius promises a future discussion of the nature of the moon, which does not appear in the extant work (*nam hoc postea videro*). However, the direction in which the *De Deo Socratis* moves after this point more or less precludes the inclusion of this topic, even if the ending is lost, and such prospective assertions do not have the same veridical force as retrospective statements such as that at 150, since there is room for a change of mind or omission. Two possible explanations suggest themselves. The first is that Apuleius here seems to imitate the famous claim at Lucretius 5. 155 *quae tibi posterius largo sermone probabo*, which promises a full treatment of the gods, not to be found in the extant *De Rerum Natura:* the apparent verbal links *postea* (~ *posterius*) and *videro* (~ *probabo*) in Apuleius support this, as does the quotation from the same book of Lucretius (5. 575 *notham iactat de corpore lucem*) which occurs immediately before the Apuleian statement (*DDS* 118). In this case Apuleius' claim would allude to that of Lucretius, presumably in the full knowledge that the Lucretian promise was similarly unfulfilled. This would be a subtle literary allusion, perhaps oversubtle. The second explanation is more basic. *postea* could refer not to the *De Deo Socratis* but to a future discourse in which the speaker will deal with this topic, and if as already suggested the *De Deo Socratis* is being delivered to Apuleius' habitual audience at Carthage, this would make very good sense.[26] Whichever of these is the more plausible, Apuleius' promise must above all be considered in its rhetorical context, where its prime function is as a token of his learning: he is able and willing to dis-

---

[24] Buffière (1956), 365–91, Stanford (1963), 121–7, Lamberton (1986), 360.

[25] e.g. *Flor.* 9. 40, 16. 48.

[26] Precisely the same point is made by Max. Tyr. *Dial.* 8. 7, tr. Trapp (1997a): 'This is a topic about which I must speak to you again on a subsequent occasion.'

course on the rival theories of the source of the moon's light, but he must get on with the business in hand, which is another topic, and it is simply not important that he never returns to this interesting subject. Given this rhetorical aspect and the explanations just offered, the promise is not conclusive evidence that there is a lacuna in the text of the *De Deo Socratis* somewhere after 119.

3. STRUCTURE AND ANALYSIS OF THE WORK

(i) *Structure*

The *De Deo Socratis* clearly divides into four main parts: the initial classification of beings into gods and men, the former including *daimones* (115–32), the general account of *daimones* (132–56), the discussion of the *daimonion* of Socrates (157–67), and a concluding exhortation to follow the example of Socrates more generally in the practice of moral philosophy (168–78).[27] This structure clearly shows that Apuleius' main interest is the general exposition of Platonic theory about *daimones*, and that the particular issue of Socrates' *daimonion*, which provides the title of the work but takes up less than a sixth of its space, is evidently subordinate. Here we should be cautious, since as Helm argues it is perfectly possible that a lost opening section of the work contained more material about Socrates.[28] But the extant arrangement is not unlike the treatment of the same topic in Maximus *Dialexeis* 8 and 9, where Socrates' *daimonion* takes about a third of the space and *daimones* in general two-thirds, or even Plutarch's *De Genio Socratis*, where the issue of Socrates' *daimonion* eventually becomes subordinate to the historical setting (see Sect. 1 above), though the work provides a more detailed discussion of the *daimonion* than either Apuleius or Maximus, and does not say much about *daimones* in general. Of course, the *daimonion* of Socrates was not an inexhaustible topic in itself, and the linking with it of a discussion of *daimones* in general was an obvious strategy, but Apuleius seems to concentrate disproportionately on the latter.

Also original to the Apuleian treatment is the final section, encouraging his audience to turn to self-contemplation and the good life of philosophy. In theme this is a standard προτρεπτικὸς λόγος, following a

[27] For further discussion of the structure cf. Beaujeu (1973), 5–7, and Bingenheimer (1993), 72–3.

[28] Helm (1900), 601–3.

tradition which goes back to Plato's *Euthydemus*, Aristotle's lost *Protrep-ticus*, and Cicero's lost *Hortensius*;[29] its presentation is in diatribe mode, and strongly recalls the *Epistles* of Seneca (see Sect. 3 (ii) III below). Its relation to the remainder of the subject matter of *De Deo Socratis* is some-what tenuous; Apuleius makes the link by presenting Socrates as the exemplar of philosophical virtue which all are urged to follow (168), but the section has no concern with *daimon*-theory, being largely a tissue of general and familiar topics of popular ethics. As suggested in Section 2 above, this final section may once have been followed by further material, whether more of the same or different in tone, since there is some possi-bility that an original ending has been lost.

(ii) *Analysis*

I. *Gods and Men* (115–32)

The work begins from the tripartite division of beings into astral gods, non-astral gods, and men, ascribed to Plato (115). In fact, this division is not found in the works of Plato, though it is similar to several of his clas-sifications; it is first firmly encountered in the writings of Pythagorean theorists in the first century BC. This is a good example of the way in which views not held by Plato but which had come to be accepted by the flexible and eclectic Middle Platonism of the second century AD could be retrospectively ascribed to the master himself, a phenomenon frequently encountered both in the *De Deo Socratis* and in the other philosophical writings ascribed to Apuleius, and Apuleius himself seems particularly fond of tripartite divisions in his philosophical expositions.[30] The three parts are then dealt with in order: the astral or visible gods, the invisible gods, and men and their distance from the gods.

(a) *Astral gods* (115–20). From the first Apuleius shows that literary and rhetorical interests are as important as philosophical doctrine in this work: the account of the astral gods begins with a quotation from the proem of the first *Georgic* (116 = *Georg.* 1. 5–6), suggesting perhaps an analogy between Apuleius' didactic speech and Vergil's didactic poem (we have noted already the strong Lucretian didactic colouring in the *De*

---

[29] See conveniently Rutherford (1989), 23–4.

[30] On the flexible interpretation of Plato in Apuleius cf. Hijmans (1987) and Gersh (1986), 215–328; on Apuleian tripartition see Gersh (1986), 227–53, though he is perhaps over-disposed to find it.

Deo Socratis).[31] The order in which the astral bodies are treated is that of Cicero's *De Natura Deorum*, which is a significant model here for Apuleius as writer of philosophical didactic prose, just as the forensic speeches of Cicero provide an important model for the *Apologia*.[32] Particularly notable is the *ekphrasis* of the moon (116–17):

diei opificem lunamque, solis aemulam, noctis decus, seu corniculata seu dividua seu protumida seu plena sit, varia ignium face, quanto longius facessat a sole, tanto largius conlustrata, pari incremento itineris et luminis, mensem suis auctibus ac dehinc paribus dispendiis aestimans.

The archaic and poetic vocabulary, the balancing clauses in apposition or articulated by correlatives, the use of rhythm and rhyme (*quanto longius . . . tanto largius*), the multiple anaphora of *seu*, the colourful and continued financial metaphor of *incremento, auctibus, dispendiis*, and *aestimans*—all these elements are typical of the high Apuleian epideictic style which we see also in the *Florida* and the heightened parts of the *Apologia* and *Metamorphoses*.[33] And this stylistic richness is expended on the moon, a topic which is, as Apuleius himself implies, only marginally relevant to the topic of the work in hand. It would be difficult to find clearer evidence that this work is at least as much concerned with rhetorical and literary display as with philosophical content, a strongly sophistic sense of priorities.

The discussion of the other stars continues in much the same vein, incorporating a quotation from Lucretius, specifically named (118 *notham iactat de corpore lumen* = *DRN* 5. 575, see Sect. 2 above), and an unattributed second citation, from the *Aeneid* (120 *Arcturum pluviasque Hyadas geminosque Triones* = *Aen.* 1. 744 and 3. 516); typically for this work, the authority of Plato is joined with that of these Latin poets (120 *qui cum Platone sentis*). The *Aeneid* citation is immediately preceded by an archaic imperative (*locato*, 120) of a type particularly common in didactic contexts from Cato's *De Agri Cultura* to the *Georgics*,[34] and by another typically epideictic paragraph on the traditional topic of the majestic motion of the planets (120):

---

[31] On Lucretius see n. 18; note that *Georg.* 3. 80–1 are cited at *DDS* 173.

[32] Note too that the *De Mundo* begins with an obvious allusion to the opening of Cicero *Tusc.* 5 (see Ch. 5, Sect. 3 (i)); on Ciceronian colour in the *Apologia* see Ch. 2 n. 17.

[33] On this style see the careful analyses of Bernhard (1927).

[34] See Thomas (1988), 231–2; this type of imperative is found only here in the philosophical works of Apuleius (it is relatively common in the higher style of the *Metamorphoses*).

varia quippe curriculi sui specie, sed una semper et aequabili pernicitate, tunc progressus, tunc vero regressus mirabili vicissitudine adsimulant pro situ et flexu et instituto circulorum, quos probe callet qui signorum ortus et obitus conperit.

Again, note the balances and rhymes, especially in the cleverly chiastic interweaving of the two rhyming pairs *aequabili pernicitate/mirabili vicissitudine* and *tunc progressus, tunc vero regressus*; the paragraph ends with a clear allusion to Catullus 66. 2 *qui stellarum ortus comperit atque obitus*, echoing another of Apuleius' favourite poets.[35] The whole section on the astral gods ends (121) with another poetic quotation, this time from Ennius, another writer cited elsewhere by Apuleius;[36] apart from the typically archaizing colour, we should also remember that Cicero, already seen as a model for Apuleius here (see above), was apt to cite Ennius in his philosophical works.[37]

(b) *The non-astral gods* (121–4).   Having rounded off his account of the planets with an Ennian quotation, Apuleius brings out another, Ennius' famous two-line list of the twelve Olympian gods from the *Annales* (121), to introduce his brief section on the conventional gods.[38] This is followed by an attack on the ignorant who do not worship the gods properly (122–3), interesting not only for its style (more balanced clauses and rhyme) but also for its presentation of the speaker as pious and possessed of correct religious and philosophical knowledge. This is precisely the self-characterization of Apuleius not only in the *Apologia*, where it might be expected in a defence against a charge of magic (which included implications of irreligion), but also in the *Florida*, where *Flor.* 1 presents Apuleius almost in the light of a permanent religious pilgrim.[39] Indeed, his later reputation as a holy man, which Augustine is so concerned to refute, suggests that this piece of image-making on Apuleius' part was consistent and successful (the clear knowledge of religious cult deliberately displayed in the *Metamorphoses* is also relevant here).[40] The doctrine

---

[35] On Catullus in Apuleius see Ch. 1 and esp. *Apol.* 11–13; the particular parallel is picked up by Barra (1962–3), 104, and Beaujeu (1973), 209.

[36] Cf. *Apol.* 39 and Ch. 1 n. 127.

[37] Cf. e.g. *Div.* 1. 40–1, 1. 107–8, 2. 116, *Off.* 1. 38.

[38] *Ann.* 240–1 Skutsch: *Iuno Vesta Minerva Ceres Diana Venus Mars / Mercurius Iovis Neptunus Volcanus Apollo.* In fact Apuleius is the earliest source for these lines, and the only other is Martianus Capella, who probably takes them from Apuleius. For commentary and location in the *Annales* cf. Skutsch (1985), 424–6.

[39] Cf. n. 19 above on the *Apologia*; on *Flor.* 1 see Scotti (1988).

[40] For the accuracy of the depiction of the Isis-cult in the *Metamorphoses* see the commentary of Gwyn Griffiths (1975).

on the nature of the gods given here is standardly Platonic, but, given the strong Lucretian colour in this work, it is interesting to note that Apuleius stresses both the separation of the gods from men and man's wrong superstitious fear of the gods, both elements prominent in the Epicurean theology of the *De Rerum Natura*.

The final part of the section (124) is devoted to the supreme god, a feature of Plato's teaching much emphasized in Apuleius and in second-century Platonism generally.[41] In a rhetorical question which fills a whole fifteen-line paragraph, Apuleius accomplishes a witty *praeteritio*: why should he tell of the supreme deity when the divinely eloquent Plato frequently states that its sublime nature cannot be expressed in mortal discourse (a hyperbolic allusion to a single passage of the *Timaeus*)?[42] Even the greatest wise men can have only an intermittent perception of the deity, attained by removing themselves as far as possible from the corrupting influence of the body (a clear allusion to the *Phaedo*).[43]

(c) *Man and his separation from the gods* (125–32). The transition in subject matter from the highest god to humble mortals is marked in a typically stylish self-conscious link passage (125):

missum igitur hunc locum faciam, in quo non mihi tantum, sed ne Platoni quidem meo quiverunt ulla verba pro amplitudine rei suppetere, fac iam rebus mediocritatem meam longe superantibus receptui canam tandemque orationem de caelo in terram devocabo.

Again, as in the description of the moon at 116–17, the sentence is held together by a continuing metaphor, this time a military one—*missum . . . faciam, longe superantibus*, and *receptui canam* (dismissal, victory, and retreat). The final sentence *orationem . . . devocabo* is another possible echo of Cicero's *philosophica*; at *Tusc.* 5. 10 Cicero says that Socrates, in contrast to the interests of Archelaus in heavenly bodies, was the first to bring philosophy down to earth and the actions of humans: *primus philosophiam devocavit a caelo et in urbibus conlocavit.*[44]

The treatment of man points out the paradox of his condition, endowed with rationality and an immortal soul, but also capable of bestial vice. Once again Apuleius rises to the occasion with a full panoply of rhetorical colours (126–7):

---

[41] Hijmans (1987), 436–40, Dillon (1977), 454.
[42] *Tim.* 28 c—cf. Beaujeu (1973), 211.   [43] *Phaed.* 64e ff.—cf. Beaujeu (1973), 211.
[44] Note that the opening of the *De Mundo* already alludes to the opening of *Tusc.* 5—cf. n. 31 above.

Igitur homines ratione gaudentes, oratione pollentes, immortalibus animis, moribundis membris, levibus et anxiis mentibus, brutis et obnoxiis corporibus, dissimillimis moribus, similibus erroribus, pervicaci audacia, pertinaci spe, casso labore, fortuna caduca, singillatim mortales, cunctim tamen universo genere perpetui, vicissim sufficienda prole mutabiles, volucri tempore, tarda sapientia, cita morte, querula vita, terras incolunt.

Rhyme, alliteration and balance are in full flow here, with the sentence consisting mostly of asyndetic contrasting pairs. The phrase *oratione pollentes* is introduced partly for the jingle with *ratione*, but also appropriately stresses the human power of speech in the context of a performance by a professional human speaker.[45]

These fragile men are naturally separated from the perfect gods, as Apuleius goes on to argue. In fact, the gods are like the great men of the real world, who are difficult to approach for the rest of mankind, an illustration given in detail (128–9):

inter homines, qui fortunae munere opulenti elatus et usque ad regni nutabilem suggestum et pendulum tribunal evectus est, raro aditu sit, longe remotis arbitris in quibusdam dignitatis suae penetralibus degens. parit enim conversatio contemptum, raritas conciliat admirationem.

The comparison of gods and kings is a traditional one, but Apuleius gives it some Roman colour; *suggestus* can refer to the speaking-platform in the Forum Romanum, the Rostra, while *tribunal* naturally indicates the dais in the same location on which Roman magistrates normally sat.[46] But there are echoes of emperors as well as magistrates: the mention of difficulty of access and of spending one's time away from the eyes of men in inner rooms suggests the mystique of monarchy.[47] The pair of *sententiae* which provide a neat gnomic closure for the passage (*parit enim . . . admirationem*) look proverbial, and although it would be pleasing to credit Apuleius with coining the proverb 'familiarity breeds contempt' and its opposite, both these sayings are very likely to derive from a previous source.[48]

At 129 Apuleius introduces an imaginary objector. This is a trick found in Cicero's forensic speeches, but also in the style of diatribe; Lucretius, already seen as a model for Apuleius as a writer of philosophical didactic,

---

[45] It may also recall the popular etymology *oratio quasi oris ratio*—cf. Maltby (1991), 432.

[46] *Suggestus*: Livy 31. 29. 9. *Tribunal*: *OLD* s.v. 1.

[47] For *penetralia* of monarchic seclusion cf. *Gloss. Lat.* 4. 457, *TLL* 10. 1. 1062. 23 ff.

[48] Though in fact I can find no earlier source for either; for Apuleian interest in paroemiography cf. Ch. 1, Sect. 2 (ii) 2.

incorporates several imaginary objectors in his demolition of the fear of death at the end of *De Rerum Natura* 3, a passage which makes extensive use of diatribe techniques.[49] The objector in Apuleius points out the obvious difficulty: if the gods have no real contact with men, as Plato and the speaker argue, then to whom must prayers and oaths be addressed? The objector's language is colourful and powerful; the string of short rhetorical questions at 130, each introduced with a relative pronoun, is very forceful, as is the doubly anaphoric sequence *cui . . . cui . . . cui . . . quem . . . quem . . . quem . . . quem . . . quem denique*. The concern with oaths adds a very Roman colour, stressed by the accompanying quotation from an oath-scene in the *Aeneid* (9. 300) which is then studied in its literary context, and supplemented by another Vergilian oath-scene (10. 773), the perverted oath of Mezentius (a figure of interest to Apuleius, as the *Apologia* shows).[50] The knowledge shown of the text of the *Aeneid* is a typical example of paraded sophistic learning; Apuleius, for his Latin-speaking audience, treats Vergil just as writers of the Greek Second Sophistic treat Homer—as a universally familiar text on which all self-respecting intellectuals should be able to comment,[51] though his apparent ease of quotation can sometimes bring him to grief, as at 145 (see below). Once again, at 132, the weighty and fashionable authority of Ennius is invoked at a point of closure (though the line is characteristically likely to be taken from its use in Cicero's *De Officiis* (3. 104) rather than from a direct reading of Ennius),[52] and his word-play between *ius* and *Iovis* is used to support the traditional view that the gods are concerned with oaths. This proposition is further supported by a final rhetorical question, introduced by the Ciceronian formula *quid igitur censes*,[53] which characteristically combines an antiquarian allusion with a *reductio ad absurdum*. Referring to the early Roman cult of Jupiter Lapis[54] and playing on the god's cult-title, the objector is made to argue that if Plato really believes that there is no communication between god and man, we are better off praying to a stone than to Jupiter.

[49] Cf. Wallach (1976).

[50] *Apol.* 56, 89. For Apuleius' manipulation of the Vergilian quotations for his own purposes here see Bingenheimer (1993), 148–9.

[51] See esp. Kindstrand (1973).

[52] This passage of Cicero is clearly a source of Apuleius in the *De Deo Socratis*: cf. n. 63. For Apuleius and Ennius see n. 36.

[53] Cf. *ND* 1. 82, *Phil.* 13. 6.

[54] For this cult and its antiquarian interest in the second century AD cf. Polybius 3. 25. 6–9 with F. W. Walbank *ad loc.*, and Gellius *NA* 1. 21. 4.

II. *The Account of Daimones* (132–56)

This is the central part of the work, in terms of both position and length of treatment. It falls into four sections, the first dealing with the general function of *daimones* as intermediaries between god and man (132–8), the second with their specific location within the universe, also intermediate (138–45), the third with their possession of emotion and other differences from the gods (145–50), and the fourth with their various particular types (151–6), which provides a natural transition to talking about the particular *daimonion* of Socrates at 157.

(a) *The function of* daimones (132–7). Here Apuleius, like all subsequent expositors of *daimon*-theory, builds on the famous account of *daimones* in Plato's *Symposium* (202d–203a), specifically alluded to at 133, and on other lost intermediate sources.[55] Having presented an imaginary objector retailing a false idea of Platonic teaching in sections 129–32, Apuleius now answers him with Plato's true doctrines, and shows that he has misunderstood. The two central arguments of the objector, that the gods seem to be so separated from men that they cannot hear their prayers, and that consequently they have no care for humans, are of course familiar Epicurean doctrine, and their presentation indeed recalls Lucretius in some verbal details.[56] The answer is that all traffic between gods, whether through prayer or divination, is accomplished through *daimones*, and that the gods do therefore concern themselves with mankind.

In his emphasis here Apuleius reflects the concern of a Roman culture which placed great weight on forms of divination. Plato's brief assertion that *daimones* are concerned with all forms of foretelling (*Symp.* 202e) is characteristically expanded by Apuleius into a long and rhythmical list of individual aspects of divination, with a strongly Roman colour (134):

proinde ut est cuique tributa provincia, vel somniis conformandis vel extis fissiculandis vel praepetibus gubernandis vel oscinibus erudiendis vel vatibus inspirandis vel nubibus coruscandis ceterisque adeo, per quae futura dinoscimus.

Here Apuleius, beginning with the formal term *provincia* to designate the *daimon*'s sphere of operations as if that of a Roman magistrate, uses the official language of augury, incorporating in his list not only a number of

---

[55] Cf. Beaujeu (1973), 215–19.
[56] *DDS* 132 *seiunctos a nobis deos . . . a cura rerum humanarum removi* ~ Lucretius *DRN* 1. 51 [*divum natura*] *semota a nostris rebus seiunctaque longe*, a resemblance unnoted elsewhere.

technical terms but also the well-known threefold division of divination according to the *Etrusca disciplina*, the Etruscan system of religious lore at Rome—from entrails, *haruspicina* (*extis*), from the flight and cry of birds (*praepetibus*), and from lightning (*nubibus coruscandis*).[57] This Roman system, no doubt culled from Cicero's *De Divinatione* or Varronian antiquarianism, is here combined with two elements from the *Symposium*, the concern of *daimones* with dreams and their inspiration of prophets, showing that Apuleius is directly reworking the passage of Plato.[58]

This passage on *divinatio* is immediately followed by another paragraph of strong Roman colour, which digresses from the argument about *daimones* to give a list of moments in Roman history where prodigies or other forms of divine warning have played an important role (135–6). The great men to whom such signs have been given are given in a Ciceronian-type list of *exempla*—Hannibal, Flaminius, Attius Navius, Tarquinius Priscus, and Servius Tullius, and further Roman modes of divination are mentioned (135 *cuncta hariolorum praesagia, Tuscorum piacula, fulguratorum bidentalia, carmina Sibyllarum*).[59] These signs to great men are taken either from the earliest Roman history or from the era of the Second Punic War, and probably derive ultimately from a reading of Cicero and Livy.[60] Such vulgar interventions are below divine dignity, Apuleius argues (this attitude, which appeals neatly to the Roman sense of hierarchy, seems to derive from a Stoic source);[61] these things are the task of the *daimones*, lower in status (137).

(b) *The location and physical substance of* daimones (137–45). The linking of the four elements with the various orders of beings goes back to Plato and Aristotle, although Apuleius and Philo of Alexandria are the first to locate the *daimones* specifically in the *aer*, the thicker air to be found between the earth, the home of men, and the *aether*, the fine fiery air which is the traditional home of the gods.[62] Apuleius presents this part of the exposition in a particularly rhetorical mode, no doubt because

---

[57] For the *Etrusca disciplina* and its standard threefold division the standard treatment is still Thulin (1906–9); Apuleius no doubt culls his material from Cicero *Div.* and *ND*, where the topic is much discussed.

[58] So Beaujeu (1973), 215–17.

[59] Here Sibylline prophecies (connected with Tarquinius Superbus) are added to the *disciplina Etrusca* (n. 57 above).

[60] For the references see Beaujeu (1973), 218.

[61] See Beaujeu (1973), 219, citing Seneca *NQ* 2. 32. 2, Cicero *Div.* 1. 118.

[62] Cicero *Div.* 1. 64 with A. S. Pease's commentary.

there is little effective proof he can bring to bear apart from the appropriateness of an intermediate location for intermediate beings. After an apparently learned allusion (138) to Aristotle's *Historia Animalium* on the subject of fire-tolerant creatures, probably drawn from Cicero's use of the same passage,[63] Apuleius' line of attack (139) is simply to stress the improbability of one whole element (the *aer*) being without its own class of beings, when the other three each have one (the *aether* has the gods, the earth men, the sea fish and other fluid creatures). Birds, he argues, which one might see as the natural occupants of the *aer*, never fly above the height of Mount Olympus (given in elaborate detail, ostensibly from a technical source),[64] and this leaves the whole remainder of the *aer*, which extends much further, to the lowest orbit of the moon: is this space to be wholly unoccupied? Has it not creatures of its own? Two rhetorical questions follow one another swiftly, interlarded with other forceful phrasing of Ciceronian colour (*quid tandem? immo enim . . .*).[65]

This texture of argument, strongly rhetorical in form, short on relevant evidence and laced with items of casual learning (Aristotle, Mount Olympus), recalls many passages in the *Apologia*. The audience is carried along to the next stage of the argument, once again from analogy and similarity: if the intermediate region of the *aer* is occupied by creatures, these creatures must themselves be intermediate between god and man in nature (140), and their mass must be heavy enough to prevent their rising to the *aether*, but light enough to prevent their sinking to the earth, a Stoic idea (141).[66] This reasoning from bare probability is supplemented by its presentation as the common intellectual enterprise of speaker and audience, reflected in 140 by the use of first-person plural verbs, a common Lucretian device;[67] note how Apuleius cleverly shifts from *disseramus*, a 'royal we' describing what he is about to do, to the more

---

[63] *DDS* 138 *siquidem Aristoteles auctor est in fornacibus flagrantibus quaedam [propria] animalia pennulis apta volitare totumque aevum suum in igni deversari, cum eo exoriri cumque eo extingui* ~ Cicero *Div.* 1. 103 *sunt* quaedam *etiam quae* igne nasci *putentur appareantque* in ardentibus fornacibus *saepe* volitantes, a much closer resemblance than to Aristotle *Hist. An.* 5. 19 552b.

[64] *DDS* 139 *ut geometrae autumant,* apparently a formula of cross-reference to a technical body of work—cf. Varro *RR* 3. 16. 5 *quod geometrae . . . ostendunt,* Gellius *NA* 1. 20. 1 *quae* σχήματα *geometrae appellant.*

[65] For this *quid tandem?* cf. Cicero *Clu.* 70, *Mur.* 76, *Dom.* 24.

[66] Cf. Beaujeu (1973), 222–4.

[67] For the Lucretian first-person plural cf. n. 68 below. *DDS* 140 *disseramus . . . et gignamus* also echoes Lucretian vocabulary: *disserare* is used of the poet's didactic activity at *DRN* 1. 55, 6. 940, while *gigno* is a typically Lucretian archaic verb (forty-eight times in *DRN*).

cooperative *mente formemus et gignamus animo,* linking himself and his listeners in a shared search for the truth. He is clearly aware of the airiness of his argument (141 *quod ne vobis videar poetico ritu incredibilia confingere*), and proceeds at 142 to support it with a Lucretian-type example from the visible world, once more coloured with Lucretian vocabulary as well as the express quotation of *De Rerum Natura* 6. 96–8.[68] He appeals to the sight of heavy clouds descending to crown the peaks of mountains; they, like *daimones,* are of intermediate mass, too heavy to ascend to the heavens and too light to descend to the earth. The application to *daimones* is accomplished by a typically Lucretian *a fortiori* analogy: if clouds can hover in mid-air like this, how much more so *daimones,* who are composed of finer material (143–4)? Their finer material further means that they are visible to men only when they wish to be so; this thought occasions a short purple passage about their delicate texture (145) which is again strongly Lucretian in character:[69]

sed *fila corporum possident rara* et *splendida* et *tenuia* usque adeo ut *radios* omnis nostri tuoris et raritate *transmittant* et *splendore* reverberent et *subtilitate* frustrentur

This poetic connection is continued by the final examples in this section. The first is the famous example of Minerva (Athene) appearing to Achilles in the first book of the *Iliad,* referred to in the 'casually improvized' translation of Homer already mentioned as indicating both the Latin-speaking audience of the *De Deo Socratis* and the superior bilingualism of the speaker,[70] followed by one each from Vergil and Plautus.[71] The first two quotations refer to the invisibility which divine status or favour can confer and imply that the literary Olympians are in fact *daimones*; this was a view of Xenocrates, if not of Plato himself.[72] The

---

[68] *Videmus* at DDS 142 is a first-person plural form used seventy times in the *De Rerum Natura*; with 142 *ab hac corporis subtilitate nubes concretas* compare Lucretius *DRN* 5. 466 *corpore concreto . . . nubila,* and with *ut saepenumero animadvertimus* compare Lucretian expressions such as *saepe cernimus* (3. 526), *saepe videmus* (4. 61), and *saepe ostendimus* (4. 672).

[69] For the italicized expressions see Lucretius *DRN* 3. 383 *tenuia fila,* 2. 586 *vis multas possidet in se,* and the common Lucretian uses of *rarus* (1. 743; 2. 107, 230; 3. 235; 4. 196), *tenuis* (fourteen times in *DRN*) for atomic texture, *splendidus* (seven times in *DRN*), and *splendor* (also seven times in *DRN*). *Subtilis* is used eight times in Lucretius, though *subtilitas* is not found there.

[70] DDS 145 *versum Graecum* [i.e. *Il.* 1. 198], *si paulisper opperiamini, latine enuntiabo:* 'soli perspicua est, aliorum nemo tuetur'.

[71] On Apuleius and Plautus cf. Ch. 3 n. 21.

[72] Cf. Beaujeu (1973), 225–6.

Vergilian quotation shows a memory error: the context Apuleius refers to (Juturna bringing help to Turnus on the battlefield in Latium) occurs in *Aen.* 12 (468 ff.), while the line actually cited is *Aen.* 1. 440, where Aeneas is concealed from sight by a divine mist by his mother Venus. The line used of the male and divinely protected Aeneas is here turned to describe the female and divine protector Juturna; this error in fact has the added benefit of bringing in two Vergilian contexts where goddesses aid men, rather than one. The Plautine citation is a familiar one, the fourth line of the *Miles Gloriosus*, the play's title being alluded to in the words introducing the quotation (*Plautinus* miles *super clipeo suo* gloriatur); it shares with the Homeric and Vergilian passages the idea of impairing the sight of others, this time not by divine intervention but by a brilliantly shining shield, a battle context which clearly links up with the allusion to Juturna. This grouping of authoritative quotations again provides some sense of closure, as at 130–2, and concludes the section on the location and physical substance of *daimones*.

(c) Daimones, *emotions, and the higher gods* (145–50). Having cited three poetical examples, Apuleius goes on to use the first two, both examples of divine favour conferred, as proofs of the love and hatred which *daimones* can bear for men. This susceptibility of *daimones* to emotion contrasts with the imperturbability of the true heavenly gods, presented in traditional Platonic manner as free from pleasure and pain; the arguments here are closely derived from Plato's dialogues, though there is the occasional trace of Lucretius' descriptions of the similarly passionless gods of Epicurus.[73] The emotional capacity of *daimones* which brings them closer to humans than the celestial gods is elegantly expressed in a sequence of balanced rhythmical clauses at 147:

nam proinde ut nos possunt omnia animorum placamenta vel incitamenta, ut et ira incitentur et misericordia flectantur et donis invitentur et precibus leniantur et contumeliis exasperentur et honoribus mulceantur aliisque omnibus ad similem nobis modum varient.

The crucial point of similarity to man is stated at the beginning and the end of this elaborate sentence (*proinde ut nos, ad similem nobis modum*). Further, the whole is governed by the twin opposing ideas of rousing the gods to action and of placating or deprecating them, introduced in the initial noun pair *placamenta vel incitamenta*, and maintained in the three

[73] On the Platonic colouring cf. Beaujeu (1973), 226–7; there is much common ground with Lucretius *DRN* 2. 646–51 (cf. also n. 55 above).

careful noun–verb pairings which follow before the summarizing ending.

This openness of *daimones* to emotion is used by Apuleius to explain the diversity of religious practice in human cult (148–50). The logical connection here is presumably that each *daimon* is an individual with particular preferences and needs to be worshipped in a different way, but this is never made explicit; the speaker is too keen to launch into a catalogue of differing religious rites, clearly to his taste. We recall that here and elsewhere Apuleius represents himself as a man of deep religious interests and knowledge;[74] the allusions to Egypt and 'barbarians' (149) gives a Herodotean ethnographic flavour, as well as implying Apuleius' own knowledge of such matters (although here, unlike in the *Apologia*, he does not allude to his own religious experience and qualifications). Once again, the catalogue gives the opportunity for characteristic stylistic ornamentation (149):

itidem pro regionibus et cetera in sacris differunt longe varietate: pomparum agmina, mysteriorum silentia, sacerdotum officia, sacrificantium obsequia: item deorum effigiae et exuviae, templorum religiones et regiones, hostiarum cruores et colores.

The balanced clauses are deployed with typically Apuleian rhythm and assonance; noteworthy here is *religiones et regiones*, which alludes to a prominent word-play in Lucretius,[75] an author already seen as influential on Apuleius' didactic project in the *De Deo Socratis*. The subject matter of processions, mysteries, priests, sacrifices, cult-statues, and temples constitutes the normal apparatus of ancient religion, but readers of Apuleius' novel will note that all these items recur in the description of the cult of Isis in *Met.* 11. These multiple ceremonies are accompanied, claims Apuleius, by an equally multiple set of possibilities for error and omission, and consequent divine wrath; he claims to have many examples of such neglect of the gods, but prefers not to air them in case he fails to include more than he mentions. Here one thinks immediately of the ritual omissions which led to the sacrifice of Iphigenia at Aulis, the death of Protesilaus, or the appearance of the Calydonian boar,[76] but there is

---

[74] Cf. nn. 19 and 38 above.

[75] Lucretius *DRN* 1. 63–4 *in terris oppressa gravi sub* religione / *quae caput a* caeli regionibus *ostendebat.*

[76] All available to Apuleius in convenient Latin sources—for Iphigenia cf. Ovid *Met.* 12. 27–31 as well as Lucretius *DRN* 1. 80–101, for Protesilaus cf. Catullus 68. 75–80, for the Calydonian boar cf. Ovid *Met.* 8. 273–83.

wit here as well as implied mythological allusion: Apuleius himself does not wish to commit a sin of omission in listing sins of omission. He also appeals to the learning of his audience, who will all be at least vaguely familiar with such stories.

(d) *Types of* daimones (150–6). The somewhat self-conscious passage which immediately follows allows Apuleius an ingenious link *a propria persona* with his next topic: he will not retail mythological learning, implied perhaps to be Greek, but rather give an account in Latin of the types of *daimones*, in order for the reader to have a fuller understanding of the *daimonion* of Socrates. As already noted in Section 2 above, this mention of Socrates is the first allusion to what the title presents as the main subject of the work, and it occurs well over half-way through the extant text. This fact is surely strong evidence for the loss of the work's beginning in which its subject and procedure was set out (the *daimonion* of Socrates, prefaced by a general account of *daimones*), especially when linked with the empty cross-reference at 150 (*ut iam prius dictum est*), which is also best explained by the work's acephalous nature (see Sect. 2).

The account of *daimones* themselves begins (150) with a famous quotation from the *Aeneid*, Nisus' words to Euryalus (*Aen.* 9. 184–5 *dine hunc ardorem mentibus addunt, / Euryale, an sua cuique deus fit dira cupido?*);[77] this technique of searching the great epics for allusions to *daimones* has already been deployed at 145, and the listener/reader feels here as there the comfort of familiar literary territory in attempting to grasp unfamiliar philosophical ideas. The quotation is used to introduce the important notion, present already in Plato's *Timaeus* (90d), that one form of *daimon* is the soul of man itself : *daemon bonus, id est animus virtute perfectus* (150). But this Platonic idea is at once given a Roman form: the idea of a 'good *daimon*' is identified with that of the traditional Roman *genius*, the spirit thought to accompany each human being.[78] This identification, like those which follow with Lemures, Lares, and Larvae, is clearly as old as the generation of Varro and Cicero;[79] and the term 'Genius' is used by Apuleius to support the general idea of the union of body and soul (151–2):

ut eae preces, quibus Genium et genua precantur, coniunctionem nostram nexumque videantur mihi obtestari, corpus atque animum duobus nominibus comprehendentes, quorum communio et copulatio sumus.

---

[77] Note that here *deus* fits the title of this work: cf. n. 23 above.
[78] Cf. R. Schilling in *RAC* 10. 53–64.　　　　　　　　　　[79] Cf. Beaujeu (1973), 233.

The jingle *Genium et genua,* itself an apparent antiquarian allusion to prayer-language, is used in the manner of a Varronian significant etymology to suggest union between guardian spirit and limbs and therefore between soul and body.[80] This is stressed once again in language which recalls Lucretius' lines on the same union of body and soul.[81]

Having argued that the souls of the living can count as *daimones,* Apuleius proceeds to argue the same for the souls of the dead (152–3). The identification of types of *daimones* with the traditional Roman types of spirits (152–3), drawn from Varro as already stated, is again expressed as if it were the product of the speaker's own investigation rather than material derived from elsewhere: the phrase *vetere Latina lingua reperio* (152) lays a claim to personal research into archaic Latin, an appropriately fashionable claim for the period in which Apuleius was writing.[82] The distinction made between *Lares,* beneficent home-protecting spirits, and *Larvae,* wandering malevolent spirits, and the use of *Manis* for spirits which may be either, is not specifically made in any previous source, but it would be astonishing if Apuelius were formulating it for the first time in a passage which is otherwise so tralatician. As Beaujeu has pointed out,[83] these three types correspond to the three types of souls (good, bad, and intermediate) described (without being called *daimones*) in the mystical eschatology of the *Phaedo* (113d–114a), a translation of which is recorded amongst the lost works of Apuleius (see Chapter 1); if this equivalence has not been adopted wholesale from an earlier writer such as Varro, Apuleius may be combining a Roman antiquarian source and a reading of Plato in applying this classification to *daimones.*

A final class of the souls of the dead which count as *daimones* is presented in the list of virtuous humans who have been deified and who are given the appellation *deus,* clearly treated by Apuleius as in the work's title as an equivalent of *daimon* (154),[84] Amphiaraus, Mopsus, Osiris, and Aesculapius. For once, this group of names seems to have several elements personalized to the particular context. Mopsus and Osiris with their African associations suggest a Carthaginian audience for the speech (as suggested in Sect. 1 above), as does the climactic stress on Aesculapius,

---

[80] Though the etymology itself is not explicitly recorded by Varro or other writers (cf. Maltby (1991), 256), its alliterative character is typical of the language of Roman prayer (on which see Appel (1909)).

[81] Cf. Lucretius *DRN* 3. 845–6: *nil tamen est ad nos qui comptu coniugioque / corporis atque animae consistimus uniter apti.*

[82] Cf. Ch. 1 n. 68, and esp. Fronto *Ep.* 4. 3. 3 on the seeking-out of archaic words.

[83] Beaujeu (1973), 235.   [84] See n. 23.

the Greco-Roman version of the local Carthaginian god *'smun*, and we note that Apuleius elsewhere proclaims his personal devotion to Aesculapius and shows some knowledge of the cult of Osiris.[85] These *daimones* who are or were combined with the body in human beings are then distinguished from a further class, intermediate divine powers who are always separate from bodily forms. Somnus and Amor, the latter an evident allusion to the *Symposium*, the former to Vergil and Homer, are immediately brought forward as examples, not without humour: Amor takes away the sleep which Somnus brings.[86]

It is clear that Apuleius maintains that the *daimonion* of Socrates belongs to this external class of *daimones*, described as witnesses and guardians of men's behaviour and thoughts, and later as attending souls in their trial after death (155):

hominibus in vita agenda testes et custodes singulis additos, qui nemini conspicui semper adsint arbitri omnium non modo actorum verum etiam cogitatorum. at ubi vita edita remeandum est, eundem illum, qui nobis praeditus fuit, raptare ilico et trahere veluti custodiam suam ad iudicium atque illic in causa dicunda adsistere, si qua commentiatur, redarguere, si qua vera dicat, adseverare, prorsus illius testimonio ferri sententiam.

Here Apuleius is thinking of a famous Platonic passage, the eschatological myth of the *Phaedo*, already alluded to in this section of *De Deo Socratis*, where it is the job of the guardian *daimon* to brings its soul to the place of judgement (*Phaed.* 107 d–e). The judicial function of the *daimon* is characteristically elaborated by Apuleius, adding detail and technical terminology, suitable for a Roman audience.[87] In particular, the curious triple role of the *daimon* as policeman ensuring that its soul attends its trial, as defence counsel speaking for it as client, and as a neutral cross-examiner of its evidence seems to be Apuleius' own elaboration of the Platonic view, but it does reflect both the protective role of the *daimonion* of Socrates and its unflinching regard for the truth, both stressed in prominent Platonic texts.[88]

---

[85] Aesculapius: *Apol.* 55. 10, *Flor.* 18. 37–43. Osiris: *Met.* 11. 36. 4 ff.

[86] For the god Sleep in Homer and Vergil cf. *Il.* 14. 231, *Aen.* 5. 838; their conjunction might also suggest the topos of erotic insomnia, also found in epic—cf. A. S. Pease's note on Vergil *Aen.* 4. 522.

[87] *Testes, custodes, arbitri, custodiam, iudicium, in causa dicunda, adsistere, redarguere, adseverare, testimonio, sententiam* are all in some sense technical terms of law (see *OLD* on each of them): for Apuleius' legal knowledge cf. Ch. 3 n. 108.

[88] Plato *Apol.* 31d, *Phaedr.* 242b–c, [Plato] *Theages* 128–9 (protection from error); Plato *Apol.* 40b (concern for truth/the right).

For this description of the external *daimon*'s function, and the fact that it is placed last in the typology of 150–6, clearly forms the culmination of Apuleius' classification of *daimones* and prepares for the introduction of the *daimonion* of Socrates at 157. This climactic effect is underlined by the purple passage of 156–7, which concludes this section with some splendid rhetorical fireworks. This passage is introduced by a moralizing exhortation, which itself anticipates the way in which the audience will be urged in the last section of the speech (167–78) to follow the example of Socrates, and which serves to point to the applied ethical function of all this abstract metaphysical doctrine (155–6):

proinde vos omnes, qui hanc Platonis divinam sententiam me interprete ausculatis, ita animos vestros ad quaecumque agenda vel meditanda formate, ut sciatis nihil homini prae istis custodibus nec intra animum nec foris esse secreti, quin omnia curiose ille participet; omnia visitet, omnia intellegat, in ipsis penitissimis mentibus vice conscientiae deversetur.

The idea of the inner god who knows the secrets of our hearts and acts as conscience has interesting parallels in other ancient religious traditions,[89] and seems to elaborate Platonic ideas in the light of subsequent developments. It is difficult to find evidence for an idea of conscience in the modern sense in the age of Plato, though this is not far from the inner voice of the *daimonion* which told Socrates to refrain from action which would be wrong (*Apol.* 40a); but ideas of conscience, or at least of *conscientia*, are well developed by the second century AD.[90] Likewise, the inner god is an obvious development of the 'inner voice', which could be misrepresented by Socrates' opponents as a 'new god'.[91]

The concluding purple passage itself once again combines stylistic ornament with adaptation to a Roman context:

hic, quem dico, privus custos, singularis praefectus, domesticus speculator, proprius curator, intimus cognitor, assiduus observator, individuus arbiter, inseparabilis testis, malorum improbator, bonorum probator, si rite animadvertatur, sedulo cognoscatur, religiose colatur, ita ut a Socrate iustitia et innocentia cultus est, in rebus incertis prospector, dubiis praemonitor, periculosis tutator, egenis opitulator, qui tibi queat tum insomniis, tum signis, tum etaim fortasse coram,

---

[89] e.g. Jewish (*Psalms* 44. 21 'Shall not God search this out? for he knoweth the secrets of the heart'); the man/god relationship sketched here is also not far from that of the Hermetic/Gnostic tradition—cf. Fowden (1986), 104–15.

[90] On the emergence of the idea of conscience, especially in early imperial Stoicism, and its connection with one's *daimon* see the material gathered by Rutherford (1989), 229 n. 14.

[91] Plato *Apol.* 26b ff., 31d.

cum usus postulat, mala averruncare, bona prosperare, humilia sublimare, nutantia fulcire, obscura clarare, secunda regere, adversa corrigere.

The short balanced clauses with rhyme and assonance form an impressive, almost overwhelming list, expressing the diversity and importance of the *daimonion*'s functions and the need to obey it, a suitable ending for a section on the nature of *daimones* and a fitting transition to the particular treatment of the *daimonion* of Socrates, carefully flagged by a specific mention (*ita ut a Socrate iustitia et innocentia cultus est*). Once again Roman technical terminology places the discussion in a context familiar to Apuleius' audience: *custos, praefectus,* and *speculator* are drawn from military life, *curator, cognitor, arbiter,* and *testis* from legal language.[92] These public terms are paradoxically juxtaposed with the private and intimate dimension through their epithets (*privus, singularis, domesticus, proprius, intimus, assiduus, individuus, inseparabilis*), a striking and carefully calculated rhetorical effect. Apuleius' fondness for rhyme and for agent nouns in -*tor* leads him to add further nouns with that termination, non-technical terms and in some cases quite possibly his own coinages (*observator, improbator, probator, prospector, praemonitor, tutator, opitulator*);[93] the purpose is clearly to personify the *daimon* and stress that all these characteristics are inherent rather than transient. Archaic and poetic vocabulary also play a role in the solemn and climactic tone of this passage: note especially the verbs *queat, averruncare, sublimare,* and *clarare*.[94] The audience is now fully apprised of the moral importance of the internal *daimonion,* and ready for a discussion of its role for Socrates.

III. *The* Daimonion *of Socrates* (157–67)

The work at last reaches its ostensible main subject. As stressed in Section 1, the parallel of the opening of Apuleius' exposition with that of Maximus of Tyre suggests a common origin, and that Apuleius is drawing on traditional material here. The comparison of the external *daimonion* with a Lar is not quite consistent with the identification previously drawn between the Lares and internal soul–*daimones,* and suggests that

---

[92] See *OLD* on all these words, and compare n. 87 above.

[93] All these words except *observator* are first recorded in Apuleius: for a list of Apuleian nominal neologisms, including a number of other similar agent nouns in –*tor*, cf. Koziol (1872), 267–73.

[94] All except *clarare* (a poeticism with some archaic colour) are strongly archaic—see *OLD*.

this is Apuleius' own addition, the other identification with the Lares being a traditional one. The question asked in this opening is the fundamental one which appears also in Plutarch: if Socrates was so wise, as Plato and others maintain (cf. *Phaed.* 118a), why did he need this strange *daimonion*?

Apuleius replies by invoking a Platonic dichotomy between human wisdom and divine foresight (157–8): even the wisest men have recourse to divination. This dichotomy is then illustrated, in a manner which is familiar in *De Deo Socratis* with examples from Homer and other Greek literary texts, given in paraphrase rather than quotation for this Latin-speaking audience (158–62). The praise of Nestor, the wise man of the *Iliad*, here with particular reference to his diplomatic intervention in the quarrel between Achilles and Agamemnon in *Il.* 1, is traditional in contexts pointing to Homer's emphasis on the importance of rhetoric,[95] and Apuleius' description of Nestor incorporates a number of Homeric elements (158):[96]

nempe Pylius orator, eloquio comis, experimentis catus, senecta venerabilis, cui omnes sciebant corpus annis hebere, animum prudentia vigere, verba dulcedine adfluere.

In 159 Odysseus, commonly paired with Nestor as an example of eloquence in Homer,[97] is briefly mentioned in a reference to the night-expedition of *Il.* 10. But the human wisdom of both Nestor and Odysseus is seen to fail in the context of Aulis, where it is only the divine prophecy of Calchas which can ensure the departure and success of the Greek expedition. This example, like the brief allusions to Helenus and Cassandra as unsuccessful prophets at 162, seems to echo Cicero's *De Divinatione*, where all three occur; once again Cicero's *philosophica* are a suitable source for Apuleius in didactic mode.[98] In a neat balance which sets Trojans alongside Greeks, Priam's council, whose individual names are drawn from *Il.* 2, are likewise presented as equally resourceless when divination was needed.[99] All these examples are compared with Socrates,

---

[95] Cicero *Brut.* 40, Pliny *Ep.* 1. 20. 22, Quintilian 12. 10. 64.

[96] Esp. from Nestor's first appearance at *Il.* 1. 249 ff.

[97] So in all three of the passages cited in n. 95 above.

[98] Cicero *Div.* 1. 87–9 (cf. Beaujeu (1973), 240).

[99] *DDS* 161 *vel Hicetaon vel Lampo vel Clytius ~ Il.* 3. 147 (= 20. 238) Λάμπον τε Κλυτίον θ' Ικετάονά τ'. Apuleian editors should surely read *Lampos* as the nominative: *Lampo*, read by both Beaujeu (1973) and Moreschini (1991), is a Renaissance conjecture for the garbled *iambo* or *iampo* of the manuscripts here, but cannot be the nominative of Homer's name (it would naturally reflect a feminine ending in Greek, and a masculine is clearly needed).

who was similarly in need of prophetic guidance when his wisdom was insufficient (162). This link brings us back to the ostensible subject of the section; note how 163 *vir adprime perfectus* exactly repeats a phrase from 157, returning to Socrates on both the linguistic and thematic levels. So far two-thirds of the space since 157 has been devoted to Homeric examples,[100] and only one-third to Socrates, mirroring the structure of the work as a whole.

At 162–7 the case of Socrates is at last discussed in detail. Apuleius says that the *daimonion* characteristically prevented wrong actions rather than encouraging right ones, Socrates being wise enough to act correctly in most cases; this is generally in accordance with the instances of the *daimonion*'s action in Plato's dialogues. The Platonic characterization of the *daimonion* as a voice, a topic much discussed by Plutarch in *De Genio Socratis* and mentioned by Maximus of Tyre,[101] is raised next, with an allusion to its famous appearance in the *Phaedrus* (242b–c), a dialogue much read in the Second Sophistic,[102] though the quasi-legal *extra pomoerium* gives a strongly Roman colour.[103] Like Plutarch and Maximus, Apuleius is concerned in this context to defend Socrates against the charge that the *daimonion* was merely a form of credulous superstition, on a par with regarding the casual utterances of others as prophetic and directing one's life accordingly (this charge of superstition is aptly coloured again with reminiscence of Lucretius, the scourge of *religio*).[104] The example from the *Phaedrus* seems partly meant to defend Socrates through its consequences, showing that the *daimonion*'s intervention was not casual but led to the real and important exposition of Socrates' views on love (and is perhaps therefore rather more positively directive than Apuleius would have us believe).

The same purpose underlies Apuleius' assertion that Socrates in the *Phaedrus* heard a voice which was not necessarily human, thereby differentiating him from the vulgarly superstitious; much play is made with the details of Plato's text, which says τινα φωνήν (242c2), 'some voice', closely

---

[100] Very much in the tradition of Greek discussions of the *daimonion* of Socrates: Max. Tyr. *Dial.* 8. 5 has a similar set of Homeric examples.

[101] Plutarch *De Gen. Socr.* 580c, Max. Tyr. *Dial.* 14. 5—cf. Beaujeu (1973). 243.

[102] See the evidence collected by Trapp (1990).

[103] Here uniquely of Athens—cf. similarly *Met.* 1. 21. 3 *extra pomoerium* (of Hypata in Thessaly); Apuleius seems to be the only writer to use this term of the boundaries of non-Italian towns, presumably in order to appeal to a Roman audience—cf. *OLD* s.v.

[104] *DDS* 164 *non suopte corde sed alterius verbo reguntur ac . . . consilia ex alienis vocibus colligunt* ~ Lucretius *DRN* 5. 1133–4 *quandoquidem sapiunt alieno ex ore petuntque / res ex auditis potius quam sensibus ipsis* (noted by Beaujeu (1973), 242).

translated by Apuleius as *vocem quampiam* (165), the indefinite stressing that it was not a normal type of voice. This grammatical analysis is supported by a line from Terence (*Eun.* 454 *audire vocem visa sum modo militis*), a school author throughout Roman antiquity, though less favoured in the second century AD than the more colourfully archaic Plautus, which gives the genitive ascribing the voice to a person which Plato avoided by using the indefinite adjective.[105] Apuleius moves on to the notion that the intervention of Socrates' *daimonion* sometimes had a visual element (166). This is difficult to justify from the Platonic evidence, where the language either refers explicitly to an aural experience or simply says that the *daimonion* 'occurred' to Socrates.[106] Apuleius' *nam frequentius non vocem sed signum divinum sibi oblatum prae se ferebat* (166) certainly exaggerates with *frequentius*, and the only passage which might support it is that in the *Apology* (40a) where Socrates claims that the *daimonion* did not 'oppose' him on the way to the trial, which might imply some degree of visual contact (but certainly need not do so).[107] Here Apuleius is undoubtedly influenced by post-Platonic theory which interpreted the dialogues for its own purposes, no doubt resembling the Pythagorean and Aristotelian authority which he claims for the visibility of *daimones* in general at 166–7;[108] that he is here dealing with traditional material, despite his own assertions of originality, is confirmed by the Homeric example of Athene appearing to Achilles in *Il.* 1 (166), which has already been used at 150 and occurs also in Plutarch and Maximus.[109]

As at other points in the work, he is fully aware (166) of the weakness of his ground in arguing for the visibility of *daimones*, especially as he himself had earlier (121) seemed to class them among the invisible gods: *credo plerosque vestrum hoc, quod commodum dixi, cunctantius credere et impendio mirari formam daemonis Socrati visitatam*. This vulnerability is shown not only by his appeal to the Pythagoreans and Aristotle as authorities, but also by the final paragraph of the argument, which as often relies strongly on rhetoric rather than logic (167):

---

[105] On Terence in second-century AD literature cf. Holford-Strevens (1988), 158. The quasi-scholarly discussion of *vocem quampiam* here has a distinct flavour of the writings of the Roman *grammatici*, amongst whom Terence was a favourite author for discussion because of his 'pure' Latin and consequent use in the school curriculum—cf. Bonner (1977), 216.

[106] See the passages cited in n. 6: the verb generally used is γίγνομαι or its compounds.

[107] The phrase πυκνὴ ἀεὶ ἦν there perhaps implies aural contact.

[108] Cf. Beaujeu (1973), 243.

[109] Max. Tyr. *Dial.* 8. 5; for the probability of a common source see Sect. 1 above.

quod si cuivis potest evenire facultas contemplandi divinam effigiem, cur non adprime potuerit Socrati obtingere, quem cuivis amplissimo numini sapientiae dignitas coaequarat? nihil est enim deo similius et gratius quam vir animo perfecte bonus, qui hominibus ceteris antecellit, quam ipse a diis immortalibus distat.

The analogy of gazing on a cult-statue, a familiar part of ancient religion and reminiscent of Apuleius' own religious practice as detailed in the *Apologia*,[110] with Socrates' visual contact with the *daimonion*, a bizarre and unusual form of private communion, is clearly tendentious. It is buttressed by the idea of the equality of the truly wise man and the gods, a topos of ancient philosophy found in the *De Platone* but not restricted to Platonism;[111] why should equals not see each other? But this is immediately weakened by the idea that the sage is equally distant both from other inferior men and from the gods, which is inconsistent with the notion of his equality with divinity. Thus the arguments for visual contact between Socrates and his *daimonion* are weak in the extreme. Why are they included here? No doubt they existed in the literary tradition of discussing the *daimonion*, but Apuleius was free to take or leave such tralatician material according to personal preference. The intellectual context of the *De Deo Socratis* may provide an answer. The idea of private communion with a god was a highly popular one in the age of the Second Sophistic; many claimed to have had such experiences—Aelius Aristides in the *Sacred Tales*, enjoying repeated contact with Aesculapius, Maximus of Tyre, who claimed to have seen the same god (as well as various other heroic figures), and of course Lucius in Apuleius' own *Metamorphoses*, who has a personal revelation of the goddess Isis.[112]

IV. *Following the Moral Example of Socrates* (167–78)

Many have noted that this final section is rather different from the material which has preceded it.[113] There is no mention of Socrates' *daimonion*, and only one mention of the term *daimon* (170), though the personal virtues of Socrates are a running link in the section (167, 169, 174, 175), and its central theme of cultivating one's own soul (i.e. *daimon*) provides a degree of continuity with what has gone before. It is a tissue of

---

[110] *Apol.* 63. 3.

[111] Cf. also Epicurus *Ep.* 3. 135, Aristotle *EN* 10. 7 1177b.

[112] Max. Tyr. *Dial.* 9. 7, Apuleius *Met.* 11. 3–6; for the general cultural background cf. Festugière (1954), Dodds (1965), Lane Fox (1986), 375 ff.

[113] Beaujeu (1973), 244 n. 3.

commonplaces from the protreptic tradition, and shows a diatribic style highly reminiscent of the works of Seneca, which like the *philosophica* of Cicero and the *De Rerum Natura* of Lucretius presented a natural model for Apuleius.[114] The section falls into two parts: an introductory encouragement to turn to virtue and philosophy and cultivate one's soul (167–9), and an extended proof that wisdom and virtue are the only true goods (169–78). As argued in Section 2, the work shows signs of having lost its ending as well as its beginning, and it is likely that there was originally more material, including perhaps a formal ending returning to the subject of the *daimonion* of Socrates, the ostensible subject of the work.

(a) *Encouragement to virtue and philosophy* (167–9). As noted above (Sect. 3 (i)), this section clearly belongs to the ancient tradition of philosophical protreptic. The use of Socrates as a moral example, implicit of course in the Socratic dialogues of Plato, is common: he is a major character in the *Epistles* and philosophical essays of Seneca, and in the *philosophica* of Cicero, all models and sources for the *De Deo Socratis*.[115] Apuleius begins with a sentence which embodies several elements of the protreptic tradition (167):

quin potius nos quoque Socratis exemplo et commemoratione erigimur ac nos secundo studio philosophiae pari similitudini numini caventes permittimus?

The rhetorical question, the first-person plural verb, suggesting that the speaker and audience are at one, and the metaphor of *erigimur* all locate the passage in the dimension of diatribe and popular protreptic. The first and second are prominent in Seneca's *Epistles*, which also seem to provide the immediate source for the metaphor of *erigimur* (*Ep.* 71. 6): *erige te, Lucili virorum optime, et relinque istum ludum litterarium*, a similar exhortation to philosophy which is swiftly followed by a reference to the shining example of Socrates (71. 7). The metaphor of cultivating the soul (168 *animus colendus sit*) comes from Plato;[116] this in turn introduces the analogy between care of the body and care of the soul, another Platonic favourite which entered the diatribic tradition.[117] This image is rhetorically elaborated at 168, showing Apuleian balance but Senecan point and force in the brevity of the clauses:

[114] On Senecan colour here see Beaujeu (1973), 244–5.
[115] Socrates is mentioned nineteen times in the *Dialogi* of Seneca, twenty-two times in his *Epistles*, and 124 times in the philosophical writings of Cicero.
[116] *Crat.* 440c, *Rep.* 3. 410a, c, *Laws* 1. 649b.
[117] e.g. *Gorg.* 480b; see the material gathered by Bramble (1974), 35 nn. 2–3.

at si quis velit acriter cernere, oculi curandi sunt, quibus cernitur; si velis per-
niciter currere, pedes curandi sunt, quibus curritur; itidem si pugillare valde velis,
bracchia vegetanda sunt, quibus pugillatur.

The evident reference to athletic performance recalls, as has been
noted,[118] another passage of Seneca's *Epistles*, where the analogy between
physical and spiritual training is used in similarly protreptic fashion (*Ep.*
80. 3):[119]

si corpus perduci exercitatione ad hanc patientiam potest qua et pugnos pariter
et clades non unius hominis ferat . . . quanto facilius animus conroborari possit
ut fortunae ictus invictus excipiat.

The analogy also occurs at Horace *Ep.* 1. 1. 28–31, a similar context of
philosophical protreptic, where the average man is encouraged to strive
for virtue by the analogy of care for the body; even though he is unlikely
to be a great hero or athlete, he still seeks to prevent physical illness:

> non possis oculo quantum contendere Lynceus,
> non tamen idcirco contemnas lippus inungi;
> nec quia desperes invicti membra Glyconis,
> nodosa corpus nolis prohibere cheragra.

The mention of Lynceus' sharp sight and the might of Glycon, a leading
contemporary exponent of the *pankration*, all-in boxing, match the elements of sharp-sightedness and boxing in Apuleius, though the fact that
a general form of the analogy is found in Epictetus might suggest a common source for Apuleius and Horace in earlier Cynic or Stoic moralizing.[120]

   This traditional texture continues in the final part of this section,
which uses the common theme of the worthwhile nature of making an
attempt at something even if one is unlikely to become a leading exponent (169):[121]

---

[118] Cf. Beaujeu (1973), 244–5.

[119] Cf. similarly *Ep.* 78. 16, not adduced by Beaujeu: *nos quoque evincamus omnia, quorum praemium non corona nec palma est nec tubicen praedicationi nominis nostri silentium
faciens, sed virtus et firmitas animi et pax in ceterum parta, si semel in aliquo certamine debel-
lata fortuna est.*

[120] Cf. Epictetus *Discourses* 1. 2. 37 'I shall never be a Milo, and yet I do not neglect my
body; nor shall I be a Croesus, and yet I do not neglect my property; nor, in general, do we
cease to take pains in any area, because we despair of arriving at the highest degree of per-
fection'—tr. Hard (1995).

[121] Again, the parallel of this element with both Epictetus and Horace argues for a common moralizing source.

nescio ut Ismenias tibiis canere, sed non pudet me tibicinem non esse; nescio ut Apelles coloribus pingere, sed non pudet me non esse significem; itiden in ceteris artibus, ne omnis persequar, licet tibi nescire nec pudeat.

Underlying this is the common Platonic analogy between virtue and other technical crafts, here flute-playing and painting.[122]

(b) *Virtue as the only real good* (169–78). This final section begins by invoking in the mouth of an interlocutor (another diatribic touch) the three great figures of Middle Platonism—Socrates, Plato, and Pythagoras.[123] Its topic is certainly relevant to Socrates, since the point is repeatedly made in Plato's *Apology* and elsewhere that Socrates was a poor man and pursued virtue rather than wealth. Human unwillingness to spend time and effort on what really matters is stressed in a typically Roman image from doing daily accounts (170):[124]

igitur cotidiana eorum aera dispungas: invenias in rationibus multa prodige pro-fusa et in semet nihil, in suo dico daemonis cultum, qui cultus non aliud quam philosophiae sacramentum est.

The image may again owe something to a passage of Seneca (*De Ben.* 4. 32. 4), but two further points are more significant. First, the use of the term *daemon* for the only time in this last section of the *De Deo Socratis*; this suggests a thematic continuity with the earlier parts of the work, but also creates a possible inconsistency with it (the *daemon* here is clearly a soul-*daimon* of an internal kind, but this is not analogous to the case of Socrates and his *daimonion*, since that was earlier said to be an external spirit). Second, the clever play on the ambiguity of the word *cultus* here: *daemonis cultum* uses *cultus* in the sense of 'care, looking after', but *sacra-mentum* stresses that *cultus* can also refer to religious worship, appropri-ate for the *daimon* as a divine being (and we have already seen that it is the *daimones* who according to Apuleius are the effective recipients of human cult-activity directed towards the gods).

The attack on extravagant builders (171) is again highly traditional

---

[122] The *tibicen* Ismenias seems to be culled from Pliny *HN* 37. 8, 86, 10. For flute-playing as an analogy or contrast for virtue in Plato cf. *Phil.* 56a, *Prot.* 323a, *Gorg.* 501e, and for paint-ing in a similar role cf. *Gorg.* 503e; the two crafts are found together in a similar compara-tive context at [Plato] *Theages* 126e.

[123] For interest in Socrates in Middle Platonism see for example his constant mentions in Plutarch, Dio, and Maximus; for Pythagoras in Middle Platonism cf. Dillon (1977), 341–83.

[124] *Dispungere* = 'mark off, check' (Ulpian *Dig.* 40. 7. 6. 7): once again, the image is derived from Seneca (*De Ben.* 4. 32. 4, *Dial.* 10. 7. 7).

material in Roman moralizing, going back to Cato;[125] close links have rightly been seen between Apuleius' long and artistically constructed list of architectural extravagances with Seneca's similar condemnatory catalogues.[126] The contrast between outward luxury and inner poverty is another common theme; Apuleius' formulation alludes directly to the famous preface of Sallust's *Catiline*,[127] and there are further points of contact with the preface to the *Jugurtha*,[128] but it is also a feature of Greek diatribe.[129] Likewise, the symbolic use of the example of Tantalus (171–2) recalls a passage of Horace's *Satires* (1. 1. 68 ff.), which itself derives from the Greek diatribic tradition,[130] and the illustration of buying a horse uncovered and well inspected and its application to the moral scrutiny of men (173–4) is derived from Seneca *Ep.* 80. 9 (already suggested as a source at 168):

equum empturus solvi iubes stratum, detrahis vestimenta venalibus ne qua vitia corporis lateant: hominem involutum aestimas? mangones quidquid est quod displiceat, id aliquo lenocinio abscondunt, itaque ornamenta ipsa suspecta sunt; sive crus alligatum sive bracchium aspiceres, nudari iuberes et ipsum tibi corpus ostendi.

The example also occurs in a more literal context at Horace *Sat.* 1. 2. 86 ff., but the conjunction of this with Seneca once again suggests an ultimate origin in the Greek diatribe tradition.[131] Once again, Apuleius elaborates his traditional material in his own characteristic manner, demonstrating his learning by listing a number of technical items of horse-equipment (*phaleras, baltei, frena, ephippia, cingula*) in rhythmical and balanced clauses (*dependent . . . circumiacent, caelata . . . fucata . . . aurata*), and ornamenting the whole with a quotation from the third book of the *Georgics* (3. 80–1), the classic Latin literary text on horse-selection.[132]

---

[125] Cf. Nisbet and Hubbard (1978), 288.

[126] Beaujeu (1973), 245.

[127] *DDS* 171 *indocti incultique* ~ Sallust *Cat.* 2. 8 *indocti incultique*. For Apuleius and Sallust see now McCreight (1998).

[128] *Jug.* 2. 4; see the comments of Beaujeu (1973), 245.

[129] Cf. Beaujeu (1973), 246.

[130] Cf. Lejay (1911), 21.

[131] A distant, more technical source may be Xenophon *De Re Eq.* 1. 2; Apuleius mentions Xenophon as a historian at *Flor.* 20. 6, though he may not have read all his *opuscula*.

[132] The quotation as transmitted concludes with the word *honesti* in 3. 81, which in Vergil's text begins the next sentence, but can be made to belong to *pectus* with some plausibility; this syntactical modification of the original is either Apuleian (in which case editors are correct to print it) or scribal, literal-mindedly copying out all the words in the line with no regard for syntax (in which case *honesti* should be excluded).

The application of the illustration of horse-selection to choosing the virtuous man brings in Socrates once again, described with affection as *meum Socratem* (174); Socrates like the horse is to be considered divested of all trappings such as riches, easy enough since Socrates was proud of his poverty. The classification of such accidental goods as riches and birth as *aliena* (174), things which do not really belong to an individual, derives ultimately from Plato, though it also reflects the Stoic doctrine of ἀδιά-φορα, things to which the wise man is indifferent.[133] The mythological allusion at 175 *sat Porthaonio gloriae est, qui talis fuit, ut eius nepotem non puderet* is a learned one, and the proper name has been corrupted in transmission, but has been successfully unscrambled as a reference to the virtuous Oeneus (son of Porthaon) appropriately being honoured and restored to his kingdom by his grandson Diomedes.[134] Its point in context is evident (even those of great descent count virtue and its recognition as the most important thing), but its apparently recondite nature suggests either that this was a piece of mythology relatively familiar from a lost literary source, or that Apuleius was characteristically intent on impressing his audience with a particularly obscure piece of legendary lore.

This is followed by the reintroduction of a fictional interlocutor (cf. 169–70) and a piece of pointed dialogue (175):

'generosus est': parentes laudas. 'dives est': non credo fortunae . . . 'validus est': aegritudine fatigabitur. 'pernix est': stabit in senectute. 'formosus est': expecta paulisper et non erit. 'at enim bonis artibus doctus et adprime est eruditus et, quantum licet homini, sapiens et boni consultus': tandem aliquando ipsum virum laudas.

Here we see a verbal stripping-off of external and irrelevant qualities; each apparent virtue is dismissed, until we reach the essential qualities of

---

[133] Cf. Beaujeu (1973), 246.

[134] Cf. Beaujeu (1973), 246 n. 4, and the story given in Hyginus *Fab.* 175; the text cited is his conjecture (the manuscripts have *sateprothaonio*): *sat* was originally suggested by Baehrens (1912), 119, while a reference to Porthaon, father of Oeneus, was first argued for by Ribbeck (1878), who proposed *sate e Porthaone*. If Beaujeu's restoration is right (and I would agree with Moreschini (1991) in cautiously accepting it), the grandiloquent patronymic *Porthaonio*, and perhaps some of the surrounding words, are very likely to be a direct quotation from a tragedy, as Ribbeck (1878) suggests. Euripides' *Oeneus* contained the relevant plot about Oeneus and his restoration by his grandson Diomedes (fr. 558–70 Nauck²), and both Pacuvius' *Periboea* (cf. D'Anna (1967), 139–50) and Accius' *Diomedes* (cf. Dangel (1995) 356–7) reworked the plot in Latin; the latter is perhaps more attractive as a source for Apuleius here given the explicit quotation from Accius' *Philoctetes* which follows in *DDS* 176–7 (see n. 138 below).

the man, which begin with education and learning, those which an intellectual of the second century AD might have rated most highly. The form of brief question and answer is found in the *Apologia* and recalls Ciceronian rhetoric,[135] but here in this moralizing context the model is rather Senecan diatribe-style—compare Seneca *Ep.* 12. 10, 43. 9–10, and especially 47. 1:

'servi sunt'. immo homines. 'servi sunt'. immo contubernales. 'servi sunt'. immo humiles amici. 'servi sunt'. immo conservi …

The point is carried home by an elegantly ornamented final sentence, which also brings us back to the figure of Socrates (175):

hoc enim nec a parentibus hereditarium est nec a casu pendulum nec a suffragio anniculum nec a corpore caducum nec ab aetate mutabile. haec omnia meus Socrates habuit et ideo cetera habere contempsit.

Here *a suffragio anniculum* evidently refers to the competition for annual magistracies, indifference to which was a common topic of Roman moralizing,[136] while *a corpore caducum* suggests the metaphor of beauty's flower, which will wilt and fall, a poetic touch.[137]

This section, and the work in its extant form (for the possibility of a lost ending see Sect. 2 above), concludes with another great moral example to rival Socrates—Odysseus, or Ulysses (176–8). This figure is introduced through a quotation of Accius' *Philoctetes*, a suitably archaic literary allusion for the second century AD and a poet often cited by Apuleius.[138] By the second century AD Odysseus has been carefully cleaned up and presented as a model hero in the philosophical tradition of the Stoa and the Academy; similar exemplary versions of him are found in Greek writers of the Second Sophistic,[139] but this is already an established tradition in mainstream Latin literature.[140] The treatment of Odysseus continues the theme of external goods; the quotation from Accius names his parent last, and Apuleius uses this to stress that parentage is the least of his virtues (though in the passage of Accius the patronymic clearly forms a rhetorical climax), and that the moral qualities which precede this in the quotation are much more important.

[135] Cf. *Apol.* 27. 5–12, 103. 2–3, and Ch. 2, Sect. 4. IV above.
[136] Cf. e.g *Dial.* 1. 4. 2, 9. 4. 5.
[137] Recalling famous contexts such as Catullus 11. 21–4 and *Aen.* 9. 435–7.
[138] On Apuleius and Accius cf. Ch. 3 n. 60.
[139] Dio *Or.* 55, 56, Max. Tyr. *Dial.* 26, [Plutarch] *De Vit. et Poes. Hom.* 133–44, and n. 23 above.
[140] Cf. Stanford (1963), 121–7.

The work ends with the idea that Athene (Minerva) represents wisdom accompanying Odysseus in the *Odyssey* (177). This is a standard allegorization,[141] and Apuleius elaborates the idea in typical manner, in a passage which concludes our extant text (178):

> igitur hac eadem comite omnia horrenda subiit, omnia adversa superavit. quippe ea adiutrice Cyclopis specus introiit, sed egressus est; Solis boves vidit, sed abstinuit; ad inferos demeavit et ascendit; eadem sapientia comite Scyllam praeternavigavit nec ereptus est; Charybdi consaeptus est nec retentus est; Circae poculum bibit nec mutatus est; ad Lotophagos accessit nec remansit; Sirenas audiit nec accessit.

Once again the style strongly recalls Seneca, with its build-up of short contrasting clauses; the episodes chosen are those most often treated by the allegorizing interpreters of the *Odyssey*,[142] and the Sirens and Circe are specifically alluded to by Horace in the famous epistle already mentioned.[143] This splendid catalogue provides a striking ending, with its vivid 'vignette' effect in recalling famous moments from a literary classic, but the closure seems too abrupt, especially in a text originally conceived for performance. I have argued above (Section 2) that we are here missing the formal conclusion, which no doubt included a return to the figure of Socrates and his *daimonion*, the ostensible subject of the work.

4. CONCLUSION

This literary consideration of the *De Deo Socratis* has stressed several central factors. First, its genre of popular philosophical lecture and its subject of the *daimonion* of Socrates firmly link it with the contemporary activities of Greek sophistic writers, especially with the *Dialexeis* of Maximus of Tyre. We know of another (lost) Apuleian popular lecture *De Aesculapii Maiestate*,[144] and no doubt there were others; such stylish epideictic performances, clearly analogous to the speeches from which the *Florida* are extracted, must have been central to Apuleius' rhetorical and literary activity, and are clearly different from the more doxographical

---

[141] Cf. Buffière (1956), 278–89.

[142] For the ancient testimony for these allegories see Buffière (1956), 359–62 (Cyclops), 243–5 (cattle of the Sun), 379–80 (Scylla and Charybdis), 379 (Circe), 378 (Lotus-eaters), 380–6 (Sirens).

[143] Horace *Ep.* 1. 2. 23.

[144] *Apol.* 55. 10.

work of *De Platone*. Second, this contemporary Greek flavour is modified by the work's clear colouring of this material for a Roman audience, shown not only by constant allusions to Roman cultural institutions, but also by continuous use of the Roman literary and moralizing tradition, especially of Cicero and Seneca. Once again Apuleius is seen to be purveying something of the culture of the Greek Second Sophistic to a Roman North African audience, adapting his protreptic discourse as a capable professional orator to local cultural horizons and preferences, and presenting himself as an eloquent and literate intellectual as well as a *philosophus Platonicus*.

5

Philosophical Exposition: *De Mundo*
and *De Platone*

1. SHARED PROBLEMS OF AUTHENTICITY
AND DATING

The *De Mundo* and *De Platone* are respectively a free translation of the
extant pseudo-Aristotelian Περὶ Κόσμου, and a two-book handbook to
the doctrines of Plato, which is also likely to be a translation or paraphrase of an earlier Greek text; both are thus attempts to expound in
Latin the doctrines of Greek philosophers.[1] These two works are transmitted along with the *De Deo Socratis* and the *Asclepius* in a group of
manuscripts of the philosophical works attributed to Apuleius, a group
separate from the F tradition which contains the more literary works.[2] As
argued in Chapters 2 and 4, the existence of the 'false preface' at the
beginning of the *De Deo Socratis*, which I and others believe to have been
the original final section of the *Florida*, suggests that the two extant
branches of the manuscript tradition derive from a late antique division
of the collected works of Apuleius, possibly at the moment when their
texts were copied from papyrus to codex. Of the four philosophical works
thus transmitted together, I have already argued that the *Asclepius* is a
later and un-Apuleian accretion,[3] while the *De Deo Socratis* is indubitably

---

[1] The texts of both works used here are those of Moreschini (1991); the excellent Budé
edition of Beaujeu (1973) has useful notes. For *De Mundo*, there is a useful edition by Bajoni
(1991), with Italian translation, which also conveniently gives a text of the Περὶ Κόσμου. For
De Platone, there is an edition with German translation by Siniscalco and Albert (1980),
which has a short introduction and a few useful notes. A helpful account of the central
issues of the work is given by Schmutzler (1974), 1–48 (I am most grateful to Regine May for
lending me a copy of this work). I have found no modern English translation of either work,
or of *De Mundo* at any date; *De Platone* was translated into English by Burges (1876),
323–404. Further bibliography can be found in the editions mentioned, and (above all) in
Bajoni (1992) and (1994).

[2] See Reynolds (1983), 16–18, for a brief summary, Moreschini (1985), 267–88, for a fuller
treatment.

[3] Cf. Ch. 1 n. 48.

Apuleian (see Chapter 4). The issue of the authenticity of *De Mundo* and *De Platone* has been much discussed over the last century.[4] No one has doubted that the two works are by the same author, given their common transmission, shared style, and identical addressee, Faustinus (*Mu.* 285 *Faustine fili*, *Pl.* 2. 219 *Faustine fili*).[5] But are they Apuleian, and do they show sufficient doctrinal, literary, and stylistic consistency with the genuinely Apuleian works? I will summarize the main lines of argument from a point of view in favour of authenticity, suggest a date and place in Apuleius' works, and then move to a closer consideration of these two texts against that background. Here, as in my account of the *De Deo Socratis*, both space and my lack of expertise exclude extended investigation of the more detailed philosophical issues, which have been much discussed elsewhere.[6]

Indirect ancient testimony suggests that both these works were attributed to Apuleius by the early fifth century. Augustine cites a substantial passage from *De Mundo* (XXXIV. 364) in the *City of God* (*Civ.* 4. 2), with a specific attribution: *quae uno loco Apuleius breviter stringit in eo libello quem de mundo scripsit*, and Servius' commentary on Vergil *Aen.* 8. 275 cites as Apuleian the use of the term *medioximus* at *Pl.* 1. XI. 204, though the work itself is not named (*quos deos Apuleius medioximos vocat*).[7] The evidential weight of such citations is, of course, not by itself convincing (the Περὶ Ἑρμηνείας, which I would incline to deny to Apuleius, is assigned to him as early as the sixth century);[8] on the other hand, Augustine at least is a witness of importance, since he clearly knew a great deal about the works and the career of Apuleius.[9]

One issue which has been connected on a general level with that of authenticity is the question of the accuracy of the translation in *De Mundo*. Apuleius, it has been argued, must have been highly competent

---

[4] See esp. Axelson (1952), reprinted in Axelson (1987), Redfors (1960), Barra (1966), and Marchetta (1991); for summaries of the discussion see Beaujeu (1973), ix–xxix, and Marchetta (1991), 1–67.

[5] The vocative *fili* can of course indicate a person other than the writer's son, as in Fronto's addresses to M. Aurelius (*Amic.* 2. 3. 1, 2. 7. 1, etc.), but 'son' is the most natural translation and fits the long Latin tradition of addressing didactic treatises to one's son, which dates from Cato the Elder's *De Agri Cultura*, *De Medicina*, and *De Rhetorica*—cf. Cicero *Off.* 1. 1, echoed here, Seneca *Controv.* praef. 1, Macrobius *Sat.* I praef. 1.

[6] See esp. Regen (1971), Moreschini (1978), and Gersh (1986).

[7] For a balanced discussion of the indirect evidence for *De Mundo* and *De Platone* see Beaujeu (1973), x.

[8] For the sixth-century attribution of the Περὶ Ἑρμηνείας to Apuleius by Cassiodorus see Ch. 1 n. 40.

[9] For Augustine's knowledge of Apuleius and his works cf. Ch. 1 n. 1.

in Greek, since he proclaimed his bilingualism in Latin and Greek, and translated other Greek philosophical works as well as often closely adapting a Greek source-text in the *Metamorphoses*;[10] *De Mundo*, on the other hand, seems to show a number of places where the translator has misunderstood the Greek original, which suggests that Apuleius could not have been its author. But this argument has little to commend it. The occasional inaccuracies of *De Mundo*'s translation, which have been listed in detail by other scholars, are not great in number or quality, and are more often due to loose adaptation rather than poor translation (see Sect. 3 (ii) below); further, some at least may be due to variants in the textual transmission of Περὶ Κόσμου, and to the corruption of *De Mundo* itself in transmission.[11] In fact, though the Περὶ Κόσμου is not at all an easy text to translate, being often terse and cryptic in style, the author of the *De Mundo* seems no better and no worse a translator from Greek than other learned Romans such as Cicero or the elder Pliny, and this profile would fit Apuleius very well.[12]

In terms of doctrine, we find both continuities with and differences from the exposition of philosophical doctrines in genuinely Apuleian works. The mildly Stoicizing Peripatetic flavour of the Περὶ Κόσμου is naturally retained in *De Mundo*; this is of course a philosophical standpoint of a somewhat different kind from that of the *philosophus Platonicus*, though it is important to note that Apuleius follows the contemporary trend of Middle Platonism towards syncretism and the eclectic use of other schools.[13] On the other hand, we can see clear points where Apuleian interests might be said to emerge, especially in the second, theological part of the work. At Περὶ Κόσμου 394 b 8 ff. the Greek text refers to the controlling power (δύναμις) of the supreme god spread through the universe, while *Mu.* XXVII. 350–1 renders this singular term with the plural *potestates*, implying a level of divine powers below the supreme god, which strongly suggest the *mediae potestates*, the *daimones* or intermediate active divinities, in which Apuleius is so interested in the *De Deo Socratis* and the *Apologia*.[14] More generally, in the account of the

---

[10] For Apuleian professions of bilingualism see *Flor.* 9. 29, 18. 38–9, *Apol.* 4. 1, *DDS* 'false preface' V; for his translation of Plato's *Phaedo* cf. Ch. 1; and for his use of a Greek model in the *Metamorphoses* cf. Ch. 6.

[11] On the accuracy of the translation in *De Mundo* see Müller (1939), Redfors (1960), 13–18, and Marchetta (1991), the last stressing the possibility of corruption in transmission of both Greek and Latin texts.

[12] On Pliny as translator of Greek see André (1959), on Cicero see Powell (1995).

[13] For this tendency see the surveys by Dillon (1977), Gersh (1986), and Whittaker (1987).

[14] See esp. the discussion of Regen (1971), 33–83.

supreme god as ruler of the universe, there is much common ground with the accounts of the supreme god given in the *Apologia, De Deo Socratis,* and the *Metamorphoses*.[15] For its part, *De Platone* gives an account of Plato's doctrines which stresses some points of Apuleian interest, for example (again *daimones* and the supreme god), but which is also inconsistent in some points with other Apuleian Platonic expositions.[16] This has been regarded as firm evidence for different authorship, but could equally be derived from the tralatician nature of the ancient handbook genre, where translators or revisers are prone to repeat existing material regardless of inconsistency with their own views elsewhere.[17] Evidence from the consistency of doctrine seems therefore mixed and indecisive.

In terms of general literary texture, there is no doubt that *De Mundo* shares much with the more philosophical parts of the *Apologia* and (especially) the *De Deo Socratis*; though its quotations of poetry and other elements of literary colour derive in technique from its source text, the Περὶ Κόσμου, we can see how Greek literary allusions (and indeed cultural allusions) are adapted for a Roman audience (see further Sect. 3 (ii) below), just as Roman colour is plainly added to Greek material in the *De Deo Socratis*, and more especially how allusions are made to the same range of Latin texts as are used in the *De Deo Socratis*—echoes of Plautus, Ennius, Lucretius, and Vergil amongst the poets, and echoes of Cicero and Seneca as the classic Latin writers of philosophical exposition.[18] The way in which many passages, often located at key points in the argument, are rhetorically expanded into longer paratactic sentences of a particularly Apuleian type is especially noteworthy.[19] *De Platone*, on the other hand, is written in the dry style of a handbook with little literary colour: there are no explicit poetic quotations, practically no implicit poetic allusions, and the use of periodic sentence structure and other syntactical elaboration is extremely limited.[20] In vocabulary, *De Mundo* and

[15] For parallels with the *Apologia* and *DDS* see Regen (1971) 92–103; for links with the similarly supreme and polyonymous Isis in the *Metamorphoses*, compare *Mu.* XXXVII. 370 *et cum sit unus, plurimis nominibus cietur <propter> specierum multitudinem, quarum diversitate fit multiformis vis* with *Met.* 11. 3. 1 *cuius numen unicum* multiformi specie . . . *totus veneratur orbis*, each introducing a catalogue of the different names given to the single god.

[16] See Redfors (1960), 18–24, Moreschini (1978), 51–128.

[17] A good parallel is Cicero's *Orator* (168–236), where its traditional Aristotelian (and other) precepts on prose-rhythm are strangely dissonant in their details with Cicero's own practice (for the sources see Kroll (1913), 13–16).

[18] Cf. Müller (1939), 144–50, Redfors (1960), 73–5, and the annotations in Bajoni (1992) and (1994).

[19] e.g. at 295, 297–8, 323, 332, 339, 355, 357–8, 359–60, 364–5.

[20] Cf. the analysis of Bernhard (1927), 325–34.

De Platone clearly hang together, with some common elements not found in the undisputed Apuleian works; but even the painstaking work of Redfors concludes that there are just as many linguistic features linking these works to the elaborate and archaizing lexicon of the genuine Apuleian corpus, and that the evidence is clearly ambiguous.[21]

More substantial is the evidence of prose-rhythm. It is clear since Axelson's pioneering work that the *clausulae* (rhythmical ends of clauses and sentences) in *De Mundo* and *De Platone* show use of the accentual *cursus mixtus*, in which both the natural word-accent of Latin (as in later and less elaborate texts) and the metrical quantity of the syllables (in classic Ciceronian manner) seem to be at work in combination, and of *Scheinprosodie*, the 'apparent scansion' by which naturally long final syllables are shortened for clausular purposes.[22] These two features are not found in the indubitably Apuleian works, and would indeed normally suggest a dating rather later than the lifetime of Apuleius: accentual rhythm is first found for certain in the works of Cyprian, from the mid-third century, *Scheinprosodie* in Firmicus Maternus in the mid-fourth century. Of the two features, *Scheinprosodie* is the less firm criterion: the shortening of such long final syllables for metrical reasons had long been practised in Latin poetry, and its extension to prose may well have happened selectively in prose in the second century AD, even if we have no firm evidence of this outside the two works under discussion.[23] But the apparent innovation in *De Mundo* and *De Platone* of accentual *clausulae*, not found in the indubitably Apuleian works, is the strongest argument against Apuleian authorship, and needs to be considered at greater length.

Crucial here is the fact that we have relatively few Latin prose texts from the vital period AD 150–350, the transitional time within which the move from quantitative to accentual *clausulae* took place, and that what we do have may not be typical. Significantly for Apuleius, it also looks as if North Africa is our first source for the development of the *cursus mix-*

---

[21] Cf. Redfors (1960), 46–75, Bernhard (1927), 323–44, and the collection of material in Bajoni (1994). It is worth stressing the linguistic resemblances in *De Mundo* to the firmly Apuleian works listed in sects. 3 (i) and 3 (ii) below (here I add something to the treatments just mentioned; for *De Platone* see Sect. 5 below).

[22] Axelson (1952), (1987); cf. Redfors (1960), 75–114.

[23] On one type of poetic shortening cf. Hartenberger (1911), and on the general unreliability of *Scheinprosodie* as a dating criterion (again due largely to paucity of evidence) see Redfors (1960), 109–11.

tus in Latin prose: Cyprian, the first firmly dated user in the mid-third century, was born *c.* 200 and probably learnt his Latin style in Carthage, scene of Apuleius' career fifty years previously, in the first quarter of the century, and it could well be that *De Mundo* and *De Platone* show the same feature from the same province at an earlier date than previously thought. The evidence of Latin prose from Roman Africa closer to Apuleius in time is mixed, according to the latest detailed investigations;[24] of the works in my view most probably falsely attributed to Apuleius but akin to him in style and probably close to him in date and origin (by a pupil in the next generation?),[25] both the Περὶ Ἑρμηνείας and the *Asclepius* display the *cursus mixtus*, and so does the *Octavius* of Minucius Felix, variously dated between the AD 190s and 240 by modern scholars;[26] on the other hand, the works of Tertullian, which share something with Apuleius in vocabulary and syntax and which begin in the 190s, possibly during Apuleius' lifetime, show no trace of the *cursus mixtus*.[27] This need not mean that it is not then available; we can see in later texts that the same writer can choose whether or not to use the *cursus mixtus*, depending on the level of literary elaboration of the particular work. A central example is Augustine, more than two centuries after Apuleius: the self-consciously literary *Confessions* is according to modern research wholly non-accentual (i.e. Ciceronian) in its *clausulae*, while the less obviously literary *City of God* uses the *cursus mixtus*.[28] Similar choices are found in Jerome, who in different works could move freely between the three possibilities then available of Ciceronian *clausulae*, the *cursus mixtus*, and the purely accentual cursus.[29] Tertullian, with his classicizing literary ambitions, might well have chosen the Ciceronian mode against the *cursus mixtus* for all his work.

My own view is that the *De Mundo* and the *De Platone* are genuine Apuleian works, and that their differences in prose rhythm (and indeed of style) from other Apuleian texts are due to a combination of their later date and the availability of the *cursus mixtus*, and their lower level of literary ambition. On the matter of date, if Faustinus, the addressee of both

---

[24] See Oberhelman (1988*a*) and (1988*b*), refining his previous work with R. M. Hall, e.g. Oberhelman and Hall (1985).

[25] See Ch. 1 nn. 42 and 48.

[26] For the *cursus mixtus* in these texts cf. Oberhelman (1988*a*), 142; for the issue of the date of the *Octavius* see conveniently Beaujeu (1964), liv–lxviii.

[27] Oberhelman (1988*a*), 142, 145.

[28] Oberhelman (1988*a*), 144, 147.

[29] Scourfield (1993), 233–42,provides a good account.

works, is a son of Apuleius by Pudentilla or a later wife (the most likely interpretation of the address *Faustine fili*), and is of the usual age to study philosophy, the two works are almost certainly after 170,[30] and perhaps rather later; they may indeed be the latest works of Apuleius we possess.[31] Another possible dating criterion for *De Mundo* (and by association for *De Platone*) is its use of a slightly altered version of Gellius' *NA* 2. 22. 3–25, Favorinus' views on the winds, at *Mu.* XIII. 318–XIV. 321. Scholars are agreed that this is a clear reuse of Gellius' Latin text (see 3 (i) below);[32] but there is a notorious problem about the dating of the *Attic Nights*, which has been put as early as the mid-150s, or (as in the most recent and convincing account) after 177.[33] The issue is further complicated by the likelihood of informal personal contact between Apuleius and Gellius in the 150s, which might mean that Apuleius had access to some of Gellius' material before publication, as perhaps in the *Apologia*.[34] The use of Gellius therefore cannot provide a firm dating criterion for *De Mundo*, though it would be fully consistent with my preferred date for both works after 177.

But even if *De Mundo* and *De Platone* date as early as the 170s, it is (as we have seen) not impossible that the *cursus mixtus* may already be becoming established in Roman North Africa in that period. This need not, however, mean that the two accentually influenced works must necessarily post-date the non-accentual *Metamorphoses*, which I would want to put in the late 170s or later.[35] Here the issue of authorial choice in prose-rhythm is crucial. For Apuleius' self-consciously literary masterpiece, the *Metamorphoses*, as for Augustine's *Confessions*, the hallowed quantitative *clausulae* of Cicero were the obvious literary choice. For the less ambitious translation of a Greek work, and for the basic reworking of a Platonic handbook tradition, the less elevated but still respectable combination of the *cursus mixtus* might be appropriate, as it might have been for many of the other lost technical works listed in Chapter 1.

---

[30] This assumes that Apuleius' marriage to Pudentilla in 157–8 was his first, that if Faustinus was the son of that marriage he was not born before 158, and that the teenage years were commonly the earliest starting-point for learning philosophy (cf. Bonner (1977), 85–7).

[31] For a discussion of the various possible dates see Marchetta (1991), 65–9.

[32] See especially the detailed treatment in Müller (1939), 97–102.

[33] Holford-Strevens (1988), 12–19.

[34] See the good discussion in Holford-Strevens (1988), 16–19.

[35] Cf. Ch. 6.

2. THE *DE MUNDO*: GENERAL CHARACTER
AND STRUCTURE

The *De Mundo* is a relatively faithful translation of the extant pseudo-Aristotelian Περὶ Κόσμου, an influential treatise on the nature of the universe most probably written in the first century BC, with considerable literary pretensions which *De Mundo* follows.[36] Overall, *De Mundo* adheres fairly closely to its model's order of material and literary structure, but adapts its detailed content in a number of places, making considerable cuts, and adding some small-scale expansions as well as two larger interpolations from Gellius and about Hierapolis (see Sects. 3 (i) and 3 (ii) below), and the Latin version is some 10 per cent longer than the Greek.[37] Though it is plainly a translation, it claims in effect to be an original work, suggesting that its material is drawn by independent research not just from (Ps.-)Aristotle but also from Theophrastus (I. 289 *nos Aristotelen prudentissimum et doctissimorum et Theophrastum auctorem secuti*); this kind of plagiarized erudition is found again in the silent use of Gellius in *Mu*. XIII–XIV, and would be typically Apuleian.[38] Like the *De Deo Socratis, De Mundo* plainly pays close attention to the needs of its Latin-speaking readership: Greek terms when cited are usually glossed in some way,[39] and the Greek poetic quotations common in the Περὶ Κόσμου are usually explicitly translated, paraphrased in the surrounding context, or replaced by Latin equivalents.[40] The range of Latin authors quoted and otherwise alluded to, as already noted, corresponds closely to that found in the *De Deo Socratis* and other Apuleian works, and shows an evident archaizing taste for Ennius and Plautus.[41]

The structure of *De Mundo* can be analysed as follows:

1. Preface (285–9). The virtues of philosophy and its power to investigate natural phenomena, and the importance of the universe as a topic.

2. The composition of the universe (I. 289–XXIII. 341).
   (a) The *aether* and its heavenly bodies (I. 289–II. 293).
   (b) The *aer* and its contents (III. 293–5).

---

[36] For a convenient text and translation and a useful discussion of date see Furley (1955).

[37] For a detailed analysis cf. Müller (1939).

[38] There is a great deal of similar unsignalled literary borrowing in the *Apologia* (see Ch. 2), and scholars have noted the similar pairing of Theophrastus and Aristotle as explicit sources at *Apol.* 51. 4–5 and as models for Apuleius' biological works at *Apol.* 36. 4.

[39] Cf. e.g. 290, 317–18, 323–5, 355, 362, 372–4.

[40] Cf. e.g. 335–6 (Heraclitus glossed), 343 (Homeric citation not signalled), 363 (Ennius substituted for Homer), 368 (Lucretius replacing Sophocles).

[41] Cf. Redfors (1960), 73–5.

   (c) The earth, seas, and islands (IV. 296–7).
   (d) Interlude: the interconnectedness of all the elements (V. 297–8).
   (e) Seas and islands again (VI. 298–VII. 305).
   (f) The earth and associated phenomena (VIII. 305–XIX. 332).
        (i) Damp exhalations: mist, dew, ice, frost, rain, snow, hail (VIII. 305–IX. 309).
        (ii) Intermediate exhalations: combinations of damp and dry (X. 309–11).
        (iii) Dry exhalations: the winds and their general taxonomy (XI. 311–XIV. 321).
        (iv) Above the earth: clouds and associated weather features (XV. 321–XVI. 325).
        (v) Below the earth: volcanoes, entrances to the Underworld, earthquakes, and other seismic phenomena (XVII. 326–XIX. 332).
   (g) The wonder of the world's concord of disparate elements (XIX. 332–XXI. 337).
   (h) *Laudes mundi*: formal and elaborate praise of the universe for its order, regularity, abundance, and capacity for self-renewal (XXII. 337–XXIII. 341).

3. The supreme divine ruler of the universe (XXIV. 341–XXXVIII. 374).
   (a) The divine ruler as the single moving power of the universe, diffused and available equally through all creation; his powers of distant action without personal intervention (XXIV. 337–XXV. 346).
   (b) An extended comparison of the divine ruler's actions with the Great King of Persia and his hierarchical delegation of tasks (XXVI. 346–9).
   (c) The divine ruler's capacity to move the universe with his single power in all its diverse and differently moving physical parts (XXVII. 349–XXXI. 358).
   (d) His capacity to control the main activities of human life, and his role as the guarantor of the world's continuation (XXXI. 359–XXXII. 361).
   (e) His habitation in the highest heaven, in a dimension of immutable order contrasting with the disorder and mutability of the world below (XXXIII. 362–XXXIV. 365).
   (f) His role as the principle of order and equilibrium in the universe, reflected in the order of urban life and of flora and fauna (XXXV. 365-XXXVI. 369).
   (g) His uniqueness and single nature despite his many titles (XXXVII. 369–72).
   (h) His links with ideas of fate and predestination (XXXVIII. 372–4).

The main section of the treatise is thus fundamentally bipartite: after the elaborate preface (285–9), the first part of its exposition is concerned with the various physical elements of the universe (I–XXIII), the second with the divine ruler of the universe and his nature (XXIV–XXXVIII). This second part is treated explicitly as climactic (XXIV. 341 *quod caput est sermonis huius*). The first part is subdivided into a number of sections, and there is a logical order in its development: sections 2(a)–(c) go through the four parts of the universe in order (*aether, aer*, land, and sea, corresponding to the four elements fire, air, earth, and water), and 2(d) stresses the interconectedness of the different elements, reflecting the coming climax of this part of the work in 2(g) and (h), the celebration of the harmony and unity of the universe. Before then, however, various natural phenomena connected with the earth are treated in particular detail, no doubt because they are particularly open to human observation. Seas and islands, here seen as part of the earth, are treated in 2(e), and then in 2(f) follow other phenomena: the progression in 2(f)(i)–(iii) from damp to dry is clear, and a clear division is drawn at XVII. 325 between 2(f)(i)–(iv), concerned with atmospheric phenomena, and the concluding section 2(f)(v), which turns to the operation of air and fire under the earth in seismic phenomena. The climactic *laudes mundi* in 2(g), a splendid purple patch in the Περὶ Κόσμου elaborated even more in the Latin version, are prepared for in 2(f): the wondrous nature of the universe leads naturally to its praise.

The shorter second part has less structural variety, being closely focused on the divine ruler of the universe and his supreme powers. Sections 3(a)–(d) are basically concerned with the means by which the ruler controls the universe, a theme varied and illustrated by the extended comparison in 3(c) with the Great King of Persia, while 3(e)–(h) look at the nature of the ruler himself—where he fits into the universe physically and ideologically in 3(e) and 3(f), his unique and single character in 3(g), his relation to other traditional forms of divine power in 3(h). As it stands, sections 3(e)–(g) seem to be the stylistic climax of the work, with 3(h) as something of an appendix; the whole work does, however, end with a substantial quotation from Plato, bolstered in the Latin version with a Vergilian allusion, which avoids a feeling of anticlimax.[42] In general, counterbalancing its unity of theme, the second part has a greater variety of texture than the first in terms of poetic quotation, literary ornament, and illustration from human life, a variety which allows the translation extensive opportunity to adapt the Greek original for a Latin-speaking readership of Roman culture—see further Section 3 (ii) below.

---

[42] Plato *Laws* 715e–716a and 730a, run together; *De Mundo* adds Vergil *Georg.* 4. 221–2.

3. THE *DE MUNDO*: LITERARY AND STYLISTIC ASPECTS

Recent literary work on the *De Mundo* has been relatively effective in cataloguing its stylistic sources in general, but has been less successful in using this research to establish its overall literary character.[43] Here space precludes a full literary analysis of *De Mundo*, but I will pick out a few of the questions crucial to the work's assessment and interpretation.

(i) *Literary Affinities*

As already noted, *De Mundo* follows the Περὶ Κόσμου its relatively high literary ambitions: there seems no doubt that Cicero and Lucretius (and to a lesser extent Seneca) provide it with important thematic and linguistic models, and that other poets such as Vergil are alluded to for literary effect.[44] The work thus frames itself in a distinguished Latin tradition of philosophical and other didactic, and turns to texts which are also prominent intertexts for the *De Deo Socratis*, providing a further argument for Apuleian authorship. This colouring is particularly evident in the elaborate preface, which may be taken as programmatic in terms of the work's literary tradition as well as in terms of its thematic content. As has often been noted, *De Mundo* begins with a clear allusion to well-known Ciceronian didactic openings (*praef.* 285): *Consideranti mihi et diligentius intuenti et saepe alias, Faustine fili, virtutis indagatrix expultrixque vitiorum, divinarum particeps rerum philosophia videbatur . . .* Here the alterations to the original are clearly for intertextual purposes: both the change of addressee from Alexander, quasi-son to the supposed writer Aristotle, to Faustinus, son of the author of *De Mundo*, and the addition of the paired dative participles with *mihi* and *saepe* recall the address of the *De Officiis* (1. 1) to *Marce fili*, and especially the opening of the *De Oratore* (1. 1), *cogitanti mihi saepe numero et memoria vetera repetenti . . . Quinte frater*. The paired agent nouns in *-trix* recall verbatim the praise of philosophy near the beginning of the last book of the *Tusculans* (5. 5): *o vitae philosophiae dux, o virtutis indagatrix expultrixque vitiorum*, and the commendation of philosophy in general occurs in several of the proems of Cicero's philosophical works (*Off.* 1. 3–6, *Tusc.* 1. 1–6, *Fin.* 1. 2–3).

---

[43] I think of the scholarly but sometimes unfocused collections of material in Bajoni (1991) and (1994).

[44] See on echoes from all these authors Müller (1939), 144–50.

This Ciceronian colour is closely followed by a complex of Lucretian allusions (*praef.* 287).[45] The theme of philosophy entering the heavens recalls the famous praise of Epicurus for opening up the secrets of the universe in the proem of *DRN* 1, a link confirmed by specific verbal echoes: *mundum eiusque penetralia . . . adire* (287) recalls the *moenia mundi* penetrated by Epicurus (Lucretius *DRN* 1. 73), while *homines . . . animo peregrinari ausi sunt per caeli plagas* (287) clearly looks to Epicurus' cosmic mind-travel at Lucretius *DRN* 1. 74 *omne immensum peragravit mente animoque*, and to his mortal daring at 1. 66–7 *primum Graius homo mortalis tollere contra / est oculos ausus*, though there are also Ciceronian echoes here.[46] The mention of the *inventa* of philosophy (287) might also look to Lucretius' praise of Epicurus elsewhere as *rerum inventor* (3. 9) and his commendation of Epicurean philosophical *reperta* (5. 2). Likewise, at 289, the programmatic closure of the preface, *dicemus de omni hac caelesti ratione naturasque <et> officia complexi, et cur et quemadmodum moveantur explicabimus* recalls the equally programmatic Lucretius *DRN* 1. 54–5, *nam tibi de summa caeli ratione deumque / disserere incipiam et rerum primordia pandam.*

Though allusions to them are most dense in the preface, Cicero and Lucretius remain models throughout the work—Lucretius usually for the occasional poetic phrase, Cicero more extensively. The purple patch in praise of the earth at IV. 296, which substantially expands the Greek original, does so by echoing a similar passage at Cicero *ND* 2. 98–9, and it is worth juxtaposing the two,[47] especially as the anaphora, alliteration, balance, and rhythm of the passage from *De Mundo* is strongly indicative of Apuleian authorship.

Mu. IV. 296 haec frequentatur animantibus, haec silvarum viriditate vestitur, haec fontium perennitate recreatur, haec fluminum frigidos lapsus nunc erroribus terrenis vehit, modo profundo in mari confundit; eadem infinitis coloribus floret, altitudine montium, camporum aequore, nemorum opacitate variatur, sinuosis inflexa litoribus, distincta insulis, villulis urbibusque collucens, quas sapiens genus, homo, communibus usibus fabricatur.

Cicero *ND* 2. 98–9 ac principio terra universa cernatur . . . vestita floribus herbis arboribus frugibus . . . adde huc *fontium* gelidas *perennitates,* liquores perlucidos amnium, riparum vestitus viridissimos, speluncarum concavas altitudines, saxorum asperitates, impendentium *montium altitudines* immensitatesque

---

[45] Here I add considerably to Bajoni (1994).
[46] Cicero *Div.* 2. 30 *caeli plagas,* *ND* 1. 54 *animus . . . peregrinatur.*
[47] As done by Bajoni (1994), 1801–2.

camporum . . . quid iam de hominum genere dicam . . . quorumque operibus agri insulaeque litoraque collucent distincta tectis et urbibus.

Apart from the strong verbal and thematic echoes, both passages show a strongly Stoicizing feel, with their stress on divine providence and its demonstration in the order of the universe, a central theme of *De Mundo*, and the Stoic account of the cosmos and its divine government given by Balbus in *ND* 2. 73–173 serves as a source for *De Mundo* in a number of other places.[48]

The use of Gellius *NA* 2. 22 at *Mu.* XIII. 318–XIV. 321 has already been mentioned in the discussion of the work's date in Section 1; a consideration of *De Mundo*'s adaptation of this source can give a useful insight into its literary character. The Gellian passage reports Favorinus' account of the winds as given orally at a dinner party (cf. 2. 22. 1–2), and a comparison between the two texts shows that *De Mundo* is the imitator, turning the looser style of table-talk into the tighter frame of philosophical didactic.[49] Though *De Mundo* alters much of the language, it retains some of the Gellian phrasing, and plainly edits down the colloquial expansiveness of the original, introducing a more literary and periodic sentence structure and smoothly incorporating it into its exposition of the winds as if citing a scholarly work of Favorinus;[50] the effort to conceal the second-hand source matches the initial self-promoting pose that *De Mundo* is culled from personal research in Aristotle and Theophrastus rather than a translation of a single work attributed to Aristotle (*Mu.* I. 289; see Sect. 2 above). The editing is instructive. On the one hand, *De Mundo* cuts out the Gellian part which discusses Homer's use of the winds (2. 22. 16–18), appropriate for the Greek-cultured Favorinus but less so for a Latin-speaking readership, gives the text (XIV. 320) of a passage of Vergil (*Aen.* 8. 709–10)[51] merely alluded to without quotation in Gellius, thus matching the technique of verse-quotation in the remainder of *De Mundo*, and (naturally enough) removes Favorinus' final *praeteritio* about the winds he had no space to discuss, rounding off its discussion instead by supplying its own allusion to Cato's *Origines*, a fashionably archaic text for Apuleius. Particularly indicative of *De Mundo*'s derivative status here is

---

[48] See Müller (1939), 144–5.

[49] See Müller (1939), 97–102.

[50] XIII. 318 *Favorinus . . . refert* strongly suggests citation of Favorinus' own writings, as in the use of *refert* in citing the life of Plato by Speusippus at *Pl.* 1. II. 183.

[51] The lines of Vergil are in fact omitted in the transmission of *De Mundo*, but XIV. 320 *sic meminit* makes it certain that modern editors are right in restoring them.

the way in which the anonymous Greek tragic fragment cited by Gellius from Aristotle remains unusually untranslated and unparaphrased in *De Mundo*;[52] in its eagerness to incorporate the Gellian passage, *De Mundo* has for once neglected the interests of the Greekless reader.

(ii) *Apuleian Adaptations*

The discussion of *De Mundo*'s use of Gellius leads on to the central issue of adaptation of the Περὶ Κόσμου. Amongst scholars the issue of correct or incorrect translation has been more prominent than that of adaptation for a Roman readership, largely because of its connection with the issue of authenticity (see Sect. 1 above).[53] Here I will concentrate on some of the various ways in which *De Mundo* adapts the Περὶ Κόσμου for its Latin-speaking readers; there is no space here to give more than a brief flavour, and I shall examine only a few significant examples, giving where necessary the closest possible rendering of the Greek original.[54]

(a) The opening of the work's main exposition (Περὶ Κόσμου 391 b 9 ff.):

The universe is a combination of the heaven and the earth and of the natures contained in them. 'Universe' (κόσμος) can also be defined as the ordering and arrangement (διακόσμησις) of all things, preserved by and through god. The middle part of this arrangement, unmoveable and firmly seated, has fallen to the life-sustaining earth, the home and mother of all kinds of living creatures. The part above this, complete and limited in every direction at the highest point, the home of the gods, is called the heaven.

Compare *De Mundo* I. 289–90:

mundus omnis societate caeli et terrae constat et eorum natura, quae utriusque sunt; vel sic: mundus est ornata ordinatio dei munere, deorum recta custodia, cuius cardinem—sic enim dixerim κέντρον—robustum et immobilem genetrix atque altrix animantium omnium habet tellus, supernis omnibus, ut videri potest, aeris liquiditate ad modum tegminis saeptis et opertis. ultra deorum domus est, quod caelum vocamus.

Here several strategies of adaptation can be seen. *Eorum natura, quae utriusque sunt* is no mistranslation of 'the natures contained in them' but

---

[52] See n. 40 above for *De Mundo*'s usual practice of Latinizing Greek quotations; of course, it is possible that the translation was lost in transmission, as the Vergilian lines have been (see previous note).

[53] See especially Marchetta (1991).

[54] I use the Greek text of Furley (1955), but my own more literal translation.

an elegant way of avoiding the clumsy-sounding genitive plural *natu-rarum*, rare in Latin,[55] while *vel sic* keeps the sentence going, a contrast with the Greek and a common technique in *De Mundo*, which (in true Apuleian manner) has many more periodic sentences than Περὶ Κόσμου. The important word-play in the Greek text between κόσμος 'universe, order' and διακόσμησις 'arrangement', bringing out a central theme of the work, the orderly nature of the universe, cannot be directly reproduced in Latin, but instead *De Mundo* provides two related word-plays (a very Apuleian element)[56] of equivalent ideological importance within the work. The first is between *mundus* and *munere*, stressing that the universe is the gift of god, looking forward to the theological part of the work; and the second is between *ornata* and *ordinatio*, drawn from Cicero and repeated later in the work,[57] and emphasizes the connection between beauty and order, looking forward to the climax of the first part of the work, the *laudes mundi* of XXII. 337–XXIII. 341. The variation *dei... deo-rum* is an elegant avoidance of homoeoteleuton, and there is no need to argue that *De Mundo* may be translating a variant genitive plural in the Greek.[58] The substitution of the Greek term κέντρον corrects the μέσον of Περὶ Κόσμου, using Cicero,[59] and provides an example of both personal intervention[60] and the glossing of Greek terms[61] which are both charac-teristic features of *De Mundo*. The hanging ablative absolute clause, *supernis... opertis*, again lengthens the sentence, and unpacks the some-what cryptic original to bring out firmly the distinction between the lower air, *aer*, immediately above the earth, and the upper air, *aether*, home of the gods, rather than referring to the heaven in general as the Greek does. In general, this is not unthinking linguistic transposition, but an active and engaged literary adaptation of the original for which accu-rate rendition is not the first priority.

(b) A passage from the geographical section, describing the divisions of the Mediterranean sea (Περὶ Κόσμου 393 a 27 ff.):

---

[55] The PHI CD-ROM, covering all pre-Apuleian Latin, gives only seven instances of the form—four in Cicero and one each in Varro, Lucretius, and Quintilian.

[56] For Apuleian word-plays see conveniently the sections entitled 'Wortspiel' in Bernhard (1927).

[57] *Mu.* XXII. 337 and Cicero *ND* 2. 127. *Mundus* and *munus* occur in adjacent sentences at Cicero *ND* 2. 90, which may possibly have influenced the word-play in *De Mundo*.

[58] So Marchetta (1991), 63.

[59] *Tusc.* 1. 40 *quod* κέντρον *illi vocant.*

[60] See the further examples of authorial intervention in *De Mundo* collected by Bajoni (1994), 1797 n. 55.   [61] See n. 39 above.

it makes three seas, the Sardinian, the Galatian and the Adriatic, and following on from these at an angle, the Sicilian, and after that the Cretan, and continuous with that on one side the Egyptian and Pamphylian and Syrian, on the other the Aegean and the Myrtoan.

Compare *Mu.* VI. 300:

sed in maxima divisus est maria, quorum unum Gallicum dicitur, alterum Africum, quod quidem Aristoteles Sardiense maluit dicere, tertium Hadriaticum pelagus. his iungitur Siculum et post Creticum, eo indiscretis finibus Pamphylium, Assyrium, Aegyptium, sed ante Aegaeum et Myrtoum sunt maria.

Here the interest lies primarily in the Latin text's more Roman perspective. *De Mundo* uses *Gallicus* where *Galaticus*, the exact equivalent of the Greek word, was available,[62] using the proper adjective for 'Gallic', which belongs strictly to the familiar western Gauls but is sometimes applied to the Eastern and ethnically linked Galatians;[63] it also explicitly replaces 'Sardinian' with 'African', the normal Roman name for this sea but perhaps particularly apposite for a North African readership, very likely if the work is Apuleian. The allusion to Aristotle's use of a different name looks like a casual learned reference rather than an allusion to the source text being translated (cf. 320); this is clearly part of the overall strategy of *De Mundo* in its concealment of its translation origins (see Sect. 2 above). In the last sentence, the angular position of the Sicilian sea is omitted, but the Aegean and Myrtoan seas, the name given to the south-west Aegean, are seen as 'before' the more eastern parts of the Mediterranean rather than just on the other side from them: this view is clearly from a Roman perspective.

(c) A transition between geographical and meteorological material (*Περὶ Κόσμου* 394 a 4 ff.):

Such is the account we have given of the nature and situation of the land and sea, which we are accustomed to call the inhabited world.

    Let us speak now of the most remarkable phenomena within it and about it, summing up the necessary chief points.

Compare *Mu.* 305:

de mari satis dictum. terreni casus ita se habent.

---

[62] *Galaticus* occurs e.g. at Pliny *HN* 21. 160.
[63] For this use of *Gallus* cf. Livy 33. 18. 3, Horace *Epode* 9. 18.

Here we see a clear reduction of the original (as often), but also a re-interpretation of the link between the two sections. The inclusive polar expression 'land and sea' in the Greek is recast in Latin as a dichotomy between the two (*de mari . . . terreni*). This may look like poor translation, but in fact it is a comprehensible response to the surrounding material: *Mu.* VI. 298–VII. 305 have in fact been about the sea and its islands, while *Mu.* VIII–XIX. 332 will be very largely about the earth and its surrounding phenomena (see the structural analysis in Sect. 2 above). The Latin formulation, though the division it marks is not in fact entirely effective (I. 289–V. 298 had dealt with elements other than the sea, and some of the volcanic phenomena in XVII. 326–XIX. 332 are located in the sea), nevertheless recognizes that in some sense the account of the land and sea has not finished, and that the summarizing sentence in the Greek is in fact misleading.

(d) Subterranean sources of fire (*Περὶ Κόσμου* 395 b 18 ff.):

Of these some are invisible beneath the earth, while many have breathing and bubbling points such as Lipara, Aetna, and those on the islands of Aeolus; these also often flow like rivers and throw up fiery lumps. And some, being under the earth close to spring waters, heat them up, and some of the springs come up luke-warm, others boiling, some with a pleasant mixture of temperatures. Likewise many mouths for exhalations are open all over the world, of which some make those who come near them divinely possessed, others make them need no food, others make them prophesy, like those in Delphi and Lebadia; but some completely destroy them, like the ones in Phrygia. Often . . .

Compare *Mu.* XVII. 326–9:[64]

nam quibusdam sub terris occulti sunt spiritus et flant incendia indidem, ut Liparae, ut Aetna, ut Vesuvius etiam noster solet. illi etiam ignes, qui terrae secretariis continentur, praetereuntes aquas vaporant et produnt longinquitatem flammae, cum tepidiores aquas reddunt, viciniam, cum ferventiores opposito incendio aquae uruntur, ut Phlegethontis amnis, quem poetae sciunt in fabulis inferorum. at enim illos quis non admirandos spiritus aribitretur, cum ex his animadvertat accidere, ut eorum religione lymphantes alii sine cibo potuque sunt, pars veri praesagiis effantes futura? quod in oraculis Delphicis est ceterisque.

vidi et ipse apud Hierapolim Phrygiae non adeo ardui montis vicinum latus nativi oris hiatu reseratum et tenuis neque editae marginis ambitu circumdatum. sive illa, ut poetae volunt, Ditis spiracula dicenda sunt, seu mortiferos anhelitus eos credi prior ratio est, proxima quaeque animalia et in alvum prona atque proiecta venenati spiritus contagione corripiunt et vertice circumacta inter-

---

[64] I have here reparagraphed Moreschini's text to highlight the interpolated material.

imunt. antstites denique ipsos semiviros esse, qui audeant propius accedere ad superna semper sua ora tollentes; adeo illis cognitum est vis mali, ad inferiora aeris noxii crassitate densa, inferiores quoque facilius adire atque percellere.

saepe accidit ut . . .

It will be seen at once that *De Mundo* doubles the length of this part of *Περὶ Κόσμου* by inserting the passage about Hierapolis with a claim to autopsy; apart from the summary of Gellius at *De Mundo* XIII. 318--XIV. 321, this is the longest addition to the original, and unlike the Gellian summary it is apparently unconstrained by the limits of imitating a source text. This makes it an especially valuable locus for the consideration of *De Mundo*'s own style, which I shall discuss shortly.

Less extensive but equally characteristic adaptation of the Greek original is clear in the paragraph which precedes the reference to Hierapolis (*nam quibusdam . . . ceterisque*). The reference to lava ('these also often flow like rivers and throw up fiery lumps') is left out in *De Mundo*, the kind of brief omission we often find in its version of the Greek, here perhaps in order to allow the final ascending tricolon *ut Liparae, ut Aetna, ut Vesuvius etiam noster solet*. Again, as in (b) above, we see a Roman perspective in the fact that the list of volcanic locations in *Περὶ Κόσμου*, Lipara, Aetna, and the islands of Aeolus, is modified to include Vesuvius instead of the islands of Aeolus, with *noster* indicating that this is a feature familiar to writer and reader alike, as it would be to Romans, especially after the eruption of Vesuvius in AD 79; this may also show an awareness, more appropriate to Roman culture, that Lipara/Liparae (both spellings are found in Latin)[65] is itself one of the 'islands of Aeolus', the Lipari group off Sicily, as was generally recognized in antiquity,[66] and that the Greek text's formulation is in fact tautologous. The addition of the infernal fiery river Phlegethon and the information that it is to be found in the poets also appeals to Roman culture. The reference is clearly to a Vergilian account of the Underworld (cf. *Aen.* 6. 550–1), a theme which will importantly reappear in the inserted passage about Hierapolis (see below), and the formula with which the allusion is introduced has an appropriate poetic/archaic flavour which (like the Vergilian quotation itself) is fully Apuleian.[67] Note too the way in which the sentence *at*

---

[65] The singular at e.g. Pliny *HN* 3. 93, the plural at e.g. Livy 21. 49. 2.

[66] Cf. e.g. Vergil *Aen.* 8. 417–19, Pliny *HN* 3. 92, Strabo 6. 2. 10, Thucydides 3. 88. 1.

[67] *In fabulis*, similarly referring to literature, is found at *Met.* 6. 29. 7, while the archaic/poetic use of *scire* in the sense 'know of' is found at *Apol.* 80. 2. On Apuleian use of Vergilian quotation and allusion see the extensive material and bibliography gathered in Harrison (1997*a*) and Finkelpearl (1998).

enim . . . futura reworks its original into an elaborate period. Περὶ
Κόσμου gives religious possession, abstinence from food, and prophecy as
three separate and equally possible reactions to contact with subterranean exhalations, while *De Mundo* regards all contact as religious possession, with the consequence of either abstinence or prophecy: again,
this is reworking rather than translation, and the colourful language used
is typically Apuleian.[68] Finally in this paragraph, the Greek's 'like those in
Delphi and Lebadia; but some completely destroy them, like the ones in
Phrygia' is thoroughly altered for its new context: Lebadia, relatively
obscure to non-Greeks, is omitted completely, while the references to
deadly vapours in Phrygia are greatly expanded in the interpolated paragraph on Hierapolis.

This interpolated paragraph, as already noted, provides useful evidence for *De Mundo*'s non-translation style, and for Apuleian authorship. First, the claim to autopsy (*vidi et ipse*) with which it begins is
thoroughly in the manner of Apuleius, anxious to present himself as a
well-travelled sophistic intellectual: Phrygian Hierapolis is an exotic
location from a Roman perspective, and to claim to have been there is a
mark of sophistication and glamour. We find the same self-promoting
boast at XXXII. 361, where the writer of *De Mundo* claims to have seen the
shield of Athena Parthenos in Athens (*vidi ipse*), something which is only
hearsay for the author of Περὶ Κόσμου (399 b 33 'they say that . . .'). Both
these match *Flor.* 15 where Apuleius, speaking to a North African audience, claims autopsy of Samos, home of Pythagoras (*Flor.* 15. 4, 6).
Second, the clear allusion to *Aen.* 7. 568 *spiracula Ditis* in *sive illa, ut poetae
volunt, Ditis spiracula dicenda sunt*, which picks up the previous allusion
to the *Aeneid* in the river Phlegethon a few lines earlier, not only carefully
integrates the interpolated passage into *De Mundo* by continuing the
theme of Vergilian infernal allusion, but also uses a phrase employed by
Apuleius in the *Metamorphoses* (6. 18. 2 *spiraculum Ditis*). Third, the language and phrasing of the passage seems especially Apuleian: particularly
significant here are the balanced and rhyming elements *nativi oris hiatu
reseratum . . . editae marginis ambitu circumdatum* and *alvum prona atque
proiecta . . . corripiunt et vertice circumacta interimunt*, and the colourful
and poetic/archaic vocabulary matched in genuinely Apuleian texts
(*mortiferos anhelitus, ad superna*).[69]

---

[68] For *cibo potuque* cf. *Apol.* 50. 5 *potu et cibo*, while *praesagium* is an Apuleian favourite
(thirteen times, nearly 20 per cent of all the uses in Latin before AD 200—the PHI CD-ROM
gives some seventy examples).

[69] *Mortifer* occurs three times in the *Metamorphoses*, *anhelitus* five times (though never

(e) Roman colour in the concluding theological part of the work (*Mu.* XXIV. 341–XXXVII. 374). This part of Περὶ Κόσμου, with its more abstract argumentation about the nature of the invisible ruler of the universe, is appropriately varied and illustrated with a number of examples from Greek life and history. The most extensive of these, comparing the supreme deity with the Great King of Persia, is translated in *De Mundo* more or less directly, with some minor expansions (Περὶ Κόσμου 398 a 11–35 ~ XXVI. 346–9), but there are one or two elements which adapt it to a Roman context: the names of some of the Great King's officials are Romanized (347 *dispensatores pecuniae, quaestores vectigalium, tribunos aerarios*), and the specific mention of the Persian cities Sousa and Egbatana, of no Roman interest, are omitted. Other illustrations are similarly recast. Περὶ Κόσμου 397 b 24 ff. reads '[The god] himself holds the highest and first seat, and is called "most high" for this reason, settled (in the words of the poet) "on the loftiest peak" of the whole heaven'; in *Mu.* XXV. 343 this becomes *nec ambigitur eum praestantem, sublimem sedem tenere et poetarum laudibus eius consulum ac regum nuncupationibus praedicari et in arduis arcibus habere solium consecratum.* Here the Homeric quotations of the original[70] are elided into the general *poetarum laudibus* for the benefit of the Roman reader, and the term ὕπατος, the Homeric epithet meaning 'most high', is translated as its most common Latin equivalent, the noun 'consul', with kings thrown in for good measure (*consulum ac regum*). This has been seen as a simple translation mistake,[71] but is a conscious adaptation: the writer of *De Mundo* surely knew that the same word which Homer used for 'most high' as an epithet of Zeus also meant 'consul' in contemporary Greek, and exploits the ambiguity in order to bring home to a Roman readership the analogy of the supreme god with the supreme magistrate.

The most extensive example of this kind of adaptation occurs in the version of Περὶ Κόσμου 400 b 15 ff., where the control of the supreme deity over the universe is compared to the rule of *nomos* (law or custom) over Greek civic life. The Greek runs as follows:

for it is clearly in obedience to it [i.e. *nomos*] that the archons go out to their offices, the thesmothetes to their own court-houses, the members of the *boule*

together), while the v. rare *ad superna* occurs in the *De Deo Soctratis* (IX. 141). For Apuleian rhyming see the material gathered by Bernhard (1927).

[70] ὕπατος itself is a Homeric epithet of Zeus (*Il.* 8. 22 etc.), while *arduis arcibus* renders the Homeric ἀκροτάτῃ κορυφῇ (*Il.* 1. 499).

[71] See the extensive discussion of Marchetta (1991), 209–24.

and the *ecclesia* to their appropriate councils, and one man walks to the Prytaneum to get grain, another to defend himself in front of a jury, another to prison to die. And there are public feasts appointed by law and annual festal assemblies and sacrifices to the gods and worship of heroes and libations to the dead; and acting in many different ways according to a single ordinance and power of law it truly maintains its creator's intention, that 'the city is all together full of sacrifices, all together full of hymns and groaning'.

The Latin version is as follows (*Mu.* XXXV. 366–XXVI. 368):

ex scitis eius magistratus tribunalia, principia milites frequentabunt, recuperatores iudiciis praesidebunt, decuriones et quibus ius est dicendae sententiae ad consessum publicum commeabunt; et alius ad Minuciam frumentatum venit et aliis in iudiciis dies dicitur; reus purgandi se necessitate, insectandi studio accusator venit; ille moriturus ad supplicii locum ducitur, hic ad convivii repotia et vespertinus comissator adventat. sunt et publicarum epularum apparatus et lectisternia deorum et dies festi, ludi scaenici ludique Circenses; diis sacrificatur, geniis ministratur, obitis libatione profunditur, aliusque alio fungitur munere parentque omnes iussis legum et communis imperii. videasque illam civitatem pariter spirantem Panchaeis odoribus et graveolentis caenis, resonantem hymnis et carminibus et canticis, eandem etiam lamentis et ploratibus heiulantem.

The long list of Athenian civic institutions is elaborately transformed into one of the Roman equivalents, expanded and embellished. The four types of officials going to their place of work in Athens are expanded to five, while the three individuals going to the Prytaneum to get corn, to the courts to face charges, and to the prison to die, surely an allusion to the trial and death of Socrates,[72] are expanded to three opposed pairs, adding the contrast between prosecutor and defendant and the final picture of the reveller. The five types of public festival in the Greek are expanded to eight, and the picture of the whole city sharing joy and grief is mildly embellished. Again, the particular needs of an audience of Roman culture are evident. The technical terms of Roman officialdom, religion and law are carefully applied; a specific landmark in Rome, the Porticus Minucia Frumentaria, is explicitly mentioned; and the Greek quotation at the end of the extract, even though taken from such an obvious source as the beginning of Sophocles' *Oedipus Tyrannus* (lines 3–4), is paraphrased rather than being explicitly treated as a citation, though an allusion to Lucretius in the phrase *Panchaeis odoribus* shows that the

---

[72] Socrates as displayed in Plato's *Apology* defended himself in court and was condemned to death after proposing as his alternative punishment that he be fed for life at public expense in the Prytaneum (*Apol.* 36d 7).

translator is aware of its literary status.[73] Clear, too, are specific Apuleian traits. The mention of the Porticus Municia Frumentaria with its specific topographical reference to the centre of the city of Rome is very like the allusion to the similarly located *metae Murtiae* at Apuleius *Met.* 6. 8. 2, where the purpose in the fictional tale of Cupid and Psyche is clearly to give a point of reference for a Roman readership. The overall style of the passage seems strongly Apuleian, with its rhyming verbs at the end of clauses: *frequentabunt . . . praesidebunt . . . commeabunt,* all relatively uncommon words which occur in the indubitably Apuleian works,[74] and *sacrificatur . . . ministratur,* like the repeated *-abunt* a typically Apuleian sound-pattern in rhyming clauses.[75] Apuleian too is the colourful vocabulary: *ad convivii repotia* recalls Apuleius *Apol.* 59. 3 *ad repotia cenae obeunda,* while *ploratibus heiulantem* uses two archaic Apuleian words.[76]

4. THE *DE PLATONE*: TRANSMISSION, STRUCTURE, COMPARISON WITH ALCINOUS

As noted in Section 1 above, the *De Platone* shares its textual transmission, its addressee and its problems of authenticity with *De Mundo*. Its full title, to be found in B, the oldest and best manuscript, and its associated tradition,[77] is *De Platone et eius Dogmate,*[78] and it is plainly a work of philosophical doxography summarizing the key doctrines of Plato as perceived in the second century AD. As it stands, the work contains two books, the first dealing with natural philosophy, physics, the second with moral philosophy, ethics; statements in the opening section of the first book suggest that there will be a third book dealing with rational philosophy, logic, thus covering the three traditional parts of philosophy.[79] The treatise as a whole shows the syncretism typical of Platonism in the

---

[73] Cf. Lucretius *DRN* 2. 417 *araque Panchaeos exhalat propter odores.*

[74] *Praesidere* occurs four times (*Met., Flor.*) as well as twice in *De Mundo, frequentare* eleven times (*Met., Apol., DDS*) and three times in *De Mundo, commeare* eleven times (*Met., DDS*) and twice in *De Platone* as well as once in *De Mundo.*

[75] Cf. *Met.* 5. 22. 1 *roboratur . . . mutatur,* 5. 1. 52 *sonatur. . . cantatur,* 9. 19. 1 *carpebatur . . . distrahebatur;* and also 6. 28. 5 *adornabo . . . discriminabo,* 6. 32. 2 *habitabit . . . aestuabit,* 9. 27. 4 *necabo . . . vocabo . . . tractabo.*

[76] *Ploratus* occurs at *Met.* 7. 21. 5, *heiulare* five times in the *Metamorphoses.*

[77] See Moreschini (1985), 267–88, on the manuscript tradition.

[78] The Grecism *dogmate* already provides a link with the work of Alcinous (see below), the full title of which is Διδασκαλικὸς τῶν Πλάτωνος δογμάτων (Whittaker (1990), xiii–xv).

[79] For the history of these three divisions of philosophy, implicit in Plato, explicit in Xenocrates and the early Academy, see conveniently Dillon (1993), 57–8.

second century AD, which could happily absorb and claim for its own subsequent and diverse philosophical ideas such as logic.[80] The third book of *De Platone* on logic announced in *Pl.* 1 is not extant in our manuscripts of the philosophical works of Apuleius. However, there exists a work attributed to Apuleius in a separate textual tradition, the Περὶ Ἑρμηνείας, which plainly covers the territory of logic, and which scholars have often seen as the lost third book of *De Platone*.[81] As I argued in Chapter 1, it is not impossible that the Περὶ Ἑρμηνείας is Apuleian and originally part of *De Platone*,[82] but the most likely interpretation of the evidence, in my view, is that the work was composed by a later follower of Apuleius as a supplement to the two existing books of *De Platone*, supplying the missing treatment of logic promised at the beginning of *De Platone*. Hence the Περὶ Ἑρμηνείας will not be considered in this section; in any case, owing to its highly technical nature, its prime interest is not for literary commentators but for historians of logic, who have done much recent work on it.[83] Though the third book of *De Platone* on logic was probably never written rather than being lost in transmission or preserved in the Περὶ Ἑρμηνείας,[84] there are clear signs of textual disturbance in our extant text of *De Platone*. Its second book has a formal address to the writer's son Faustinus, while the first book begins abruptly *in medias res* with no preface, starting at once with the biography of Plato, and is plainly without its ending, since it finishes with an incomplete sentence and indeed an incomplete word, though it seems likely that not much text has been lost there. This suggests that both the beginning and the ending of Book 1 have been lost in transmission, and that Book 1 of *De Platone*, like *De Mundo*, originally contained a prefatory section including an address to Faustinus.[85]

As already noted, *De Platone* is clearly a summary of Platonic doctrine as perceived in the second century AD. In its title,[86] its selection and mildly haphazard treatment of material from Plato, and its generous admixture of Stoic and Peripatetic views which are presented as Platonic, it shows a

[80] Cf. Gersh (1986), Whittaker (1987).
[81] e.g. Londey and Johanson (1987).
[82] See Ch. 1 n. 42.
[83] See the literature gathered in Londey and Johanson (1987); Dr Suzanne Bobzien is currently working on the treatise from this angle.
[84] Here I agree fully with Beaujeu (1973), 53.
[85] Sallmann (1997), 300–1, suggests that the separate address of Book 2 indicates that the two books may have been published separately, but the loss of a preface to Book 1, given the other evidence of textual loss and incompleteness, provides a more probable explanation.
[86] See n. 78.

considerable resemblance to another Platonic handbook, the extant *Didaskalikos* now generally ascribed to Alcinous.[87] Though it has been claimed that the two texts together represent the teachings of the Platonist Gaius,[88] who seems to have been operating in the early decades of the second century AD,[89] the material shared by the two very likely goes back much earlier to the first-century BC Arius Didymus and before, and the differences between them, though relatively minor, suggest that they are not together promoting the view of an individual Platonist. Thus those who are sceptical about the 'School of Gaius' seem to have the weight of evidence on their side;[90] both *De Platone* and the *Didaskalikos* are better viewed as independent witnesses to a large and tralatician body of Platonic doxography circulating in the period of Middle Platonism. It is unlikely that either treatise depends directly on the other: their verbal coincidences are very few and are very likely to point to a common source rather than to each other, and though neither treatise can be accurately dated, both are perhaps most likely to belong to the end of the second century AD, though a third-century date cannot be ruled out for the *Didaskalikos*.[91] My own view is that *De Platone* is a translation or close adaptation of a Greek handbook belonging to the same Middle Platonist doxographical tradition as the *Didaskalikos*. This would make it resemble *De Mundo* in its 'plagiarizing' literary character as a Latin work claiming to present Greek doctrine from the writer's own researches, but in fact closely following a single Greek source. That *De Platone* differs markedly from *De Mundo* in its almost complete lack of literary colour and ornament is due to the especially dry and jejune nature of its source text, though there are moments when the compiler's attention is particularly engaged by a topic—topics which would be of interest to Apuleius (see below).

The structure of *De Platone* is clear enough, and it is worth juxtaposing that of the *Didaskalikos* to show both the similarities and the differences between the two (see the chart on the following page).[92]

---

[87] For comparisons cf. Dillon (1977), 311–38, Göransson (1995), 137–81. On the identification of the author of the *Didaskalikos* as Alcinous rather than Albinus, and its consequences for the history of Middle Platonism, see the convenient discussion of Göransson (1995), 13–28.

[88] Most notably now by Moreschini (1978).   [89] Dillon (1977), 266–7.

[90] Dillon (1977), 266–340, Whittaker (1987), and Göransson (1995); the last helpfully summarizes the history of the issue.

[91] For discussions of the date of Alcinous cf. Dillon (1993), x–xiii, Whittaker (1990), viii–xiii, Göransson (1995), 132–6.

[92] For more detailed comparisons see the works cited in n. 87.

De Platone	Didaskalikos
Book 1	A *Introductory* (152. 1–154. 5)
A. *Life of Plato* (I. 180–IV. 189)	(a) Definition of philosophy and the
(NB I. 187, 189—the parts of philosophy)	philosopher
Physics	(b) The contemplative and the practical
B. *God, matter, cosmology* (V. 190–XII.	life
207)	(c) The parts of philosophy
(a) God	
(b) The Forms	B. *Dialectic* (154. 6–160. 43)
(c) The two essences	(a) Theory and criterion of knowledge
(d) The four elements and their forma-	(b) Dialectic
tion	(c) Syllogistic
(e) The formation of the universe	
(f) The world-soul	C. *Theoretical Science* (160. 43–179. 33)
(g) Time	(a) Mathematics
(h) Celestial bodies	(b) Theology and first principles
(i) Classification of beings	(i) Matter
(j) Providence and destiny	(ii) The Forms
C. *Humans* (XII. 207–XVIII. 218)	(iii) God
(a) The tripartite soul	(iv) The incorporeality of qualities
(b) The senses	(c) Physics
(c) The parts of the body	(i) The formation of the universe
(d) The diseases of soul and body	(ii) The four elements and their for-
	mation
Book 2	(iii) The world-soul and celestial bod-
Ethics	ies
D. *Outline of moral theory* (I. 219–VIII. 231)	(iv) Other divine beings
(a) Classification of goods	(v) Creation of humans and other
(b) Intermediate natural state; virtues as	beings
intermediate qualities	(vi) The parts of the body
(c) Vices—excesses and deficiencies	(vii) The senses
(d) Virtue	(viii) Weight
(i) General characteristics	(ix) Breathing
(ii) The four cardinal virtues	(x) Human diseases
(iii) The central importance of justice	(xi) The soul: its relation to the body,
E. *Means of promoting virtue* (VIII.	its parts and its immortality
231–XIV. 240)	(xii) Man and fate
(a) Two types of rhetoric and the art of	
politics	D. *Ethics* (179. 34–189. 11)
(b) Teaching virtue	(a) The highest good and happiness
(c) The choice of good and evil	(b) Similarity to God the human end
(d) The involuntary nature of vice	(c) The role of intellectual disciplines in
(e) Friendship and love	this
F. *Degrees of virtue and vice* (XIV. 240–	(d) Virtue
XXIII. 255)	(i) The four cardinal virtues
(a) The four types of vicious man	(ii) Good dispositions and progress to
(b) The worst man of all	virtue
(c) Evil its own punishment	(iii) Other virtues classified and
(d) The average moral man	described
(e) The perfect sage	(iv) The involuntary nature of vice
(f) Similarity to God the human end	(f) The emotions and pleasure
G. *Organization of states* (XXIV.	(g) Friendship and love
255–XXVIII. 263)	(h) Various types of political constitu-
(a) The ideal state	tion
(b) The well-run state	E. *Miscellaneous* (189. 12–27)
	(a) The philosopher and the sophist
	(b) Their objects: being and non-being
	F. *Conclusion* (189. 28–33)

The two texts plainly differ in length: the *Didaskalikos* is a longish single book, just over half the volume of *De Platone* as we have it. But their plans are clearly similar. Both set out to treat Plato's doctrines under the three headings of logic, physics, and ethics, though in a different order: in the *Didaskalikos* logic comes first, under the more Platonic heading of dialectic but including Aristotelian syllogistic, while in *De Platone* it seems to have come last in the lost third book (see above). *De Platone's* opening life of Plato is not found in the *Didaskalikos*, and is in fact the earliest extant life of Plato apart from a fragmentary papyrus text from Herculaneum.[93] There is little in it that is not found in other biographical accounts, and its particular closeness to the life of Plato in Diogenes Laertius (3. 1–47), which probably belongs to the early third century AD, strongly suggests a single previous source common to the two. Three elements in the biography in *De Platone* might be argued to be particularly Apuleian. First, its stress on Plato's literary genius in remoulding the doctrines of his predecessors (1. II. 185 *labore, quo adserere eam nisus est, elegantia, per quam venustatem et maiestate verborum ei plurimum adhibuit dignitatis*, 1. III. 188 *impolitas sententias . . . cum ratione limando tum ad orationis augustae honestissimam speciem induendo perfectas atque admirabiles fecit*): this particular concern with Plato's literary art would naturally fit Apuleius, the Platonic philosopher and self-conscious *littérateur*. The second Apuleian element is the special emphasis on the Pythagorean influence on Plato (1. III. 186): as can be observed from *Flor.* 15, Apuleius seems to have had a particular interest in Pythagoras, and indeed in that speech again characterizes Plato as strongly Pythagoreanizing (*Flor.* 15. 26 *porro noster Plato, nihil ab hac secta vel paululum devius, pythagorissat in plurimis*). The third Apuleian element is the general topic and particular style. The potted biography of the philosopher is a feature of the *Florida*,[94] especially (again) of *Flor.* 15, where Apuleius gives a brief biography of Pythagoras (15. 12–25), which like that of Plato in *De Platone* relates closely to the equivalent life in Diogenes Laertius and is plainly dependent on the Greek tradition of philosophical

---

[93] On this, and on the traditional anecdotal material in *De Platone's* biographical section, see the useful collection of material by Riginos (1976). There is a fuller but less readily available treatment of Apuleius' Plato biography in Schmutzler (1974), 49–96.

[94] Cf. also *Flor.* 2 (Socrates), 9. 15 ff. (Hippias), 14 (Crates), 18. 19 ff. (Protagoras), 18. 30 ff. (Thales), 22 (Crates again); it has been plausibly argued that Apuleius' interest in famous philosophers, especially in Pythagoras, reflect his own self-image as an eminent philosopher—cf. Ch. 2 n. 82.

biography.[95] The biography of Plato also contains more typical elements of Apuleian style than any other passage in *De Platone* of comparable length.[96] This is perhaps because the writer here has more flexibility than in the more strictly transcribed doxographical sections; though in the biography too there is close dependence on Greek sources, there is no complex argument or set of doctrines to summarize or follow.

I suggested earlier on other grounds that the opening of the first book of *De Platone* might have been lost in transmission, as its end plainly was.[97] Given this, *De Platone* might well have originally begun with an introductory set of definitions like those which open the *Didaskalikos* (A). Such a suggestion might be supported by the beginning of the second book of *De Platone*, which starts by defining the nature of ethics (2. I. 219 *moralis philosophiae caput est, Faustine fili, ut scias quibus as beatam vitam perveniri rationibus potest*), and by the repeated mention of the three parts of philosophy towards the end of the biographical section of *Pl.* 1 (1. I. 187, 189), perhaps suggesting a topic already broached in a lost introduction. But in general its more expansive and colourful Apuleian interest in philosophical biography sets the opening of *De Platone* apart from the more austere and matter-of-fact approach of the *Didaskalikos*, and this is symptomatic of the general contrast of the two works. Though both are jejune and compressed handbooks, the *Didaskalikos* is rather more so than *De Platone*.

After the section on dialectic (B), the *Didaskalikos* begins its treatment of what it calls 'theoretical science' (C). This has three divisions, mathematics, theology, and physics, the last two of which correspond to what *De Platone* calls 'natural science' or physics, but its initial concern with mathematics (C(a)) highlights an important Platonic area largely ignored in *De Platone*; we find it again in the *Didaskalikos* at D(c), which stresses the role of mathematics amongst the intellectual disciplines in enabling men to achieve similarity to God. Generally, however, the two works give broadly similar accounts of physics and theology. God, the forms, the elements, the formation of the universe, the classification of beings, the human body and soul, and the issue of fate are treated in more or less the same order. But there are instructive differences: *De Platone*

---

[95] Cf. Ch. 2 n. 81; for the close links of the biography of Plato in *De Platone* with Diogenes Laertius see Riginos (1976).

[96] As well as many elements of archaic and poetic vocabulary, note the Apuleian rhythmical phrasing (otherwise v. rare in *Pl.*) at 1. III. 188: *impolitas sententias et incohatas . . . limando . . . induendo.*

[97] See n. 84.

has a separate treatment of time not found in the *Didaskalikos* (B(g)), while the *Didaskalikos* deals with topics not found in *De Platone* such as weight and breathing (C(c)(viii)–(ix)) and the incorporeality of qualities (C(b)(iv)), the earliest Platonist discussion). Particularly striking is the return in *De Platone*'s section on the operation of divine providence (B(j)) to the nature of *daimones*, already listed in the classification of beings in B(i), as they are in the matching section of the *Didaskalikos* (C(c)(v)); the B(j) passage not only stresses a topic of major Apuleian interest in the *Apologia* and *De Deo Socratis*, but even shows clear verbal links with the *De Deo Socratis* in its identitification of Roman equivalents for *daimones*.[98] Similarly interesting is the absence in C(a) and (d) of the immortality of the soul and of metempsychosis, both central Platonic doctrines emphasized in the *Didaskalikos* (C(c)(xi), C(c)(v) respectively); the immortality of the soul does get a brief mention in the account of the perfect sage (F(e), 2. XX. 249), and it is not wholly impossible that a treatment of the immortality of the soul has fallen out at the damaged end of Book 1, where it might naturally have occurred. Nevertheless, in our extant text of *De Platone* immortality is not treated as a defining characteristic of the soul; here we might see the influence of Aristotle, firmly against the immortality of the soul in the *De Anima* and plainly more influential on *De Platone* than on the *Didaskalikos* in their accounts of virtue and vice.

And it is indeed in their treatments of ethics that the two texts most diverge. The *Didaskalikos* provides a summary account which takes only 25 per cent of its space, whereas ethics occupy about 60 per cent of the extant space of *De Platone* (though Book 1 may have been longer originally). Within this, *De Platone* spends considerable space on the types of political constitution (G), treated in a single page by the *Didaskalikos* (D(h)); the material for this section of *De Platone* is drawn almost entirely from the *Republic* (G(a), the ideal state) and the *Laws* (G(b), the well-run state), and in general *De Platone* uses more extensive paraphrase of Platonic dialogues than the *Didaskalikos*, which tends to provide analytical précis. Interestingly, *De Platone* never mentions the title of a Platonic work, though it comes close to it, while the *Didaskalikos* alludes frequently to specific dialogues.[99] This partly reflects the Latin-only readership of *De Platone*, which would not expect to appreciate or pursue

---

[98] 1. XII. 206 *daemonas vero, quos Genios et Lares possumus nuncupare* ~ *DDS* XV. 150 *daemon bonus . . . eum nostra lingua . . . poteris Genium vocare* (cf. also *DDS* XV. 152–3 on *Lar* ~ *daemon*).

[99] Cf. Whittaker (1990), xviii–xxx.

cross-references to Plato in the original, but also points to the more cav-
alier attitude of the writer of *De Platone*, simply giving his readership his
personal and unreferenced version of 'what Plato said'. This kind of
authoritative and self-confident discourse would be very Apuleian.

The main differences between *De Platone* and the *Didaskalikos* in their
presentations of ethics seem to derive from two main causes. First, as
already suggested, *De Platone* takes rather more of its moral doctrine
from the Peripatetic tradition than the *Didaskalikos*, though both works
freely combine Platonic teachings with Stoic and Peripatetic views. *De
Platone*'s description of virtues as intermediates between extremes, and
of vices as excesses and deficiencies (D(b)–(c)), owes an obvious debt to
Aristotle's celebrated account of virtue as the mean in the *Nicomachean
Ethics*,[100] and its apparent innovation in viewing the natural state of man
as intermediate between vice and virtue (D(b)) might have links with the
general stress on intermediate positions between extremes as well as
looking forward to Neoplatonic doctrine on moral dualism.[101] And
though *De Platone* concurs with the *Didaskalikos* on the cardinal virtues
and the primary role of justice (D(d)(ii)–(iii)), and on the involuntary
nature of vice (E(d)), it spends a good deal more space on the means of
promoting virtue. This points to the second strand in *De Platone* where
its interests diverge from those of the *Didaskalikos*—its strong moral
didacticism. This emerges not only in its paradigmatic display in section
F of the various degrees of human moral character, focusing with particular expansion (and Platonic precedent)[102] on the most wicked man of
all, but also in its particular interest in the teaching of virtue and the art
of rhetoric (E(a)–(b)). In these sections *De Platone* clearly draws on the
discussion of different types of oratory in the *Gorgias* (463a–465d), but
makes some interesting modifications. In particular, the Platonic attack
on rhetoric as an art of flattery directed towards the judicial power is
replaced by an attack on the *professio iuris*, expertise in the law (2. IX. 233),
directed towards the legislative power.[103] The exclusion of rhetoric as
such from this context suggests that *De Platone* is not prepared to follow
Plato in condemning it. This rescuing of rhetoric in turn suggests that the
author of *De Platone* wishes to promote it, and if that author is Apuleius
this makes considerable sense—a character who was not only a Platonic

---

[100] This feature is also found briefly in the *Didaskalikos* at 30. 4, but *De Platone* emphasizes it a good deal more, in the manner of Aristotle's own elaborate treatment at the end
of the second book of the *Nicomachean Ethics* (2. 6. 1106a–2. 9. 1109b).

[101] Beaujeu (1973), 284–5.

[102] *Rep.* 9. 571a–580c.   [103] Beaujeu (1973), 292–3

philosopher but also a professional display orator and effective advocate in the law-courts, as the *Florida* and *Apologia* attest.

This particular stress on rhetoric, a central element of ancient education, also fits the general didactic cast imposed on its material by *De Platone*; the work is addressed to a son for didactic purposes, and there are a number of occasions in Book 2 where references to education or learning are particularly pointed. The innovative introduction of the intermediate natural moral state (D(b), already mentioned), places an explicit stress on the value of moral education (2. II. 223):

habere semina quidem quaedam utrarumque rerum cum nascendi origine copulata, quae educationis disciplina in partem alteram debant emicare, doctoresque puerorum nihil antiquius curare oportet quam ut amatores virtutum velint esse, moribus, institutis eos ad id prorsus imbuere, ut regere et regi discant magistra iustitia.

Other passages point the same way: apart from a brief assertion of the partial teachability of virtue (E(b)), there is also in the account of the perfect sage (F(e)) a brief passage directed specifically to the moral education of young boys, recalling perhaps the addressee Faustinus (2. XXII. 251): *sapientia amatorem boni adulescentem facit, sed eum qui probitate ingenii sit ad artes bonas promptior.* Though moral education is fundamental to Platonic ethics, especially in the *Republic*, its stress here seems to reflect a specifically pedagogic context for the writer of *De Platone* as against the *Didaskalikos*; though both are Platonic handbooks of information and instruction, *De Platone* seems to have a particular interest in the training of the young. If *De Platone* is, as I believe, Apuleian, it may belong to a period in Apuleius' career when teaching was important in his activities.[104]

5. THE *DE PLATONE*: LITERARY AND STYLISTIC ASPECTS

De Platone offers much less than *De Mundo* in the way of literary ornament and colour, and has attracted much less literary analysis.[105] This is

---

[104] On the didactic cast of much of Apuleius' work cf. Opeku (1993), and for the possibility of a didactic stage in Apuleius' later career see Ch. 1, Sect. 1, above.

[105] The only major treatment of the style of *De Platone* is Redfors (1960), 46–75; cf. also the brief remarks in Bernhard (1927), and the study of *De Platone*'s technical terminology in Moreschini (1978), 193–210.

unsurprising given its different character as a tralatician handbook, very likely a translation of a relatively colourless Greek original resembling the jejune *Didaskalikos*; this kind of source text presents an obvious contrast with the Περὶ Κόσμου, a work of somewhat richer literary texture which *De Mundo* closely matches. *De Platone*'s lack of literary ambition is a clear consequence of its relative narrow concern with the paraphrase of Platonic texts, doxographical summary, and the rendering of Platonic and other technical terminology (in which it apparently makes a number of contributions to the Latin philosophical lexicon).[106] Even its Roman readership is given little to enliven the doxography, apart from the mere translation into Latin: there are only a few allusions to Roman culture, mostly to Roman political life.[107] There are no verse citations such as are common in *De Mundo*, following its model in Περὶ Κόσμου, and relatively few recognizable literary allusions. Those allusions which can be found use Plautus, Cicero, and Lucretius, authors which are also quarried in *De Mundo* and *De Deo Socratis*, lending some support for the view that *De Mundo* and *De Platone* are, like *De Deo Socratis*, genuinely Apuleian.

First, Plautus, a typically Apuleian archaizing taste.[108] At 1. XI. 204 in describing the *daimones*, the lowest grade of god, *De Platone* uses the term *medioximus*: *quos medioximos Romani veteres appellant*. This rare and archaic term is found before Apuleius only twice in Plautus, and one of the Plautine passages seems to be referred to here (*Cist.* 512): *di deaeque, superi atque inferi et medioximi*, similarly describing the *daimones*, presented in Plautus as the divine powers intermediate between the gods of the aether and the gods of the underworld.[109] Likewise, at 2. XV. 240–1, seeking Latin equivalents for Plato's φιλότιμος and φιλοχρή-ματος or φιλοκερδής (cf. *Rep.* IX. 581a–b), *De Platone* uses *honoripeta* and *lucricupido*(?)[110] or *accipiter pecuniae*: the last phrase is itself Plautine (*Persa* 409 *pecuniae accipiter*), while the two archaic compounds seem to

---

[106] Cf. Moreschini (1978), 193–210.

[107] Cf. 1. XI. 205 *quos medioximos Romani veteres appellant*, 1. XII. 206 *Genios et Lares*, 1. XV. 212 *optimatium praestantiam*, 2. VII. 230 *suffragator bonorum*, 2. IX. 233 *professionem iuris*.

[108] Cf. Ch. 3 n. 21 (Apuleius and Plautus) and Ch. 1 n. 68 (Apuleius and archaism).

[109] The other Plautine use occurs in the same play, *Cist.* 611; after Apuleius there are only five uses listed in *TLL* (8. 569. 51 ff.), one of which is certainly an allusion to Apuleius (Servius on *Aen.* 8. 275: see n. 7 above), and three of which may have Apuleian links (another Servian reference, and one each in Sidonius and Claudianus Mamertus—on whose Apuleian connections see Ch. 1 n. 92).

[110] It has been plausibly suggested that the transmitted *lucricupidinem*, a rather anomalous accusative, should be emended to the more regularly formed *lucricupidum* (Skutsch) or *lucricupidonem* (Sinko): see *TLL* 7. 2. 1714. 47 ff.

be coined on Plautine models (*Trin.* 100 *turpilucricupidum,* Arg. *Most.* 6 *lucripeta*).[111]

Second, Lucretius, a Latin didactic model in *De Mundo* and *De Deo Socratis*.[112] At 1. IX. 200 *De Platone* asks for indulgence for its coinage of technical terms to elucidate its obscure subject matter: *detur enim venia novitate verborum rerum obscuritatibus servienti.* It has been noted that the *De Platone* passage plainly recalls Lucretius' famous apology for the inadequacy of Latin in rendering Greek philosophical material (*DRN* 1. 136–9) *nec me animi fallit Graiorum* obscura *reperta / difficile inlustrare Latinis versibus esse, / multa* novis verbis *praesertim cum sit agendum / propter egestatem linguae et* rerum novitatem.[113] A second passage of possible Lucretian colour is found at 2. XIII. 239, disapproving of passionate sexual love:

ille alius [*sc.* amor] abhorrens ab humanitatis clementia, qui vulgo amor dicitur, est appetitus ardens, cuius instinctu per libidinem capti amatores corporum in eo quod viderint totum hominem putant. eiusmodi calamitates animarum amicitias idem appellari vetat, quod nec mutuae sint nec reciprocari queant, ut ament atque redamentur, nec constantia illis adsit et diuturnitas desit amoresque eiusmodi satietate ac paenitentia terminentur.

Though this passage claims as ever in *De Platone* to represent Plato's views (e.g. *vetat*), there is no obvious Platonic source, and commentators have questioned why the passage is included at all.[114] I would argue that one motivation for the appearance of this topic is an allusion to the famous Lucretian attack on the same phenomenon at the end of *DRN* 4. 1058–1191. *De Platone*'s condemnation of erotic passion as vulgar physicalism, stress on its attachment to the outer person, and criticism of its destructive and unreciprocated nature pick up some central strands in Lucretius' argument,[115] though clear verbal reminiscences are admittedly difficult to find here.[116]

More prominent in *De Platone* than any poet is Cicero, already seen as a fundamental model for Latin philosophical didactic much used in *De*

[111] So Redfors (1960), 49–51. The *argumentum* to *Mostellaria* probably belongs to the second century AD, but as in the *De Platone* it coins words on a Plautine model—cf. *Pseudolus* 1133 *lucrifugas.*

[112] See n. 44 above and Ch. 4 n. 18.

[113] Beaujeu (1973), 266.   [114] Beaujeu (1973), 296.

[115] Cf. Brown (1987), 69–87

[116] *Qui vulgo amor dicitur* has some affinity with Lucretius *DRN* 4. 1058 *haec Venus est nobis, hinc autem est nomen amoris,* similarly pointing to common belief; *vulgo* may pick up *vulgivaga . . . Venere* at 4. 1071, while *appetitus ardens* may echo the stress in the Lucretian account of the physical burning of love (4. 1086 *ardoris,* 1090 *ardescit*).

Deo Socratis and *De Mundo.*[117] Much of the physics of *Pl.* 1 paraphrases Platonic doctrine in the creation account of *Timaeus,*[118] and it seems clear that *De Platone* makes use of Cicero's convenient Latin version of the dialogue, of which a part survives.[119] In general, *De Platone* seems to avoid complete repetition of Ciceronian phrases, though the two naturally share much technical vocabulary. One problem which both texts have is in providing Latin terms for the creator god, referred to in Plato as δημιοργός. Both Cicero's translation and *De Platone* feel the need to generate various periphrases for this term, and the two versions are sometimes close: *Tim.* 6 *fabricator huius tanti operis* ~ *Pl.* 1. VIII. 198 *fabricatore deo,* 1. X. 201 *fabricatore mundi deus, Tim.* 7 *eius [sc. mundi] aedificatore* ~ *Pl.* 1. VII. 194 *illo aedificatore mundi deo, Tim.* 17 *effector mundi et molitor deus* ~ *Pl.* 1. V. 190 *genitor rerumque omnium extructor.*[120] Similarly indicative of *De Platone*'s use of Cicero's translation is the fact that in the account of ethics in *Pl.* 2, the term *medietas* is used (2. II. 224); this word is explicitly coined by Cicero as an equivalent for the Greek μεσότης at *Tim.* 23 *vix enim audeo dicere medietates, quas Graeci μεσότητας appellant,* and does not appear in Latin between then and Apuleius, who uses it three times in the firmly Apuleian works.[121] *De Platone* is also the first text after Cicero to use another Ciceronian coinage, this time *redamare* (2. XIII. 239), explicitly coined at *Lael.* 49 *eo qui amare vel (ut ita dicam) redamare possit.*[122]

There are also possible traces in *De Platone* of the account of Stoic theology and cosmology given by Balbus in the second book of Cicero's *De Natura Deorum,* an exposition which has already been seen as an important source for *De Mundo.*[123] *ND* 2 deals first with the existence of the supreme god and his nature, then passes to an account of the riches of the universe as evidence of divine providence, an interdependent mixture of theology and cosmology which resembles the central section of *Pl.* 1 (B in my scheme above, V. 190–XII. 207). Interesting parallels are also

[117] Cf. n. 44 above and Ch. 4 n. 18.

[118] As does the *Didaskalikos*; the *Timaeus* is the normal source for Middle- and Neo-Platonist cosmology—cf. Baltes (1976, 1978), though he treats neither the *Didaskalikos* nor the *De Platone.*

[119] The version of 27d–47b; for a convenient text with facing Greek original cf. Giomini (1975).

[120] For similar language cf. also Cicero *ND* 2. 90 (from Balbus' Stoic theology and cosmology, echoed elsewhere in *Pl.*—cf. n. 123 below) *non solum habitatorem in hac caelesti ac divina domo sed etiam rectorem et moderatorem et tamquam architectum tanti operis tantisque muneris.*

[121] *Met.* 2. 4. 3, *DDS* IX. 140, X. 142—cf. further *TLL* 8. 554. 40 ff.

[122] Powell (1990), 104.   [123] Cf. n. 48.

to be found in the treatments of the senses and body parts in the two texts (C(b) and (c) in *De Platone* in my scheme, *ND* 2. 140–3). Both use the metaphor of military fortification against attack in describing the function of the eyelids in protecting the eyes: *Pl.* 1. XV. 212 *et superciliorum* saepes praemunire *oculis, ne desuper* proruat[124] *quod teneras visiones mollesque perturbet* ~ *ND* 2. 143 munitaeque *sunt palpebrae tamquam* vallo pilorum, *quibus et apertis oculis si quid incideret* repelleretur. The two also have similar passages concerned with eating: *Pl.* 1. XV. 213 *ventrem hiris intestinarum circumplexum et nexibus impeditum esse,* ne esculenta et potulenta *sese penetrarent* ~ *ND* 2. 141 *iam gustatus . . . habitat in ea parte oris quam* esculentis et potulentis *iter natura patefecit.*[125] Though these echoes are relatively vague, the likelihood that *De Platone* is using this Ciceronian text is generally high, and, as in his use of Cicero's *Timaeus,* the author of *De Platone* may be keen to avoid exact verbal repetition.

The lexicon of *De Platone* is, as scholars have recognized, close to that of the firmly Apuleian works in its use of select, archaic, and poetic vocabulary;[126] this I would regard as indicative of Apuleian authorship. Some of the more striking links are worth observing in detail. The prepositional usage *ad instar,* found fourteen times in the *Metamorphoses* and perhaps an Apuleian innovation, occurs five times in *De Platone* (and three times in *De Mundo*);[127] the archaic-colloquial adverbial combination *verum enimvero,* otherwise found only on eight scattered occasions before Apuleius, is found twice in *De Platone,* once in *De Mundo,* and once in *De Deo Socratis.*[128] At *Pl.* 1. XV. 211 the Homeric formula ἕρκος

---

[124] *Proruere* can elsewhere refer to the violent breaching of military defences—cf. *OLD* s.v. 3a.

[125] The combination *esculenta/potulenta* is found elsewhere only once in an archaic quotation in Gellius, once in Festus, twice in Donatus' commentary on Terence and once in the *Digest* (Ulpian); for the evidence, and for the variant spellings of *potulenta* (*posc-* and *poc-* are also found) cf. *TLL* 9. 2. 363. 40 ff.

[126] Redfors (1960), 46–75.

[127] An instance could be provided at *Pl.* 1. VIII. 198, where *mundo ad instar pulchrae et perfectae sphaerae* could easily be read for the manuscripts' *mundo instar;* this seems consistent, since *De Platone* has otherwise only *ad instar* prepositionally and not *instar,* which is never used prepositionally without *ad* in Apuleius (in fact, the only Apuleian example of simple *instar* is *Flor.* 12. 1 *instar illi minimo minus quam columbarum,* which is plainly substantival, as at *Pl.* 2. XXVI. 260 *cum utriusque instar similitudinis traxerint*). For *ad instar* generally see *TLL* 7. 2. 1970. 14; Apuleius is the earliest user.

[128] The PHI CD-ROM gives otherwise one example of the combination (sometimes divided into three words) from Plautus, one from Terence, two from Cato (both in speeches), one from Cicero (a speech), two from Sallust (both in speeches), seven from Livy (all but one in speeches), and one from Curtius (again in a speech). Cf. *TLL* 5. 2. 594. 26 ff., which also lists only two post-Apuleian examples.

ὀδόντων (*Il.* 4. 350, ten times in *Iliad* and *Odyssey*), is translated by *dentium vallum*, as at Gellius *NA* 1. 15. 3; the only other renditions in Latin are *Flor.* 15. 23 *murum . . . dentium* and *Apol.* 7. 4 *dentium muro*, which, though different versions, establish Apuleian interest in translating this Homeric phrase. At *Pl.* 1. XV. 212 there occurs the word *promptuarium*, 'cupboard', otherwise known only from a single occurrence in the *Digest* (33. 9. 4. 1) and another at *Met.* 1. 23. 8; at *Pl.* 2. V. 228 we find the word *meditullium*, found five times in the *Metamorphoses* and otherwise found before Apuleius only once in Cicero, once in a passage of Festus plainly dependent on Cicero, and once in Plautus.[129] At *Pl.* 2. X. 235 occurs the word *infortunium*; this passage and ten occurrences in the *Metamorphoses* are the first uses of the term since Horace and Livy,[130] while at 2. XIX. 246 we find the rare agent noun *cupitor*, which apart from two instances in Tacitus' *Annals* occurs only here, at 2. XXII. 251, and in the firmly Apuleian works (twice in the *Metamorphoses*, once in the *Florida*),[131] and at 2. XXVII. 261 the archaic noun *suadela*, which occurs twice in the *Metamorphoses* but is otherwise found only twice before Apuleius.[132]

These stylistic affinities do not prove Apuleian authorship. But they do suggest strong links with Apuleian language, and with the fashionable archaizing of the second century, thus providing corroboration for assertions of Apuleian authorship on other grounds.

6. CONCLUSION: APULEIAN PHILOSOPHICAL EXPOSITIONS?

Both these works fit Apuleius' self-presentation elsewhere as a *philosophus Platonicus*: *De Platone* represents a typical set of Middle Platonic doctrines, as comparison with Alcinous' *Didaskalikos* plainly shows, and the eclectic mix of Peripatetic, Platonic, and Stoic material in *De Mundo* is again consistent with second century Platonism. Stylistically, though *De Mundo* rises at times to a high literary level, neither work matches the impressive rhythmical, linguistic, and literary textures of the *Metamorphoses*, *Apologia*, *Florida*, and *De Deo Socratis*. Their tralatician and doxographical character is in my view adequate explanation of these differences, and sufficient stylistic affinities with the firmly Apuleian works remain to suggest common authorship; though the issue of the

---

[129] Redfors (1960), 63.   [130] Source: PHI CD-ROM.
[131] Redfors (1960), 61.   [132] Redfors (1960), 63.

accentual prose-rhythm of *De Mundo* and *De Platone* remains problematic in the current partial state of the evidence, I would regard it as indicating both the humble literary level of the two works and their possible later date, towards the end rather than the middle of the second century AD, perhaps connected with teaching activity by the older Apuleius. The fact that both treatises are in effect concealed versions of Greek originals, which is undoubtedly the case with *De Mundo*, and very likely the case with *De Platone* given its similarities to the *Didaskalikos*, is also some support for Apuleian authorship; apart from the *Metamorphoses*, which is clearly in some sense a version of a Greek work, translations and adaptations of Greek works figure prominently amongst the lost works of Apuleius catalogued in Chapter 1, and the picture given by *De Mundo* and *De Platone* of a Latin writer presenting Greek doctrines for a Latin-speaking audience with little knowledge of the pillaged Greek originals suits very well what we know of Apuleius' works in general, and of his operations in Carthage as mirrored in the *Florida* and (probably) the *De Deo Socratis*. *De Mundo* and *De Platone* show the more pragmatic and workmanlike aspect of Apuleius' literary personality. Such a practical and no-nonsense approach suits such a prolific writer keen to demonstrate apparent competence in many intellectual disciplines, to whom breadth and rapid composition must have often been more important than depth and elaborate literary craftsmanship. Many of the large and varied catalogue of technical works attributed to Apuleius and discussed in Chapter 1 must surely have been more like the humbler *De Mundo* and *De Platone* than the more ambitious literary works, which dominate the extant material and which we consequently regard as typically Apuleian.

6

A Sophist's Novel:
The *Metamorphoses*

The eleven-book *Metamorphoses*[1] of Apuleius, the longest and most interesting of the few surviving prose fictions in Latin,[2] has been aptly described as 'a sophist's novel'.[3] A summary of the novel is provided below for readers' convenience and orientation, but my present purpose is not to provide a complete interpretation of this celebrated work,[4] or even to give a basic guide to it, as I have done in other chapters for other less-known Apuleian texts, since several good introductions already exist.[5] My intention here is briefly to set the *Metamorphoses* in its intel-

---

[1] This was clearly the title of the novel at the end of the fourth century when edited by the scholar Sallustius (see the *subscriptio* to Book 9 in F) though Augustine's reference to it as the *Golden Ass* (*Civ.* 18. 18. 2 *sicut Apuleius in libris quos Asini Aurei titulo inscripsit*) occurs not long afterwards, and Fulgentius in the sixth century uses both titles (*Metamorphoses* at *Myth.* 3. 6 and *Expos. Serm. Ant.* 36, *Asinus Aureus* at *Expos. Serm. Ant.* 17, 40); for a recent discussion see Sandy (1997), 233–4. Given that both titles circulated in late antiquity, I am happy to accept a joint title '*Asinus Aureus/Metamorphoses*', along with Münstermann (1995), 46–56, though I would not agree with his Isiac arguments for it; other ancient novels had similar double titles (see the discussion in Winkler (1985) 292–320), though I do not agree with his final solution *Asinus Aureus* περὶ μεταμορφώσεων. Nevertheless, *Metamorphoses* is the key element because of its connections with the homonymous works of Lucius of Patras and Ovid; on Lucius of Patras see n. 34, while on the links between the *Metamorphoses* of Ovid and Apuleius cf. Scotti (1982), Bandini (1986), Krabbe (1989), and n. 115 below.

[2] Petronius' *Satyrica*, likely to have been even more ambitious in scale (perhaps twenty-four books) is of course preserved in a very fragmentary state; otherwise we have only the brief and less colourful *Historia Apollonii Regis Tyrii*, possibly a translation of a Greek original (cf. Schmeling in Schmeling (1996), 528–38), and the ps.-Clementine *Recognitiones*, certainly a direct translation of a Greek original (cf. Pervo (1996), 706–7).

[3] Tatum (1979), 135. See also the characterization of the novel as 'epideictic', discussed by Winkler (1985), 6, which roughly describes my approach here.

[4] It will become clear that I have some sympathy with Winkler (1985), 124, in his view that the *Metamorphoses.* is 'a philosophical comedy about religious knowledge', but that (unlike Winkler) I regard the religious content as part of the work's agenda of entertainment and cultural display. I have written a brief interpretative sketch in Harrison (1996), with which this chapter inevitably shares attitudes and material.

[5] See again Harrison (1996) for some recent brief orientation. Charting the *vastum aequor* of scholarly writing on the *Metamorphoses* is a major task which cannot be

lectual context, and to relate its character and contents to Apuleius' career as a sophistic performer, and to his philosophical and literary interests.[6] The first part of this chapter will deal with the sophistic and literary character and texture of the novel, and the narratological problems which it prominently presents; the second will treat its more general cultural context and ideological aspects, especially its relationship to contemporary religion and philosophy.

1. SOPHISTIC LITERARY TEXTURE IN THE *METAMORPHOSES*

(i) *Plot-Summary*[7]

Book 1. After the prologue, in which an unidentified speaker promises an entertaining series of tales from a Greek source, the narrator (who later turns out to be Lucius) tells of his journey to Hypata in Thessaly, on which he encounters Aristomenes. Aristomenes tells him of his friend Socrates, who while in Aristomenes' company was murdered by magic after becoming sexually involved with a witch. The travellers arrive at Hypata, where Lucius is received by his miserly host Milo. Forced to find his own dinner, he goes to the market, where he encounters an old school-friend, Pythias, now a magistrate, who names Lucius for the first time, rejects as unfit the fish he has bought, and destroys it. Lucius goes back to Milo's house still unfed, and, after a conversation with him but still no dinner, goes to sleep.

Book 2. The next day, Lucius meets Byrrhaena, an old family friend, and visits her house, where a statue of Diana and Actaeon clearly prefigures his later bestial

---

attempted here; the reader is referred to the introduction to Harrison (1999), where I have tried to pick out the most important contributions on the *Metamorphoses* since 1900. For a critical bibliography of the *Metamorphoses* to 1970 see Schlam (1971), to 1992 see Bowie and Harrison (1993); for more recent material see the indispensable on-line bibliographies maintained on the ancient novel for the *Petronian Society Newsletter* by Gareth Schmeling at http://www.chss.montclair.edu/classics/petron/PSNOVEL.html, and for Apuleius by Luca Graverini at http://www.unisi.it/ricerca/ist/anc_hist/online/apuleio/bib/. For Latin-less readers, the best modern English translations of the *Metamorphoses* are those of Hanson (1989), Walsh (1994), and Kenney (1998); the best general introductions are Walsh (1970), Tatum (1979), and Schlam (1995); the most influential recent interpretation Winkler (1985). The best texts of the whole work remain those of Robertson and Vallette (1940–5) and Helm (1931[3]), though more modern texts are available in editions of individual books, for which see the list in the introduction to Harrison (1999).

[6] Some good work has been done here by Tatum (1979), Winkler (1985), and Sandy (1997), 233–55, but there is (I think) more to say.

[7] This summary is taken from Harrison (1996), with a few minor alterations.

metamorphosis. Byrrhaena warns him of the magic arts of Pamphile, Milo's wife; far from heeding this, Lucius rushes back to Milo's house to investigate. There he makes an assignation with Pamphile's slave, Photis. Meanwhile, he dines with Milo, and they talk of the prophet Diophanes, believed in by Lucius but discredited by a story of Milo's. After dinner, he retires to bed with Photis, and they become sexually involved. A few days later, Byrrhaena invites him to dinner, where he hears the story told by Thelyphron, who describes how he was humiliated and physically maimed through incautious contact with witches at Larissa. On his way back to Milo's, late and drunk, Lucius is set upon by three robbers at Milo's door; he kills them all with his sword.

Book 3. The next day, Lucius is arrested and tried for murder. Surprisingly, the people laugh at him. Despite an elaborate and exaggerated plea of self-defence, he is convicted and forced to uncover the bodies of the three victims, which turn out to have been wine-skins. All laugh uproariously, and the chief magistrate explains that the trial is a practical joke to celebrate the Festival of Laughter in the city. Lucius is angry and offended, but pacified by civic honours. Back at Milo's house, Photis confesses that she is to blame: the animated wine-skins resulted from her own errors in aiding her mistress' magic activities. Lucius begs to be initiated into the mysteries of magic; Photis reluctantly agrees, and a few nights later allows Lucius to see Pamphile turning herself into a bird. Photis tries to provide the same metamorphosis for Lucius, but uses the wrong ointment and turns him into an ass. She promises to provide him with the antidote, roses, at dawn the next day and puts him in the stable for the night. That same night, robbers break into Milo's house, and steal Lucius-ass with the other animals to carry away their booty.

Book 4. Lucius-ass suffers as the robbers travel on, but decides against collapsing when another ass who does so is killed. They arrive at the robbers' cave, where their companions tell over dinner of their three expeditions which ended in comic failure and the loss of the great robbers Lamachus, Alcimus, and Thrasyleon. The same night, the robbers go out and return with a prisoner, a beautiful young girl of high birth, kidnapped on the very point of marriage. She is distraught, and the aged housekeeper of the robbers tells her a tale to soothe her, that of Cupid and Psyche.

'There was once a princess so beautiful that she was worshipped as Venus. Venus, outraged, asked Cupid to ensure that the princess made the most degrading of marriages. But none dared to marry her (her name was Psyche) because of her extreme beauty; the Delphic oracle, consulted, said she should be placed on a cliff and would marry a terrifying winged monster. Her parents sadly complied with the oracle; no monster appeared to Psyche, but a gentle breeze carried her down and set her in a grassy valley.'

Book 5. 'When she woke up, she saw a beautiful palace, equipped with disembodied voices, which answered her bidding and provided for all her comforts.

When she went to bed, she was visited by an unknown male who slept with her, and who returned each night. Eventually, Psyche asked her unknown partner for contact with her family; he objected but eventually allowed her to summon her sisters to the palace, on condition that she resist any pressure on their part to discover his identity. The sisters visited and were jealous of Psyche's luxurious lifestyle, especially when they heard that she was pregnant. They tricked her into fatal curiosity and finding out her husband's identity—he was Cupid, who had taken her for himself; on the discovery he left her. Psyche, realizing her loss and her sisters' trick, took deadly revenge on them. Venus, informed of Cupid's activities with Psyche, was enraged with both the lovers.'

Book 6. 'Psyche began her search for her lost Cupid. Ceres and Juno were sympathetic, but could not help for fear of Venus' wrath. Venus asked Mercury to advertise for Psyche's return to her as a runaway slave, but Psyche gave herself up of her own accord. To punish and humiliate Psyche, Venus set her a number of almost impossible tasks to do, which friendly animals under Cupid's influence helped her to complete. The final task was to descend to the Underworld to get a little of Proserpina's beauty for Venus in a box. Psyche managed to fill the box and bring it back, but at the last moment her curiosity again got the better of her; she opened the box and a deadly sleep flew out, making her unconscious. Cupid rescued her, and persuaded Jupiter to allow him to marry Psyche; even Venus agreed, and Psyche was made an immortal and Cupid's wife, giving birth to a daughter, Pleasure.'

Shortly afterwards, Lucius-ass takes the opportunity of the robbers' absence to try to escape; the girl jumps on his back, but they are recaptured. The robbers plan a dire fate for Lucius and the girl.

Book 7. The next day, these plans are forestalled by the arrival of a stranger, who claims to be the famous bandit Haemus. Telling the robbers tales of bravado, which include a story of a resolute wife who takes male disguise and saves her husband, he offers himself as leader to them. They accept; he advises them not to kill the girl as planned, but to sell her instead. Lucius-ass is indignant at Haemus' overtures to the girl and her warm response, but soon realizes that Haemus is her fiancé Tlepolemus in disguise. Tlepolemus/Haemus drugs the robbers' wine and then, with the help of his fellow-citizens, rescues the girl, now finally named as Charite; he and the girl are married. Lucius-ass is rewarded by being sent to their country estate. Remaining there for some weeks, he is mistreated by a herdsman's wife and a cruel boy. Eventually, the boy is eaten by a bear; Lucius-ass is blamed and attacked by the boy's mother, but repels her with a stream of liquid dung.

Book 8. A slave arrives at the estate from the town, bringing the dreadful news that both Tlepolemus and Charite are dead; Tlepolemus has been treacherously murdered by Thrasyllus, in love with Charite, while she, after discovering the murder and blinding Thrasyllus by a trick, has killed herself. All the slaves panic at a change of ownership, and run away, taking Lucius-ass with them. On their perilous journey they risk attack by wolves, have dogs set on them, and encounter an old man who turns out to be a devouring serpent in disguise. Eventually, they reach the safety of a town, where Lucius-ass is sold to a group of travelling priests of the Syrian Goddess. They are charlatans, dedicated to making money and to passive sexual gratification, and visit various places, exploiting the superstition of the locals. In the course of their travels, Lucius-ass is faced with the possibility of being butchered to replace a stolen joint of venison.

Book 9. He escapes this fate by pretending to be rabid. Travelling on with the priests, Lucius-ass hears the tale of a deceived husband. The priests are arrested for stealing from a shrine; Lucius-ass is sold again, this time to a miller, who puts him to arduous work in a mill. There he is mistreated by the miller's adulterous wife and overhears her conversation, which includes a tale about the exploits of her potential new lover; her new lover visits, but the pair are surprised by the miller's return. The wife hides the lover; he remains concealed while the miller narrates yet another tale of adultery, but is discovered by the help of Lucius-ass, and punished appropriately by the miller. The miller's wife, expelled from her home, takes dreadful revenge, killing the miller by witchcraft. Lucius-ass is sold to a poor gardener and endures more hardship; the pair encounter a rich man whose family is tragically destroyed. Finally, a soldier attempts to commandeer Lucius-ass; the gardener resists, escapes, and hides with the ass, but Lucius-ass's braying betrays them, and the gardener is arrested.

Book 10. The soldier takes Lucius-ass for himself, and leaves him temporarily at a house where Lucius-ass learns the story of a wicked poisoning stepmother whose crimes were discovered by the good sense of a doctor. The soldier sells Lucius-ass; he is bought by a pair of cooks, and enjoys their food secretly; they discover him and turn his apparently strange eating into a spectacle for public entertainment. Their master buys Lucius for himself, and has him taught more tricks and taken to Corinth. There a noble matron enjoys sex with Lucius-ass; this leads Lucius-ass's master to plan to display him in sexual congress in the arena with a condemned woman, another vicious poisoner, whose story is then narrated. Lucius-ass dreads this as the ultimate degradation. The show in the arena begins with an elaborately staged pantomime; Lucius-ass escapes just before his own ordeal is due, runs to Cenchreae, the port of Corinth, and falls asleep on the beach.

Book 11. He wakes, and seeing the moon, prays to the universal mother-goddess for help. She appears to him in the form of Isis, and gives him instructions for his re-transformation through participation in her festival, about to occur in that very location, and for future happiness as her initiate. The festival is described; Lucius-ass follows Isis' instructions and is changed back to human form. A priest of Isis explains that Lucius' ass-form and sufferings were just punishment for his former curiosity and slavish pleasures. Lucius becomes a devotee of the goddess, and receives initiation, with some payments needed; after a brief visit home, he travels at her suggestion to Rome. There he undergoes two further initiations into the mysteries of Osiris, a surprise to him, each requiring more payments and accompanied by dream-instructions from the god; money is provided through Lucius' work as an advocate, and he ends the novel as a minor priest of the cult in Rome, joyfully performing his duties.

(ii) *Lucius: A Sophistic Protagonist?*

One of the most obvious ways in which the *Metamorphoses* is a 'sophist's novel' is the characterization of its protagonist and first-person narrator Lucius as a sophist in the making, or at least as a figure with recognizably high status and ambitions within the cultural world of the Second Sophistic.[8] Apart from the novel's problematic prologue, where the speaker is not named and the biographical details seem to fit not Lucius but rather the personified book itself,[9] Lucius himself is immediately introduced on his first unambiguous appearance in the work as connected with a well-known intellectual dynasty, that of Plutarch (1. 2. 1 *originis maternae fundamenta a Plutarcho illo ac mox Sexto nepote eius prodita gloriam nobis faciunt*), and we are reminded of this distinguished ancestry again when he meets his relative Byrrhaena (2. 3. 3 *Plutarchi familia ambae prognatae sumus*). He is presented as a Greek from Corinth (1. 22. 4, 2. 12. 3);[10] his father is named as Theseus at 1. 23. 6, but since the point of that passage is to make a comparison with the literary Theseus of Callimachus' *Hecale* we may justly suspect that the name is invented for that momentary purpose (it is not mentioned again in the *Metamorphoses*).[11] More important is the family information given by Lucius' relative Byrrhaena, who as well as confirming the Plutarchan connection (above) names his mother as Salvia (2. 2. 8), indicating that she was born a Roman citizen,[12] and suggests that his father was of distinguished social rank (2. 3. 2 *quod illa clarissimas ego privatas nuptias*

---

[8] Mason (1983) is an important treatment of Lucius' social distinction, on which I here build by stressing specifically intellectual and educational aspects.

[9] As argued in Harrison (1990*b*).

[10] Note that *Onos* 55, reflecting the Greek *Metamorphoses*, states that Lucius is from Patras.

[11] On the Hecale connection see Harrison (1997*a*), 56–7. Note that at *Onos* 55 the name of Lucius' father is omitted in an apparent lacuna in the manuscripts (we are given the rather uninformative name of his brother, Gaius). Mason (1983), 139, argues for Theseus as a real Athenian name pointing to an ultimately Attic origin for Lucius, but this seems very unlikely given its literary function in alluding to Callimachus.

[12] So Bowersock (1965), 289, associating her with C. Salvius Liberalis Nonius Bassus, governor of Macedonia under Domitian (*PIR* S 105). For a later consular Salvius cf. n. 188 below.

fecerimus).[13] This high social position is confirmed by the magistrate presiding at the Festival of Laughter at Hypata in his fulsome apology to Lucius, indignant after the practical joke of a false accusation of murder (3. 11. 1 *neque tuae dignitatis vel etiam prosapiae tuorum ignarae sumus, Luci domine; nam et provinciam totam inclitae vestrae familiae nobilitas complectitur*). The further honours offered by the magistrate, that Lucius is to be inscribed as Hypata's *patronus* and have a statue erected to him there (3. 11. 5), are realistic for the second-century empire, and such as would be paid to a Roman grandee.[14] Lucius is thus clearly presented as an elite Greek, almost certainly with Roman citizenship (note his *praenomen*, the only name we hear of)[15] and able to speak Latin,[16] from a socially elevated background in an important Greek city; in other words, he shares the social origins of almost all the major Greek sophists of the first and second centuries AD.[17]

We also find a number of indications of Lucius' cultural and educational background in the *Metamorphoses*, which confirm his social elite status but also suggest particular intellectual interests. The Plutarchan connection already remarked of course links Lucius with two significant Middle Platonist philosophers, Plutarch himself and his nephew Sextus. Sextus, like the Claudius Maximus of the *Apologia*,[18] was a teacher of Marcus Aurelius, and may have been heard by Apuleius himself;[19] the

---

[13] Mason (1983), 139–40, argues that *clarissimus* here refers specifically to consular rank, but this seems too precise for the vague novelistic context; *clarissimas ... nuptias* here seems just as unspecific as 4. 32. 3 *beatas nuptias* (in the fantasy world of Cupid and Psyche).

[14] For Roman grandees as patrons of provincial communities in the Roman empire see Harmand (1957); he records a number of examples in Roman Africa at 233–6 (e.g. Fronto as patron of Calama—*CIL* 8. 5350), and three examples of aristocratic youths as patrons of African cities at 240–1. This again suggests Lucius' high social status and that the honours given him at Hypata, though in an absurd scenario, are not in themselves unrealistic.

[15] By contrast, Lucius' other two names (which indicate Roman citizenship) were almost certainly revealed at *Onos* 51, where the text says that Lucius has his other two names in common with his father, but the father's name is lost—see n. 11. It is intriguing but no doubt coincidental that Lucius shares his sole name with a Platonist philosopher of Apuleius' own generation (see n. 188), especially since the name is inherited from Apuleius' Greek source.

[16] At 9. 39. 3 Lucius-ass understands the Latin question of the soldier which his more humble human owner requires to be repeated in Greek, while at 11. 28. 6 the human Lucius turns without linguistic preparation to earning money by acting as an advocate in the Roman courts (*per patrocinia sermonis Romani*).

[17] See especially Bowie (1982).

[18] Ch. 2 n. 21.

[19] Marcus *Med.* 1. 9, *SHA Marcus* 3. 2; the latter passage suggests that Marcus attended Sextus' lectures at the time normal for philosophical study, i.e. the late teens and early twenties (c. 135–45; Marcus was born in 121). Dillon (1977), 338, and Dowden (1994), 428–9, plausibly suggest that Apuleius himself heard Sextus in the 140s—cf. Ch. 1 n. 19.

suggestion is surely that Lucius has inherited some of his family's intellectual interests, though the stressing of this connection at the beginning
of Lucius' narrative has also been plausibly viewed as a hint that Platonic
philosophy is to have some role in the novel, just as the mention of Egypt
in the prologue (1. 1. 1) seems to look forward to the Isiac conclusion of
the work.[20] Stress is also laid on Lucius' more general education and intel-
lect as well as these philosophical connections. His learning is flattered in
a wheedling speech by the slave-girl Photis at 3. 15. 4 (*sed melius de te doc-
trinaque tua praesumo, qui praeter generosam natalium dignitatem praeter
sublime ingenium sacris pluribus initiatus . . .*), he is rebuked for not living up to his education by the priest Mithras at 11. 15. 1 (*nec tibi natales ac
ne dignitas quidem, vel ipsa, qua flores, usquam doctrina profuit*), and
comments on his own learning in oratory at 11. 30. 4 (*studiorum meorum
laboriosa doctrina*). The first of these three passages highlights not only
education in general but initiation in particular, a by-product of elite
educational travel; those visiting famous cult-sites in the Greek world
could have themselves initiated into the cult, just as (for example)
Augustus was initiated into the Eleusinian mysteries,[21] and Apuleius himself claimed to have been initiated into several cults in Greece (*Apol.* 55.
8).[22] Finally, there are two passages where future literary glory of some
kind is foretold for Lucius: at 2. 12. 5 he himself reports a Chaldaean
prophet at Corinth as predicting that *nunc enim gloriam satis floridam,
nunc historiam magnam et incredundam fabulam et libros me futurum,*[23]
while at 11. 27. 9 the priest Asinius Marcellus reports to Lucius a vision he
experienced of the god Osiris concerning the future intellectual glory of
the 'man from Madauros' (*Madaurensem*), apparently taken by Lucius to
refer to himself: *nam et illi* (Lucius?) *studiorum gloriam et ipsi* (Asinius)
grande compendium sua (Osiris') *comparari providentia.*[24]

The mention of the notorious 'man from Madauros' passage, which
will be fully discussed below, raises an important issue—the resemblance
between Lucius, the narrator of the novel, and Apuleius, its author.[25]
Apart from this famous moment, where the two have seemed to many to
be at least temporarily identified, Lucius and Apuleius seem to have a

---

[20] Cf. Grimal (1971) and n. 133 below.   [21] Suet. *Div. Aug.* 93, Dio 51. 4. 1, 54. 9. 10.

[22] Cf. Hunink (1997), ii. 149.

[23] *Floridam* here could look forward to Apuleius' *Florida*, just as *libros* plainly looks forward in metafictional manner to the *Metamorphoses*; for the term 'metafiction' cf. n. 110
below. For a similar metafictional interpretation of 11. 27. 9 see Sect. 1 (iv) below.

[24] For a fuller analysis of this passage see Sect. 1 (iv) below.

[25] Cf. esp. van der Paardt (1981), Walsh (1970), 250, Smith (1972), 530 n. 40. Hicter (1944),
(1945) goes too far in identifying the two.

good deal in common: both belong to a provincial elite, both have connections with Platonic philosophy,[26] both have a first-class education
including study at Athens and visits to Rome,[27] both have Greek intellectual credentials as well as seeking a literary or rhetorical career in Latin,[28]
both are subject to jealous rivalries in that career,[29] both have been initiated into several Greek mystery-cults,[30] both receive honorific statues,[31]
and both are trained orators and emerge successfully from defending
themselves in a trial in which the charges can be seen as fabricated.[32]
These resemblances do not require that the *Metamorphoses* should be
read as a fictionalized autobiography, though there were apparently
ancient readers who thought Apuleius himself might really have been
turned into an ass.[33] Like many modern novelists, Apuleius is adapting
elements of his own life and experience in order to make the characterization of his first-person protagonist more realistic and effective, and to
set him in his own contemporary cultural background.

The affinities of Lucius' education and intellectual interests in the
Metamorphoses with the Greek sophistic world are even clearer in the
characterization of Lucius in the pseudo-Lucianic Greek *Onos*, which I
with the majority of modern scholars regard as an epitome of the Greek
Metamorphoses of Lucius of Patras,[34] now generally agreed to be the common source of both Apuleius and the *Onos*.[35] Thus in the *Metamorphoses*

---

[26] Cf. Lucius' connection with Plutarch and Sextus at *Met.* 1. 2. 1, discussed below.

[27] Lucius' education at Athens: *Met.* 1. 24. 5. Apuleius' education at Athens and visits to Rome: *Flor.* 20. 4, 17. 4.

[28] For Apuleius' Greek intellectual credentials see the discussion of his Greek works at Ch. 1, Sect. 2 (ii).

[29] Lucius' jealous rivals: *Met.* 11. 30. 4. Rivals of Apuleius at Carthage: *Flor.* 9. 1, Ch. 3 n. 49.

[30] Lucius: *Met.* 3. 15. 4 *sacris pluribus initiatus.* Apuleius: *Apol.* 55. 8 *sacrorum pleraque initia in Graecia participavi.*

[31] Lucius: *Met.* 3. 11. 1. Apuleius: Ch. 1 nn. 30, 32.

[32] The mock-trial of *Met.* 3. 1–12 and the trial of the *Apologia*.

[33] This seems to be the implication of Augustine *Civ.* 18. 18. 1 *sicut Apuleius . . . sibi ipsi accidisse ut accepto veneno humano animo permanente asinus fieret aut indicavit aut finxit*; though Augustine's own scepticism is clear, the conflation of author and narrator in some other minds is evident.

[34] I see no reason to attribute this work to Lucian, with Lucius (as in Apuleius) as the protagonist and first-person narrator, as many have done following Perry (1967), 211–35;
Photius' summary (see next note), our only real evidence, plainly regards Lucius as the
author, as does his further cross-reference at *Bibl. cod.* 166 (111b34). For further good arguments against Lucianic authorship cf. Hall (1981), 354–67.

[35] The *Onos* is extant, while the Greek *Metamorphoses* are preserved only in a problematic summary by Photius (*Bibl. cod.* 129). For brief summaries of the arguments on the relations between the three texts, and further literature on this vast issue, see conveniently
Walsh (1974), Harrison (1996), 500–1.

as in many of his other works[36] we can see Apuleius translating and adapting a Greek work for a Roman audience, as he explicitly admits (for once)[37] in the novel's prologue (1. 1. 6 *fabulam Graecanicam incipimus*). Two passages in the *Onos*, presumably inherited from the Greek *Metamorphoses*, make it clear that Lucius' background in that work is specifically sophistic. The author of Lucius' letters of recommendation to his host in Hypata (Hipparchus in the *Onos*, Milo in Apuleius) in the *Onos* (2) is Decrianus, a sophist from Patras, who in Apuleius (1. 21. 8, 1. 22. 4) becomes Demeas of Corinth whose profession is not named; and when Lucius states his family origin to the governor of Macedonia at the climactic point of his retransformation from asinine to human shape at *Onos* 55, a scene omitted in Apuleius' adaptation of the story, he claims that he himself is a 'writer of stories and other things' and that his brother is 'an elegiac poet and a fine prophet'.[38] Here we find more specific details about the intellectual distinction of Lucius, namely that he is a professional man of letters and comes from a family of professional writers;[39] and though Apuleius has chosen to play down this aspect of his protagonist by giving less focused information (see above), the general world of Lucius, that of the elite intellectual with literary ambitions, seems to be much the same in both works.

Though Lucius has many traits of the elite intellectual in the *Metamorphoses*, his education does not prevent him from making many foolish decisions and choices, and his intellectual capacity is usually shown in the novel as ineffectual and comically ambiguous. In general terms, Lucius is credulous (not least as a member of a religious cult in Book 11),[40] foolish, too easily swayed by momentary sensual pleasure, and above all, too inquistive for his own good (*curiosus*). On the other hand, he can produce a persuasive and highly inventive forensic oration of Ciceronian character[41] when required to at the mock trial in Book 3 (3. 4. 3–7. 3), and can earn money easily as an advocate in the Roman law-courts (11. 28. 6), clear signs of a good rhetorical education. But his

[36] See Ch. 1 for a survey of Apuleius' works, which include a number of translations from Greek (e.g. the lost *Phaedo* and the extant *De Mundo*—for the latter see Ch. 5) and a number of popularizations in Latin of Greek thought (e.g. the *De Platone*—see Ch. 5).
[37] Contrast e.g. the *De Mundo*, where it is at no point admitted that it is a translation of a Greek work.
[38] Tr. J. P. Sullivan in Reardon (1989), 617.
[39] An obvious parallel is the literary family of the Philostrati—on these (and their complex prosopography) see Anderson (1986), 291–6.
[40] See further Sect. 2 (ii) below.
[41] See below, n. 77.

literary training emerges otherwise in his narrative only in trite and self-important mythological and textual references, as if he is anxious to tell us what he has recently learnt:[42] his killing of the three supposed assailants at the end of Book 2 is like Hercules' slaying of the three-bodied monster Geryon (2. 32. 7),[43] the old woman's attempts to stop the girl Charite's escape attempt on the back of Lucius-ass are compared to Dirce's struggle with the bull (6. 27. 5), a rider of Lucius-ass is ironically referred to as Bellerophon (7. 26. 3),[44] and Lucius describes his adventures as an ass as a form of odyssey, showing that he knows the (trite) opening lines of the *Odyssey* (9. 13. 4-5).[45] Similarly, his blustering attack on the unjust judgements against Socrates, Palamedes, and Ajax (10. 33. 1–4) rehearses well-known examples,[46] and he knows that seven is the Pythagorean ritual number (11. 1. 4). Lucius' expensive education, much stressed by other characters as a token of his elite status, in fact does him relatively little credit, and his intellectual ambitions achieve little owing to his general foolishness and immaturity.

(iii)　*Novel as* Paideia: *Sophistic and Literary Learning in the* Metamorphoses

The literary texture of the *Metamorphoses* contains elements which can be labelled 'sophistic', whether we take this as characterizing the voice of the intradiegetic narrator Lucius or the extradiegetic narrator Apuleius.[47] To take perhaps the most obvious example, the Apuleian fondness for

---

[42] This character of the youthful narrator with half-baked learning resembles that of the 'mythomaniac' Encolpius in Petronius' *Satyrica* as recently characterized by Conte (1996)—an element of Petronian influence on Apuleius, perhaps?

[43] Note the similar comparison to Ajax by the witty but relatively uneducated slave-girl Photis at 3. 18. 5.

[44] The Bellerophon/Pegasus/Chimaera myth is (unsurprisingly) a favourite of Lucius-ass (cf. also 8. 16. 3, 11. 8. 4), but is also alluded to by one of the robbers at 6. 30. 4. The upper-class Charite also shows mythological learning—cf. 4. 26. 8 (Attis, Protesilaus: has she been reading Catullus 63 and 68?), 6. 29. 4 (Phrixus, Arion, Europa). For mythological analogies in the *Metamorphoses* in general, often voiced by semi-educated characters, cf. Bernhard (1927), 208–9.

[45] Cf. Harrison (1990a).

[46] For Socrates as an unjust victim of legal judgement see Plato's *Apology* and the whole subsequent tradition; for Ajax and Palamedes paired in this role cf. *Rhet. Her.* 2. 28, Ovid *Met.* 13. 34–62.

[47] For these useful terms see Genette (1980), 228–31: 'intradiegetic' = within the text's narrative, 'extradiegetic' = outside the text's narrative. Winkler (1985) makes the further distinction for the *Metamorphoses* between Lucius-*actor* (acting protagonist) and Lucius-*auctor* (retrospective narrator of action). As we shall see, identifying these different voices in the novel is often problematic.

ekphrasis (elaborate formal description, especially of artefacts, places, or persons) which is evident in the *Florida* is also clear in the *Metamorphoses*.[48] This technique, with its opportunity for stylistic display and ornament, is commonly viewed as characteristic of sophistic writing in general as well as of the ancient novels in particular.[49] The *Metamorphoses* has a number of these *ekphraseis* in prominent locations, commonly introduced by rhetorical flourishes; some of these also function as literary allusions as well as pieces of epideictic writing. In Book 2, when Lucius visits the house of his wealthy relative Byrrhaena, we have a formal description of her palatial residence and in particular of a sculptural group of Actaeon and Diana in the middle of the house (2. 4. 1–10); this sculpture is highly significant, as scholars have noted, since it is a warning to Lucius not to show *curiositas* towards powerful females and a prediction of his forthcoming bestial metamorphosis.[50] A similar elaborate *ekphrasis* of a sumptuous palace occurs at the beginning of *Met.* 5 (5. 1. 3–7) when Psyche wakes up in Cupid's house, which may again have epic antecedents.[51] Natural landscapes receive the same treatment—for example, the robbers' cave at 4. 6. 1–4 and a cliff at 6. 14. 2–4. There are also detailed descriptions of persons and their features—for example, an appreciative account of the hair of the slave-girl Photis at 2. 8. 2–9. 7, which has a specific parallel in sophistic literature in the form of the encomium of hair written by Dio Chrysostom,[52] and a full word-picture of the goddess Isis at 11. 3. 3–4. 3.[53] The longest *ekphrasis* in the whole work describes the appearance of a pantomime performance on the subject of the Judgement of Paris, 10. 30. 1–32. 4;[54] a description of the elements of pantomime was the subject of a work of Lucian from the 160s, the *De Saltatione*,[55] showing the currency of the topic in sophistic literature.

[48] Cf. Slater (1998).

[49] For *ekphrasis* in the *Florida*, and its general sophistic character, see Ch. 3 n. 80.

[50] So e.g. Tatum (1979), 38–9, Peden (1985), Winkler (1985), 168. It can also be argued that this narrative function is an imitation of Vergilian *ekphrasis*-technique—cf. Harrison (1997*a*).

[51] Resembling both the palace of Alcinous in *Od.* 6 and the Palace of the Sun at Ovid *Met.* 2. 1 ff.—cf. Harrison (1998*b*), 59–60.

[52] Preserved in the *Praise of Baldness* of Synesius, and conveniently found in Crosby (1951), 331–43; see Hunink (1997), ii. 25, and Englert and Long (1972–3) on Apuleian interest in hair generally.

[53] Note that this includes a brief appreciation of her hair (11. 3. 3), one of the elements linking her and Photis—cf. Alpers (1980), 200–1. For the Photis/Isis resemblance see n. 173 below.

[54] On this episode see Fick (1990), Zimmerman (1993).

[55] For the date and character of this work cf. Jones (1986), 69–75.

More frequent than such specifically 'sophistic' elements are the many allusions to classic literary texts, demonstrating the literary learning of the author. It is not an exaggeration to state that the *Metamorphoses* (like Petronius' *Satyrica*) often has a depth of literary texture and allusion which rivals that of the richest Augustan poetry, and much has been done in recent scholarship to bring this out, especially in the emergence of detailed commentaries on the individual books of the *Metamorphoses*.[56] This literary texture is located not only in the most overtly 'literary' parts of the novel, such as the long mythological tale of Cupid and Psyche (4. 28–6. 24),[57] but is a constant part of its character.

Primary amongst intertexts for the *Metamorphoses* are the great epic poems of Greece and Rome.[58] One fundamental reason for this is clearly the display of the author's *paideia*, the literary learning which was the stock-in-trade of sophists and elite intellectuals:[59] in the second-century Roman empire, as now, the epics of Homer and Vergil held a central place in literary and educational culture, and to demonstrate close acquaintance with them was to demonstrate the basic standard of learning for a man of letters.[60] Another reason is the nature of the novel genre, for which the epic was a natural precursor: as has been pointed out, the ancient novel is essentially the successor of the epic as the vehicle of lengthy fictional narrative.[61] Though (as we shall see) the *Metamorphoses* is full of literary allusions to many kinds of writing, it seems to be particularly concerned with highlighting its similarities with and differences from the epic in particular. The epic affinities of the *Metamorphoses* are evident from its structure. It has eleven books, almost but not quite an epic number; the two-book inserted tale of Cupid and Psyche, taking up approximately one-sixth of the work, clearly recalls inserted tales of similar size in epic, such as that of Aeneas in Books 2 and 3 of the twelve-book *Aeneid* and that of Odysseus in Books 9–12 of the twenty-four-book

---

[56] Walsh (1970), 52–63, provided an important corrective to previous treatments which underestimated the literary artistry and texture of the *Metamorphoses* (especially the influential Perry and Helm). For commentaries on the *Metamorphoses* see the critical bibliography in the introduction to Harrison (1999); for the most recent large-scale treatment of literary allusion in the *Metamorphoses* see Finkelpearl (1998).

[57] Here Kenney (1990a) has been particularly useful in detecting literary allusions. See also now the studies in Zimmerman *et al.* (1998), which add many further echoes.

[58] See the considerable bibliography conveniently collected in Harrison (1990b), (1997a), and (1998b), and much of the material in Finkelpearl (1998).

[59] See e.g. Anderson (1993), 69–85.

[60] For Homer in the Second Sophistic see Kindstrand (1973); for Vergil in Roman imperial education cf. Bonner (1977), 213–14.

[61] Perry (1967), 45–57, Bakhtin (1981), 1–41.

Odyssey. Even the way in which the tale of Cupid and Psyche begins before the end of Book 4 and ends before the end of Book 6, evidently not matching the Homeric or Vergilian model where the tales of Odysseus and Aeneas begin and end with books, clearly derives from the tension between episode and book in the structure of Ovid's *Metamorphoses.*[62]

Epic imitations are also found in significant number in specific episodes of the *Metamorphoses*, as well as in its overall structure. Best-known are the echoes of the *katabasis* of *Aen.* 6 in the descent of Psyche to the Underworld,[63] but epic imitation in the *Metamorphoses* is not confined to the loftier style of Cupid and Psyche. For example, the journey of Lucius to Hypata and his dealings with strangers in the opening books recall the similar experiences of Telemachus in the opening books of the *Odyssey*; the Haemus/Tlepolemus episode in Book 7, where Tlepolemus disguises himself in order to infiltrate and defeat the robbers, echoes the cunning of the disguised Odysseus amongst the suitors;[64] the story of Charite in Book 8, the romantic heroine who loses her partner and resolutely commits suicide, echoes that of Dido;[65] and (as we have seen) Lucius' time as an ass is specifically compared with the adventures of Odysseus as a formative learning process in Book 9.[66] Of course, Apuleius is likely to be conscious of the tradition of the Greek ideal novel, which owes more than a little to the *Odyssey*,[67] but the detailed reworkings of both Greek and Roman epic in particular episodes are meant to be noticed as such, and are of a different order of imitation from the use of epic in the Greek novel, which usually provides only themes and a general narrative framework. Crucially, the epic episodes mentioned above are almost all transformed in their new novelistic context; reworked with the comic or sensational tone of Milesian stories, their metamorphosis stresses the difference of literary kind between a low-life novel and the lofty epic level.

Of course, literary learning in the *Metamorphoses* is not restricted to use of epic.[68] Amongst poetic genres other than mythological epic, the influence of Lucretius is felt as well as that of Vergil,[69] and love-elegy

---

[62] On these issues see in more detail Harrison (1997*a*) and (1998*b*), 58–60.

[63] See Finkelpearl (1990) and (1998), 110–14.

[64] On these two Odyssean echoes see Harrison (1990*b*), and for further Odyssean echoes in the Tlepolemus episode see Frangoulidis (1992).

[65] See Forbes (1943–4), Harrison (1997*a*), Shumate (1996*b*), Finkelpearl (1998), 115–48.

[66] 9. 13. 4–5   [67] Perry (1967), 45–57.

[68] Again Walsh (1970), 52–63, is important in stressing its variety of literary sources; see also Finkelpearl (1998).   [69] Kenney (1990*a*), 121.

provides occasional erotic colour.[70] Imitations of Greek tragedy can also
be seen, whether in Psyche's apparent tragic fate of death instead of marriage (*Met.* 4. 33. 4),[71] or in the parodic *lecti invocatio* where the comically
suicidal Aristomenes bids farewell to his hotel bed (*Met.* 1. 16. 2–3),[72] or
in the marked evocation of the Hippolytus story in the tale of the mur-
derous stepmother (*Met.* 10. 2. 4).[73] Of prose genres, traces of historiography, so influential on the Greek novels, can also be detected—whether
in the story of the market-gardener with its Livian *prodigia* in *Met.* 9.
32–8,[74] or in the Thucydidean military tales told by the robbers in Book
4. 9–21.[75] The world of literary *declamatio*, much more familiar to the second century than to the twentieth, is seen in the story of *Met.* 9. 35–8,
where the aggressive rich neighbour, the dispute between a rich and a
poor man, and the tragic father who loses all his sons are all common
declamatory themes.[76] And forensic oratory of the classic Ciceronian
type is very much to the fore in the speeches of the prosecution and
defence at the mock-trial of Lucius in *Met.* 3. 3. 1–3. 7. 1, both astonish-
ingly addressed to *Quirites* though spoken by Greeks before Greeks,[77] just
as there is strong Ciceronian colour in the *Apologia*, to which the mock-
trial scene may well be a witty allusion.[78]

There are also prominent echoes of Platonic dialogues. As I will argue
later in this chapter, these mostly convey literary learning and entertainment, and their ideological content has commonly been overvalued. To
the allusions to Plato's *Phaedrus* discussed below (*Met.* 1. 18. 8 ~ *Phaedr.*
229a, 5. 24. 1 ~ *Phaedr.* 248c), we might add two echoes of Plato's *Sym-*

---

[70] See esp. the considerable collection of Ovidian parallels in Kenney (1990*a*), 242.
[71] Schiesaro (1988).   [72] Mattiacci (1993*b*).
[73] Zwierlein (1987), though I would not agree with all of his reconstruction of Sophocles'
Phaedra from Apuleius' text.
[74] Graverini (1997).   [75] Loporcaro (1992).
[76] Aggressive rich neighbour: Ps.-Quintilian *Decl. Mai.* 7, 9, 11. Dispute between rich and
poor man: Seneca *Contr.* 5. 2, 10. 1, Calpurnius Flaccus *Decl.* 7, 11, 17, 27, 28, 29, 38, 50, 53, Ps.-
Quintilian *Decl. Min.* 271, 305, 337, 379. Father who loses sons: Seneca *Contr.* 4. 1, 7. 4. 9. Some
of these echoes are picked up by Hijmans *et al.* (1995), 297, with further references.
[77] For a good analysis of the two speeches, pointing out standard forensic expressions
and techniques, cf. van der Paardt (1971), 46–7 and 63–4; for some specifically Ciceronian
echoes cf. e.g. *Met.* 3. 6. 1 *dux et signifer ceterorum* ~ Cicero *Mur.* 50 *dux et signifer calami-
tosorum,* and *Met.* 3. 3. 9 (in the *peroratio*) *habetis itaque reum tot caedibus impiatum, reum
coram deprensum, reum peregrinum* ~ Cicero *Caec.* 104 (also in the *peroratio*) *habetis
hominem singulari pudore, virtute cognita et spectata fide, amplissimae totius Etruriae
nomine.* For *Quirites* cf. 3. 3. 2, 3. 5. 6, and the comments of van der Paardt (1971), 41.
[78] For Ciceronian colour in the *Apologia* cf. Ch. 2 n. 17; for allusion to the *Apologia* in
Lucius' mock-trial cf. van der Paardt (1971), 63 n. 1.

posium.[79] This famous symposiastic dialogue, plainly familiar to Apuleius (*Apol.* 12. 2),[80] is surely behind the symposiastic setting for the competing tales of the robbers at *Met.* 4. 9–21, just as Petronius' *Satyrica* clearly echoes the *Symposium* in the symposiastic tale-telling of the *cena Trimalchionis*.[81] It also seems to be some kind of model for the tale of Cupid and Psyche. In the *Symposium*, the assembled company at the symposium compete in praising the god Love (Cupid). The climax occurs when Socrates tells the assembled company of how the true nature of Love was revealed to him by the priestess Diotima of Mantinea (201d–212c): Diotima claims that Love's true object is the beauty of the soul, not the body, and that thus he is the greatest of the gods, drawing man towards contemplation of the divine. Here is an inserted tale in which a woman gives an account of love and the soul, Cupid (*Cupido/Amor*)[82] and Psyche (ψυχή, soul), a Platonic model for the narrative frame of the tale of Cupid and Psyche in the *Metamorphoses*. In Apuleius the tale about Love and the Soul is narrated not by a dignified priestess with a ponderous name, Diotima, 'honoured by Zeus', but by a nameless and undignified old woman, a *delira et temulenta anicula* (*Met.* 6. 25. 1); this comic touch stresses the lower literary character of the *Metamorphoses*, more concerned with literary entertainment than philosophical exposition, as we shall see in Section 2 below.

The learning of the *Metamorphoses* is not of course restricted to literary allusion; many of the broad range of Apuleian intellectual interests evident from his many and varied technical works (see Chapter 1) also emerge in his novel. Readers of the *Metamorphoses* are (for example) told the length of an elephant's pregnancy (1. 9. 6), given medical views on dreaming with a full stomach (1. 18. 4) or on remedies for biliousness (10. 25. 3), and reminded of the *lex Julia de adulteriis* (6. 22. 4)[83] and of scientific views on rabies (9. 3. 3–4);[84] these are snippets of learning from fields in which Apuleius shows extensive interest elsewhere—zoology,

[79] For the second of these echoes see Harrison (1998*b*).

[80] Kenney (1990*b*) argues (perhaps over-ingeniously at times) for a close use of the *Symposium* in Apuleius' characterization of Venus in the tale of Cupid and Psyche.

[81] Cf. Cameron (1969), Bessone (1993), Conte (1996), 120–1.

[82] Interestingly, Cupid is normally called 'Cupido' in the *Metamorphoses* and named as 'Amor' only once in a specific word-play (5. 23. 3 *sic ignara Psyche sponte in Amoris incidit amorem*). For similar puns on the allegorical possibilities of the names Cupid and Psyche cf. 5. 6. 9 *tuae Psyches dulcis anima*, 5. 13. 4 *Psychae animam*, 5. 23. 3 *cupidine fraglans Cupidinis*, 6. 2. 5 *miserandae Psyches animae* (see Kenney (1990*a*) on all these passages).

[83] Cf. also *Apol.* 88. 3, where Apuleius alludes to the *lex Julia de maritandis ordinibus*.

[84] Cf. the discussion in Mattiacci (1993*a*).

medicine, and law.[85] Perhaps the most sustained display of technical
knowledge is in the account of the Isis-cult in Book 11: there we are given
a great deal of detailed information concerning the Isis-cult—the
appearance of the cult-statue of the goddess herself (11. 3. 4–11. 4. 3), the
names and cults under which Isis claimed to appear in the Mediterranean
world (11. 5. 1–4), the procession of the Ploiaphesia, the Isiac festival in
which Lucius-ass finds himself (11. 8. 1–11. 12. 2). Though some at least of
this material is adapted to the narrative framework of the novel (see
below), its general accuracy is beyond question.[86] But (as I will discuss
below) this is not a token of Apuleian promotion of the Isis-cult, though
Apuleius himself may well have been an initiate[87] (hence perhaps his
detailed information). As in the display of other literary and non-literary
learning, what we have here is self-display by a member of a social and
intellectual elite, a demonstration of cultural capital:[88] only the intellectual elite would care for the minute details of the Isiac cult, a cult which
had been brought into fashion in the Greek sophistic world by its treatment in the *De Iside et Osiride* of Plutarch, and only the social elite would
be able to afford the costs of initiation.[89]

(iv) *Novel as Epideixis: Narrative Complexity and Sophistic Self-Display in the* Metamorphoses

A key element of the *Metamorphoses*, and one of its fundamental problems for the literary interpreter, is the complex function of the first-person narrative voice in this largely autodiegetic novel.[90] The main
narrative voice we hear within the text, the primary intradiegetic voice,[91]
is that of Lucius, the elite young Greek; but we are aware from information both inside and outside the text that the novel is in fact written by a
person of Roman culture, the extradiegetic author and narrator
Apuleius. The title and author's name at the head of the text would have

---

[85] For Apuleian interests in Aristotelian-type zoology see Ch. 1, Sect. 2 (ii) 12, for medicine
cf. Ch. 1, Sect. 2 (ii) 7, and for law Ch. 2 n. 108.

[86] Cf. n. 160.   [87] Cf. n. 162.

[88] For the concept of 'cultural capital', prestige and knowledge acquired through elite
education, see the work of the sociologist Pierre Bourdieu, esp. Bourdieu (1984).

[89] Another reason for the stress on expenditure in *Met.* 11—see Sect. 2 (ii) below.

[90] i.e. with a first-person narrator who tells a story in which he/she is the central character; this is the strongest form of the 'homodiegetic' narrative mode, in which the narrator
tells a story in which he/she participates, as opposed to the 'heterodiegetic', a narrator telling
a story in which he/she does not feature. For these terms see Genette (1980), 245.

[91] For the terms 'intradiegetic' and 'extradiegetic' see n. 47.

instantly revealed the facts of authorship for an ancient as for a modern reader; and there are several occasions in the novel when the author's Roman identity is indicated in a way which compels the reader to look to Apuleius rather than Lucius.[92] This problem of the narrative voice is famously highlighted at the novel's opening (1. 1. 1–6):[93]

at ego tibi sermone isto Milesio varias fabulas conseram, auresque tuas benivolas lepido susurro permulceam, modo si papyrum Aegyptiam argutia Nilotici calami inscriptam non spreveris inspicere. figuras fortunasque hominum in alias imagines conversas et in se rursum mutuo nexu refectas, ut mireris, exordior. quis ille? paucis accipe. Hymettos Attica et Isthmos Ephyrea et Taenaros Spartiatica, glebae felices aeternum libris felicioribus conditae, mea vetus prosapia est. ibi linguam Atthidem primis pueritiae stipendiis merui; mox in urbe Latia advena studiorum Quiritium indigenam sermonem aerumnabili labore, nullo magistro praeeunte, aggressus excolui. en ecce praefamur veniam, si quid exotici ac forensis sermonis rudis locutor offendero. iam haec equidem ipsa vocis immutatio desultoriae scientiae stilo quem accessimus respondet: fabulam Graecanicam incipimus. lector intende: laetaberis.

Thessaliam—nam et illic originis maternae nostrae fundamenta a Plutarcho illo inclito ac mox Sexto philosopho nepote eius prodita gloriam nobis faciunt— eam Thessaliam ex negotio petebam.

But let me join together different stories in that Milesian style, and let me soothe your kindly ears with an agreeable whispering, if only you do not scorn to glance at an Egyptian papyrus inscribed with the sharpness of a reed from the Nile. I begin a tale of men's shapes and fortunes transformed into different appearances and back again into themselves by mutual connection, that you may wonder at it. 'Who is this?' Hear in brief. Attic Hymettus and the Corinthian Isthmus and Spartan Taenarus are my origin of old, ever-fertile regions recorded in even more fertile books. There it was that I acquired the Attic tongue in the first campaigns of boyhood; thereafter in the Latin city as a foreigner to the studies of Rome I took on and developed the local language with laborious effort and without the lead of a master. Look then, I ask your pardon at the beginning, if I commit any offence, being an inexperienced speaker of the language of the forum which is foreign to me. Indeed, this very change of language corresponds to the style of switch-back lore (?) which I have approached (?): I begin a story of Greek origin. Reader, pay attention: you will be pleased.

---

[92] See esp. van der Paardt (1981), the mention of *Quirites* at *Met.* 3. 3. 2 (cf. n. 77), and the mention of the Roman *metae Murciae* at *Met.* 6. 8. 2 (see Kenney (1990a), 199–200).

[93] On the prologue see the forthcoming collective volume edited by Kahane and Laird (2000). The text and translation of the prologue which follow are those of the contribution of Harrison and Winterbottom to that volume, which also discusses the problems of text and interpretation in the prologue (a translation is given here for once because of those difficulties).

It was Thessaly—for it was from there that the foundations of my mother's line, coming from the famous Plutarch and then Sextus the philosopher his nephew, emerged to bring glory on our family—it was that very Thessaly that I was heading for on business.

The *Metamorphoses* thus begins with a prologue in which the opening speaker is not named or closely identified and which indeed raises explicitly the question of the speaker's identity (1. 1. 3 *quis ille?*), a question which cannot easily be answered; the main story opens at 1. 2. 1 *Thessaliam . . . petebam*, plainly in the voice of Lucius, as the references to Plutarchan descent show,[94] but it is not at all clear that Lucius speaks the prologue, even though the text simply begins abruptly in the first person (1. 1. 1 *at ego tibi sermone isto Milesio varias fabulas conseram . . .*), and a reader would naturally expect the speaker to be identical with the first-person speaker of 1. 2. 1. For the autobiographical details supplied in the prologue, that the speaker is from Athens, Corinth, and Sparta and has learned Latin recently and with difficulty as a foreigner in Rome, seem to apply neither to the Latin-speaking author Apuleius, nor to the novel's main narrator Lucius, who comes from Corinth (1. 22. 4, 2. 12. 3), not from Athens, Corinth, and Sparta, and who seems to have no difficulty in turning to pleading in the Latin law-courts when he arrives in Rome (11. 28. 6), which implies that he has not learnt Latin painfully and recently as the prologue-speaker claims to have done. Whether one solves this difficulty by postulating a separate Plautine-type prologue-speaker, which would fit some of the other comic colour in the novel,[95] or by presenting the book itself as the speaker of its own prologue, which makes sense of a number of further details in the text,[96] such an initial enigma marks out what kind of work the *Metamorphoses* is—one involved with questioning the status and authority of its own narrator and narrative, an 'interrogative' text, to use a convenient critical term.[97]

Such deliberate problematizing of narrator and narrative at such an early stage clearly sets an agenda for the novel as a whole. The problems of the prologue are famously redoubled at the novel's end, where the narrator, up to now clearly Lucius of Corinth, is apparently named by the

[94] Though Lucius is of course not named in the novel until addressed by his schoolfriend Pythias at 1. 24. 6 *mi Luci*, another example of Apuleius' teasing approach to identity in his novel, the Plutarchan connection is alluded to elsewhere (2. 3. 3) and confirms that Lucius is the speaker at 1. 2. 1 and following.

[95] So Smith (1972), followed by Winkler (1985), 200–3.

[96] So Harrison (1990*b*)

[97] For this term cf. Belsey (1980), 90–103.

god Osiris appearing to the priest Asinius Marcellus as *Madaurensem* (11. 27. 9):

Nam sibi visus est quiete proxima, dum magno deo coronas exaptat, ... et de eius ore, quo singulorum fata dictat, audisse mitti sibi Madaurensem, sed admodum pauperem, cui statim sua sacra deberet ministrare; nam et illi studiorum gloriam et ipsi grande compendium sua comparari providentia.[98]

This passage seems to identify Lucius with Apuleius himself, born at Madauros. Some have tried to emend *Madaurensem*,[99] but most regard it simply as a signal that the initiation-narrative in Book 11 is in some sense autobiographical, a mark that we are now entering Apuleius' personal religious testament.[100] Though there are as we have seen clear similarities between Apuleius himself and the Lucius of his novel,[101] this notion at its end that they are effectively identical and that amusing fiction becomes earnest personal religious witness is a sudden and unprepared metamorphosis, even in a text where metamorphosis is the central theme, and where the identity of the narrator was prominently marked out as a problem in the prologue. We shall see in Section 2 that an earnest reading of Lucius' activities in the cult of Isis and Osiris is difficult to arrive at. But even supposing that there were a metamorphosis of the protagonist from Lucius to Apuleius here, it can only be momentary, since a subsequent passage about the protagonist plainly refers back to Lucius' previous career as narrated earlier in the novel.[102]

How is this vexed problem to be approached? Winkler's sophisticated interpretation of the celebrated 'man from Madauros' passage as a deliberate puzzle for the reader which admits of no authoritative solution, but which simply draws attention to the inconsistency and paradox of the identity of Lucius with Apuleius without letting go of the possibility of the 'religious testament' explanation, seems too indeterminate.[103] More attractive in my view are interpretations of a more overtly narratological cast, which would fit the self-conscious game on the identity of the novel's narrator which the text has already played on the reader in the prologue. This lays firm emphasis on an essential symmetry, the way in

---

[98] Robertson and Vallette (1940–5) and Griffiths (1975) rightly follow Helm's lacuna after *exaptat* in this passage, since the referent of *eius* (presumably Osiris) clearly needs to be named.

[99] See the discussions of Griffiths (1975), 334, and van der Paardt (1981).

[100] See esp. Nock (1933), 138–55, Festugière (1954), 68–89, Dodds (1965), 3.

[101] See above, Sect. 1 (ii).

[102] *Met.* 11. 29. 5 *quas in provincia sumpsisti* clearly looks back to Lucius' first initiation in Cenchreae—see Griffiths (1975), 339.   [103] Winkler (1985), 199, 219.

which the novel both begins and ends by raising fundamental questions about the identity of its narrator.

Here two views have been propounded. Van der Paardt has argued[104] (though without using the term) that *Madaurensem* is effectively a metalepsis,[105] a momentary and deliberate conflation of different narrative levels, an intrusion by the extradiegetic narrator Apuleius into the world of the intradiegetic narrator Lucius. He points out that this matches the way in which the extradiegetic narrator seems to intrude into the world of the metadiegetic (i.e. second-degree or embedded)[106] narrator of Cupid and Psyche, the unnamed old woman, at *Met.* 4. 32. 6, where Apollo is said to speak in Latin for the benefit of *huius Milesiae conditorem*, 'the composer of this Milesian tale', which can only be Apuleius. The effect, as in other metalepses, is one of humorous sophistication. But this momentary metalepsis seems in the end too surreal an approach: the god's prediction is then simply not true but a joke for the benefit of the knowing reader, which makes no sense other than to advertise what the reader already knows, that Apuleius and not Lucius is the actual author of the work in progress. More satisfying for me is the view of Penwill, in which the god's prediction does come true, but his message is distorted through the misunderstanding so often applied to the ambiguities of ancient prophetic discourse:

> The god of course does not lie; there is a sense in which Asinius will encounter a man from Madauros, but this does not happen when he meets Lucius. What Osiris predicts is the incorporation of Asinius into the Madauran's book, not the metamorphosis of fictive narrator into actual author.[107]

Asinius gets it wrong in the sense that he has misidentified Lucius as Apuleius, who will 'be sent' later to Asinius as the author of the story in which both Asinius and Lucius appear as characters. Apuleius is here a metonym for his book, a usage common in Roman thought,[108] and *Madaurensem* may be chosen with the future book in mind, since it specifically anticipates the appearance of the author's toponym in the title-inscription of the *Metamorphoses*.[109]

---

[104] Van der Paardt (1981)   [105] For the term cf. Genette (1980), 234–7.
[106] Genette (1980), 231–4.   [107] Penwill (1990), 223–6, at 225.
[108] For example, see the metonymic use in the (ancient) titles of Martial 14. 186–95 of 'Vergil', 'Cicero', 'Livy', 'Sallust', 'Tibullus', 'Lucan', and 'Catullus' to describe editions of these writers' works.
[109] As in the MS Φ, copy of F, which at the beginning of the *Metamorphoses* gives *Apulei Platonici* Madaurensis *Prosae de Magia Lib. II expl.* . . . *Apulei Meta. I.*

This metafictional[110] interpretation seems to me to respond most effectively to the evidence of the text. Most notably, it fits with the extraordinarily ambiguous use of pronouns, possessive adjectives, and indirect speech at *Met.* 11. 27. 9, where we find in the same sentence *sibi* (reflexive, referring to the speaker Asinius, summarized by Lucius to the reader), *eius* (demonstrative, presumably referring to Osiris), *sua* (reflexive, referring to the speaker Osiris, summarized by Asinius to Lucius), *illi* (demonstrative, referring to *Madaurensem*), *ipsi* (referring to the summarizer Asinius), and *sua* (reflexive, referring to the reported speaker Osiris). Here, if anywhere, is a context where identities might become confused and misinterpreted. Such an interpretation of confused identity also goes well with the otherwise extraordinary manner in which Lucius receives the prophecy: though a natural reaction to *Madaurensem* would be to say 'you have the wrong man', Lucius in fact makes no objection or correction to Asinius' speech. This derives from two aspects of Lucius' character as displayed in the novel. First, from his general gullibility when he is in the hands of the cult in Book 11 (see further below): he will take on trust whatever is told him, whatever the consequences for himself, and however illogical it appears. Second, from his as yet unfulfilled literary pretensions: the prophecy of literary glory which Osiris makes (*studiorum gloriam*) is naturally and instantly accepted by Lucius (as we have seen, an ambitious member of the intellectual elite) as applying to himself, easy enough if one loses the thread of identity in the highly ambiguous prophecy. Lucius' true literary glory is not to be a celebrated writer himself but to be the subject of a major work of literature, just as (on this reading) the *grande compendium* for Asinius would be not be the large fee to be paid by Lucius, but rather the great reward of appearing as a character in the novel of Apuleius.

This interpretation, looking forward in the voice of Lucius to the novel of Apuleius, matches another prophetic point in the text. At *Met.* 2. 12. 5 Lucius reports to his host Milo a prediction made about him at Corinth by the Chaldean prophet Diophanes: he and the journey he is about to embark on will be famous and turn into a fantastic narrative in several books:

---

[110] For metafiction, the tendency of fictional texts to highlight their own fictionality, see the guides of Waugh (1984) and Currie (1995), esp. the useful definition at Waugh (1984), 2: 'Metafiction is a term given to fictional writing which self-consciously and systematically draws attention to its status as an artefact in order to pose questions about the relationship between fiction and reality'. Cf. also Waugh (1984), 14–19, on the entry of the (extradiegetic) narrator into the text.

mihi denique proventum huius peregrinationis inquirenti multa respondit et
oppido mira et satis varia: nunc enim gloriam satis floridam, nunc historiam
magnam et incredundam fabulam et libros me futurum.

As Warren Smith has indicated, this is plainly a reference to the inclusion
of Lucius in Apuleius' novel: 'Diophanes' prophecy is clearly a tongue-in-
cheek reference to the *Metamorphoses* itself: the *libri* which will record
Lucius' adventures are the eleven books which make up the novel as we
have it.'[111] Lucius' literary fame is again foretold, and again Lucius latches
eagerly on to the prediction; though this time the prophecy seems to be
correctly interpreted as a prediction of Lucius' fame as the *subject* of a
work of literature (Lucius does not seem to interpret the *libri* as an autobiographical story by himself), Lucius cannot possibly imagine the future
framework of the Latin novel of Apuleius in which he will be celebrated.[112] As in 11. 27. 9, the novel looks forward to its own completion,
above and beyond the world of its characters.

Such undoubted literary and narratological complexity can be seen as
typical of sophistic narrative texts in general, as well as of Apuleius in particular. The normal mode of literary communication for sophistic writers was the live rhetorical performance, and its written record in the
normal sophistic declamation, as for example in Apuleius' own *De Deo
Socratis* or the orations of Dio Chrysostom.[113] In the different framework
of a fictional narrative, where the author, even if himself the first-person
narrator, is naturally less prominent than when in the act of delivering
his own work or as the speaker of the written speech which mirrors that
live delivery, there is a danger of diminishing or losing the element of self-
display and self-promotion which is absolutely fundamental to the
sophistic mode of existence.[114] The problem for a self-promoting sophistic intellectual in writing fictional narrative is that of how to keep the
spotlight on himself when not talking about himself, the characteristic
frame and frequent subject of sophistic declamation, as for example in
Apuleius' own *Florida*. The kind of complex presentation of narrative

[111] Smith (1972), 532–3. *Incredundam* clearly picks up the fantastic element of the
Metamorphoses prominently mentioned in its prologue (*Met.* 1. 1. 2 *ut mireris*); in such an
evidently metaliterary context, *floridam* could be an oblique hint at the *Florida* as a work
preceding the *Metamorphoses* (note the sequence *nunc . . . nunc*).
[112] As Smith (1972), 533, notes, the status of the prediction is typically and comically complicated by Milo's immediately following story which thoroughly discredits Diophanes as a
prophet—*Met.* 2. 13–14.
[113] Cf. conveniently Anderson (1993), 55–68.
[114] For sophistic self-presentation cf. Anderson (1993), 216–33, Gleason (1995).

voice which we have identified in the *Metamorphoses* is precisely the kind of strategy which draws attention to the existence and virtuoso status of the work's author.[115] Moreover, such a strategy is recognizably related to the narrative strategies of other sophistic texts.

A straightforward use of the speaker's identity is to be found in the opening of the Euboean speech of Dio Chrysostom (*Or.* 7).[116] This work, which after an extensive narrative of the utopian lifestyle of Euboean hunters turns to moralizing on the contrast between the simple rural life and urban luxury and vice, begins by drawing attention to the speaker and his credentials (7. 1):

> What follows I shall narrate from my own experience, and not through hearing from others. For it may be a characteristic not only of old age to speak at length and not easily to thrust away any of the words which occur to one; it may also be characteristic of a wanderer as well as of an old man. The reason for this is that both have had things happen to them which they recall with some pleasure. I will tell you, then, of the kind of men I encountered in virtually the middle of Greece, and what kind of life they live.[117]

Here the status of the speaker as a garrulous old man, and his implied sophistic glamour as an experienced traveller in the Odyssean mould, are highlighted at the beginning of the work in a *captatio benevolentiae* which will have importance in the later parts of the speech: Dio has learnt moral lessons from his visit which he will later convey to his audience. There is here a claim to historical-type authenticity[118] rather than any Apuleian-type problematizing of the narrator's identity and veracity, but there is also a clear focus on his personal knowledge and authority, as we would expect for a sophistic performer. This more conventional model is at the root of Apuleius' comic version in the *Metamorphoses*. Similar to Apuleius' prologue in its clever variation on this model is the opening of the first of Lucian's *True Histories*.[119] There the speaker presents a first-person set of traveller's tales, famously prefaced with an amusing assertion of their untruthfulness (*VH* 1. 4): 'My subject, then, is things I have neither seen nor experienced nor heard tell of from anybody else: things, what is more, that do not in fact exist and could not ever exist at all. So

---

[115] Parallels with the narratorial stance of Ovid's *Metamorphoses* are clear (cf. e.g. Solodow (1988), 47–73, esp. 73), another link between these two homonymous texts.

[116] See the excellent commentary of Russell (1992), and for the novelistic aspects of this text Holzberg (1996), 640–4.   [117] My translation.

[118] So also Holzberg (1996), 641.

[119] For modern assessments of the *True Histories* and their links to fiction cf. Anderson (1996), 555–61, and esp. Fusillo (1988).

my readers must not believe a word I say.'[120] This self-conscious drawing
of the reader's attention in the work's preface to the status of its narra-
tor/speaker, and the explicit inversion of the speaker's usual claim to
veracity and authenticity seen in Dio Chrysostom, has an obvious link
with the problematic prologue of Apuleius' *Metamorphoses*; the effect in
both cases is comic and entertaining, as well as indicating the literary
sophistication and sophistic self-promotion of the writer.

This concern with the authority of the speaker, and with the possibilities of narrative complexity which the presence and variation of a narrative voice can offer, is also seen in the three Greek novels which are
normally referred to as 'sophistic', which are contemporary with or later
than Apuleius and match the *Metamorphoses* in literary and narratological complexity; even if all of these are later than Apuleius, they may well
represent a tradition which was known to him. Longus' *Daphnis and
Chloe*, very likely from the second century ad,[121] is presented by an initial
speaker as his own summary of an account given by an exegete of a picture in a grove of the Nymphs (1 *praef.*); thus we have a double distancing effect, with the speaker giving the version of another voice which is
itself summarizing a work of art representing the plot of the novel. The
prologue to Achilles Tatius' *Leucippe and Clitophon* (1. 1–1. 2), another text
which very likely dates from the second century,[122] presents the novel as
reporting the words of Clitophon spoken to the author, without returning at the end to this original frame; again, there is through the use of this
metadiegetic narrator a clear distancing of the plot of the novel from the
voice of the author, while the failure to return to this frame at the end,
surely deliberate, adds to the impression of complexity in the matter of
narrative voice. In Heliodorus' *Aethiopika*, considerably later in date than
Longus or Achilles Tatius[123] and told in the third person, a similar impression of narrative complexity arises with the novel's opening *in medias res*
(1. 1), beginning enigmatically with a dramatic tableau which the reader
is finally equipped to interpret much later in the work (5. 33); that information is not only suspensefully postponed, but also forms the climax of
the long inserted tale of Calasiris (2. 24–5. 33), which appears to give the
reader necessary information but itself may also mislead.[124]

[120] Tr. B. P. Reardon, from Reardon (1989), 622.

[121] On the date of *Daphnis and Chloe* see Hunter (1983), 3–15.

[122] On the date of Achilles Tatius see Plepelits (1996), 387–90.

[123] On the date of Heliodorus (probably fourth cent. AD) cf. Morgan (1996), 417–21.

[124] Cf. Winkler (1982); on this and other aspects of the complex narrative technique of
Heliodorus see now esp. the first four papers in Hunter (1998).

Such deliberate complexity not only serves to intrigue and entertain the reader; it also aims to display for admiration the ingenuity and sophistication of the writer, a thoroughly sophistic attitude. Heliodorus' novel gives us an indication that such complex narrative proems as we find in Apuleius, Longus, and Achilles Tatius, which involve a sophisticated interrelation between the voice of the author and that used in his main narrative, are a characteristically sophistic feature; this can be plainly linked with sophistic performance and the relationship between the prefatory discourse of the *lalia* or *prolalia*, commonly a light-hearted self-presentation, and the main part of a declamation, often dealing with weightier material.[125] As Calasiris begins his long and complex tale, he says (*Aethiopica* 2. 24. 5) 'But first I shall tell you briefly about myself. This is not, as you think, a sophist's trick to avoid telling the story, but the logical way to present my narrative and an indispensable preliminary'.[126] A general lack of straightforwardness in beginning, and especially in beginning in the first person, in order to draw attention to the speaker/narrator's cleverness, is a sophistic technique which the *Metamorphoses* enthusiastically adopts. In its protagonist, its rich literary texture, and its complex concern with narrative voice, the *Metamorphoses* is indeed a 'sophist's novel'.

2. CONTEMPORARY CULTURE AND IDEOLOGY IN THE *METAMORPHOSES*

(i) *The* Metamorphoses: *A Serious Novel of Ideas?*

Perhaps the most crucial question in the overall interpretation of the *Metamorphoses* is that of whether the novel has a serious 'message' of a religious or philosophical nature. This is naturally a central issue in any attempt to set the novel in its contemporary intellectual context, and faces any linear, first-time reader of the work with considerable urgency. After the 'Milesian'[127] melodramatic, low-life, and entertaining narratives of the first ten books, the last book, with its sudden appearance of the goddess Isis in person and its extensive account of religious experience and cult-practice, seems to introduce an entirely different kind of material. Moreover, the inclusion of this material must have been an authorial

---

[125] See conveniently Anderson (1993), 53–64.
[126] Tr. Winkler in Reardon (1989).
[127] On the literary tradition of the Milesian Tales see conveniently Harrison (1998a).

choice. The different and openly comic ending of the *Onos*, in which the narrative concludes with Lucius' homecoming after his sexual rejection in human form by a woman he had pleasured as an ass (*Onos* 56), strongly argues that the Isis-book is added by Apuleius to the material he took over from the Greek *Metamorphoses*. The adventures of Lucius-ass, previously enjoyed for their bawdiness and entertainment value, are famously reinterpreted by the priest Mithras as symptomatic of Lucius' concern with low pleasures and self-gratification, from which he is now to be released by devoting himself to the chaste cult of the goddess Isis (11. 15. 1):

lubrico virentis aetatulae ad serviles delapsus voluptates curiositatis improsperae sinistrum praemium reportasti. sed utcumque Fortunae caecitas, dum te pessimis periculis discruciat, ad religiosam istam beatudinem improvida produxit malitia.

Interpreters have reacted in different ways to this apparent authorial imposition of a religious structure on the novel, and to the issues of unity which it plainly raises. The most reductively minded, and those with the lowest view of the author's literary capacities, have followed Perry in holding that the work simply has no unity: the account of Lucius' religious experiences is 'sincere' and a clear contrast with the previous low-life and entertaining material, but is merely put in to ensure intellectual respectability for the work as a whole by raising the tone at the end. In Perry's own words, 'Apuleius is content merely to tack on at the end a piece of solemn pageantry as ballast to offset the prevailing levity of the previous ten books'.[128]

This approach is less favoured by recent critics than other possibilities which assume an essential unity in the work.[129] Perhaps most popular has been to accept the priest's words as giving both the moral and the narrative structure of the novel: Lucius falls into low sensuality, is punished by his asinine metamorphosis, and is eventually enlightened and redeemed in the cult of Isis. The low-life elements of the earlier books, narrating Lucius' worldly errors and wanderings, serve as an instructive contrast with the elevated material of Book 11, which reveals the underlying religious truth.[130] The most extreme form of this approach is found in the work of Merkelbach, who following Kerényi argued that Books 1–10, and

---

[128] Perry (1967), 240.

[129] For a history of interpretations since 1900 see the introduction to Harrison (1999).

[130] This approach is argued in the most sophisticated way by Penwill (1975), and is for example implicit in the influential articles of Tatum (1969) and Wlosok (1969).

especially the tale of Cupid and Psyche, contain a symbolic and anticipatory exposition of the rites of initiation into the cult of Isis which emerge
explicitly in Book 11.[131] Though the strong form of this thesis has convinced relatively few,[132] most would now favour an interpretation of the
work in which the Isiac material of Book 11 was in some sense and to some
degree anticipated in earlier parts of the novel, even as early as the prologue itself.[133] But such a structural unity can be seen as a purely formal
link, providing a strand of unity which works with a number of others,
and need not require the Isiac material or the priest's moralizing to contain the central 'message' of the work. Modern unitarians can hold that
the religious elements of the novel are 'sincere',[134] but they can also see
them as deeply ambiguous in allowing both a 'sincere' and a satirical/par-
odic interpretation.[135]

This last interpretation is that of Winkler, the most influential modern view of the *Metamorphoses*: in his own words,

> my ultimate assessment of the *Golden Ass* is that it is a philosophical comedy
> about religious knowledge. The effect of its hermeneutic playfulness, including
> the final book, is to raise the question whether there is a higher order that can
> integrate conflicting individual judgements. I further argue that the effect of the
> novel and the intent of Apuleius is to put that question but not to suggest an
> answer.[136]

Winkler suggests that the *Metamorphoses* resembles a detective story in
that its whole plot turns out to need reinterpretation when the final twist
of Isiac 'conversion' is revealed in Book 11, and that even then the solution to the mystery is not determined: we are not sure whether the religious climax of the novel is to be taken seriously, whether at the end
Lucius is a true shaven devotee or a clownishly bald dupe. The power of
his interpretation comes from its close link with the complexity of narrative voice which we have already seen as a prime feature of the
Metamorphoses (see Section 1 (iv) above). The general divided narrative
structure of the novel in Books 1–10, with the omniscient *auctor*, the retrospective first-person narrator, commenting with hindsight on the
actions of the naive *actor*, the first-person character acting in the story,

[131] Kerényi (1927), Merkelbach (1962).
[132] See the important review of Merkelbach by Turcan (1963); for a partial resuscitation
of Merkelbach's views see Münstermann (1995); for a recent balanced view, Beck (1996).
[133] Isis in prologue: Grimal (1971). Isiac links throughout: Griffiths (1978).
[134] Sincere: e.g. Wlosok (1969), Alpers (1980).
[135] Ambiguous: Anderson (1982), 83, though not as penetrating as Winkler (1985).
[136] Winkler (1985), 124.

breaks down in Book 11, and the reader is given no retrospective analysis by the narrator with which to judge the events of that book; hence the remaining indeterminacy at the end.

It is against this critical background and in response to these formulations of the issues that I turn to interpreting the religious material in *Met.* 11. It is difficult after the work of Winkler to take Lucius' account of his Isiac initiations as an unproblematically straightforward first-person account of religious experience: there are too many comic elements in the narrative of Book 11 to allow this view, previously widely held, especially by scholars of ancient religion.[137] On the other hand, I find it equally hard to accept the indeterminate view propounded by Winkler himself; for me, the evidence of the text does not lead us to suspend judgement on the issue of religious seriousness, but pushes strongly towards an interpretation of a largely parodic and satirical kind.

(ii)   *The* Metamorphoses *and Religion: Sermon or Satire?*

The period of the composition of Apuleius' *Metamorphoses*, the second half of the second century AD, falls at the beginning of what has been famously described by E. R. Dodds as an 'age of anxiety' in the Greco-Roman world.[138] Whether or not one subscribes to Dodds's implicitly psychologizing model, this period seems to have witnessed increased interest in religion, cult-activity, and the pursuit of personal spirituality in the Roman empire, and these themes are consequently prominent in the *Metamorphoses* as in other literary texts of the period.[139] In this section I will first give a reading, heavily influenced by the work of Winkler, of Lucius' experiences within the cults of Isis and Osiris as recounted in the novel, relating this to other contemporary texts with religious connections. I conclude that the *Metamorphoses* shows an undoubtedly detailed knowledge of Isiac religion, but that this interest is used for cultural and intellectual display and satirical entertainment rather than to assert any ideological or personal commitment.

Book 11 begins with Lucius-ass asleep on the beach at Cenchreae, the port of Corinth, exhausted after his stressful escape from the arena in Book 10. He awakes to see the moon shining, and immediately identifies

---

[137] For use of the narrative of Lucius' cult-initiations as straightforward evidence for ancient religious experience see the scholars cited in n. 100.

[138] Dodds (1965), designating the period from Marcus to Constantine.

[139] For the prominence of 'personal' religion and cult-activity in this period see Dodds (1965), Festugière (1954), and Turcan (1996).

it with the supreme goddess, to whom he prays elaborately under many names, first submerging his head seven times under the sea for the purposes of purification (11. 1–2). He then falls asleep again, but soon awakes once more to see the goddess herself emerging from the sea; he describes her appearance in great detail, which leaves no doubt that she is Isis (11. 3–4); she confirms this in her answer to his prayer, in which she matches his initial polyonymous invocation of her by identifying herself with a whole list of goddesses, but ends with her true name of Isis (11. 5. 1–3). She then offers him salvation through initiation into her cult, instructing him to join in the celebration of her impending spring festival of Ploia-phesia.[140] There he is to shed the shape of an ass, traditionally hated by Isis (as she says) through its association with her enemy Seth/Typhon,[141] become one of her initiates, and reap the reward of service to her through a happy life and further bliss in the Underworld (11. 5. 4–11. 6. 7).

For a linear first-time reader of the novel's narrative, nothing could be more surprising than these developments. This grand scene of divine epiphany, with its elaborate use of the language of prayer and hymn, and its invocation of the serious topics of cult-initiation, felicity in life, and existence after death, is, as we have already noted, a complete change of tone from the atmosphere of Books 1–10, largely concerned with melo-dramatic and entertaining stories with little apparent further meaning or content. For the second-time reader and the literary scholar, the surprise is less complete, since various hints from the prologue onwards have sug-gested that an Isiac climax is in prospect, particularly the tale of Cupid and Psyche, in which Psyche, like Lucius, encounters much tribulation as a result of her own weakness and *curiositas* before receiving divine salva-tion.[142] Suggestive, too, perhaps, of future rescue is the increasingly depressing and desperate nature of the events and tales narrated in Books 9 and 10, concluding with the melodramatic biography of the mass-mur-deress whom Lucius-ass is intended to pleasure in the arena.[143]

All seems to be elevated and serious in the great scene at the beginning of Book 11: Lucius' plea to Isis appears genuinely pathetic and moving, her answer comes across as both grand and merciful, and the syncretic

[140] *Met.* 11. 5. 5 makes it clear that this is indeed the occasion of Isis' epiphany, though the name of the festival is there elaborately paraphrased rather than directly mentioned.

[141] *Met.* 11. 6. 2 *mihique iamdudum detestabilis beluae istius corio te protinus exue;* for the association see Griffiths (1975), 162, and for the Egyptian mythological background to Isis' detestation for Seth–Typhon in a likely Apuleian source cf. Plutarch *De Iside et Osiride* 30.

[142] See n. 133.

[143] Tatum (1969), 518–19, 522–3.

identification of Isis with other goddesses in both Lucius' prayer and Isis' reply closely reflects the practice of contemporary Isis-cult and the phrasing of known Isis-aretalogies.[144] On the other hand, there are elements which make one think twice. The ritual washing of the head seven times in the sea, and the accompanying statement that this is the Pythagorean ritual number (11. 1. 4), seems odd and comic when we remember that this is an ass speaking and visualize the action. Likewise, the fact that both the miraculous visions of Lucius-ass, that of the moon and that of Isis herself, wake him from sleep opens up the possibility that these may be merely dreams experienced as if reality. This would be only natural for the physically and emotionally exhausted Lucius, likely enough to be open to such autosuggestion, and gullible enough to believe it, as we will see in his dealings with the cult of Isis and Osiris.

Such considerations might seem to point to Winkler's indeterminate approach: the text of Book 11 seems to suggest both a serious and a comic interpretation of the religious experience narrative in these opening pages,[145] and to make no decision between the two. As suggested earlier, my own view is that Book 11 is ultimately comic and parodic, that the satirical material in the end outweighs the 'serious' elements, following Winkler's own powerful analysis of the subversive and comic elements in Book 11.[146] The narrative sequence is here important: the undoubted elevation and literary power of Lucius-ass's encounter with the divine Isis herself is soon debased by his contact with the human personnel of her cult, and things go downhill from that point, until we find Lucius at the end of the novel as a shaven-headed official of the Osiris-cult in Rome, having gullibly surrendered his social status, career ambitions, and financial resources to an exploitative religious organization.

The subversive and playful elements which for me point to this interpretation begin in earnest when Lucius-ass first encounters the cult-followers of Isis in the procession of the Ploiaphesia (11. 8–11). In particular, the various costumed figures in the vanguard of the procession (*anteludia*), described fully in 11. 8, do not seem to have Isiac or other religious symbolism, and perhaps rather reflect contemporary Roman public

---

[144] With the list of syncretisms and local names for Isis at *Met.* 11. 5. 2–3 compare the similar much longer list in the invocation of Isis in *P. Oxy.* 1380, with the comments of Griffiths (1975), 147–8.

[145] Shumate (1996a) stresses the psychological realism of Lucius' religious experience in *Met.* 11 while accepting ultimate Winklerian ambiguity, a somewhat ambivalent position; see my discussion in Harrison (1997b).

[146] Winkler (1985), 209–27.

shows.[147] In the context of the novel, their effect is undoubtedly comic: not only do these participants present a motley and gaudy appearance in themselves, but many of their costumes also amusingly look back in some detail to the previous adventures of Lucius-ass.[148] Since this episode begins Lucius' contact with the human ministers of the Isiac cult and can be viewed as in some sense programmatic for his involvement with them, I will here treat it at some length. Of the eleven figures described in sequence, (i), the soldier, recalls the soldier who commandeers Lucius-ass from a poor gardener at 9. 39; (ii), the hunter, alludes to the tragic end of the Charite story in Book 8, where Charite's husband Tlepolemus is treacherously killed by his friend Thrasyllus when both are engaged in hunting (8. 4–6),[149] while (iii), the man disguised as a woman, is another allusion to Tlepolemus, who tells the robber band of a supposed daring exploit from which he escaped only by disguising himself as a woman (7. 8).[150]

Of the remaining figures, (iv), the gladiator, surely recalls the *ludi* from which Lucius-ass has escaped at the end of Book 10, since these were principally gladiatorial games (10. 18),[151] while (v), the magistrate, looks back to Lucius' school-friend Pythias, the officious magistrate who deprives Lucius of his dinner at the end of Book 1 (1. 24),[152] and (vi), the philosopher, recalls Lucius-ass's comic self-characterization as a *philosophantem . . . asinum* at 10. 33, and may reflect the philosophical

---

[147] Here I agree with Griffiths (1975), 172–80, and (1978), 158–9, against Merkelbach (1962), 89. For a more subtle religious/philosophical interpretation, with some awareness of the narrative echoes, see Gianotti (1986), 78–94.

[148] I here follow the important approach briefly sketched by Fick-Michel (1991), 421–3, though I do not agree with her overall view of the novel—cf. n. 208 below.

[149] Tlepolemus, like the hunter of the *anteludia*, bears a *venabulum* on this expedition (8. 5 *en cape venabulum*).

[150] Tlepolemus' imagined elaborate description of his disguise is clearly picked up here (7. 8)—*sumpta veste muliebri florida in sinus flaccidos abundante, mitellaque textili contecto capite, calceis femininis albis illis et tenuibus indutus et in sequiorem sexum incertus atque absconditus*. The two descriptions share a particular interest in coloured footwear (*soccis obaurati /calceis . . . albis*) as well as elaborate female dress in general. The theme of disguise has dramatic irony at this point in the plot, where Tlepolemus is again disguised as the robber Haemus. Fick-Michel (1991), 421, also suggests an allusion to the quasi-transvestite priests of Book 8, who can address each other as *puellae* (8. 27. 2).

[151] Fick-Michel (1991), 422, suggests an additional echo of the gladiatorial games for which the bear of 4. 13. 1 was being prepared, but the more immediate reminiscence is the stronger.

[152] Especially as Lucius remarks there on Pythias' similarly conspicuous insignia (1. 24): *nam et lixas et virgas et habitum prorsus magistratui congruentem in te video*. Fick-Michel (1991), 422, adds the magistrates presiding at a trial in Book 10 (10. 6. 4), but they are far less memorable for the reader.

connections of Lucius' family through their link with Sextus and Plutarch.[153] Figure (vii), the bird-catcher, seems to have no parallel in the novel,[154] but (viii), a fisherman, recalls the fisherman who at the end of Book 1 (1. 24) sells Lucius the fish which the magistrate Pythias bizarrely orders to be trampled into pieces, a scene already recalled in the *anteludia* with the representation of the magistrate (see figure (v) above).[155] The last three figures in the *anteludia* clearly allude to the general idea of man/beast metamorphosis, central of course to the *Metamorphoses*, but also recapitulate earlier scenes in the novel: (ix), a bear disguised as a woman, looks like a clever reversal of the scene where the bandit Thrasyleon disastrously disguises himself as a bear, also a she-bear (4. 15–21);[156] (x), a monkey dressed up as Ganymede, recalls 1. 12, where in the tale of Aristomenes the witch Meroe refers ironically to her errant lover Socrates as *Catamitus meus*, meaning Ganymede;[157] while (xi), an ass with artificial wings walking next to an old man, comically compared to Pegasus and Bellerophon, not only reminds the reader of earlier amusing comparisons of Lucius-ass to Pegasus (6. 30, 8. 16) and of one of his riders to Bellerophon (7. 26), but also looks back to the various human owners of Lucius-ass, especially perhaps to the poor gardener of Book 9 who walked with Lucius along the roads.

The effect of this symbolic recapitulation of various themes from the novel, unrecognized as usual by the thoughtless Lucius, who here as in the obviously cautionary inserted tales fails to see what is plainly relevant to himself,[158] is entertaining and witty. The stress for the alert reader is

[153] See Sect. 1 (ii) above. Fick-Michel (1991), 422, suggests more distant links with other images of philosophers.

[154] Fick-Michel (1991), 422, suggests an echo of the supposed boy trying to catch a sparrow in a lying tale at *Met.* 8. 20. 2, but this seems a tenuous link with the fully equipped professional bird-catcher of the *anteludia*.

[155] So Fick-Michel (1991), 422. This would be another appropriate echo, since the fish-trampling scene has been interpreted as an anticipation in the plot of Isiac ritual (cf. Fick (1991)): to recall it here when Lucius is about to enter the cult of Isis is clearly fitting.

[156] Fick-Michel (1991), 422, adds the devouring bear of 8. 24. 4–5, but the aspect of bestial metamorphosis is clearly the most important. Commentators have suggested that in the immediate context of the parade this figure is meant to suggest Callisto, metamorphosed into a bear by Juno for having an affair with Jupiter (Ovid *Fasti* 2. 177–86), and this seems likely enough, given the connection of the next figure with Ganymede, another sexual partner of Jupiter resented by Juno (cf. e.g. Vergil *Aen.* 1. 28).

[157] This parallel is suitable for Lucius looking back at his previous life, since the dire fate of Socrates in perishing because of excessive interest in sex and magic is an obvious (but unheeded) warning for Lucius himself, who goes on to get involved in much the same way with Photis in Hypata.

[158] Cf. Tatum (1969), 499–500.

plainly on comic effect and the anticipation of the work's coming closure, implicit in such a resumptive summary of past events in the plot. Though such a synoptic view of the adventures of his previous life might be a suitable prelude to a transforming religious experience for Lucius, his past life (as it were) passing before him at the moment of truth,[159] there is no suggestion of such a function in the text. This is an entertaining narrative structure for the delectation of the reader, an amusing cavalcade of past events wittily transformed.

The rest of the procession is then fully described (11. 9–11). Here there seems to be no doubt that the descriptions of the cult-followers, musicians, initiates, and officials carrying cult-objects reflect in their detail actual elements of contemporary Isiac cult.[160] This display of acquaintance with the Isis-cult, particularly strong here but a feature throughout Book 11, has usually been presented as the worshipful inside knowledge of the initiate Lucius, narrating the procession retrospectively from his later privileged status as an official in the cult; but there is another possibility. These details, as well as characterizing the narrator Lucius as initiate,[161] also have the effect of a display of knowledge on the part of the author Apuleius; as we have seen above, initiation into cults and consequent knowledge of them was a feature of elite intellectual life in the second century AD, and Apuleius, who elsewhere asserts his own status as initiate of several Greek cults,[162] may well be displaying here for his elite readership the cultural capital he has thus acquired. The Isis-cult in particular seems to have appealed particularly to the Greek intellectuals of the Second Sophistic: good evidence of this is the *Isis and Osiris* of Plutarch, in which the Isiac myths are recounted and given a Platonist interpretation.[163] As we shall shortly see, such religious knowledge and implied special status was particularly attractive to sophists, providing an additional means for the self-promotion and self-glamorization characteristic of sophistic life.

[159] This point is not made by Shumate (1996a), though it might have fitted her argument. The whole notion of monotheistic conversion in antiquity is interestingly challenged in Bradley (1998) with specific reference to Lucius in Book 11.

[160] Cf. the full treatment of Griffiths (1975), 180–233.

[161] Though of course his status is ambiguous at this point in the narrative—as *actor*, experiencing protagonist, he is ignorant of the cult, while as *auctor*, subsequent narrator, he is describing these details retrospectively as an initiate.

[162] *Apol.* 55. 8 *sacrorum pleraque initia in Graecia participavi.*

[163] See the excellent edition by Griffiths (1970); for links between Apuleius and Plutarch more generally cf. Walsh (1981). Given Apuleius' concern to advertise Lucius' supposed links with the family of Plutarch (see above, Sect. 1 (ii)), it seems very likely that this work was a source for Apuleius' understanding of the Isis-cult.

At the end of the procession (11. 12) comes the high priest shortly to be named as Mithras, who bears the sacred *sistrum* of Isis and a garland of roses. Lucius-ass then approaches and eats the roses, previously stressed in the novel as the antidote which will restore his human shape; accordingly he becomes a man again, a miracle proclaimed by the crowd (11. 13). After ordering a tunic to be given to Lucius to cover his nakedness (11. 14), the priest speaks to him, showing detailed knowledge of his name and history and claiming that Lucius, having now paid the penalty for his interest in low pleasures, has escaped from the tribulations of ill fortune into the peace and joy of the Isis-cult (11. 15). Like the epiphany of Isis, the speech shows elevation and dignity. But the reaction of the crowd at 11. 16. 3, as Winkler has crucially stressed, injects a note of complexity and a suggestion of a parodic or satirical interpretation. In her speech to Lucius at 11. 6. 4 Isis had promised Lucius that none of her followers would react adversely to Lucius' change back to human shape, implying that she would modify this natural reaction; but at 11. 16. 3 her followers interpret the change to human shape and dedication to the service of Isis as the token of great virtue on Lucius' part and great favour from Isis. Isis has influenced her followers indeed; but this reaction is entirely at odds with the account given by Mithras the priest, that Lucius' animal shape was a punishment for low desires, the change back to human form being a mark of his restoration to humanity from subhuman form and behaviour, not of his superhuman virtue and divine favour. The gap between these two interpretations, as Winkler has stressed, encourages the reader to think that not everything in the narrative of the Isis-cult is to be taken at face value. Every time an elevated and dignified religious moment is narrated, it is followed by material which suggests another approach.

As I have noted, Winkler himself argued that this pattern leads to an ambiguously balanced interpretation for the reader: even by the end of the book, he claims, the evidence of the text does not allow us to choose between a religious and a parodic interpretation, to decide whether Lucius is a bald dupe or privileged initiate.[164] My contention is that the evidence of the text after 11. 16 pushes the reader firmly towards the parodic interpretation, that the cults with which Lucius has become involved are both venal and exploitative, and that he is their gullible victim. Here again I am heavily dependent on Winkler's collection of evidence in the text,[165] but interpret it less ambivalently. Apart from the extraordinary

---

[164] Winkler (1985), 223–7.   [165] Winkler (1985), 204–27.

twist of *Madaurensem* at 11. 27. 9, already discussed as a supreme example of the author's display of narratological complexity and wit, the narrative of Lucius' experiences in the cults of Isis and Osiris in 11. 18–30 has three features which particularly undermine a 'sincere' religious interpretation.

First, the theme of money. As already discussed, cult-initiation in the ancient world was a feature of elite culture, and was therefore likely to be expensive. But the frequency with which Lucius is required to pay money for the various stages of his initiations, and the stress on his consequent need for money in the narrative, is quite extraordinary. The main benefit from Lucius' meeting with his long-lost family and friends at 11. 18. 3 is not so much the joy of reunion as the fact that they bring money needed for Lucius' expenses in the cult (*quo ad cultum sumptumque largiter succederet*); likewise, he has to beg from his friends to get the items needed for his first Isiac initiation (11. 23. 1). As he leaves Cenchreae for his long-postponed but in fact brief visit home, Lucius pays a gratuity to the cult-members, at the highest level his slender means can afford (11. 24. 6), and in his farewell prayer to Isis he regrets that his relative poverty restricts the sacrifices he can make to her (11. 25. 5). At Rome, his final initiation into the cult of Osiris is delayed from lack of means (11. 28. 1), and the priest Asinius appears to be promised a large profit for initiating Lucius (11. 27. 9);[166] Lucius finally raises the fee for initiation by selling even the clothes from his back (11. 28. 3). Eventually, Lucius is able to pay his cult-fees through acting as an advocate in the Roman law-courts, though even he recognizes their exorbitant level, which he displays as a token of his great piety (11. 30. 1–2). These constant mentions of the high costs of Lucius' various initiations, and of his difficulties in meeting them, suggest to the reader less naive than Lucius that he is being duped by the cults of Isis and Osiris, and systematically deprived of his money.

A second theme of 11. 16–30 which points in this direction is the way in which the narrative constantly provides false endings for the initiations and story of Lucius, each climax seeming to be the final one before the revelation of another stage. This might seem suitable for a narrative of religious devotion, stressing the obedience of the devotee to the complexities of the divine will, but it might also suggest that Lucius is gullible and being manipulated in order for the cults of Isis and Osiris to profit from him as much as possible, and that this is compounded by

---

[166] For a discussion of this passage see Sect. 1 (iv) above.

self-deception and autosuggestion on Lucius' part:[167] it seems that he can even deceive himself when the cult and its staff are not there to do it for him. After the much-postponed and elaborately narrated first Isiac initiation is eventually concluded at 11. 23. 7, Lucius at last takes his leave of the cult at Cenchreae and goes home after effusive thanks to the goddess (11. 25. 1–11. 26. 1). The first-time reader might well think that this is the end of the story, especially since the hero's return home after giving thanks to the gods forms the conclusion of the pseudo-Lucianic *Onos*, and presumably therefore of the Greek *Metamorphoses*.[168] However, after only a few days at home, and even before the very sentence describing his journey home has had time to conclude, Lucius is called by a vision of the goddess to travel to Rome (11. 26. 1):

> recta patriam larem revisurus meum post aliquam multum temporis contendo paucisque post diebus deae potentis instinctu raptim constrictis sarcinulis, nave conscensa, Romam versus profectionem dirigo.

The breathtaking suddenness of Lucius' change of plan, the casual introduction of his major relocation to the Great City, and his tremendous facility for seeing life-changing visions of the goddess, which he himself has already remarked on earlier in the narrative,[169] suggest that we are now dealing with a hyperdutiful and autosuggestive religious maniac, motivated by self-induced miraculous visions. The effect of this, in my reading, can only be comic: Lucius is so deeply devoted to Isis, or to his imagined version of Isis, that she has taken over his whole life to a ridiculous extent. He is duped by his own gullibility as well as by the rapacious cult.

This first false closure and new start is then immediately succeeded by another one. At 11. 26. 3 Lucius seems to be settled as a worshipper of Isis on the Campus Martius in Rome,[170] and the story seems to conclude in a sentence which does in fact bear a close thematic resemblance to the actual close of the novel, as well as recalling details from the prologue:[171] *eram cultor denique adsiduus, fani quidem advena, religionis autem indi-*

---

[167] For another instance of Lucius' possible autosuggestion see p. 240 above.

[168] *Onos* 56.

[169] *Met.* 11. 19. 2 *nec fuit nox una vel quies aliqua visu deae monituque ieiuna.*

[170] On this shrine and its strongly Egyptian character see Lembke (1994) and Brenk (1999).

[171] *Met.* 11. 30. 5, the actual ending, similarly describes Lucius' habitual cult-activity in the imperfect tense: *collegii ... munia ... gaudens obibam,* while *advena* and *indigena* recall *Met.* 1. 1. 4 *mox in urbe Latia advena* (exactly like Lucius in Book 11) *indigenam sermonem ... excolui,* suggesting closure through ring-composition.

gena. But the story continues: Lucius spends a year as worshipper of Isis, but then receives another of his visions urging further initiation. Not unnaturally, even he wonders what all this is about, since he thinks himself already fully initiated (11. 26. 4); this is surely a hint to the reader to share Lucius' doubts, one of several in these last pages of the novel. The authorities at the shrine (naturally) explain the meaning: he must be initiated into the cult of Osiris, an interpretation strengthened by the vision of Osiris experienced by Asinius Marcellus (11. 27. 7–9), a vision which we have seen to be complex and tricky in other ways as the source of the famous *Madaurensem.* After this complex and expensive further initiation, Lucius settles down as a devotee of this new cult, supporting himself through legal advocacy, and we again seem to have reached a point of closure (11. 28. 6).

Once again, however, our expectations are disappointed, and the effect is surely witty and comic. The story goes on: Lucius has even more visions, this time suggesting a third initiation. Again, he has doubts, addressing himself, and questioning the good faith of the priests who performed the two previous initiations (11. 29. 3): *'nimirum perperam vel minus plene consuluerunt in me sacerdos uterque'; et hercules iam de fide quoque eorum opinari coeptabam sequius.* Once again this is a prompt to the reader, who has for some time been feeling the suspicions that Lucius here voices, and the effect is comic: even the dupe Lucius suspects that all is not well. His extreme emotional agitation is noted (11. 29. 3 *cogitationis aestu fluctuantem ad instar insaniae percitum*) immediately before he has another consoling divine vision, another suggestion that his continuing series of divine encounters has more to do with his state of mind than with the actual visitation of the gods. The third initation, with a personal vision of Osiris himself, provides the final closure of the book: Lucius is left as a pastophor of the cult of Osiris in Rome, rejoicing in his divine devotions and shaven head.

A third comic theme apparent in 11. 16–30, closely linked with the two already examined, is that of Lucius' characteristically naive misunderstanding and hopeful interpretation of elements which to the cautious reader suggest complexity and subversion. At 11. 20. 1 Lucius has one of his many visions, this time of the high priest suggesting that Lucius is about to receive money and resources from Thessaly including a slave called Candidus ('White'). Lucius puzzles over this, since he has no slave of that name, but regards the prophecy as fulfilled when his slaves arrive from Thessaly bringing his white (*candidus*) horse (1. 20. 7). More critical readers might regard this as a hopeful identification; Lucius clearly wants to believe his vision, and will ignore unhelpful details in order to do so. Likewise, at 11. 27. 7 the priest Asinius Marcellus, who is to carry out the first of Lucius' two initiations in the Osiris-cult, has a pronounced limp; this is bizarre, since as Griffiths has noted, 'it seems doubtful whether lame or crippled persons were normally admitted to the priesthood of the Egyptian cults'.[172] Having been given the information of Asinius' limp in a dream, Lucius is only too glad to spot the confirmation of his identity, and wholly ignores what ought to be a worrying sign. Similar to this is Lucius' failure to understand the import of *Madaurensem* at 11. 27. 9, or at least to query it as one would expect, as we have already seen:[173] here as elsewhere Lucius hopefully hears what he wants to hear.

These ambivalences and clever underminings of Lucius' apparent religious testament suggest to me that the text in the end, despite the carefully created elevated tone of a number of the religious passages, prompts the reader to treat Lucius' account of the cults of Isis and Osiris in *Met.* 11 as an amusing satire on religious mania and youthful gullibility. This gives the novel as a whole a clear unity: the tone throughout remains fundamentally amusing and entertaining. It also gives unity to the characterization of the protagonist: Lucius retains in Book 11 the credulity and lack of sense and proportion which have been his main characteristics throughout the novel, and there is a strong suggestion that the cults are exploiting for financial gain his gullibility and his remarkable tendency to have religious visions. At the same time there is an impressive display of knowledge of the Isis-cult, involving details which can be fully substantiated from other literary and archaeological evidence; the two can surely co-exist in an account which is both a display of authorial elite religious knowledge, possibly from personal experience, and a satire on the narrator's youthful derangement and credulity.

This satirical reading of Lucius' cult-narrative can be supported by other evidence in both Apuleius himself and other contemporary writers. The only other religious cult which appears in the main narrative of the novel, that of the Syrian goddess in Books 8–9, is shown as unambiguously corrupt: its priests are plainly charlatans dedicated to the lowest pleasures of the flesh who exploit the credulity of the people they encounter and finally come to grief as temple-robbers. It might be argued that as such it forms a narrative precursor to the genuine and climactic cult of Isis, praising the latter by providing an inferior and repulsive lower

---

[172] Griffiths (1975), 333.   [173] Cf. p. 231 above.

form of cult which is surpassed by the true religious experience of the novel's end.[174] However, continuity could be the point just as much as difference. The suggestion could equally be that all cult-officials are at bottom corrupt and venal, something which is at least hinted at in Book 11. Similar is the famous reference to the enthusiastically monotheistic baker's wife at *Met.* 9. 14. 5, whether we read it as an allusion to Judaism or to Christianity:[175] though the narrator Lucius suggests that she is impious for rejecting polytheism,[176] there is clearly a satirical agenda, for this religious devotee is characterized as a hypocritical sink of all the vices.[177]

An Apuleian satire on the Isis-cult in Book 11 would also match the attitude of Apuleius' Greek contemporary Lucian, who often engaged in religious satire. Particularly interesting as a point of comparison here is the devastating critique of religious charlatanry in his *Alexander.*[178] This narrative of the recent life, religious career, and death of the false prophet Alexander of Aboutneichos recounts his fraudulent establishment of the new god Glycon, a supposedly oracular snake, and includes his invention of a new mystery-cult at Aboutneichos. All this charlatanry is thoroughly debunked by Lucian, who knew Alexander and treats him partly as a professional intellectual rival. This work must post-date the death of Marcus Aurelius in 180, and might have been available to Apuleius if the *Metamorphoses* belongs to the 180s;[179] but in any case it shows a contem-

---

[174] So Schlam (1992), 54 The same argument can be made either way about the evident similarities between the slave-girl Photis, her 'perverted' initiation of Lucius into the mysteries of sex and magic, and the false illumination implicit in her name (cf. Greek φῶς, 'light'), and the divine Isis with her chaste service, true illumination, and 'proper' mystical initiation (cf. *Met.* 11. 15. 3); either Photis is an inferior foreshadowing of Isis' greatness (cf. Wlosok (1969), 78–9, Alpers (1980), 199–205), or the two figures show Lucius' susceptibility to female purveyors of enlightenment without ranking the two (as I would hold).

[175] I agree with Schmidt (1997), who provides a good account of the long controversy on this passage, that a hit at Christianity is intended; the casual attack recalls the equally casual allusion to Christ as a 'crucified sophist' at Lucian *Peregrinus* 13.

[176] *Met.* 9. 14. 5 *spretis atque calcatis divinis numinibus in vicem certae religionis mentita sacrilega praesumptione dei, quam praedicaret unum.*

[177] Cf. the highly vituperative description at 9. 14. 3–4, and 9. 14. 5 *confictis observationibus vacuis fallens omnis homines et miserum maritum decipiens matutino mero et continuo stupro corpus maniciparat.*

[178] On the *Alexander* and its context cf. Hall (1981), 207–12, Jones (1986), 133–48. For Lucianic religious satire in general cf. Hall (1981), 194–220. Lucian's *De Dea Syria*, which purports to give a straight Herodotean account of the same cult so satirized by Apuleius in the *Metamorphoses*, has been interpreted as satirical, but this is controversial: cf. Anderson (1976), 68–82 (satirical), Jones (1986), 41–3 (sceptical of this).

[179] *Alexander* 48 'the god Marcus' gives the clear *terminus post quem* of the death of Marcus; for the possibly Commodan date of the *Metamorphoses* see Ch. 1, Sect. 1 above.

porary context of religious satire in the form of an attack on a figure known to the writer.

In this context, it is worthwhile to suggest a particular target for Apuleius' satirical approach to Lucius' religious experience in *Met.* 11, a target which would firmly locate the novel within the sophistic world. Some time in the 170s, perhaps in 175, the famous sophistic performer Aelius Aristides[180] wrote down the many visions of the god Aesculapius and other deities by which his health, personal life, and professional career had been directed over nearly thirty years; the book may have been published to coincide with a visit to Smyrna by Marcus and Commodus in spring 176.[181] Part of this extraordinarily self-important text, aptly described as demonstrating 'a monstrous conceit'[182] on the author's part, is extant as the six books of *Sacred Tales* (*Or.* 47–52). These yield a number of interesting parallels with the narrative of Lucius' experiences of the Isis-cult in *Metamorphoses* Book 11.[183] In both texts the narrator is presented as in close communication with and as a priest of a particular deity,[184] receives and obeys divine instructions in repeated visions, including detailed predictions which come true and orders to go to a different place,[185] expresses his inability adequately to describe the ineffable deity,[186] and acquires or improves his powers of public speaking through the god's agency.[187] We even find Isis as one of the various deities appearing to Aristides, and a vision-initiation of Aristides into the cult of Sarapis, the more Hellenized form of Osiris, both of course close parallels with Lucius' experiences in *Met.* 11.[188]

Though the *Sacred Tales* also contain much material not picked up in Apuleius, especially the continual references to Aristides' state of bodily

[180] Though he denied the label 'sophist': cf. Stanton (1973), 355.

[181] This is the thesis of Weiss (1998), 38–9, who argues convincingly against the publication date of 170–1 advanced by Behr (1968), 108–10, and for 175; the question hinges on the text and interpretation of *Or.* 48. 9—is the Salvius there 'the present consul' (so the transmitted text, a reference to the consul of 175, *PIR* S 104), or 'one of the consulars' (so Behr's not wholly satisfactory emendation, a reference to the consul of 148, *PIR* S 103)?

[182] Lane Fox (1986), 160.

[183] See my more detailed discussion in Harrison (2000).

[184] For Aristides as priest of Aesculapius cf. *Or.* 47. 41, 50. 102.

[185] e.g. *Or.* 49. 21–2 (dream prediction fulfilled in temple—cf. *Met.* 11. 27. 4–8), *Or.* 51. 1, 51. 17 (commanded to travel—cf. *Met.* 11. 26. 1).

[186] *Or.* 48. 8, 48. 49—cf. *Met.* 11. 3. 3.

[187] *Or.* 50 and 51 are continually concerned with Aesculapius' promotion of Aristides' rhetorical career (see especially the narrative of help over a decade at *Or.* 50. 14–70, and Aristides' own summary of the god's help at *Or.* 51. 36); for Isis' help for Lucius' forensic oratory cf. *Met.* 11. 30. 2.

[188] *Or.* 49. 6 (Isis), 49. 48 (Sarapis initiation)—cf. *Met.* 11. 23. 7, 11. 27. 4.

health, it seems difficult to believe that these parallels are coincidental.[189]
If they are not, parody in Apuleius' playful novel of the work of Aristides,
evidently 'sincerely' intended as a portentous account of the writer's
experiences and personal importance as a privileged communicant with
the gods, seems the most likely relation. The gullible and self-deceiving
Lucius with his minor literary and oratorical ambitions is an apt carica-
ture of the self-proclaimed religious and rhetorical superstar Aristides.
There is no great problem about the chronology of the two texts, since
Apuleius could easily have written the *Metamorphoses* after 175–6.[190]
Apuleius, then, would be sending-up his age's taste for writing about religious cults and personal religious experience, and in particular attacking
the self-important pretensions of a well-known sophistic author, with
whom he may have had at least indirect contact: an associate of Apuleius
mentioned in the *Florida* was probably a friend of a character mentioned
in the *Sacred Tales*.[191] This would be close to the approach of Lucian in
Alexander, who not only debunks religious charlatanry but also mounts
a personal attack on a rival professional intellectual. Thus the
Metamorphoses would have something of the same parodic relation to the
contemporary literature of religious experience as it does to the romantic plots of the Greek ideal novels,[192] and its religious satire in Book 11
would be connected with the sophistic tendency to attack rivals.[193]

Thus the satirical interpretation of Apuleius' narrative of Lucius' experiences in the Isis-cult in *Met.* 11 is not only a plausible reading of the text;
comparison with the religious satire of Lucian shows that it is just as well
rooted in a contemporary context as the 'religious testament' interpretation. This parodic reading can also be argued to have specific connections with the sophistic literary world in an attack on the religious and

---

[189] Note too that an acquaintance of Aristides, represented as miraculously knowing of
Aristides' self-congratulatory vision of Marcus and Verus at *Or.* 47. 49, is named Diophanes
like the discredited prophet at *Met.* 2. 12–14; that the consular Salvius (for his identity see n.
181), sharing a name with Lucius' mother Salvia in the *Metamorphoses* (cf. n. 12), is mentioned at *Or.* 48. 9; that Alcimus is the name of Aristides' steward at *Or.* 50. 97 as well as of
a robber at *Met.* 4. 12. 1; and that Lucius (possibly the Platonist Lucius of Macedonia—
Philostratus *VS* 2. 1. 556–7) is the name of one of Aristides' fellow-intellectuals (*Or.* 51. 57–9;
cf. Behr *ad loc.*). These may all be coincidences.

[190] Ch. 1, Sect. 1.

[191] The Julius Perseus mentioned in *Flor.* 18 (cf. Ch. 3 n. 120) is probably identical with the
T. Julius Perseus commemorated in an inscription at Pergamum set up by the praetor Sex.
Iulius Maior Antoninus Pythodorus (Habicht (1969), 63, no. 27); Champlin (1980), 155 n. 70
points out that this Pythodorus is presumably the friend of Aristides mentioned at *Or.* 47.
35. I owe this point to Dr Charles Weiss.

[192] Cf. Harrison (1996), 502–3.   [193] Cf. Ch. 2 n. 49.

intellectual pretensions of Aelius Aristides. Furthermore, the account of the Isis-cult simultaneously provides an epideictic display of elite religious knowledge, possibly derived from personal experience, stressing the high cultural status of the author. Both these functions of the book can be described as pleasurable entertainment for an alert and educated audience.

(iii) *The* Metamorphoses *and Philosophy: The Pertinence of Platonism*

Interpreters have often characterized the *Metamorphoses* as a novel of Platonic philosophical ideas.[194] This is promising in principle, since Apuleius plainly presents himself in public contexts as a Platonic philosopher (*Apol.* 10. 6, *Flor.* 15. 26), and it seems probable that something of his interest in the Isis-cult is owed to the syncretistic Platonizing account of the myth of Isis and Osiris to be found in Plutarch's *De Iside et Osiride*, especially given that the narrator Lucius' supposed relationship to Plutarch is highlighted at the beginning of the *Metamorphoses*.[195] The episode of Cupid and Psyche (*Met.* 4. 28–6. 24) has been a particular target for those who wish to argue that the plot of the *Metamorphoses* involves Platonizing allegory.[196] There not only do we have an inserted tale with a pair of leading characters possessing overtly etymologized allegorical names implying a Platonising agenda about Love and the Soul;[197] we also have clear reminiscences of the *Phaedrus* at the famous moment when Cupid abandons Psyche,[198] and of the *Symposium* in the characterization of Venus[199] and in the overall narrative structure of the inserted 'myth'-tale.[200] Within the novel as a whole, as well as in the tale

---

[194] The most thorough treatments in their different ways are Thibau (1965), Fick-Michel (1991), and Gianotti (1986); see also Moreschini (1978) and (1993).

[195] See Sect. 1 (ii); the allusion to Lucius' Plutarchan genealogy may of course be an indication of the work's literary indebtedness.

[196] Beginning of course with Fulgentius *Myth.* 3. 6 (p. 66. 16–70. 2 Helm), and picked up in the Italian Renaissance; see the good survey of the reception of the Cupid and Psyche episode in the introduction to Moreschini (1994b). For a modern Platonizing allegory of the Cupid and Psyche story cf. Hooker (1955).

[197] For overt etymologies of *Cupido* and *Psyche* cf. *Met.* 5. 6 *tuae Psyches dulcis anima*, 5. 13 *Psychae animam*, 6. 2 *Psyches animae*; 5. 23 *in Amoris incidit amorem . . . cupidine fraglans Cupidinis* (see Kenney (1990a) on all these passages).

[198] Cf. p. 256 below.

[199] Cf. Kenney (1990b), though I find much of his argument excessively ingenious.

[200] Cf. Harrison (1998b), where the narrative framework of the anonymous old woman's tale about Love and Soul relayed by Lucius-ass to the reader is linked with the priestess Diotima's account of Love relayed by Socrates in the *Symposium*.

of Cupid and Psyche, there is also the element of *curiositas*, the meddle-someness which is the fault common to Psyche and Lucius and a favourite topic of Apuleian interpreters. This has been convincingly argued to be a version of Platonic *polypragmosyne*, psychic imbalance, in which the lower appetitive part of the soul exercises an undesirable dominance over the higher and more intellectual parts.[201] Thus the unique prominence of *curiositas* as a theme in Apuleius' novel[202] may be explained by its Platonic connections.

It would thus be foolish to deny the importance of Platonic literary and philosophical material in the shaping of Apuleius' novel. Indeed, the overall frame of the work can be seen as fundamentally connected with a Platonizing epistemology. In its own terms as a narrative by Lucius, which must be distinguished from any personal view or ideology of the author, the *Metamorphoses* presents us with a series of events which are apparently shown in the final book to have a coherence and meaning not fully apparent before. The priest's words at *Met.* 11. 15, as we have already seen,[203] present an overt interpretative framework for the novel, that Lucius' experiences in the first ten books have been controlled by a divine force which, by punishing him by metamorphosis and suffering, has shown him the inappropriateness of the sensual existence which he previously sought, and which now offers him the 'true' existence of divine service. His previous ideas and view of the world were wrong, and he is now being given a chance to correct them with the benefit of 'true' perception.[204]

We have already examined the priest's speech in discussing the religious interpretation of the novel. But there is no doubt that it also appeals to a specifically Platonizing construction of the world. The condemnation of moral degradation and servile pleasure alludes to elements of Platonic moral theory, even down to the famous phrase *serviles voluptates*, 'slavish pleasures'.[205] And the dualistic distinction it implies between

---

[201] De Filippo (1990), who also gives references to the many scholarly discussions of *curiositas* in Apuleius.

[202] Though the adjective *curiosus* is common from Plautus on, the noun *curiositas* occurs only once before Apuleius but eleven times in the *Met.* (PHI CD-ROM, TLL 4. 1489. 69 ff.).

[203] Sect. 2 (ii) above.

[204] Compare the view of Photis as a 'false' anticipation of Isis, discussed in n. 176. There as in Book 11 it is possible to accept a dualistic epistemological structure without accepting any moralizing or didactic consequences.

[205] This seems to pick up Plato's δούλαις ... ἡδοναῖς at *Rep.* 9. 587c (a parallel unnoted by commentators) and the general Platonic idea that low pleasures enslave (*Phaed.* 65c, *Rep.* 9. 589e).

the partial and false knowledge of the non-initiate and the true knowledge of the initiate clearly recalls Platonic epistemology and the theory
of Forms, with which Apuleius as translator of the *Phaedo* certainly had
some acquaintance.[206] There only the trained and 'initiated' philosopher
can perceive the true version of the world in the dimension of the Forms,
while most mortals move in the shadowy world of sense-perception. In
terms of the famous analogy of the Cave in Plato's *Republic*, those elements of Lucius' unenlightened experience prefiguring his future as an
initiate are mere dark shadows on the wall of the Cave, whereas the real
knowledge of Isis achieved by Lucius in the last book corresponds to the
knowledge of the Good, which Plato describes, as Apuleius describes Isis,
as the source of light and illumination.[207]

However, this use of Platonic moral theory and epistemology as one
of the novel's structural frameworks in no way necessitates that the story
of Lucius is a Platonizing moral fable presented for a didactic purpose.
Such Platonic allusion could be purely a demonstration of cultural learning, just as the use of epic structures and frameworks makes no serious
claim for the novel as an epic.[208] The general treatment of Lucius as a
gullible fool and the satirical parody of the Isis-cult and its functionaries
in Book 11 suggest that this Platonizing colour in his narrative is not to be
taken at its ideological face value.[209] If we attribute it to Lucius, it is only
the analysis of a narrator whose judgement even (or especially) in the last
book of the novel has little moral or intellectual authority; if we attribute
it to Apuleius, the plot of the novel suggests that moral didacticism cannot be the author's goal. After all, Lucius is not fundamentally improved
as a character by his experiences, and does not gain wisdom or insight
into the true nature of the world, for at the end of the novel he plainly
remains a gullible dupe.

All this suggests that the novel is not fundamentally concerned with
advocating the doctrines and values of Platonism, something confirmed
by the fact that the terms *Plato* and *Platonicus* are never found in it,

---

[206] For Apuleius' translation of the *Phaedo* cf. Ch. 1, Sect. 2 (ii) 4; for a convenient exposition of the theory of Forms see White (1992).

[207] Cf. *Rep.* 7. 514a ff.

[208] Cf. Harrison (1998*b*).

[209] This is my difficulty with the interpretation of Fick-Michel (1991) who accepts the
satirical interpretation of the Isis-cult but views Lucius' initiations as representing a genuine Platonic progress towards the good. The initiations and the treatment of the Isis-cult
cannot be so neatly untangled, as I hope my reading of *Met.* 11 indicates.

though they are used in other Apuleian works.[210] There also appears to be no Platonic element in the strongly programmatic prologue of *Met.* 1. 1,[211] while the nod to Plutarch and Sextus in *Met.* 1. 2. 1, though it no doubt suggests that Middle Platonic interests are in some sense important for the novel, is (as we have seen) at least as much concerned with possible literary debts and respectable socio-intellectual status in the Second Sophistic.[212] If the *Metamorphoses* is a missionary or proselytizing text for Platonism, or even a cautionary moral tale about youthful error, it must be accounted a distinct failure. Its protagonist does not profit (even retrospectively) from the Platonizing analysis of his errors, and its general Platonizing colour is to be found at such a subtle literary, structural, and intertextual level that considerable readerly alertness is required to uncover it.

The primary function of Platonic allusion in the *Metamorphoses*, I would argue, is that of entertaining literary and cultural display. Though Apuleius may have chosen to present himself as a Platonic philosopher in public contexts, this in no sense requires his novel to present a Platonic philosophical message of a didactic kind. I have already argued above that Platonic texts form part of a larger range providing material for Apuleian literary epideixis. Indeed, Plato had a special status for the Atticizing writers of the Second Sophistic, and the *Phaedrus* and *Symposium*, the dialogues most overtly alluded to by Apuleius, were extremely popular in the Greek literary texts of the second century AD.[213] Supposedly ideological echoes can thus be seen as elements of a particularly fashionable literary intertextuality, intended to display the virtuoso learning of the author to a discerning and bilingual elite readership, and matching in a Latin text the Platonic allusions of Greek sophistic contemporaries.

Two examples support this approach. The first is the story of the character Socrates, told by Aristomenes in *Met.* 1. 5–19. This plainly contains a number of echoes of Plato's *Phaedrus*, especially at 1. 18. 8 which alludes

[210] Plato is named more than twenty times in the firmly Apuleian works other than the *Metamorphoses* (*Apol., DDS, Flor.*); the adjective *Platonicus* occurs only five times, all in the *Apologia*.
[211] I find the attempt to uncover philosophical significance here by Thibau (1965), 92–101, vague and unconvincing. Isiac elements, by contrast, are undoubtedly present (cf. n. 133 above), but anticipating the novel's ending rather than advocating an ideology.
[212] Middle Platonic interests: n. 19. Literary debts to Plutarch's *De Iside and Osiride*: n. 166. Socio-intellectual status: Sect. 1 (ii).
[213] For the *Phaedrus* see Trapp (1990), *passim*; for the *Symposium* see Trapp (1990), 143, 156–7, and Trapp (1994), 373.

to the famous setting of that dialogue under a plane-tree.[214] These have been taken as a token of Apuleius' profound concern with Plato's theory of love, the central topic of the *Phaedrus*, since the story of Socrates concerns misguided erotic behaviour.[215] But the low-life character of Apuleius' story, involving witches, bestial metamorphosis, drenching with urine, attempted midnight flight from an inn, comic attempted suicide, and a gory and sensational death, suggests that a philosophical agenda is not the point here. The allusions to the *Phaedrus* rather represent a splendid literary joke: in his darkly comic and sordid tale of adultery, black magic, and murder Apuleius recalls in the lower literary form of the novel the much more elevated Platonic treatment of love. In the same way his character Socrates, portrayed as a doomed sensualist disastrously falling for an older woman, is wittily the inverse of the sexually self-restrained Platonic Socrates, able in the *Symposium* to resist even the charms of the devastatingly handsome Alcibiades.[216] This could be presented as a serious moralizing lesson for Lucius, about to face similar erotic dangers in Hypata, but the entertaining black comedy overcomes any didactic element, especially since Lucius (as usual) fails to heed the cautionary tale.[217]

The second example occurs in the tale of Cupid and Psyche, where the *Phaedrus* is famously echoed at 5. 24. 1:

at Psyche, statim resurgentis eius crure dextero manibus ambabus arrepto, sublimis evectionis appendix miseranda et per nubilas plagas penduli comitatus extrema consequia, tandem fessa delabitur solo.

This much-discussed passage has rightly been seen as an allusion to *Phaedrus* 248c:

If any soul becomes a companion to a god and catches sight of any true thing, it will be unharmed until the next circuit; and if it is able to do this every time, it will always be safe. If, on the other hand, it does not see anything true because it could not keep up, and by some accident takes on a burden of forgetfulness and wrongdoing, then it is weighed down, sheds its wings and falls to earth.[218]

---

[214] With 1. 18. 8 *iuxta platanum istam residamus* compare *Phaedr.* 229a–d: '[Socrates] Lead the way then, and find us a place to sit. [Phaedrus] Do you see that very tall plane tree? [Socrates] Of course. [Phaedrus] It's shady, with a light breeze; we can sit, or if we prefer, lie down on the grass there.' Tr. A. Nehemas and P. Woodruff in Cooper (1997), 509.

[215] Thibau (1965), 104–17.

[216] Tatum (1979), 27, notes the ironic naming of Socrates (but without the specific reference to the Alcibiades' episode, famously narrated by Alcibiades himself in the *Symposium*, 218c–219e).   [217] Cf. n. 158.

[218] Tr. A. Nehamas and P. Woodruff in Cooper (1997), 526.

This intertextual echo has commonly been presented as justifying an allegorical interpretation of the story of Cupid and Psyche. But the difference between the context and treatment of the idea in the *Phaedrus* and in the *Metamorphoses* is instructive and crucial. In the Platonic dialogue this passage occurs in the lofty and mystical discourse spoken by Socrates, supposedly modelled on the famous palinode of the poet Stesichorus (*Phaedr.* 244a). In Apuleius' novel the moment is certainly a dramatic one, the abandonment of Psyche by Cupid, but the treatment again seems to present a comic version of the Platonic model. Unlike the Platonic soul, Psyche (soul) never has wings in Apuleius' novel,[219] and she cannot hope to follow the god Cupid; she is trying to go where she is not wanted, following the tragicomic tradition of the Ovidian Scylla, desperately grasping the stern of the departing ship of Minos, who has rejected her as a lover.[220] And though Psyche has like the Platonic soul indeed taken on 'a burden of forgetfulness and wrongdoing', forgetting Cupid's admonition not to probe his identity and acting wrongly in investigating it, Apuleius' elaborate description of her as an unwanted appendage to the rising Cupid provides a strong comic contrast with the mystical tone of the Platonic context. Here the text lingers on the undignified picture of Psyche hanging in the air in remarkably elaborate and heightened language (*appendix miseranda et per nubilas plagas penduli comitatus extrema consequia*), whose effect can only be a deliberate and humorous contrast with the heroine's ludicrous (if pathetic) posture.[221] Though there is a clear allusion to Plato's allegory, there is no profound allegorical symbolism in the Apuleian version. This initial hint at symbolism is never followed up. The romance of 'Love and Soul' is in fact seriously allegorized at no other point in the tale,[222] and generally owes more to the erotic narratives of Roman elegy and the Greek novel than to Platonic philosophy.[223]

Here, then, we have an amusing take on a lofty Platonic passage, a

---

[219] Though ironically her name means 'butterfly' as well as 'soul' in Greek.

[220] At Ovid *Met.* 8. 142–4; Kenney (1990*a*) notes the parallel, but not the tragicomic effect.

[221] Kenney (1990*a*), 173, rightly points out that *penduli comitatus extrema consequia* is 'a very artificial expression even for Apuleius', though he does not suggest humour here.

[222] Kenney (1990*a*), 16–17, regards the symbolic naming of Venus' servants as *Sollicitudo* and *Tristities* (6. 9. 2) and her enemy as *Sobrietas* (5. 30. 3) as strong evidence for allegory in the story; but he himself has made a good case for the Vergilian/Ovidian literary origin of these figures (cf. Kenney (1990*a*), 186, 202), and their names reflect the themes of Ovidian love elegy rather than Platonic theorizing. Such abstract ministers are attached to gods in literature as early as Homer (cf. e.g. *Il.* 4. 439–41).

[223] Kenney (1990*a*) provides a mass of important parallels from both these genres.

literary joke for the learned reader. We can compare the fact that the eventual daughter of Cupid and Psyche is called Pleasure (*Voluptas*) at 6. 24. 4. This looks like portentous philosophical symbolism, but matches nothing in Plato; as Kenney notes, it is in any case surprising that the pair have a daughter, since the previous narrative has suggested a son.[224] As in Psyche's mid-air suspension, this passage plays with the possibility of allegorical meaning but ultimately debunks it: the union of Love and Soul naturally leads to Pleasure without intervention from Plato, and we are reminded in both cases that this is only a novel, not a philosophical treatise. Pleasure is the issue of the story, whether for the reader, gaining through the narrative of Cupid and Psyche the literary pleasure promised in the prologue (1. 1 *lector intende: laetaberis*), or for the characters Cupid and Psyche, for whom it produces a child of that name. Learned and witty literary allusion is here combined with the self-reflexive reminder that this text is no Platonic dialogue but a low-life fictional narrative for the delectation of its audience.

Two further functions of Platonic allusion in Apuleius' *Metamorphoses* may be mentioned briefly in conclusion. First, it is worth noting that, just as Plato's dialogues provide key literary intertexts in the time of the Second Sophistic, so Platonic philosophy was the most active and fashionable of the philosophical schools in this period.[225] To show familiarity with Platonic doctrines as well as the more literary aspects of Platonic texts was again a matter of fashion and cultural display, in which Apuleius as a talented self-promoter and self-proclaimed *philosophus Platonicus* was sure to participate. In the case of Apuleius, this role meshes with a second function, the way in which (as we have already noted) Platonic ethical and epistemological ideas are used as one strategy of unity in the novel, providing an overt link between the 'true' and 'virtuous' world of the Isis-cult and the 'false' and 'vicious' world of profane existence. Once again, there is no need for this to make the *Metamorphoses* a didactic Platonic treatise. There is a crucial difference between the use and the promotion of Platonic ideas, and Platonic dualism is only one of a number of unities which can be found in the novel. Similarly, the discovery of earlier narrative foreshadowings of the Isiac conclusion does not entail an Isiac interpretation of the whole work, and other narrative unities, such as the function of the novel's inserted tales

---

[224] Kenney (1990*a*), 224, citing *Met.* 5. 11. 6 *infantem alium*, 5. 12. 5 *parvulum nostrum* (add 5. 26. 4 *puelli*).

[225] Cf. Whittaker (1987).

in reflecting and anticipating the actions of Lucius[226] or the relations of its narrative frames to those of epic poetry[227] imply no particular ideological stance or interpretation. Platonic material, like Isiac material, provides only one strand in the rich texture of Apuleius' novel, and though it must be assigned its full weight in the text's project of multifarious cultural display, that is no reason to allocate to it a dominant ideological importance.

(v) *Conclusion: Entertainment, not Enlightenment*

The view of the *Metamorphoses* sketched here suggests that literary entertainment and cultural display, rather than ideological commitment or didactic purpose, lie behind the undoubted deployment of both Isiac and Platonic elements in the novel. Neither should be treated as a key to the 'message' of the work, but both should be viewed as contributing significantly to its self-consciously complex and impressive literary and cultural texture, a texture which above all presents for the elite reader of the second century the intellectual range and claims of its author. Though Apuleius proclaimed himself a Platonic philosopher, and might have been an Isiac initiate, the treatments of Platonic ideas and of Isiac cult in his novel are fundamentally playful, filtered as they are through the amusingly foolish narrator Lucius and his entertaining and sensational experiences. Above all, it is the work's own generic self-consciousness as a novel, and not an Isiac aretalogy or Platonic dialogue, which prevents the firm establishment of a didactic ideological line or purpose. The *Metamorphoses* is always aware of its status as an entertaining narrative in the Milesian tradition, and that its self-proclaimed purpose is to bring pleasure and not enlightenment: *lector intende: laetaberis* (*Met.* 1. 1).

---

[226] Cf. Tatum (1969).   [227] Cf. Harrison (1997*a*) and (1998*b*).

BIBLIOGRAPHY

ABT, A. (1908), *Die Apologie von Apuleius von Madaura und die antike Zauberei* (Giessen).

ALIMONTI, T. (1975), 'Apuleio e l'arcaismo in Claudiano Mamerto' in *Forma futuri: Studi in onore di M. Pellegrino* (Torino), 189–228.

ALPERS, K. (1980), 'Innere Beziehungen und Kontraste als "hermeneutische Zeichen" in den *Metamorphosen* des Apuleius von Madauros', *WJA* 6: 197–207.

ANDERSON, G. (1976), *Studies in Lucian's Comic Fiction* (*Mnemosyne* Suppl. 43) (Leiden).

—— (1982), *Eros Sophistes: Ancient Novelists at Play* (American Classical Studies 9) (Chico, Calif.).

—— (1984), *Ancient Fiction* (London/Sydney).

—— (1986), *Philostratus* (London).

—— (1993), *The Second Sophistic* (London).

—— (1996), 'Lucian's *Verae Historiae*', in Schmeling (1996), 555–62.

ANDRÉ, J. (1959), 'Erreurs de traduction chez Pline l'Ancien', *REL* 37: 203–15.

—— (1986), *L'Inde vue de Rome* (Paris).

ANONYMOUS (1893), *The Works of Apuleius . . . A New Translation* (London).

APPEL, G. (1909), *De Romanorum precibus* (Diss., Giessen).

ASSFAHL, G. (1932), *Vergleich und Metapher bei Quintilian* (Stuttgart).

ASTBURY, R. (1977), 'Petronius, *P. Oxy.* 3010, and Menippean Satire', *CPh* 72: 22–31.

AUGELLO, G. (1984), *L'Apologia o la Magia, Florida di Lucio Apuleio* (Turin).

AUSTIN, R. G. (1948), *Quintilian Book XII* (Oxford).

AXELSON, B. (1952), *Akzentuierender Klauselrhythmus bei Apuleius* (Lund).

—— (1987), *Kleine Schriften zur lateinischen Philologie* (Stockholm).

BAEHRENS, W. A. (1912), 'Zu den philosophischen Schriften des Apuleius', *RhM* 67: 112–34.

BAJONI, M. G. (1991), *Apuleio: De Mundo* (Pordenone).

—— (1992), 'Apuleio filosofo platonico 1940–1990', *Lustrum* 34: 339–88.

—— (1994), 'Aspetti lingusitici e letterari del "De Mundo" di Apuleio', *ANRW* II. 34. 2: 1785–1832.

BAKHTIN, M. (1981), *The Dialogic Imagination: Four Essays*, tr. C. Emerson and M. Holquist (Austin).

BALDASSARI, M. (1986), *Apuleio—l'interpretazione* (Como).

BALDWIN, B. (1985), '*Fumum vendere* in the *Historia Augusta*', *Glotta* 63: 107–9.

BALDWIN, T. W. (1944), *William Shakespere's small Latine and lesse Greeke* (2 vols.) (Chicago).

BALTES, M. (1976, 1978), *Die Weltenstehung des Platonischen Timaios nach den antiken Interpreten* (2 vols.) (Leiden).

BANDINI, M. (1986), 'Il modello della metamorfosi ovidiana nel romanzo di Apuleio', *Maia* 38: 33–9.

BARCHIESI, A. (1986), 'Tracce di narrativa greca e romanzo latino: una rassegna', in *Semiotica della novella latina*, 219–36.

BARKER, A. (1984), *Greek Musical Writings*, i: *The Musician and his Art* (Cambridge).

—— (1989), *Greek Musical Writings*, ii: *Harmonic and Acoustic Theory* (Cambridge).

BARNES, T. D. (1967), 'The Family and Career of Septimus Severus', *Historia* 16: 87–107.

—— (1971, 2nd edn. 1985), *Tertullian: A Historical and Literary Study* (Oxford).

BARRA, G. (1960–1), 'Il valore e il significato del "De deo Socratis" di Apuleio', *Ann. fac. lett. fil. Napoli* 9: 67–119.

—— (1966), 'La questione dell'autenticità del "De Platone et eius dogmate" e del "De Mundo" di Apuleio, *RAAN* 41: 127–88.

—— and Pannuti, U. (1962–3), 'Il "De deo Socratis" di Apuleio', *Ann. fac. lett. fil. Napoli* 10: 81–141.

BARTALUCCI, A. (1985), 'Analisi testuale del frammento di Levio sui filtri magici' in Tandoi (1985), ii. 79–92.

BARTH, C. VON (1624), *Adversariorum commentariorum libri lx* (Frankfurt).

BARTSCH, S. (1989), *Decoding the Ancient Novel* (Princeton).

BEAUJEU, J. (1964), *Minucius Felix: l'octave* (Paris).

—— (1973) *Apulée: opuscules philosophiques et fragments* (Paris).

BECK, R. (1973), 'Some Observations on the Narrative Technique of Petronius', *Phoenix* 27: 42–61.

—— (1996), 'Mystery Religions, Aretalogy and the Ancient Novel', in Schmeling, 131–50.

BEHR, C. A. (1968), *Aristides and the Sacred Tales* (Amsterdam).

—— (1986), *P. Aelius Aristides: The Complete Works*, ii (Leiden).

—— (1994), 'Studies on the Biography of Aelius Aristides', *ANRW* II. 34. 2: 1140–1223.

BELSEY, C. (1980), *Critical Practice* (London).

BERNARD, W. (1994), 'Zur Dämonologie des Apuleius von Madaura', *RhM* 137: 358–73.

BERNARDO, A., and LEVIN, S. (1990) (eds.), *The Classics in the Middle Ages* (Binghamton, N.Y.).

BERNHARD, M. (1927), *Der Stil des Apuleius von Madaura* (Stuttgart).

BESSONE, F. (1993), 'Discorsi dei liberti e parodia del "Simposio" platonico nella "Cena Trimalchionis"', *MD* 30: 63–86.

BETTINI, M. (1982), 'A proposito dei versi sotadei, greci e romani: con alcuni capitoli di "analisi metrica lineare"', *MD* 9: 59–105.

BIANCO, G. (1971), *La fonte greca delle Metamorfosi di Apuleio* (Brescia).

BIGWOOD, J. M. (1993), 'Ctesias' Parrot', *CQ* ns 43: 321–7.

BILLERBECK, M., and SCHAMP, J. (1996) (eds.), *Kainotomia: Die Erneuereung der griechischen Tradition* (Freiburg).

BINDER, G., and MERKELBACH, R. (1968) (eds.), *Amor und Psyche* (Wege der Forschung 126) (Darmstadt).

BINGENHEIMER, M. (1993), *Lucius Apuleius von Madaura: De deo Socratis* (Frankfurt).

BIRLEY, A. R. (1988), *Septimus Severus: The African Emperor* (London).

BLÄNSDORF, J. (1995), *Fragmenta Poetarum Latinorum* (Stuttgart/Leipzig).

—— ANDRÉ, J., and FICK, N. (1990) (eds.), *Theater und Gesellschaft im Imperium Romanum* (Tübingen).

BLANC, N., and BUISSON, A., eds. (1999), *Imago Antiquitatis: Religions et iconographie du monde romain. Hommage offert à Robert Turcan* (Paris).

BLUMENTHAL, H. J. and MARKUS, R. A. (1981) (eds.), *Neoplatonism and Early Christian Thought* (London).

BOMPAIRE, J. (1958), *Lucien écrivain* (Paris).

BONNER, S. F. (1977), *Roman Education* (London).

BOURDIEU, P. (1984), *Distinction: A Social Critique of the Theory of Taste* (London).

BOWERSOCK, G. W. (1965), 'Zur Geschichte des römischen Thessaliens', *RhM* 108: 277–89.

—— (1969), *Greek Sophists in the Roman Empire* (Oxford).

—— (1974) (ed.), *Approaches to the Second Sophistic* (University Park, Pa.).

BOWIE, E. L. (1970), 'Greeks and their Past in the Second Sophistic', *P&P* 46: 3–41.

—— (1982), 'The Importance of Sophists', *YCS* 27: 29–59.

—— (1989), 'Greek Sophists and Greek Poetry in the Second Sophistic', *ANRW* II. 33. 1: 209–58.

—— and Harrison, S. J. (1993), 'The Romance of the Novel', *JRS* 83: 159–78.

BRADLEY, K. (1997), 'Law, Magic and Culture in the *Apologia* of Apuleius', *Phoenix* 51: 203–23

—— (1999), 'Contending with Conversion: Reflections on the Reformation of Lucius the Ass', *Phoenix* 53.

—— (forthcoming), '*Romanitas* and the Roman Family: The Evidence of Apuleius' *Apology*', in Swain.

BRAMBLE, J. C. (1974), *Persius and the Programmatic Satire* (Cambridge).

BRANCALEONE, F. (1996–7), 'Apuleio frgg. 20 e 20 bis Beaujeu', *Invigilata Lucernis* 18–19: 25–9.

BRENK, F. E. (1999), 'The Isis Campensis of Katja Lembke', in Blanc and Buisson.

BRINK, C. O. (1982), *Horace On Poetry*, iii: *Epistles Book II* (Cambridge).

BROWN, R. D. (1987), *Lucretius on Love and Sex* (Leiden).

BRUNT, P. A. (1994), 'The Bubble of the Second Sophistic', *BICS* 39: 25–52.

BÜHLER, W. (1987), *Zenobii Athoi Proverbia I* (Göttingen).

BUFFIÈRE, F. (1956), *Les Mythes d'Homère et la pensée grècque* (Paris).

BURGES, G. (1876), *The Works of Plato*, vi (London).

BUTLER, H. E. (1909), *The Apologia and Florida of Apuleius of Madaura* (Oxford).

—— and OWEN, A. S. (1914), *Apulei Apologia* (Oxford).

CALLEBAT, L. (1964), 'L'Archaïsme dans les *Métamorphoses* d'Apulée', *REL* 42: 346–61.

—— (1968), *Sermo Cotidianus dans les* Métamorphoses *d'Apulée* (Caen).

—— (1978), 'La Prose des *Metamorphoses*: génèse et spécificité', in Hijmans and van der Paardt, 167–87.

—— (1984), 'La Prose d'Apulée dans le *De Magia*', *WS* 18: 143–67.

CAMERON, ALAN (1980), '*Poetae Novelli*', *HSCP* 84: 127–75.

CAMERON, AVERIL (1969), 'Petronius and Plato', *CQ* NS 19: 367–70.

CANFORA, L. (1980), 'Crispus Sallustius autore delle *suasoriae ad Caesarem senem?*', *Index* 9: 25–32.

CARBONERO, L. (1977), 'Analogie e rapporti fra la difesa ciceroniana del poeta Archia ed il processo per la magia di Lucio Apuleio', *Sileno* 3: 245–54.

CARRATELLO, U. (1963), 'Apuleio morì nel 163–4', *GIF* 16: 97–110.

CAVALLO, G. (1987) (ed.), *Le strade del testo* (Rome).

CHAMPLIN, E. (1980), *Fronto and Antonine Rome* (Cambridge, Mass.).

CLAVAUD, R. (1974), *Demosthène: Prologues* (Paris).

COARELLI, F. (1989), 'Apuleio a Ostia?', *DArch* 6: 27–42.

CONTE, G. B. (1996), *The Hidden Author: An Interpretation of Petronius' Satyricon* (Berkeley).

COOPER, J. M. (1997) (ed.), *Plato: Complete Works* (Indianapolis/Cambridge).

COPENHAVER, B. P. (1992), *Hermetica* (Cambridge).

COURTNEY, E. (1993), *The Fragmentary Latin Poets* (Oxford).

CROSBY, H. L. (1951), *Dio Chrysostom: Orations V* (Cambridge, Mass.).

CSAPO, E., and SLATER, W. J. (1995), *The Context of Ancient Drama* (Ann Arbor).

CUCCIOLI MELLONI, R. (1969), *Richerche sul pitagorismo*, i: *Biografia di Pitagora* (Bologna).

CURRIE, M. (1995) (ed.), *Metafiction* (London).

DAHLMANN, H. (1979), 'Ein Gedicht des Apuleius? (Gellius 19. 11)', *AAWM* 8.

DANGEL, J. (1995), *Accius: les fragments* (Paris).

D'ANNA, G. (1967), *M. Pacuvii fragmenta* (Rome).

DE'CONNO, R. (1958–9), 'Posizione e significazione dei *Florida* nell'opere di Apuleio', *Ann. fac. lett. fil. Napoli* 8: 57–76.

DEFILIPPO, J. G. (1990), '*Curiositas* and the Platonism of Apuleius' Golden Ass', *AJPh* 111: 471–92.

DEL RE, R. (1966), *Apuleio: Sul Dio di Socrate* (Rome).

DEROUX, C. (1979) (ed.), *Studies in Latin Literature and Roman History*, i (Brussels).

DESERTINE, A. (1898), *De Apulei studiis plautinis* (Nijmegen).

DESIDERI, C. (1978), *Dione di Prusa* (Messina).

DIELS, H. (1901), *Poetarum philosophorum fragmenta* (Berlin).

DI GIOVINE, C. (1981), 'Sulla presenza di Lucrezio nel De deo Socratis di Apuleio', *Orpheus* NS 2: 114–23.

DILLON, J. (1977), *The Middle Platonists* (London; repr. with addenda 1996).

—— (1993), *Alcinous: The Handbook of Platonism* (Oxford).

DODDS, E. R. (1965), *Pagan and Christian in an Age of Anxiety* (Oxford).

DONINI, P. (1979), 'Apuleio e il platonismo medio', in Pennacini *et al.*, 103–12.

DOWDEN, K. (1982), 'Apuleius and the Art of Narration', *CQ* NS 32: 419–35.

—— (1994), 'The Roman Audience of the Golden Ass', in Tatum, 419–34.

EDWARDS, C. (1993), *The Politics of Immorality In Ancient Rome* (Cambridge).

EFFE, B. (1976), 'Der misglückte Selbstmord des Aristomenes (Apuleius *Met.* 1. 14–17): zur Romanparodie im griechischen Eselsroman', *Hermes* 104: 362–75.

ELSOM, H. E. (1984), 'Apuleius and the Writing of Fiction and Philosophy in the Second Century A.D.' (Diss., Cambridge).

ELSTER, M. (1991), 'Römisches Strafrecht in den *Metamorphosen* des Apuleius', in Hofmann, 135–54.

ENGLERT, J., and LONG, T. (1972–3), 'Functions of Hair in Apuleius' *Metamorphoses*', *CJ* 68: 236–9.

FANTHAM, E. (1995), 'Aemilia Pudentilla: Or the Wealthy Widow's Choice', in Hawley and Levick, 220–32.

FASCE, S. (1973), 'L'*Erotikos* di Frontone', in *Argentea Aetas: In memoriam E. V. Marmorale* (Genoa), 261–72.

FEDELI, P. (1985), *Properzio: il libro terzo delle elegie* (Bari).

FEHLING, D. (1977) *Amor und Psyche* (*AAWM* 9) (Wiesbaden).

FERRARI, M. G. (1968), 'Aspetti di letterarietà nei *Florida* di Apuleio I', *SIFC* 40: 85–145.

—— (1969), 'Aspetti di letterarietà nei *Florida* di Apuleio II', *SIFC* 41: 139–87.

FESTUGIÈRE, A-J. (1954), *Personal religion among the Greeks* (Berkeley).

FICK, N. (1990), 'Die Pantomime des Apuleius (*Met.* X. 30–34, 3)', in Blänsdorf, André, and Fick, 223–32.

—— (1991), 'Pythias et le rituel égyptien du marché d'Hypata', in Fick and Carrière, 251–63.

—— and Carrière (1991) (eds.), *Mélanges Étienne Bernard* (Paris).

FICK-MICHEL, N. (1991), *Art et mystique dans les Métamorphoses d'Apulée* (Paris).

FINKELPEARL, E. (1990), 'Psyche, Aeneas and an Ass: Apuleius *Met.* 6. 10–6. 21', *TAPA* 120: 333–48.

—— (1998), *Metamorphosis of Langauge in Apuleius* (Ann Arbor).

FLAMAND, J-M. (1989), 'Apulée de Madaure', in Goulet, 298–317.

FLORES, E. (1992) (ed.), *Miscellanea di studi in onore di Armando Salvatore* (Naples).

FORBES, C. A. (1943–4), 'Charite and Dido', *CW* 37: 39–40.

FORSTER, E. S., and FURLEY, D. J. (1955), *Aristotle*, iii (Loeb) (London).

FÖRSTER, R. (1893), *Scriptores physiogonomonici Graeci et Latini*, i (Leipzig).

FOUCAULT, M. (1986), *The History of Sexuality*, iii: *Care of the Self* (Harmondsworth).

FOWDEN, G. (1986), *The Egyptian Hermes* (Princeton).

FRANGOULIDIS, S. A. (1992), 'Epic Inversion in Apuleius' Tale of Tlepolemus/Haemus', *Mnemosyne* 45: 60–74.

FURLEY, D. J. (1955), 'On the Cosmos', in Forster and Furley.

FUSILLO, M. (1988), 'Le Miroir de la lune: *L'Histoire vraie* de Lucien—de la satire à l'utopie', *Poétique* 73: 109–35.

GAGER, J. G. (1972), *Moses in Greco-Roman Paganism* (Nashville/New York).

GAIDE, F. (1993), 'Apulée de Madaure a-t-il prononcé le De Magia devant le proconsul d'Afrique?', *LEC* 61: 227–31.

GALINSKY, G. K. (1972), *The Herakles Theme* (Oxford).

GARCÍA-HERNÁNDEZ, B. (1998) (ed.), *Estudios lingüística latina* (Madrid).

GASCOU, J. (1972), *La politique municipale de l'empire romaine en Afrique proconsulaire de Trajan à Septime-Sévère* (Paris).

GEFFCKEN, K. (1973), *Comedy in the Pro Caelio* (Leiden).

GEMOLL, W. (1883), *Untersuchung über die Quellen, den Verfasser und die Abfassungszeit der Geoponica* (Berlin).

GENETTE, G. (1980), *Narrative Discourse*, tr. J. E. Lewin (Oxford).

GERSH, S. (1986), *Middle Platonism and Neoplatonism: The Latin Tradition* (2 vols.) (Notre Dame, Ind.).

GIANOTTI, G. F. (1986) *'Romanzo' e ideologia: studi sulle* Metamorfosi *di Apuleio* (Naples).

GIOMINI, R. (1975), *Cicero: De Divinatione, De Fato, Timaeus* (Leipzig).

GLEASON, M. (1995), *Making Men: Sophists and Self-Presentation in Ancient Rome* (Princeton).

GLUCKER, J. (1978), *Antiochus and the Late Academy* (Hypomnemata 56) (Göttingen).

GOLDHILL, S. D. (1995), *Foucault's Virginity* (Cambridge).

GÖRANSSON, T. (1995), *Albinus, Alcinous, Arius Didymus* (Gothenburg).

GOULET, R. (1989) (ed.), *Dictionnaire des philosophes anciens*, i (Paris).

GOW, A. S. F. (1965), *Machon* (Cambridge).

GRAF, F. (1997) (ed.), *Einleitung in die lateinische Philologie* (Stuttgart/Leipzig).

GRANT, R. M. (1988), *Greek Apologists of the Second Century* (London).

GRAVERINI, L. (1997), 'In historiae specimen (Apul. *Met.* 8. 1. 4)', *Prometheus* 23: 247–78.

—— (1998), 'Memorie virgiliane nelle *Metamorfosi* di Apuleio', *Maia* 50: 123–45.

GREEN, R. P. H. (1991), *The Works of Ausonius* (Oxford).

GRIFFITHS, J. G. (1970), *Plutarch's De Iside et Osiride* (Cardiff).

—— (1975), *Apuleius of Madauros: The Isis-Book (Metamorphoses, Book XI)* (Leiden).

—— (1978), 'Isis in the *Metamorphoses* of Apuleius', in Hijmans and van der Paardt, 141–66.

GRILLI, A. (1982), '*Mutmut*', *Maia* 34: 259–60.

GRIMAL, P. (1971), 'Le Calame égyptien d'Apulée', *REA* 73: 343–55.

GSELL, S. (1922a), *Inscriptions latines de l'Algérie I* (Paris).

—— (1922b), *Khamissa, Mdaourouch, Announa* (Paris).

GUEY, J. (1951), 'Au théâtre de Leptis Magna: le proconsulat de Lollianus Avitus et la date de l'Apologie d'Apulée', *REL* 29: 307–17.

GUTHRIE, K. S. (1987), *The Pythagorean Sourcebook* (Grand Rapids, Mich.).

GUTSFELD, A. (1992), 'Zur Wirtschaftsmentalität nichtsenatorischer provincialer Oberschichten: Aemilia Pudentilla und ihre Verwandten', *Klio* 74: 250–68.

HABERMEHL, P. (1996), '*Quaedam divinae potestates*: Demonology in Apuleius' *De Deo Socratis*', in Hofmann and Zimmerman, 117–42.

HABICHT, C. (1969), *Die Inschriften des Asklepieions* (Berlin).

—— (1985), *Pausanias' Guide to Ancient Greece* (Berkeley).

HADOT, I. (1984), *Arts libéraux et philosophie dans la pensée antique* (Paris).

—— (1997), 'Geschichte der Bildung: artes liberales', in Graf, 17–34.

HAGENDAHL, H. (1967), *Augustine and the Latin Classics* (2 vols.) (Gothenburg).

HALL, J. A. (1981), *Lucian's Satire* (New York).

HANSEN, W. (1996), *Phlegon of Tralles' Book of Marvels* (Exeter).

HANSON, A. E., and GREEN, M. H. (1994), 'Soranus of Ephesus: *Methodicorum Princeps*', *ANRW* II. 37. 2: 968–1075.

HANSON, J. A. (1989), *Apuleius: Metamorphoses* (2 vols.) (Cambridge, Mass.).

HARD, R. (1995), *The Discourses of Epictetus* (London).

HARMAND, P. (1957), *Le Patronat sur les collectivités publiques des origines au bas-Empire* (Paris).

HARRISON, S. J. (1988), 'Three Notes on Apuleius', *CQ* NS 38: 265–7.

—— (1990*a*) 'Some Odyssean Scenes in Apuleius "Metamorphoses"', *MD* 25: 193–201.

—— (1990*b*) 'The Speaking Book: The Prologue to Apuleius' *Metamorphoses*', *CQ* NS 40: 507–13.

—— (1992), '*Apuleius Eroticus*: *Anth. Lat.* 712 Riese', *Hermes* 120: 83–9

—— (1996), 'Apuleius' *Metamorphoses*', in Schmeling, 491–516.

—— (1997*a*), 'From Epic to Novel: Apuleius as Reader of Vergil', *MD* 39: 53–74.

—— (1997*b*), review of Shumate (1996*a*), in *Petronian Society Newsletter* 27: 11–13.

—— (1998*a*), 'The Milesian Tales and the Roman Novel', in Hofmann and Zimmerman, 61–73.

—— (1998*b*), 'Some Epic Structures in Cupid and Psyche', in Zimmerman *et al.*, 51–68.

—— (1999) (ed.), *Oxford Readings in the Roman Novel* (Oxford).

—— (2000), 'Apuleius, Aelius Aristides and Religious Autobiography', in Hofmann and Zimmerman.

HARTENBERGER, R. (1911), *De O finali apud poetas latinos ab Ennio usque ad Iuvenalem* (Diss., Bonn).

HAWLEY, R., and LEVICK, B. (1995) (eds.), *Women in Antiquity: New Assessments* (London).

HEATH, T. L. (1921), *A History of Greek Mathematics* (2 vols.) (Oxford).

—— (1990), *The Thirteen Books of Euclid's Elements* (Chicago/London).

HELLER, S. (1983), 'Apuleius, Platonic Dualism, and Eleven', *AJP* 104: 321–39.

HELM, R. (1898), *Fulgentius* (Leipzig).

—— (1900), 'De prooemio orationis Apuleianae quae est De deo Socratis', *Philologus* 59: 598–604.

HELM, R. (1905), *Apulei Apologia* (Leipzig).
—— (1906), *Lukian und Menipp* (Leipzig/Berlin).
—— (1910), *Apulei Florida* (Leipzig).
—— (1931), *Apulei Metamorphoseon Libri XI* (3rd edn.) (Leipzig).
—— (1955), 'Apuleius' Apologie—ein Meisterwerk der zweiten Sophistik', *Das Altertum* 1: 86–108.
HERZOG, R. (1989) (ed.), *Restauration und Erneuerung: die lateinische Literatur von 284 bis 374 n. Chr.* (Munich).
HICTER, J. (1944), (1945), 'L'Autobiographie dans l'*Âne d'or* d'Apulée', *A.C.* 13: 95–111, 14: 61–8.
HIJMANS, B. L., JR. (1987), 'Apuleius Philosophus Platonicus', *ANRW* II. 36. 1: 395–475.
—— (1994), 'Apuleius Orator: "Pro se de magia" and "Florida" ', *ANRW* II. 34. 2: 1708–84.
—— and VAN DER PAARDT, R. TH. (1978) (eds.), *Aspects of Apuleius' Golden Ass* (Groningen).
—— —— SCHMIDT, V., WESSELING, B., and ZIMMERMAN, M. (1995), *Apuleius Madaurensis: Metamorphoses Book IX* (Groningen).
HILDEBRAND, G. F. (1842), *Apulei omnia opera* (2 vols.) (Leipzig).
HINE, H. M. (1981), *An Edition with Commentary of Seneca, Natural Questions, Book Two* (New York).
HOCK, R. F., and O'NEIL, E. N. (1986), *The Chreia in Ancient Rhetoric,* i: *The Progymnasmata* (Atlanta).
HOEVELS, F. E. (1979), *Märchen und Magie in den Metamorphosen des Apuleius von Madaura* (Amsterdam).
HOFMAN, J. B., and SZANTYR, A. (1965), *Lateinische Syntax und Stylistik* (Munich).
HOFMANN, H. (1990) (ed.), *Groningen Colloquia on the Novel,* iii (Groningen).
—— (1991) (ed.), *Groningen Colloquia on the Novel,* iv (Groningen).
—— (1993) (ed.), *Groningen Colloquia on the Novel,* v (Groningen).
—— (1995) (ed.), *Groningen Colloquia on the Novel,* vi (Groningen).
—— (1999) (ed.), *Latin Fiction* (London).
—— and ZIMMERMAN, M. (1996) (eds.), *Groningen Colloquia on the Novel,* vii (Groningen).
—— —— (1997) (eds.), *Groningen Colloquia on the Novel,* viii (Groningen).
—— —— (1998) (eds.), *Groningen Colloquia on the Novel,* ix (Groningen).
—— —— (2000) (eds.), *Groningen Colloquia on the Novel,* x (Groningen).
HOÏSTAD, R. (1948), *Cynic Hero and Cynic King* (Uppsala).
HOLFORD-STREVENS, L. (1988), *Aulus Gellius* (London).
HOLZBERG, N. (1984), 'Apuleius und der Verfasser des griechischen Eselromans', *WJA* 10: 161–78.
—— (1993), *Die Antike Fabel* (Darmstadt).
—— (1996), 'Novel-like Works of Extended Prose Fiction II', in Schmeling, 619–54.

Hooker, W. (1955), 'Apuleius's "Cupid and Psyche" as a Platonic Myth', *Bucknell Review* 5. 3: 24–38.

Horsfall, N. M. (1988) (ed.), *Vir Bonus Discendi Peritus* (Festschrift O. Skutsch) (*BICS* Suppl. 51) (London).

Horsfall Scotti, M. T. (1990), 'Apuleio tra magia e filosofia: la riscoperta di Agostino', in *Dicti studiosus: scritti di filologia offerti a Scevola Mariotti* (Urbino), 295–320.

Howald, E. (1927), *Corpus Medicorum Latinorum*, iv (Leipzig).

Hunink, V. (1992), *Lucanus, Bellum Civile III* (Amsterdam).

—— (1995), 'The Prologue of Apuleius' *De Deo Socratis*', *Mnem.* 48: 292–312.

—— (1996), 'Apuleius and the *Asclepius*', *Vig. Chr.* 50: 288–308.

—— (1997), *Apuleius: Pro se de magia* [2 vols] (Amsterdam).

—— (1998*a*), 'Comedy in Apuleius' Apology', in Hofmann and Zimmerman, 97–114.

—— (1998*b*), 'The Enigmatic Lady Pudentilla', *AJPh* 119: 275–91.

Hunter, R. L. (1983), *A Study of Daphnis and Chloe* (Cambridge).

—— (1998) (ed.), *Studies in Heliodorus* (Cambridge).

Huss, W. (1985), *Geschichte der Karthager* (Munich).

Janson, T. (1964), *Latin Prose Prefaces* (Stockholm).

Jocelyn, H. D. (1990), 'L. Caecilius Minutianus Apuleius', in Tarugi, 207–18.

Jones, C. P. (1986), *Culture and Society in Lucian* (Cambridge, Mass.).

Kahane, A., and Laird, A. (2000) (eds.), *A Companion to the Prologue of Apuleius' Metamorphoses* (Oxford).

Karttunen, K. (1997), *India and the Hellenistic World* (Helsinki).

Kassel, R., and Austin, C. (1989), *Poetae Comici Graeci*, vii (Berlin).

Kelter, E. (1890), *Apulei quae fertur physiognomonia quando composita sit* (Diss, Kiel).

Kennedy, G. A. (1978), 'Encolpius and Agamemnon in Petronius', *AJP* 99: 171–8.

—— (1983), *Greek Rhetoric under Christian Emperors* (Princeton).

Kenney, E. J. (1990*a*), *Apuleius: Cupid and Psyche* (Cambridge).

—— (1990*b*) 'Psyche and her mysterious husband', in Russell, 175–98.

—— (1998), *Apuleius: The Golden Ass. A New Translation* (Harmondsworth).

Kerényi, K. (1927), *Die griechisch-orientalische Romanliteratur in religionsgeschichtlicher Beleuchtung* (Tübingen, repr. Darmstadt 1962).

Keulen, W. (1997), 'Some Legal Themes in Apuleian Context', in Picone and Zimmermann, 203–29.

Keyser, P. T. (1994), 'On Cometary Theory and Typology from Nechepso-Petosiris through Apuleius to Servius', *Mnem.* 47: 625–51.

Kindstrand, J. (1973), *Homer in der zweiten Sophistik* (Uppsala).

—— (1981), *Anacharsis* (Uppsala).

Kotula, T. (1969), 'Utraque lingua eruditi . . .', in *Hommages à Marcel Renard* (Brussels), ii. 386–92.

Koziol, H. (1872), *Der Stil des Apuleius* (Vienna).

Krabbe, J. K. (1989), *The Metamorphoses of Apuleius* (New York/Berne).

KRAUT, R. (1992) (ed.), *The Cambridge Companion to Plato* (Cambridge).

KROLL, W. (1913), *M. Tullius Cicero: Orator* (Berlin).

KUSSL, R. (1990), 'Die *Metamorphosen* des "Lucius von Patrai": Untersuchungen zu Photius *Bibl.* 129', *RhM* 133: 379–88.

LAMBERTON, R. (1986), *Homer the Theologian* (Princeton).

LANCEL, S. (1987), 'Y-a-t'il une Africitas?', *REL* 63: 161–82.

LANE FOX, R. (1986), *Pagans and Christians* (Harmondsworth).

LASSERRE, F. (1954), *Plutarque: De la musique* (Lausanne).

LAUSBERG, H. (1960), *Handbuch der literarischen Rhetorik* (Munich).

LAZZARINI, C. (1985), 'Il modello virgiliano nel lessico delle *Metamorfosi* di Apuleio', *SCO* 35: 131–60.

LE BOHEC, Y. (1994) (ed.), *L'Afrique, la Gaule, la religion à l'époque romaine* (Brussels).

LEFKOWITZ, M. (1981), *The Lives of the Greek Poets* (London).

LEJAY, P. (1911), *Oeuvres d'Horace: Satires* (Paris).

LEMBKE, K. (1994), *Das Iseum Campense in Rom* (Heidelberg).

LEPELLEY, C. (1979), *Les cités de l'Afrique romaine au Bas-Empire*, i (Paris).

—— (1981), *Les cités de l'Afrique romaine au Bas-Empire*, ii (Paris).

LEUMANN, M. (1977), *Lateinische Grammatik: Laut- und Formenlehre* (Munich).

LINKE, H. (1880), *Quaestiones de Macrobii Saturnaliorum fontibus* (Diss., Breslau).

LIPÍNSKI, E. (1994), 'Aesculapius/Esmun en Afrique Proconsulaire', in Le Bohec, 19–26.

LONDEY, D., and JOHANSON, C. (1987), *The Logic of Apuleius* (Leiden).

LOPORCARO, M. (1992), 'Eroi screditati dal testo: strutture della parodia nelle storie di briganti in Apuleio *Met.* IV. 9–21', *Maia* 44: 65–78.

LUDWIG, W. (1963), 'Plato's Love Epigrams', *GRBS* 4: 59–82.

McCREIGHT, T. D. (1990), 'Invective Techniques in Apuleius' Apology', in Hofmann, 35–62.

—— (1998), 'Apuleius, lector Sallustii', *Mnem.* 51: 41–63.

MACLEOD, M. D. (1967), *Lucian*, viii (Loeb) (London/Cambridge, Mass.).

MAGGIULLI, G., and BUFFA GIOLITO, M. F. (1996), *L'altro Apuleio* (Naples).

MALTBY, R. (1991), *A Lexicon of Ancient Latin Etymologies* (Leeds).

MANTERO, T. (1972), 'L'Ἐρωτικός di Apuleio' in *Studi classici in onore di Quintino Cataudella III* (Catania), 435–516.

—— (1973), 'La questione del prologo del *De Deo Socratis*', in *Argentea Aetas: in memoriam E. V. Marmorale* (Genoa), 219–59.

MARACHE, R. (1952), *La Critique littéraire de langue latine et le développement du goût archaïsant au IIe siècle de notre ère* (Rennes).

—— (1957), *Mots nouveaux et mots archaïques chez Fronton et Aulu-Gelle* (Rennes).

MARAGONI, E. (1988), 'Sol qui candentem: Ennio, Accio e un lapsus di Apuleio' in Tandoi, 42–9.

MARCHESI, C. (1914), *Apuleio di Madaura: Della Magia* (Bologna).

MARCHETTA, A. (1991), *L'autenticità apuleiana del De Mundo* (L'Aquila).

MARSHALL, P. K. (1983) 'Apuleius' in Reynolds, 15–16.

MARTIN, J. (1931), *Symposion* (Paderborn).

MASON, H. J. (1971), 'Lucius at Corinth', *Phoenix* 25: 160–5.

—— (1978), '*Fabula Graecanica*: Apuleius and his Greek Sources', in Hijmans and van der Paardt, 1–15.

—— (1983), 'The Distinction of Lucius in Apuleius' *Metamorphoses*', *Phoenix* 37: 135–43.

—— (1994), 'Greek and Latin Versions of the Ass-Story', *ANRW* II. 34. 2: 1665–1707.

—— (1999), 'The *Metamorphoses* of Apuleius and its Greek Sources', in Hofmann, 103–12.

MATTIACCI, S. (1982), *I frammenti dei poetae novelli* (Rome).

—— (1985), 'Apuleio "poeta novello"', in Tandoi, ii. 235–77.

—— (1986), 'Apuleio e i poeti latini arcaici', in *Munus amicitiae: scritti in memoria di Alessandro Ronconi*, i. 159–200 (Florence).

—— (1993a), 'L'episodio della *canis rabida* e la prova dell'acqua: una innovazione apuleiana tra scienza e parodia', *Sileno* 19: 179–95.

—— (1993b), 'La *Lecti invocatio* di Aristomene: pluralità di modelli e parodia in Apul. *Met*. 1. 16', *Maia* 45: 257–67.

—— (1994), 'Note sulla fortuna di Accio in Apuleio', *Prometheus* 20: 53–68.

MATTINGLY, D. J. (1995), *Tripolitania* (London).

MAY, J. M. (1988), *Trials of Character: The Eloquence of Ciceronian Ethos* (Chapel Hill).

MÉDAN, P. (1925), *La Latinité d'Apulée dans les Métamorphoses* (Paris).

MERKELBACH, R. (1958), 'Eros und Psyche', *Philologus* 102: 103–16.

—— (1962), *Roman und Mysterium in der Antike* (Berlin/ Munich).

—— (1995), *Isis Regina—Zeus Sarapis* (Stuttgart).

METHY, N. (1983), 'Fronton et Apulée: romains ou africains?', *RCCM* 25: 37–47.

MILLAR, F. G. B. (1968), 'Local Culture in the Roman Empire: Libyan, Punic and Latin in Roman Africa', *JRS* 58: 126–34.

—— (1981), 'The World of the *Golden Ass*', *JRS* 71: 63–75.

MORESCHINI, C. (1965), 'La demonologia medioplatonica e le *Metamorfosi* di Apuleio', *Maia* 17: 30–46.

—— (1978), *Apuleio e il Platonismo* (Florence).

—— (1985), *Dell'Asclepius al Crater Hermetis* (Pisa).

—— (1990), *Apuleio: La magia* (Milan).

—— (1991), *Apulei opera philosophica* (Stuttgart).

—— (1993), 'Elementi filosofici nelle Metamorfosi di Apuleio', *Koinonia* 17: 109–23.

—— (1994a), 'Elio Aristide tra retorica e filosofia', *ANRW* II. 34. 2: 1234–47.

—— (1994b), *Il mito di Amore e Psiche in Apuleio* (Naples).

MORGAN, J. R. (1985), 'Lucian's *True Histories* and the *Wonders beyond Thule* of Antonius Diogenes', *CQ* NS 35: 475–90.

—— (1996), 'Heliodorus', in Schmeling, 417–56.

MRAS, K. (1949a), *Apuleius' Florida im Rahmen ähnlicher Literatur* (Vienna).

—— (1949b), 'Die προλαλιά bei den griechischen Schriftstellern', *WS* 64: 71–81.

MÜLLER, S. (1939), *Das Verhältnis von Apuleius De mundo zu seiner Vorlage* (Leipzig).

MÜNCHER, K. (1920), *Xenophon in der griechisch-römischen Literatur* (Leipzig).

MÜNSTERMANN, H. (1995), *Apuleius, Metamorphosen: literarischer Vorlagen* (Stuttgart/Leipzig).

NESSELRATH, H. G. (1990), 'Lucian's Introductions', in Russell, 111–140.

NISBET, R. G. M., and HUBBARD, M. (1978), *A Commentary on Horace's Odes: Book II* (Oxford).

NOCK, A. D. (1933), *Conversion* (Oxford, repr. London 1963).

—— and Festugière, A-J. (1945), *Hermès Trismegiste*, iii (Paris).

NORDEN, F. (1912), *Apuleius von Madaura und das römische Privatrecht* (Leipzig).

OBERHELMAN, S. M (1988a), 'The *cursus* in Late Imperial Latin Prose: A Reconsideration of Methodology', *CPh* 83: 136–49.

—— (1988b), 'The History and Development of the *Cursus Mixtus* in Latin Literature', *CQ* NS 38: 228–42.

—— and HALL, R. G. (1985), 'Meter in Accentual Clausulae of Late Imperial Latin Prose', *CPh* 81: 214–39.

ODER, E. (1890), 'Beiträge zur Geschichte der Landwirtschaft bei den Griechen I', *RhM* 45: 58–99.

ÖNNEFORS, A. (1964), *Corpus Medicorum Latinorum*, iv (Leipzig).

OPEKU, F. (1974), 'A Commentary with Introduction on the *Florida* of Apuleius' (Diss., London).

—— (1979), 'Physiognomy in Apuleius', in Deroux, 467–74.

—— (1993), 'Popular and Higher Education in *Africa Proconsularis* in the Second Century AD', *Scholia* 2: 31–44.

OTTO, A. (1890), *Die Sprichwörter und sprichwörtlichen Redesarten der Römer* (Leipzig).

PAGE, D. L. (1981), *Further Greek Epigrams* (Cambridge).

PASCAL, C. (1908), 'Proverbia Senecae', *RFIC* 36: 63–9.

PEARCY, L. T. (1993), 'Medicine and Rhetoric in the Period of the Second Sophistic', *ANRW* II. 37. 1: 445–56.

PECERE, O. (1984), 'Esemplari con subscriptiones e tradizione dei testi latini: l'Apuleio *Laur*. 68. 2', in Questa, 111–37.

—— (1987), 'Qualche riflessione sulla tradizione di Apuleio a Montecassino', in Cavallo, 97–124.

PEDEN, R. G. (1985), 'The Statues in Apuleius *Metamorphoses* 2. 4', *Phoenix* 39: 380–3.

PENNACINI, A., DONINI, P. L., ALIMENTI, T., and MONTEDURO ROCCAVINI, A. (1979), *Apuleio letterato, filosofo, mago* (Rome).

PENWILL, J. L. (1975), 'Slavish Pleasures and Profitless Curiosity: Fall and Redemption in Apuleius' *Metamorphoses*', *Ramus* 4: 49–82.

—— (1990), '*Ambages Reciprocae*: Reviewing Apuleius' *Metamorphoses*', in A. J.

Boyle (ed.), *The Imperial Muse*, ii: *Flavian Epicists to Claudian* (Berwick, Vic.), 211–35.

PERRY, B. E. (1927), 'On Apuleius' Hermagoras', *AJP* 48: 263–6.

—— (1967), *The Ancient Romances: A Literary-Historical Account of their Origins* (Berkeley/Los Angeles).

PERVO, R. (1996), 'The Ancient Novel Becomes Christian', in Schmeling, 685–712.

PETERSMANN, H. (1998), 'Gab es ein afrikanisches Latein?', in García-Hernández, 125–36.

PICONE, M., and ZIMMERMANN, B. (1997) (eds.), *Der antike Roman und seine mittelalterliche Rezeption* (Basel/Boston/Berlin).

PITHOEUS, P. (1565), *Adversaria subseciva* (Paris).

PLEPELITS, K. (1996), 'Achilles Tatius', in Schmeling, 387–416.

PORTOGALLI CAGLI, B. M. (1992), *Apuleio: il demone di Socrate* (Venice).

POWELL, J. G. F. (1990), *Cicero: On Friendship and The Dream of Scipio* (Warminster).

—— (1995), 'Cicero's Translations from Greek', in id., *Cicero the Philosopher*, 273–300 (Oxford).

QUESTA, C. (1984) (ed.), *Atti del convegno 'Il libro e il testo'* (Urbino).

RATHKE, A. (1911), *De Apulei quem scripsit "De deo Socratis" libello* (Diss., Berlin).

REARDON, B. P. (1971), *Courants littéraires grècques des IIe et IIIe siècles après J. -C.* (Paris).

—— (1974), 'The Second Sophistic and the Novel', in Bowersock, 23–9.

—— (1989) (ed.), *The Collected Ancient Greek Novels* (Berkeley).

—— (1991), *The Form of Greek Romance* (Princeton).

REDFORS, J. (1960), *Echtheitskritische Untersuching der apuleischen Schriften De Platone und De Mundo* (Lund).

REGEN, F. (1971), *Apuleius Philosophus Platonicus. Untersuchungen zur Apologie (De Magia) und zu De Mundo* (Berlin).

RELIHAN, J. C. (1992) 'Rethinking the History of the Literary Symposium', *ICS* 17: 213–44.

REYNOLDS, L. D. (1983) (ed.), *Texts and Transmission: A Survey of the Latin Classics* (Oxford).

RIBBECK, O. (1878), 'Apuleius de deo Socratis', *RhM* 33: 434–8.

—— (1897), *Scaenicae Romanorum Poesis Fragmenta* (3rd edn.) (Leipzig).

RICHTER, G. M. A. (1965), *The Portraits of the Greeks* (3 vols.) (Oxford).

RIGINOS, A. S. (1976), *Platonica* (Leiden).

RIVES, J. (1994), 'The Priesthood of Apuleius', *AJPh* 115: 273–90.

ROBERTSON, D. S. (1910), 'Lucius of Madaura: A Difficulty in Apuleius', *CQ* 4: 221–7.

—— and VALETTE, P. (1940–5), *Apulée: Les Métamorphoses* (3 vols.) (Paris; repr. 1956, 1965, 1971).

ROCCA, S. (1978), 'Apuleio e Nonio', *Studi Noniani* 5: 225–35.

RÖLLIG, W. (1980), 'Das Punische im römischen Reich', in Untermann, 285–99.

ROMM, J. (1992), *The Edges of the Earth in Ancient Thought* (Baltimore).

RONCAIOLI, C. (1966), 'L'arcaismo nelle opere filosofiche di Apuleio', *GIF* 19: 322–56.

ROOS, P. (1984), *Sentenza e proverbio nell'antichità e I Distici di Catone* (Brescia).

ROSS, D. W. (1969), *Style and Tradition in Catullus* (Cambridge, Mass.).

RUSSELL, D. A. (1970), 'Hermagoras', in *Oxford Classical Dictionary* (2nd edn.) (Oxford).

—— (1973), *Plutarch* (London).

—— (1983), *Greek Declamation* (Cambridge).

—— (1990) (ed.), *Antonine Literature* (Oxford).

—— (1992), *Dio Chrysostom: Orations VII, XII, XXXVI* (Cambridge).

—— (1993), *Plutarch: Selected Essays and Dialogues* (Oxford).

RUTHERFORD, R. B. (1989), *The Meditations of Marcus Aurelius* (Oxford).

SALLMANN, K, (1995), 'Erzählendes in der Apologie des Apuleius, oder Argumentation als Unterhaltung', in Hofmann, 137–68.

—— (1997) (ed.), *Die Literatur des Umbruchs: von der römischen zur christlichen Literatur, 117 bis 284 n. Chr.* (Munich).

SANDY, G. N. (1978), 'Book XI: Ballast or Anchor?', in Hijmans and van der Paardt, 123–40.

—— (1993), 'West meets East: Western Students in Athens in the Mid-Second Century AD', in Hofmann, 163–4.

—— (1994), 'Apuleius' *Metamorphoses* and the Greek Novel', *ANRW* II. 34. 2: 1511–74.

—— (1997), *The Greek World of Apuleius* (*Mnemosyne* Suppl. 174) (Leiden).

SANDYS, J. E. (1908), *A History of Classical Scholarship* (3 vols.) (Cambridge).

SCHANZ, M., and HOSIUS, C. (1935), *Geschichte der römischen Literatur*, ii (4th edn.) (Munich; repr. 1967).

—— —— and KRUGER, M. (1922), *Geschichte der römischen Literatur*, iii (Munich).

SCHEFFER, J. (1654), *De militia navali* (Uppsala).

SCHIESARO, A. (1988), 'La tragedia di Psiche: note ad Apuleio *Met.* 4. 28–35', *Maia* 40: 141–50.

SCHLAM, C. C. (1970), 'Platonica in the *Metamorphoses* of Apuleius', *TAPA* 101: 477–87.

—— (1971), 'The Scholarship on Apuleius since 1938', *CW* 64: 285–309.

—— (1992), *The Metamorphoses of Apuleius: On Making an Ass of Oneself* (Chapel Hill).

SCHMELING, G. L. (1996) ed., *The Novel in the Ancient World* (*Mnemosyne* Suppl. 159) (Leiden).

Semiotica della novella latina (1986) (Materiali e contributi per la storia della narrativa, greco-latina, 4) (Rome).

SCHMID, W. (1887), *Der Atticismus* (2 vols.) (Stuttgart).

SCHMIDT, V. L. (1997), 'Reaktionen auf das Christentum in den *Metamorphosen* des Apuleius', *VChr* 51: 51–71.

SCHMUTZLER, K-P. (1974), *Die Platon-Biographie in der Schrift des Apuleius De Platone et eius Dogmate* (Diss., Kiel).

SCIOPPIUS, G. (1594), *Symbola critica in L. Apulei opera* (Leiden).

SCOTTI, M. T. (1982), 'Il proemio delle Metamorfosi tra Ovidio e Apuleio', *GIF* 34: 43–65.

—— (1988), '*Religiosis Viantium*: Note ad Apuleio, *Florida* 1', in Horsfall, 126–8.

SCOURFIELD, J. H. D. (1993), *Consoling Heliodorus: A Commentary on Jerome, Letter 60* (Oxford).

SHUMATE, N. C. (1996a), *Crisis and Conversion in Apuleius' Metamorphoses* (Ann Arbor)

—— (1996b), ' "Darkness Visible": Apuleius Reads Virgil', in Hofmann and Zimmerman, 103–16.

SIDERAS, A. (1994), 'Rufus von Ephesus und sein Werk im Rahmen des antiken Medezin', *ANRW* II. 37. 2: 1077–1253.

SIMON, M. (1968), 'Zur Abhängigkeit spätrömischer Enzyklopädien des *artes liberales* von Varros *Disciplinarum libri*', *Philologus* 110: 88–101.

SINISCALCO, P., and ALBERT, K. (1980), *Apuleius: Platon und seine Lehre* (Sankt Augustin).

SKUTSCH, O. (1985), *The Annales of Quintus Ennius* (Oxford).

SLATER, N. W. (1998), 'Passion and Petrifaction: The Gaze in Apuleius', *CPh* 93: 18–48.

SMITH, W. S. (1972), 'The Narrative Voice in Apuleius' *Metamorphoses*', *TAPA* 103: 513–34.

SOLODOW, J. W. (1988), *The World of Ovid's Metamorphoses* (Chapel Hill).

SORABJI, R. (1997) (ed.), *Aristotle and After* (*BICS* Suppl. 68) (London).

STADTER, P. A. (1980), *Arrian of Nicomedia* (Chapel Hill).

STANFORD, W. B. (1963), *The Ulysses Theme* (Oxford).

STANTON, G. R. (1973), 'Sophists and Philosophers: Problems of Classification', *AJP* 94: 50 64.

STEINMETZ, P. (1982), *Untersuchungen zur römischen Literatur des zweiten Jahrhunderts nach Christi Geburt* (Palingenesia 16) (Wiesbaden).

STEMPLINGER, E. (1912), *Das Plagiat in der griechischen Literatur* (Leipzig).

STEPHENS, S. A., and WINKLER, J. J. (1995), *Ancient Greek Novels: The Fragments* (Princeton).

STOCK, A. (1911), *De prolaliarum usu rhetorico* (Diss. Königsberg).

STOK, F. (1985), 'Il pauperismo di Apuleio', *Index* 13: 353–86.

STRAMAGLIA, A. (1996), 'Prisciano e l'*Epitome Historiarum* di Apuleio', *RFIC* 124: 192–8.

SULLIVAN, M. (1967), *Apuleian Logic* (Amsterdam).

SUMMERS, R. G. (1967), 'A Legal Commentary on the *Metamorphoses* of Apuleius' (Diss., Princeton).

—— (1970), 'Roman Justice and Apuleius' *Metamorphoses*', *TAPA* 101: 511–31.

—— (1972), 'Apuleius' *Juridicus*', *Historia* 21: 120–6.

—— (1973), 'A Note on the Date of the *Golden Ass*', *AJP* 94: 375–83.

SÜSS, W. (1912), *Ethos* (Leipzig).

SWAHN, J. O. (1955), *The Tale of Cupid and Psyche* (Lund).

SWAIN, S. C. R. (forthcoming) (ed.), *Romanitas.*

SYME, R. (1959), 'Proconsuls d'Afrique sous Antonin le Pieux', *REA* 61: 310–19 (repr. in id. *Roman Papers*, i. 461–9 (Oxford, 1979)).

—— (1988), 'The Date of Justin and the Discovery of Trogus', *Historia* 37: 358–71 (repr. in id. *Roman Papers*, vi. 358–71 (Oxford, 1991)).

TANDOI, V. (1984, 1985, 1988) (ed.), *Disiecti membra poetae* (3 vols.) (Foggia).

TARUGI, G. (1990) (ed.), *Homo sapiens homo humanus* (2 vols.) (Florence).

TATUM, J. (1969), 'The Tales in Apuleius' *Metamorphoses*', *TAPA* 100: 487–527.

—— (1979), *Apuleius and the Golden Ass* (Ithaca, N.Y.).

—— (1994) (ed.), *The Search for the Ancient Novel* (Baltimore).

THIBAU, R. (1965), 'Les *Métamorphoses* d'Apulée et la théorie platonicienne de l'éros', *Studia Philosophica Gandensia* 3: 89–144.

THIELING, W. (1911), *Der Hellenismus in Kleinafrika* (Leipzig/Berlin).

THOM, J. C. (1995), *The Pythagorean Golden Verses* (Leiden).

THOMAS, P. (1900), 'Remarques critiques sur les oeuvres philosophiques d'Apulée: 3ème série', *Bulletins de l'Académie royale de Belgique* 37: 143–65.

THOMAS, R. F. (1988), *Virgil: Georgics I–II* (Cambridge).

THOMASSON, B. E. (1960), *Die Statthalter der römischen Provinzen Nordafrikas von Augustus bis Diocletian* (2 vols.) (Lund).

THOMPSON, L. A., and FERGUSON, J. (1969) (eds.), *Africa in Classical Antiquity* (Ibadan).

TOMASCO, D. (1992), 'Ancora sul prologo del De deo Socratis', in Flores, 173–95.

THULIN, C. O. (1906–9), *Die Etruskische Diziplin* (3 vols.) (Gothenburg).

TRAPP, M. B. (1990), 'Plato's Phaedrus in Second-Century Greek Literature', in Russell, 141–74.

—— (1994), *Maximus Tyrius: Dissertationes* (Stuttgart/Leipzig).

—— (1997a), *Maximus of Tyre: The Philosophical Orations* (Oxford).

—— (1997b), 'Philosophical Sermons: The "Dialexeis" of Maximus of Tyre', *ANRW* II. 34. 3: 1945–76.

TURCAN, R. (1963), 'Le Roman initiatique: à propos d'un livre récent', *Revue de l'histoire des religions* 163: 149–99.

—— (1996), *The Cults of the Roman Empire* (tr. A. Nevill) (Oxford).

UNTERMANN, J. (1980) (ed.), *Die Sprachen im römischen Reich der Kaiserzeit* (Cologne).

VAHLEN, J. (1903), *Ennianae Poesis Reliquiae* (2nd edn.) (Leipzig).

VALLANCE, J. T. (1990), *Asclepiades of Bithynia* (Oxford).

VALLETTE, P. (1908), *L'Apologie d'Apulée* (Paris).

—— (1924), *Apulée: Apologie, Florides* (Paris; repr. 1960, 1971).

van DAM, H-J. (1984), *P. Papinus Statius: Silvae Book II. A Commentary* (*Mnemosyne* Suppl. 82) (Leiden).

van der PAARDT, R. TH (1971), *Apuleius: Metamorphoses Book III* (Amsterdam).

—— (1981), 'The Unmasked "I": Apuleius Met. XI. 27', *Mnem.* 34: 96–106.

van THIEL, H. (1971), *Der Eselsroman* (2 vols.) (Munich).

VARDI, A. (1993), 'Why Attic Nights, or What's in a Name?', *CQ* NS 53: 298–301.

VASALY, A. (1993), *Representations: Images of the World in Ciceronian Oratory* (Berkeley/London).

VIDMAN, L. (1977), 'Die Stadtpräfektur des Q. Lollius Urbicus und Apuleius, Apologia 2–3', *AArchSlov* 28: 373–84.

VON STADEN, H. (1997), 'Galen and the "Second Sophistic"', in Sorabji, 33–54.

WALLACH, B. P. (1976), *Lucretius and the Diatribe against the Fear of Death* (Leiden).

WALSH, P. G. (1970), *The Roman Novel: The Satyricon of Petronius and the Metamorphoses of Apuleius* (Cambridge; repr. with addenda Bristol, 1995).

—— (1974), review of van Thiel (1971) and Bianco (1971), *CR* NS 24: 215–18.

—— (1978), 'Petronius and Apuleius', in Hijmans and van der Paardt, 17–24.

—— (1981), 'Apuleius and Plutarch', in Blumenthal and Markus, 20–32.

—— (1994), *Apuleius: The Golden Ass* (Oxford).

WAUGH, P. (1984), *Metafiction* (London).

WEHRLI, F. (1951), 'Der Arztvergleich bei Platon', *MH* 8: 177–84.

WEIDNER, E. (1913), 'βάρβαρος', *Glotta* 4: 303–4.

WEISS, C. G. (1998), 'Literary Turns: The Representation of Conversion in Aelius Aristides' *Hieroi Logoi* and Apuleius' *Metamorphoses*' (Diss., Yale).

WHITBREAD, L. G. (1971), *Fulgentius the Mythographer* (Columbus, Ohio).

WHITE, N. P. (1992), 'Plato's Metaphysical Epistemology', in Kraut, 277–310.

WHITTAKER, J. (1987), 'Platonic Philosophy in the Early Centuries of the Empire', *ANRW* II. 36. 1: 81–123.

—— (1990), *Alcinoos: enseignement des doctrines de Platon* (Paris).

WIGTIL, D. N. (1984), 'Incorrect Apocalyptic: The Hermetic 'Asclepius' as an Improvement on the Original', *ANRW* II. 17. 4: 2282–97.

WINKLER, J. (1985), Auctor & Actor: *A Narratological Reading of Apuleius' Golden Ass* (Berkeley/Los Angeles).

—— (1982), 'The Mendacity of Calasiris and the Narrative Strategy of Helidoros' *Aethiopika*', *YCS* 27: 93–158.

WINTER, T. N. (1969), 'The Publication of Apuleius' Apology', *TAPA* 100: 607–12.

WLOSOK, A. (1969), 'Zur Einheit der *Metamorphosen* des Apuleius', *Philologus* 113: 68–84.

YARDLEY, J. C., and HECKEL, W. (1997), *Justin: Epitome of the Philippic History of Pompeius Trogus*, i (Oxford).

ZANKER, P. (1995), *The Mask of Socrates* (Berkeley).

ZIMMERMAN, M. (1993), 'Narrative Judgement and Reader Response in Apuleius' *Metamorphoses* 10. 29–34: The Pantomime of the Judgement of Paris', in Hofmann, 143–61.

—— (1996), 'Apuleius von Madaura', in *Der Neue Pauly*, i. 910–14

—— et al. (1998) (ed.), *Aspects of Apuleius' Golden Ass*, ii: *Cupid and Psyche* (Groningen).

ZWIERLEIN, O. (1987), *Senecas Phaedra und ihre Vorbilder* (Abh. Ak. Wiss. Mainz 5) (Stuttgart).

Bibliography

INDEX

Accius 109–10, 170, 171
Aedituus, Porcius and Catulus 54
Aelius Aristides 35, 250–1
Aesculapius
  Ap.'s interest in 33–5, 159
  worship of, in Carthage 6, 123, 139
Afranius 55
Alcinous, *Didaskalikos* 197–209
Alexander Peloplaton (sophist) 103
Anacharsis, sophists' interest in 126
Antigenidas (aulete) 100
Apologia 39–88
  Ciceronian character of 44, 51
  pseudo-realism and revision of 42
  structure and composition of 47–50
  title of 42–3
Apuleius, life
  bilingualism, supposed 15, 30, 125, 132, 154
  biography, reconstruction of 1–10
  improvization, rhetorical 124, 130
  legal knowledge 81
  plagiarized erudition 181
  priesthood of 8
  rivals, rhetorical 99, 106, 111, 121
  statues of 117
  supreme god, Platonic, interest in 75, 148, 177
  teaching activities, possible 9, 125, 203, 209
Apuleius, works (see also *Apologia*; *De Deo Socratis*; *De Mundo*; *De Platone*; *Florida*; *Metamorphoses*) 11–38
  Asclepius, inauthenticity of 12
  Astronomica (?) 29
  De Aesculapii Maiestate 32, 72
  De Arboribus (?) 27
  De Arithmetica (?) 31
  De Musica (?) 31
  De Proverbiis 20
  De Re Publica 25
  De Re Rustica 26
  Epitoma Historiarum 24
  Eroticus 28

Hermagoras 21
Ludicra 16–20
medical works (*Libri Medicinales*?) 25
miscellaneous fragments of lost works 35–6
Naturales Quaestiones/Φυσικὰ Προβλήματα 29–30
Περὶ Ἑρμηνείας, likely inauthenticity of 11–12, 195
Phaedo 23
poems, lost 34–5
Quaestiones Conviviales 13
speeches and declamations, lost 32–4
spurious minor works 13
zoological works 30–1
archaizing tendency, second-century 17, 54, 87–8, 158, 207–8
Alexander the Great, sophists' interest in 104
Anacharsis, sophist's interest in 126
Archimedes (?) 56
Aristotle 71, 153
Asclepiades of Prusa 125
astronomy, Greek 29
Atticism 107
auletes, celebrated, Ap. parallels himself with 98, 100
Augustine 1, 179

bird, Apuleius parallels himself with 112

Caecilius 53
Carthage, Ap.'s connections with 1–10, 39–88 *passim*, 139
Claudius Maximus, C. (proc. Afr. 158–9) 7, 39–88 *passim*
Callimachus 215
Cato 186
Catullus 17
Christian apologetics 43
Cicero 44, 51, 53, 63, 70, 76, 78, 83, 146, 148, 150, 153, 154, 162, 184–6, 205–7, 219, 224
Claudianus Mamertus 93–4
Clemens (poet) 102